TABLE OF CONTENTS

WELCOME BACK TO SKYLANDS

Welcome back, young Portal Master!

First the bad news. Kaos has returned, and plans to awaken the ancient Arkeyan army. Once again, he is attempting to assert his control over Skylands.

Now, the good news. The Giants are back. It's true! They weren't a legend. If you hold a Skylander Giant in your hands right now, hold it tight, Portal Master.

That Giant is the key to thwarting Kaos' plan and once again returning Skylands to peace.

For Veteran Portal Masters

If you played *Skylanders Spyro's Adventure*®, welcome back! A few things have changed since the first game, and they are summarized for you here.

- There are now eight new Giant Skylanders. While you can complete the adventure without a Giant Skylander, you will miss out on many side areas (and some of the fun!). Giant Skylanders have powers that give them advantages in battle, and can solve certain challenges.

- In addition to the Skylanders from the first game, eight new Skylanders have been added to the game's roster.

- There's more to do. In addition to Heroic Challenges from the first game, there are 21 fun and rewarding Arena Challenges that will test your prowess as a Portal Master while growing the bank accounts of your Skylanders.

- There's more to buy. Auric has a wonderful store full of great things to purchase and unlock. His inventory changes in each location where you encounter him.

- There's a new game called "Skystones." Skystones is a fun diversion that tasks you to collect and build a killer deck that can take on Skystones players of all levels throughout Skylands.

- There is a new collectible called Charms. You can earn Charms in the Arenas. Every Charm is unique and each one globally provides your Skylanders with a different in-game benefit.

- Your Skylanders can now go beyond level 10, and reach level 15 in experience.

- Each Skylander has nine Quests to complete for new rewards.

ABOUT SERIES 2 FIGURES

Most of the Skylanders from the first game are being re-released as Series 2 figures. You can tell if your figure is Series 1 or Series 2 when you put it on the portal.

Series 2 figures get some additional benefits. All Series 2 Skylanders get a special Wow Pow power that enhances an existing power. Additionally, Series 2 Skylanders can change their Upgrade Paths without being reset.

SERIES 1   SERIES 2

THE SKYLANDERS

The following pages have a great deal of information about the Skylanders, including their starting stats, powers, upgrades and putting their powers to good use. Use these two pages as both a checklist of available toys and as a quick reference to find which pages in this guide have the Skylander you want to know more about.

CHECKLIST KEY

Series 1	Characters who were introduced in *Skylanders Spyro's Adventure*.
Legendary	Legendary versions of characters from *Skylanders Spyro's Adventure* and *Skylanders Giants*.
New Character	New characters introduced in *Skylanders Giants*.
Giant	New characters introduced in *Skylanders Giants* that are larger than standard Skylanders.
Series 2	New versions of characters for *Skylanders Giants* that first appeared in *Skylanders Spyro's Adventure*. Series 2 Skylanders have a special "Wow Pow" power.
Lightcore™	Lightcore are special versions of Skylanders. Their powers have a special glow, and when you place them on the Portal, they blast out an area-of-effect attack!
Alt Deco	Alternate color schemes for certain characters. This color scheme appears on both the toy and while playing the game.

GIANT SKYLANDERS

SWARM 6	TREE REX 8	EYE-BRAWL 10	CRUSHER 12	HOT HEAD 14	THUMPBACK 16	NINJINI 18	BOUNCER 20
GIANT	GIANT	GIANT	GIANT	GIANT	GIANT	GIANT	GIANT
	ALT DECO (Gnarly Tree Rex)		ALT DECO (Granite Crusher)			ALT DECO (Scarlet Ninjini)	GIANT LEGENDARY

AIR SKYLANDERS

JET-VAC 22	SONIC BOOM 24	WHIRLWIND 26	LIGHTNING ROD 28	WARNADO 30
New Character	Series 1	Series 1	Series 1	Series 1
New Character Legendary	Series 2	Series 2	Series 2	
Lightcore™		Alt Deco (Polar Whirlwind)		

LIFE SKYLANDERS

SHROOMBOOM 32	CAMO 34	STUMP SMASH 36	ZOOK 38	STEALTH ELF 40
New Character	Series 1	Series 1	Series 1	Series 1
Lightcore™		Series 2	Series 2	Series 2
				Series 2 Legendary

UNDEAD SKYLANDERS

FRIGHT RIDER 42
- ○ New Character

CYNDER 44
- ○ Series 1
- ✓ Series 2

CHOP CHOP 46
- ○ Series 1
- ○ Series 1 Legendary
- ○ Series 2

HEX 48
- ○ Series 1
- ○ Series 2

GHOST ROASTER 50
- ○ Series 1

EARTH SKYLANDERS

FLASHWING 52
- ○ New Character
- ○ Alt Deco (Jade Flashwing)

BASH 54
- ○ Series 1
- ○ Series 1 Legendary
- ○ Series 2

DINO-RANG 56
- ○ Series 1

PRISM BREAK 58
- ○ Series 1
- ○ Series 2
- ○ Lightcore™

TERRAFIN 60
- ○ Series 1
- ✓ Series 2

FIRE SKYLANDERS

HOT DOG 62
- ✓ New Character
- ○ Alt Deco (Molten Hot Dog)

IGNITOR 64
- ✓ Series 1
- ○ Series 2
- ○ Series 2 Legendary

SUNBURN 66
- ○ Series 1

ERUPTOR 68
- ○ Series 1
- ✓ Series 2
- ○ Lightcore™

FLAMESLINGER 70
- ○ Series 1
- ○ Series 2

WATER SKYLANDERS

CHILL 72
- ○ New Character
- ○ New Character Legendary
- ○ Lightcore™

ZAP 74
- ○ Series 1
- ✓ Series 2

WHAM-SHELL 76
- ○ Series 1

GILL GRUNT 78
- ○ Series 1
- ✓ Series 2

SLAM BAM 80
- ○ Series 1
- ○ Series 2
- ○ Series 2 Legendary

MAGIC SKYLANDERS

POP FIZZ 82
- ✓ New Character
- ○ Lightcore™
- ○ Alt Deco (Punch Pop Fizz)

SPYRO 84
- ○ Series 1
- ○ Series 1 Legendary
- ○ Dark Spyro
- ○ Series 2

DOUBLE TROUBLE 86
- ○ Series 1
- ○ Series 2
- ○ Alt Deco (Royal Double Trouble)

WRECKING BALL 88
- ○ Series 1
- ✓ Series 2

VOODOOD 90
- ○ Series 1

TECH SKYLANDERS

SPROCKET 92
- ○ New Character

DRILL SERGEANT 94
- ○ Series 1
- ✓ Series 2

BOOMER 96
- ○ Series 1

DROBOT 98
- ○ Series 1
- ○ Series 2
- ✓ Lightcore™

TRIGGER HAPPY 100
- ○ Series 1
- ○ Series 1 Legendary
- ○ Series 2

SWARM

"BRING THE STING!"

STATS

♥		400
⚡	20	
🛡	12	
◎	50	
◉	25	

UPGRADE PATHS

BARBEROUS AVENGER
Further develop Swarm's Barb Blade attacks.

WASP STORMER
Further develop Swarm's Swarm Form attacks.

SOUL GEM ABILITY

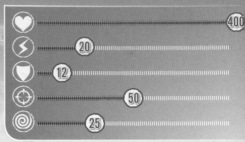

BEE IS FOR BUTT STINGER
COST: 4,000 Gold
PREREQUISITE: Find Soul Gem in Cutthroat Carnival level
DAMAGE: Low
RANGE: Long
SPEED: Fast

While flying, press **Attack 3** to fire butt stinger missiles that track enemies.

STRATEGY
One of the difficulties of the Flight of the Wasp attacks is that they are hard to redirect quickly if an enemy gets behind Swarm. Luckily, Bee is for Butt Stinger fills in this deficiency, allowing Swarm to repeatedly blast a butt stinger back at any enemies unlucky enough to be standing behind him.

SPECIAL QUEST

SWARM FEELINGS:
DEFEAT 100 ENEMIES IN SWARM FORM.

While you can complete this quest without pursuing the Wasp Stormer Path, it's extremely difficult, and you must focus on weaker enemies. With the Wasp Stormer Path, this quest is a piece of cake. Simply use your Swarm Form regularly, and it unlocks in no time.

First, you should disregard Swarm's Speed stat, his Flight of the Wasp (Attack 2) makes him the fastest Giant in the game. However, he's the least armored of the Giants, so while using him, you need to do your best to stay out of range of enemy attacks. Flight of the Wasp is an excellent form of transportation, and a great power for quickly blasting through levels.

Focus on the Wasp Stormer Path, which improves Swarm's weird Swarm Form attacks. While in Swarm Form, simply being near enemies damages them, which allows you to focus on avoiding incoming attacks. Swarm Form has deadly directed and area-of-effect attacks that are tremendously effective in all combat situations.

PRIMARY ATTACKS

ATTACK 1

BARB BLADES

COST: N/A
DAMAGE: Medium
RANGE: Short
SPEED: Average

Press **Attack 1** to slash enemies.

UPGRADES

SHARPENED BARBS

COST: 500 Gold
PREREQUISITE: None

Barb Blades melee attacks do increased damage.

STINGER SHOT

COST: 1,200 Gold
PREREQUISITE: None

Hold **Attack 1** to charge up and release to shoot a stinging energy blast.

ULTIMATE BARBS

COST: 3,000 Gold
PREREQUISITE: Barberous Avenger Path

All Barb Blade attacks do maximum damage.

STRATEGY

Swarm's Blade melee attacks are his most damaging attacks, and the upgrades serve to make them even more deadly. Stinger Shot is a particularly powerful attack that blasts enemies for bonus damage and has a short charge duration. As you upgrade Swarm's Barbs, he gets more and more effective at melee fighting. Use Flight of the Wasp to circle around enemies, drop back to the ground and finish them off with a series of melee Barb attacks.

ATTACK 2

FLIGHT OF THE WASP

COST: N/A
DAMAGE: Very Low
RANGE: Long
SPEED: Fast

Press **Attack 2** to hover in the air. While flying, press **Attack 1** to shoot Barb Blades.

UPGRADES

WINGIN' IT

COST: 700 Gold
PREREQUISITE: None

Can fly faster and for longer durations.

RAZOR WINGS

COST: 1,700 Gold
PREREQUISITE: Barberous Avenger Path

Wings damage any enemies they touch.

BETTER BARB BLAST

COST: 2,200 Gold
PREREQUISITE: Barberous Avenger Path

Barb Blades shot while flying do increased damage.

STRATEGY

Flight of the Wasp gives Swarm excellent maneuverability, and allows him to attack at long range. While the damage of Flight of the Wasp is not particularly high, it can be a very useful attack when faced with lots of small, but dangerous enemies. Enemies like archers and other ranged attackers are the ideal matchup.

Razor Wings is an impractical attack. When Swarm gets close to his enemies, they take a very low amount of damage, not unlike the basic Swarm Form attack. That upgrade can wait to be purchased when you have extra money.

ATTACK 3

SWARM FORM

COST: 900 Gold
DAMAGE: Very Low
RANGE: Short
SPEED: N/A

Press **Attack 3** to turn into a swarm of bugs which damage everything they touch.

UPGRADES

SWARM STORM

COST: 1,700 Gold
PREREQUISITE: Wasp Stormer Path

Swarm Form is bigger and does increased damage.

INSECTSPLOSION

COST: 2,200 Gold
PREREQUISITE: Wasp Stormer Path

While in Swarm Form, press **Attack 2** to do shockwave damage.

BEE CLEAVER

COST: 3,000 Gold
PREREQUISITE: Wasp Stormer Path

While in Swarm Form, press **Attack 1** to form a giant axe and swing at enemies.

STRATEGY

Swarm Form attack is one of the most unusual abilities in the game. Surrounding himself with an angry bee swarm, Swarm simply needs to walk near foes to damage them. This is a great way to attack dangerous enemies since you never need to stop moving to attack, just keep circling the enemy, inflicting damage automatically while you focus on dodging incoming attacks. Swarm Form's drawback is that it has extremely low damage. Luckily, this is offset if you pursue the Wasp Stormer Path. Both of the special attacks are very effective and bump Swarm Form's damage potential up to a "Very High" rating.

Insectsplosion is a medium-range area-of-effect attack that hits all enemies for about 30 points of damage. The bees blast out hitting anything standing nearby. Bee Cleaver is a tremendously damaging focused attack that hits enemies directly in front of Swarm. It can hit for over 100 damage!

TREE REX

"BE AFRAID OF THE BARK!"

STATS

♥		43
⚡	20	
🛡	24	
⊕	40	
◎	25	

UPGRADE PATHS

TREEFOLK CHARGER
Provides more upgrades for the Sequoia Stampede attacks.

LUMBERING LASERER
Provides more upgrades for the Photosynthesis Cannon.

SOUL GEM ABILITY

WOODPECKER PAL

COST: 4,000 Gold

PREREQUISITE: Find Soul Gem in Molekin Mountain

A woodpecker buddy joins Tree Rex in battle.

STRATEGY
This fun Soul Gem gives Tree Rex a woodpecker that hangs out on his back. When there are enemies nearby, the woodpecker swoops down and attacks for a moderate amount of damage.

SPECIAL QUEST

TIMBERRRRR!: DEFEAT 50 ENEMIES BY LANDING ON THEM. CHOMPIES DON'T COUNT!

Unfortunately, the Elbow Drop maneuver doesn't work for this quest. In order to complete it, you must crush enemies by landing on them. The best way to do this is to find a bounce pad in an area with plenty of Chompies. Repeatedly bounce on the pad as each squashed enemy counts towards this quest.

If you are looking for a crushing bruiser with massive melee and charging attacks, then look no further than this Giant. Tree Rex has a massive primary attack that does incredible damage to his foes. Additionally, his fantastic charging attack allows him to blow through enemies before they even get a chance for an initial attack. Tree Rex's final attack, Photosynthesis Cannon, harnesses the power of the sun to blast enemies at range.

Tree Rex's upgrade paths give you two clear choices: Range or Charging. Strongly consider the Treefolk Charger Path. While the Photosynthesis Cannon can inflict major damage once it has been fully upgraded, Tree Rex is best suited charging through enemies and dropping elbows on any survivors.

PRIMARY ATTACKS

ATTACK 1

SHOCKWAVE SLAM
COST: N/A
DAMAGE: High
RANGE: Medium
SPEED: Slow

Press the **Attack 1** button to slam the ground with massive fists, causing shockwaves.

UPGRADES

BIG THORN SHOCKWAVE SLAM
COST: 700 Gold
PREREQUISITE: None

Press and hold **Attack 1** for a bigger, more powerful Shockwave Slam.

STRATEGY

No one said Tree Rex was a complicated guy, and his slam attacks are the epitome of simple. Tree Rex smashes the ground directly in front of him, hurting any enemies in range. His cheap Big Thorn upgrade inflicts massive damage on enemies, even those at medium range. The Slam attack doesn't have many upgrades, but it doesn't need them to be effective. In the majority of combat situations, this is Tree Rex's go-to attack.

ATTACK 2

SEQUOIA STAMPEDE
COST: N/A
DAMAGE: Medium-Low
RANGE: Medium
SPEED: Medium

Press and hold the **Attack 2** button to charge through enemies and obstacles.

UPGRADES

SUPER STAMPEDE
COST: 900 Gold
PREREQUISITE: None

Sequoia Stampede attack does increased damage.

TITANIC ELBOW DROP
COST: 1,700 Gold
PREREQUISITE: Treefolk Charger Path

Press **Attack 1** while charging to perform one serious elbow drop move.

LIGHTFOOTED
COST: 2,200 Gold
PREREQUISITE: Treefolk Charger Path

Charge longer and faster, doing more damage in the process.

ULTIMATE STAMPEDE
COST: 3,000 Gold
PREREQUISITE: Treefolk Charger Path

Sequoia Stampede attack does maximum damage.

STRATEGY

Stampede starts off as a useful ability mostly for the extra speed it provides. However, if you choose the Treefolk Charger path, Stampede gains many extra benefits, including damage as good as his slams, and speed that makes him one of the fastest Giants in the game. The Titanic Elbow Drop upgrade inflicts massive damage on any enemy unfortunate enough to get caught in the seismic blast of Tree Rex's landing.

ATTACK 3

PHOTOSYNTHESIS CANNON
COST: 500 Gold
PREREQUISITE: None
DAMAGE: Very Low
RANGE: Long
SPEED: Medium

Press **Attack 3** to harness the power of the sun and shoot light beams.

UPGRADES

TREEFOLK TRIPLESHOT
COST: 1,200 Gold
PREREQUISITE: Photosynthesis Cannon

Photosynthesis Cannon fires triple burst shots.

SUPER-CHARGED VAPORIZER
COST: 1,700 Gold
PREREQUISITE: Lumbering Laserer Path

Hold down **Attack 3** to charge up the Photosynthesis Cannon for more damage.

SUN SKEWER
COST: 2,200 Gold
PREREQUISITE: Lumbering Laserer Path

Photosynthesis Cannon blasts through enemies and explodes for more damage.

THE POD MAKER
COST: 3,000 Gold
PREREQUISITE: Super-Charged Vaporizer

Vaporized enemies turn into exploding plant pods.

STRATEGY

Photosynthesis Cannon will never be as damaging as Tree Rex's Slam attacks, but it makes up for lack of power with massive range. A fully upgraded Cannon with the Lumbering Laserer Path empowers the weapon to wreak complete havoc on the battlefield.

Super-Charged Vaporizer is one of the most damaging powers in the game. It can be hard to hit enemies with it, but even the mightiest of them will fall to the blast. After defeating an enemy with Super-Charged Vaporizer, they turn into Plant Pods which explode, dealing even more damage to nearby foes.

EYE-BRAWL

"I'VE GOT MY EYE ON YOU."

STATS

♥	430
⚡	20
🛡	30
⊕	50
◎	25

UPGRADE PATHS

EYE BRAWLER
Further develop Eye-Brawl's melee combat skills.

EYE FOR AN EYE
Further develop Flying Eyeball abilities.

SOUL GEM ABILITY

YOU'LL SHOOT YOUR EYE OUT!
COST: 4,000 Gold

PREREQUISITE: Find Soul Gem in the level The Oracle

Hold **Attack 1** to charge up Eye-Brawl's eye, release to pop it off the body, smashing directly ahead.

STRATEGY

This is an interesting Soul Gem ability because it doesn't directly enhance any of Eye-Brawl's other powers. This attack takes some practice; you must become good at releasing **Attack 1** at the right time. When you get it down, it's an effective high-damage attack, but should only be used against stationary objects. Additionally, if you upgrade via the melee path, you can probably do more damage with normal melee attacks in the time it would take to charge and attack with this skill. Hold off on investing in this skill until you have extra money.

SPECIAL QUEST

GOLD SEARCH: COLLECT 5,000 GOLD WITH THE EYEBALL DETACHED.

Five thousand is a considerable sum of gold, but if you focus on Eye Fly skills, you should be able to get this within two to three chapters. If you don't have much invested in Eye Fly, detach your eye before collecting any treasure from chests or enemies.

Eye-Brawl is a lumbering eyeball monster with excellent melee attacks, and some interesting, albeit initially less effective alternate powers. Eye-Brawl takes a while to develop his full power.

At first the Giant seems slow, and his eyeball attacks deal very low damage. Stick with him, and the true power of the eyeball becomes more apparent. Eye-Brawl's upgrades include powerful lasers, and the ability to spawn smaller eyeballs every time the laser fires.

There's no question that the Eye for an Eye path is the better investment for Eye-Brawl. While he is a competent melee fighter, his unique flying eye attacks are where he is strongest.

PRIMARY ATTACKS

ATTACK 1

HAYMAKER

COST: N/A
DAMAGE: Medium
RANGE: Short
SPEED: Slow

Press the **Attack 1** button to throw some heavy punches. Press **Attack 1**, **Attack 1**, and then HOLD **Attack 1** for a special combo.

UPGRADES

THE PUMMELER

COST: 900 Gold
PREREQUISITE: None
Punch attacks do increased damage.

EYE-BRAWL COMBOS

COST: 1,700 Gold
PREREQUISITE: Eye Brawler Path
Press **Attack 1**, **Attack 1**, and then HOLD **Attack 2** for Eye Ball Spin.

Press **Attack 1**, **Attack 1**, and then HOLD **Attack 3** for 360 Spin.

ULTIMATE PUMMELER

COST: 2,200 Gold
PREREQUISITE: Eye Brawler Path
Melee attacks do additional damage.

BEATS AN EYE PATCH

COST: 3,000 Gold
PREREQUISITE: Eye Brawler Path
New armor provides additional protection.

STRATEGY

It doesn't get much more straightforward than Eye-Brawl's primary punch attack. The hulking eyeball smashes any enemies at close range. Later upgrades allow for more damage and more variety of attacks. The Eye Ball Spin combo (**Attack 2**) shoots an extra-damaging eye straight forward. The 360 Spin does what it says and hits any enemy within a large radius around Eye-Brawl. Of particular interest on the Eye-Brawler upgrade path are the improvements to damage and armor, which allows Eye-Brawl to more easily stand toe-to-toe with other melee enemies.

ATTACK 2

EYE FLY

COST: N/A
DAMAGE: Very Low
RANGE: Long
SPEED: Fast

Press the **Attack 2** button to detach the eyeball and fly around. While flying, press **Attack 1** to shoot eye lasers.

UPGRADES

AWESOME OCCU-BLAST

COST: 700 Gold
PREREQUISITE: None
Eye laser has a faster rate of fire.

HEADLESS, NOT HELPLESS

COST: 1,200 Gold
PREREQUISITE: None
While flying the eyeball, his headless body will punch continuously.

ASSERTING INDEPENDENCE

COST: 1,700 Gold
PREREQUISITE: Eye for an Eye Path
Eyeball can now fly faster and for a longer duration.

EYE-CRAWLERS

COST: 2,200 Gold
PREREQUISITE: Eye for an Eye Path
When enemies are hit with eye lasers, eyes form around the point of impact.

BOUNCY BOUNCY!

COST: 3,000 Gold
PREREQUISITE: Eye for an Eye Path
While flying the eyeball, press **Attack 3** to bounce the eye on the ground.

STRATEGY

This unique power detaches Eye-Brawl's eye and lets you fly it around while the body stays in place. When you earn the Headless, Not Helpless upgrade, the body follows the eye while swinging blindly with Eye-Brawl's massive arms.

Eye Fly's initial attack, an eye laser, is fairly weak. However, as you upgrade via the Eye for an Eye path, you get better avenues of attack. Eye-Crawlers and Bouncy Bouncy! both enhance the attack significantly, allowing Eye Fly to wreak serious havoc on surrounding foes. When you're going up against bosses and other highly damaging enemies, you must be careful when you leave Eye-Brawl's body alone. It is relatively helpless against incoming damage, and you won't be able to dodge any big incoming attacks with Eye Fly separated from the body.

ATTACK 3

AN EYE IN TEAM

COST: 500 Gold
PREREQUISITE: None
DAMAGE: Medium
RANGE: Medium
SPEED: Slow

Press **Attack 3** to summon more eyeballs from the earth to attack enemies.

STRATEGY

This strange power allows Eye-Brawl to summon several eyeballs from the earth that seek out and attack nearby enemies. While they don't inflict major damage on enemies, they can serve to distract them as you move in to attack with melee attacks or Eye Fly.

CRUSHER

"IT'S CRUSH HOUR!"

STATS

♥		47
⚡	20	
🛡	24	
◎	40	
◎	25	

UPGRADE PATHS

ROCK GRINDER
Further develop Crusher's Hammer attacks.

RUBBLE MASTER
Further develop Crusher's Rockslide attacks.

SOUL GEM ABILITY

ROCKSLIDIN' OUT!

COST: 4,000 Gold

PREREQUISITE: Find Soul Gem in Troll Home Security level

Hold **Attack 3** to steer Rockslide boulders around.

STRATEGY

This power further enhances Crusher's ability to control his movements while in Rockslide form. This makes it much easier to repeatedly roll over enemies and avoid incoming attacks.

SPECIAL QUEST

HIGH ROLLER:
DEFEAT 100 ENEMIES WITH BOULDERS.

This straightforward quest simply requires Crusher to use his Rockslide ability to defeat many enemies. Even if you don't choose the Rubble Master path, you can still achieve this quest by regularly using Rockslide against weaker enemies, such as Chompies.

When you first see Crusher, you might expect that he's good only for crushing things, but he also has formidable crowd control and defensive capabilities. His beam can freeze almost any enemy in its path (including some bosses!). Additionally, his Rockslide power is unique and is a great area-of-effect attack that also provides excellent defense and maneuverability in combat.

In addition to his fantastic secondary powers, Crusher is hands-down one of the best melee characters in the game. He's best suited to face off against huge enemies and bosses.

PRIMARY ATTACKS

ATTACK 1

CRUSHER'S CRUSHER

COST: N/A

DAMAGE: High

RANGE: Short

SPEED: Fast

Press **Attack 1** to swing the big hammer, also named "Crusher."

Press **Attack 1**, **Attack 1**, HOLD **Attack 1** for a special combo.

UPGRADES

GROUND GRINDER

COST: 500 Gold

PREREQUISITE: None

Hold **Attack 1** to hit the ground so hard that it makes a crack in the ground that damages enemies.

SUPER CRUSHER

COST: 900 Gold

PREREQUISITE: None

Hammer does increased damage.

CRUSHER COMBOS

COST: 1,700 Gold

PREREQUISITE: Rock Grinder Path

Press **Attack 1**, **Attack 1**, HOLD **Attack 2** for Hammer Throw.

Press **Attack 1**, **Attack 1**, HOLD **Attack 3** for 360 Spin.

HAMMER DADDY

COST: 2,200 Gold

PREREQUISITE: Rock Grinder Path

Hammer takes the face of Crusher's father and does increased damage.

TRIPLE GROUND GRINDER

COST: 3,000 Gold

PREREQUISITE: Rock Grinder Path

Hold **Attack 1** to hit the ground and make three cracks appear to damage enemies.

STRATEGY

Crusher's hammer does massive damage, swings relatively fast, and upgrades like Triple Ground Grinder help eliminate the Skylander's foes at an even faster rate. There's no doubt that to realize Crusher's full potential, you should focus on the Rock Grinder Path. The extra damage from Crusher's hammer makes rapidly cutting through boss health bars his specialty.

Crusher has three combos. The **Attack 1** combo is a simple version of the Triple Ground Grinder upgrade; a seismic rift appears in the ground and hurts enemies straight ahead. Hammer Throw (**Attack 2**) tosses Crusher's hammer a long distance straight ahead. It inflicts massive damage and is great against bosses. 360 Spin (**Attack 3**) is fantastic for situations where Crusher is surrounded by enemies; it does heavy damage to any enemy at short range.

ATTACK 2

TURN TO STONE

COST: N/A

DAMAGE: None

RANGE: Short

SPEED: Average

Press **Attack 2** to shoot eye beams that turn enemies to stone.

UPGRADES

CAVELIGHT BLAST

COST: 1,200 Gold

PREREQUISITE: None

While holding **Attack 2**, press **Attack 1** to launch a pulse of energy that damages enemies.

STRATEGY

Crusher's alternate attack literally turns his enemies to stone. Almost any foe unlucky enough to get caught in Crusher's beam is frozen for about five seconds. This attack is particularly useful against enemies with special defensive capabilities like Inhuman Shields. Crusher's beam cuts right through their defenses. While the attack initially does no damage, once you unlock Cavelight Blast, you can inflict damage on nearby enemies by repeatedly tapping the **Attack 1** button while using the beam.

ATTACK 3

ROCKSLIDE

COST: 700 Gold

DAMAGE: Very Low

RANGE: Long

SPEED: Average

Press **Attack 3** to break apart into boulders running over anything in their path.

UPGRADES

CONTROLLED ROCKSLIDE

COST: 1,700 Gold

PREREQUISITE: Rubble Master Path

Control the direction of your Rockslide attack.

BOULDER BOMBS

COST: 2,200 Gold

PREREQUISITE: Rubble Master Path

While in a Rockslide, press **Attack 1** to detonate boulders.

BEDROCK ARMOR

COST: 3,000 Gold

PREREQUISITE: Rubble Master Path

Special rock from deep within the earth provides increased armor.

STRATEGY

Rockslide is the perfect attack to utilize when Crusher is surrounded by enemies. He breaks up into several boulders and blasts out, inflicting low damage to any enemies in range (the spread is quite wide). Executing this attack makes Crusher difficult to hit. That makes it an excellent defensive tactic as well as an area-of-effect attack.

If you decide to take Crusher down the Rubble Master Path, then Rockslide only gets better, allowing for better passive defense and more control over where the rocks roll. Boulder Bombs dramatically increases the damage potential of Crusher, and allows him to quickly reform when necessary.

HOT HEAD

"I'M ON FIRE!"

STATS

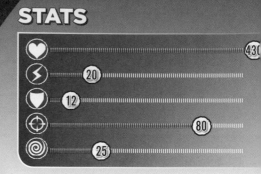

❤	430
⚡	20
🛡	12
⊕	80
◎	25

UPGRADE PATHS

THE BURNINATOR
Further develop Hot Head's cooking skills.

OIL BARON
Further develop Hot Head's Sizzle Showering skills.

SOUL GEM ABILITY

HOT ROD
COST: 4,000 Gold
PREREQUISITE: Find Soul Gem in Junkyard Isles
DAMAGE: Average
RANGE: Short
SPEED: Average
Hold **Attack 1** and **Attack 2** to transform into a hot rod!

STRATEGY
This power transforms Hot Head into a motorcycle that can run over enemies. While this transformation does give him some additional speed, Hot Head still moves slowly compared to fast Skylanders. The motorcycle inflicts average damage, but does make it much harder for enemies to hit him.

SPECIAL QUEST

BUGGY BREAKTHROUGH:
DESTROY 20 WALLS IN HOT ROD MODE.

The walls this quest is referring to are the walls that can only be crushed by a Giant or a bomb. Once you save up enough Gold to unlock the Hot Rod Power (and find the Soul Gem), you can start working on this quest.

Whenever you get to one of these walls switch to Hot Head, and you'll finish this quest in no time. A good spot with plenty of these types of walls is Chapter 2: Junkyard Isles.

Hot Head's favorite thing to do in life is to light things on fire. Luckily, he's on your side and you can use him to wreak flaming chaos on the battlefield, wiping out the Skylanders' opposition. Hot Head's primary attack is the one-two punch of Flamefire Burst and Oil Blobs. Cover your enemies with oil, then light them on fire. There are few attacks as effective for taking out enemies with loads of health.

On the other end is Hot Head's Sizzle Shower. An area-of-effect attack that starts out weak, but as you improve it with the Oil Baron Path, it dramatically improves and becomes one of the most versatile powers in the game.

PRIMARY ATTACKS

ATTACK 1

FLAMEFIRE BURST

COST: N/A

DAMAGE: Medium

RANGE: Long

SPEED: Very Fast

Press **Attack 1** to shoot a burst of fire. Hold **Attack 1** to keep flames going.

UPGRADES

TURN UP THE HEAT!

COST: 900 Gold

PREREQUISITE: None

Flamefire Burst gets even hotter and does increased damage.

ETERNAL FLAME

COST: 1,700 Gold

PREREQUISITE: The Burninator Path

Can use Flamefire Burst continuously and does maximum damage.

STRATEGY

Flamefire Burst is a flamethrower-type attack. Generally, you should hold down the button when using this attack. However, holding down the button does have a drawback: it limits Hot Head's slow movement.

Flamefire Burst hurts an enemy about once per second, as long as you keep them in the flames. This attack is designed to be used in conjunction with Oil Blobs. Light the Blobs on fire with Flamefire Burst, and enemies covered in the oil take high damage every second the flames are lit.

ATTACK 2

OIL BLOBS

COST: N/A

DAMAGE: Medium

RANGE: Medium

SPEED: Slow

Press **Attack 2** to shoot a blob of oil that can get lit on fire for serious damage.

UPGRADES

PREMIUM GRADE

COST: 500 Gold

PREREQUISITE: None

Oil Blobs and ignited Oil Blobs do increased damage.

FOSSIL FUEL

COST: 3,000 Gold

PREREQUISITE: The Burninator Path

Oil Blobs turn into fossilized monsters who attack enemies.

HOT OIL TREATMENT

COST: 2,200 Gold

PREREQUISITE: The Burninator Path

Oil Blobs and ignited Oil Blobs do maximum damage.

STRATEGY

Oil Blobs don't just cover your enemies in extremely flammable oil, but they also do pretty decent damage when they first hit. Shoot blobs on tougher enemies, and follow it up with a Flamefire Burst to inflict massive damage very quickly. If you choose the Burninator Path, not only do your blobs get more deadly, but you also get the Fossil Fuel ability which turns the blobs into strange oil creatures that seek out Hot Head's enemies. Light these pet blobs on fire to make them even more effective!

ATTACK 3

SIZZLE SHOWER

COST: 700 Gold

DAMAGE: Very Low

RANGE: Medium

SPEED: Average

Press **Attack 3** to summon a rain of fire from the sky.

UPGRADES

EXTENDED FORECAST

COST: 1,200 Gold

PREREQUISITE: Sizzle Shower

Sizzle Shower lasts longer and does increased damage.

FIRE STORM

COST: 1,700 Gold

PREREQUISITE: Oil Baron Path

Sizzle Shower does maximum damage and covers a larger area.

OIL AND FIRE

COST: 2,200 Gold

PREREQUISITE: Oil Baron Path

During a Sizzle Shower, press **Attack 2** to create an oily explosion, catching enemies on fire.

HOT WITH A CHANCE OF METEORS

COST: 3,000 Gold

PREREQUISITE: Oil Baron Path

Hold **Attack 3** to summon a gigantic meteor from the sky.

STRATEGY

Sizzle Shower starts off as a somewhat wimpy area-of-effect power. It showers Hot Head's enemies with a light lava rain that does minimal damage. The advantage of Sizzle Shower is that it lasts a relatively long time and covers a wide area. If you decide to go down the Oil Baron Path, Sizzle Shower is transformed into an extremely powerful area-of-effect attack that can be concentrated to dish out well over 100 damage in a wide area.

Oil and Fire quickly sprays oil in all directions doubling the effect of a normal Sizzle Shower's damage. To use Hot with a Chance of Meteors, start a normal Sizzle Shower, then hold **Attack 3** to charge the attack. Release the attack to smash anything standing in front of Hot Head. You don't need to charge it fully to inflict massive damage.

THUMPBACK

"HAIL TO THE WHALE!"

STATS

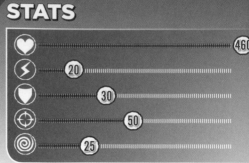

- ♥ — 460
- ⚡ — 20
- 🛡 — 30
- ⊕ — 50
- ◎ — 25

UPGRADE PATHS

ANCHOR'S A-YAY!!
Provides more upgrades for the Anchor attacks.

UP CLOSE AND PERSONAL
Provides more upgrades for the Belly Flop and Chomp attacks.

SOUL GEM ABILITY

BLOWHARD
COST: 4,000 Gold

PREREQUISITE: Find Soul Gem in Glacier Gully

While belly sliding, press the **Attack 1** button to spray water and starfish.

Thumpback represents the Water element in a big way. He has a huge anchor-based melee attack and crushing (literally) alternate attacks.

Thumpback's regular melee attack has excellent range, and can hit enemies halfway across the screen.

Additionally, Thumpback can slide on his belly, quickly dashing by enemies, but inflicting huge damage on the way. Thumpback also has a massively damaging Chomp attack that can crush enemies at close-range.

We recommend that you pick the Anchor's A-Yay!! Path when upgrading Thumpback. Thumpback's anchor attack is massively powerful in both damage and range, and improving the attack with extra combos and even more damage makes him as effective as possible in combat.

STRATEGY

This is a great add-on for the Belly Flop attack. When you hit **Attack 1** Thumpback blows a starfish and water out of his blowhole, which blasts any enemies he is sliding near. This can be done once per slide, but is very effective, especially if you miss with the Belly Flop attack directly.

The damage from this attack stacks on top of the regular Belly Flop damage. This means you can effectively hit any enemy twice with each Flop. Hit them once with the regular Flop, and hit Blowhard to blast them a second time before the slide is over. This is tremendously effective against large, cumbersome enemies.

SPECIAL QUEST

BEACHED WHALE:
DEFEAT 8 ENEMIES WITH ONE BELLY FLOP.

Thumpback's Belly Flop attack needs to be upgraded to achieve this. Once you have unlocked Slippery Belly, Thumpback can slide long distances and easily defeat enemies with low health. If you are having trouble getting this quest, invest in the Up Close and Personal Path to further increase the strength of the Belly Flop attack.

PRIMARY ATTACKS

ATTACK 1

ANCHOR ASSAULT

COST: N/A
DAMAGE: High
RANGE: Long
SPEED: Slow

Press the **Attack 1** button to swing Thumpback's anchor at enemies. Press **Attack 1**, **Attack 1**, HOLD **Attack 1** for a special combo!

UPGRADES

NOW THERE'S AN ANCHOR!

COST: 1,200 Gold
PREREQUISITE: None
Increases Anchor Assault's damage.

THUMPBACK COMBOS

COST: 1,700 Gold
PREREQUISITE: Anchor's A-Yay!! Path
Press **Attack 1**, **Attack 1**, and HOLD **Attack 2** for Power Swing.

Press **Attack 1**, **Attack 1**, and HOLD **Attack 3** for Whirlpool Ripper.

BERMUDA TRIANGLE

COST: 2,200 Gold
PREREQUISITE: Thumpback Combos, Anchor's A-Yay!! Path
Increase the power of the Whirlpool Ripper combo attack.

ULTIMATE ANCHOR

COST: 3,000 Gold
PREREQUISITE: Anchor's A-Yay!! Path
Best anchor you can find! Does maximum damage.

STRATEGY

Thumpback's primary attack is a deadly swinging attack that hits enemies both on the swing out and the swing back. The attack is slow, but its extended range and extra damage on the way back in are tremendous benefits.

If you commit to Anchor's A-Yay!!, memorize Thumpback's combos and practice them to figure out which ones you like best. Of particular interest is the upgradeable Whirlpool Ripper combo, which creates a whirlpool anywhere on the map that damages any enemies unfortunate enough to be nearby.

ATTACK 2

BELLY FLOP

COST: N/A
DAMAGE: Medium/High
RANGE: Medium
SPEED: Medium

Press the **Attack 2** button to dive into a belly flop, damaging enemies.

UPGRADES

SLIPPERY BELLY

COST: 700 Gold
PREREQUISITE: None
Slide longer after a belly flop and do increased damage.

BREAKFAST IN BED

COST: 1,700 Gold
PREREQUISITE: Up Close and Personal Path
While Belly sliding, press **Attack 3** to chomp enemies.

ARMOR OF THE SEA

COST: 2,200 Gold
PREREQUISITE: Up Close and Personal Path
Seashells make for better armor.

STRATEGY

Thumpback's trademark Belly Slide lets him power through large groups of enemies. His speed while sliding makes him hard to hit, and the Belly Flop doubles as an excellent evasive maneuver, even if you don't focus on upgrading it. Be careful, it's very easy to slide off the side of a cliff!

ATTACK 3

A WHALE OF A CHOMP

COST: 500 Gold
DAMAGE: Very High
RANGE: Very Short
SPEED: Slow

Press the **Attack 3** button for a big, whale-sized chomp.

UPGRADES

THE WHALEST CHOMP

COST: 900 Gold
PREREQUISITE: A Whale of a Chomp
Bigger, most powerful Whale Chomp attack.

BAD SUSHI

COST: 3,000 Gold
PREREQUISITE: Up Close and Personal Path
Hold the **Attack 3** button to release a stream of projectile water vomit, damaging enemies.

STRATEGY

Whale of a Chomp should be the first power you buy for Thumpback. It gives him a high damage attack to employ against particularly tough monsters. Be wary, A Whale of a Chomp can open him up to attacks from enemies. You must get pretty close with Thumpback to hit anything with his attacks. However, if you invest in the Up Close and Personal Path later on, Thumpback gets better armor.

Bad Sushi is a medium-range attack that does similar damage to a basic anchor attack. Due to its cost, you can skip and use the regular anchor attacks for your ranged attacks.

NINJINI

"ANY LAST WISHES?"

STATS

♥ (health)	410
⚡ (speed)	60
🛡 (armor)	48
◎ (critical hit)	80
◎ (elemental power)	25

UPGRADE PATHS

SWORDS OF MIGHT
Empowers Ninjini's swords to wreak destruction upon her foes!

ANCIENT DJINN MAGIC
Harness ancient Djinn magic to improve Ninjini's bottle and Surrealistic Sphere attacks.

SOUL GEM ABILITY

DAZZLING ENCHANTMENT
COST: 4,000 Gold

PREREQUISITE: Find Soul Gem in Kaos' Kastle

While inside the bottle, hold down **Attack 3** to put enemies into a trance.

STRATEGY
This power makes Ninjini's bottle attacks more practical. When you activate Dazzling Enchantment, purple smoke pours out of the top of the bottle, putting nearby small and medium sized enemies to sleep. It's important to note that this trance effect does not work against large enemies.

SPECIAL QUEST

BOTTLE BEATDOWN:
DEFEAT 5 ENEMIES WITHIN FIVE SECONDS OF EXITING YOUR BOTTLE.

This is a simple one, just transform Ninjini into the bottle and move into a large group of small enemies. Follow up the bottle attack with her swords to complete the Quest.

Ninjini is a genie who attacks head-on with gigantic dual scimitars, and more stealthily via her trusty lamp. Her skills in magic allow her to attack from range; Surrealistic Orbs track down and defeat enemies without putting Ninjini in range of her foes. Ninjini's first upgrade path is The Swords of Might, which develops her Wishblade attacks and combos. The other path, Ancient Djinn Magic, improves her ranged attacks.

Ninjini can either be a ranged fighter or a close-up melee fighter. She's equally effective both ways, but you need to decide which style you prefer before committing to an upgrade path (you can't change the path once you've chosen it without completely resetting the character).

It's also worth noting that Ninjini has excellent stats. She has good Health, Armor, and Speed, but she has superb Critical Hit; tied for the highest of any Skylander in the game!

PRIMARY ATTACKS

ATTACK 1

WISHBLADES
COST: N/A
DAMAGE: Low
RANGE: Short
SPEED: Fast

Press the **Attack 1** button to swing dual swords for hacking and slashing enemies. Press **Attack 1**, **Attack 1**, HOLD **Attack 1** for a special combo.

UPGRADES

ABRA-CA-STAB-BRA
COST: 700 Gold
PREREQUISITE: None
Wishblades do increased damage.

WISHBLADE COMBOS
COST: 1,700 Gold
PREREQUISITE: Swords of Might Path
Press **Attack 1**, **Attack 1**, HOLD **Attack 2** for Fling Blade.
Press **Attack 1**, **Attack 1**, HOLD **Attack 3** for Enchanted Blade.

WISHBLADESPLOSION
COST: 2,200 Gold
PREREQUISITE: Swords of Might Path
Hold the **Attack 1** button to charge up the swords into an explosive blast.

ULTIMATE WISHBLADE
COST: 3,000 Gold
PREREQUISITE: Swords of Might Path
Wishblades do maximum damage.

STRATEGY
Ninjini's Wishblades turn her into a whirling dervish of destruction. While the blades don't do much damage, they are extremely fast and can slice through foes quickly.

The sword combos are excellent at extending a melee-focused Ninjini's range. The **Attack 2** combo causes Ninjini to throw her sword, and the **Attack 3** combo summons a sword to Ninjini's side. Once the sword is summoned, she can follow up with Bottle and Sphere attacks.

Wishbladesplosion is an immensely damaging attack. Charge the attack, and any enemies standing in front of Nijini take a major hit to their health.

ATTACK 2

BOTTLE BLAST
COST: N/A
DAMAGE: Medium
RANGE: Short
RANGE: Very Slow

Press the **Attack 2** button to hide inside the bottle. Press **Attack 2** again to blast out in a magical explosion.

UPGRADES

BOTTLE ROCKETS
COST: 1,200 Gold
PREREQUISITE: None
While inside the bottle, press **Attack 1** to launch rockets.

ULTIMATE BOTTLE ROCKETS
COST: 2,200 Gold
PREREQUISITE: Ancient Djinn Magic Path
Bottle rockets launch faster, do more damage, and affect a greater area.

BUY A BETTER BOTTLE
COST: 3,000 Gold
PREREQUISITE: Ancient Djinn Magic Path
Bottle is stronger and moves faster.

STRATEGY
Ninjini's secondary attack is a strange one. She jumps back into her bottle, and bounces slowly towards her enemies. Once in range, tap **Attack 2** a second time to burst forth and smash any enemies at a short range.

Initially, this is Ninjini's weakest attack, and doesn't compare favorably to Wishblades. However, if you commit to upgrade the bottle, it gains Bottle Rockets which makes the attack more viable. Be wary when using this attack, as it severely reduces Ninjini's maneuverability. The bottle initially provides no extra armor, and enemies will attack her even while in bottle form.

Once you get to the Buy a Better Bottle power, the bottle becomes a great defensive tactic. Going inside the bottle dramatically increases Ninjini's armor, allowing her to completely deflect a significant number of attacks. Stay in the bottle, and blast the enemies with the upgraded rockets.

ATTACK 3

SURREALISTIC SPHERES
COST: 500 Gold
DAMAGE: Medium-High
RANGE: Long
SPEED: Slow

Press **Attack 3** to summon magical orbs and cast them towards the enemies.

UPGRADES

JUGGLING ACT
COST: 900 Gold
PREREQUISITE: Surrealistic Spheres
Hold **Attack 3** to summon four magical orbs and damage multiple enemies.

SUPER SURREALISTIC SPHERES
COST: 1,700 Gold
PREREQUISITE: Ancient Djinn Magic Path
Magical orbs do more damage and affect a greater area.

STRATEGY
Surrealistic Spheres are an excellent long-range attack that allows Ninjini to stay back from her enemies and attack them with repeated blasts of arcane power. The biggest drawback to this attack is that it's difficult to control where the spheres go. This is particularly true of the Juggling Act Upgrade, which fires the spheres in four random directions.

BOUNCER

"DEAL WITH THE WHEEL!"

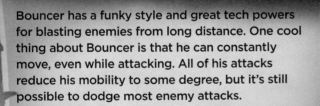

STATS

♥	43
⚡	60
🛡	24
◎	60
◉	25

UPGRADE PATHS

ROBOT ROCKETEER
Bouncer can fire off more rockets for greater damage.

I-BEAM SUPREME
Provides Bouncer with upgrades for his I-Beam and Fingerguns.

SOUL GEM ABILITY

FISTS OF DESTRUCTION!

COST: 4,000 Gold

PREREQUISITE: Find Soul Gem in Secret Vault of Secrets

While holding **Attack 1**, press **Attack 2** to fire off rocket-powered homing fists.

STRATEGY
Fists of Destruction give you extra options while using the Fingerguns. Be sure you are holding down **Attack 1** instead of rapidly tapping it to use this power. Press **Attack 2** and Bouncer fires his fists off directly ahead. The fists heat seek and turn towards any enemies in range.

SPECIAL QUEST

STAY ON TARGET!: TARGET ENEMIES 100 TIMES WITH LASER-GUIDED SHOULDER ROCKETS.

To earn this quest, you first need the Targeting Computer upgrade for your Shoulder Rockets. Once you have the upgrade, simply guide your rockets into any 100 enemies to complete the quest.

Bouncer has a funky style and great tech powers for blasting enemies from long distance. One cool thing about Bouncer is that he can constantly move, even while attacking. All of his attacks reduce his mobility to some degree, but it's still possible to dodge most enemy attacks.

Once you have purchased Bouncer's I-Beam attack, experiment with all three of his attacks to see which ones you like the best. All of them are fantastic in a variety of situations, but the upgrade paths force you to choose between continuing to upgrade Shoulder Rockets or the I-Beam and Fingerguns.

Ultimately, you should continue using all three attacks even after picking a path. They all have their place in Bouncer's arsenal.

PRIMARY ATTACKS

ATTACK 1

FINGERGUNS

COST: N/A

DAMAGE: Very Low

RANGE: Long

SPEED: Very Fast

Press the **Attack 1** button to shoot rapid-fire, ricocheting bouncy balls.

UPGRADES

MACHINE FINGERGUNS

COST: 900 Gold

PREREQUISITE: None

Press **Attack 1** to repeatedly fire Fingerguns at an accelerated rate.

SUPER MACHINE FINGERGUNS

COST: 1,700 Gold

PREREQUISITE: I-Beam Supreme Path

Rate of fire for Fingerguns increases and they do more damage too.

STRATEGY

Bouncer's primary attack is a low-damage, rapid fire ranged attack. The cool thing about Fingerguns is that the ammunition bounces off walls. This makes it much easier to hit enemies indirectly, without putting Bouncer in the line of fire. Fingerguns are a good alternate attack to pair with the I-Beam. They make up for their light damage with rapid attack; great for wiping out lots of little enemies. One important note is that you don't need to rapidly tap Fingerguns to use them. Just hold down **Attack 1** to launch an endless stream of bullets.

ATTACK 2

SHOULDER ROCKETS

COST: N/A

DAMAGE: Medium

RANGE: Medium

SPEED: Slow

Press **Attack 2** to launch rockets into the air that swiftly descend on enemies.

UPGRADES

TARGETING COMPUTER

COST: 700 Gold

PREREQUISITE: None

Hold **Attack 2** to bring up a target and control where rockets land.

ROCKETS ON DEMAND

COST: 2,200 Gold

PREREQUISITE: Robot Rocketeer Path

While holding **Attack 2**, press **Attack 1** to launch unlimited rockets.

DOUBLE TARGETS

COST: 1,700 Gold

PREREQUISITE: Robot Rocketeer Path

Now target 6 enemies at a time with laser-guided rockets.

ATOMIC CLOUDS

COST: 3,000 Gold

PREREQUISITE: Robot Rocketeer Path

Shoulder Rockets leave explosions that damage enemies.

STRATEGY

When Bouncer fires off Shoulder Rockets, they automatically track nearby enemies. The range is limited, and they fire slowly, but it's a reliable attack that allows Bouncer to keep evading incoming attacks while returning fire of his own. Once you get the targeting upgrades, you must keep Bouncer stationary while aiming, but it dramatically increases accuracy, and once you get Rockets on Demand, you can completely pound enemies with repeated rocket attacks. Few enemies can withstand a full volley of Bouncer's rockets. When you get Targeting Computer, you can still fire unguided Shoulder Rockets, just tap **Attack 2** instead of holding it down.

ATTACK 3

I-BEAM

COST: 500 Gold

DAMAGE: High

RANGE: Medium

SPEED: Slow

Press **Attack 3** to fire concentrated laser eye beams.

UPGRADES

COOLER I-BEAM

COST: 1,200 Gold

PREREQUISITE: I-Beam

Increases the damage of the I-Beam and reduces overheating.

LASER MINES

COST: 3,000 Gold

PREREQUISITE: I-Beam Supreme Path

While holding **Attack 3**, press **Attack 1** to drop laser mines.

PROFESSIONALLY COOL I-BEAM

COST: 2,200 Gold

PREREQUISITE: I-Beam Supreme Path

I-Beam does even more damage yet overheats slower.

STRATEGY

Bouncer's I-Beams take a second to warm up, but once they are ready, you can use them to pour damage relentlessly onto incoming enemies. I-Beams automatically inflict damage every second and home in on nearby enemies. I-Beams are a clear improvement over regular Shoulder Rockets, but Shoulder Rockets do get better as you upgrade them. The only disadvantage to the Beams is that it's hard for Bouncer to evade while they are activated. His turns are sluggish and you may need to stop firing for a second to avoid incoming attacks. This in turn, requires you to reheat the Beams to continue your attack.

Laser Mines are an awesome addition to the I-Beam. Just tap the **Attack 1** button three times while using the Beams to make three stationary laser mines that attack in a circular pattern. One last important note on the I-Beam is that it can overheat. However, this takes some time, and you get plenty of warning (watch for smoke to appear in Bouncer's eyes).

JET-VAC

"HAWK AND AWE!"

STATS

♥	240
⚡	50
🛡	12
⊕	20
◎	25

UPGRADE PATHS

BIRD BLASTER
Further develop Jet-Vac's Vac-Blaster attacks.

VAC-PACKETEER
Further develop Jet-Vac's Suction and Flight attacks.

SOUL GEM ABILITY

EAGLE-AIR BATTLE GEAR
COST: 4,000 Gold

PREREQUISITE: Find Jet-Vac's Soul Gem in the level Autogyro Adventure. Jet-Vac gets an enhanced armor and a pretty sweet visor.

STRATEGY

This is a straightforward power that boosts Jet-Vac's base armor and adds a sweet visor to his outfit.

SPECIAL QUEST

BIRD CLEANER:
SUCK UP 50 BIRDS IN YOUR SUCTION GUN.

Look for tiny birds on the ground throughout most levels with green grass. These birds are harmless, but that shouldn't stop you from sucking them up with your Suction Gun! Chapter 1 is a good spot for this; there are some birds right at the start point.

Jet-Vac has a super-powered vacuum device that allows him to send out a ranged attack to pick off his enemies from afar, or he can flip the switch and suck in nearby enemies.

Even though he's a bird, Jet-Vac doesn't fly naturally. Instead, he prefers to fly with the help of his vacuum device. He can only fly for a limited time, but it's enough time to attack or to evade combat, depending on what the situation warrants.

PRIMARY ATTACKS

ATTACK 1

VAC-BLASTER

COST: N/A
DAMAGE: Low
RANGE: Very Long
SPEED: Fast

Press **Attack 1** to shoot enemies with a powerful blast of air.

UPGRADES

VAC BLASTER 9000

COST: 900 Gold
PREREQUISITE: None

Vac Blaster does increased damage.

VAC MASTER-BLASTER 20X

COST: 2,200 Gold
PREREQUISITE: Bird Blaster Path

Vac Blaster does maximum damage.

PIERCING WINDS

COST: 1,700 Gold
PREREQUISITE: Bird Blaster Path

Vac Blaster does even more increased damage and pierces multiple enemies.

SUPER SUCTION AIR BLASTER

COST: 3,000 Gold
PREREQUISITE: Bird Blaster Path

Suck up enemies with the Suction Gun and it gives the Vac Blaster a super shot.

STRATEGY

The Vac-Blaster is an excellent ranged attack. It is easy to aim and can be fired rapidly to pile up the damage against Jet-Vac's foes. If you decide to go down the Bird Blaster path, the shots get more powerful, increasing damage by about 30%.

Super Suction Air Blaster, the last upgrade in the Bird Blaster Path, is a superb upgrade. Just suck any enemy up with Jet-Vac's Suction Gun (you don't need to defeat them, just damage them with the gun), and then press **Attack 1** to send out a super-blast that does tremendous damage and blows through enemy lines.

ATTACK 2

SUCTION GUN

COST: N/A
DAMAGE: Low
RANGE: Short
SPEED: Average

Hold **Attack 2** to suck enemies into the spinning fan blades.

UPGRADES

FEISTIER FAN

COST: 500 Gold
PREREQUISITE: None

Bigger spinning fan blades on the Suction Gun do increased damage to enemies.

THE MULCHER

COST: 2,200 Gold
PREREQUISITE: Vac-packeteer Path

Suction Gun attacks do maximum damage.

TURBINE SUCTION FAN

COST: 1,200 Gold
PREREQUISITE: Feistier Fan

Suction Gun attacks do even more increased damage.

STRATEGY

Jet-Vac's fan sucks nearby enemies into its whirring blades. When you use this power, it recharges the air pressure in Jet-Vac's pressure pack. This allows him to resume flying quickly if he runs out of air.

While Suction Gun's fan starts at a low-damage level, it gets three damage upgrades. By the time you get the third one, Suction Gun turns into a high-damage attack and is great against all types of enemies. You can also use Suction Gun to suck in nearby treasure.

ATTACK 3

JET-VAC JET PACK

COST: 700 Gold
PREREQUISITE: None

Press **Attack 3** to fly and perform new attacks in the air.

UPGRADES

TANK RESERVES

COST: 1,700 Gold
PREREQUISITE: Vac-packeteer Path

Can remain in flight longer and recharge faster.

FLYING CORKSCREW

COST: 3,000 Gold
PREREQUISITE: Vac-packeteer Path

While flying, press **Attack 2** to blast forward and perform a powerful corkscrew attack.

STRATEGY

Initially, the Jet Pack does not add any extra attacks, but you can still press **Attack 1** to fire a normal Vac-Blaster attack. When you launch into the air with Jet Pack, it slowly drains Jet-Vac's air pressure. This air pressure gauge is shared with the Suction Gun attack. Use the Suction Gun to recharge it quickly once you land.

Both Tank Reserves and Flying Corkscrew are great upgrades for the Jet Pack ability. Flying Corkscrew is a deadly attack that inflicts high damage to any enemy you bowl over.

SONIC BOOM

"FULL STREAM AHEAD!"

STATS

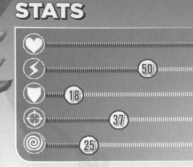

♥	280
⚡	50
🛡	18
⊕	37
◎	25

UPGRADE PATHS

MEDEA GRIFFIN
Further develop Sonic Boom's Griffin Babies.

SIREN GRIFFIN
Further develop Sonic Boom's Roar Attack.

SOUL GEM ABILITY

RESONANT FREQUENCY
COST: 4,000 Gold

PREREQUISITE: None

Roar at babies and they will roar, too!

STRATEGY

When you roar at your babies they are surrounded by a blue glow. This increases the amount of damage they deal. There's no downside to keeping this effect up. Any time you have a free moment and babies are out, use Roar.

SPECIAL QUEST

SONIC SQUEAK:
BABIES DEFEAT 50 ENEMIES.

Upgrade Sonic Boom's egg attack powers and use them to defeat enemies. The babies are effective at taking down enemies, and if you stick to the technique it does not take long to complete this quest.

Sonic Boom is a versatile Air Skylander with the ability to fly and hatch baby "pets" to help her in battle. Sonic Boom's primary attack, Roar, is a scalable medium-range blast that can knockback small and medium enemies.

While you must ultimately decide to upgrade either Egg Toss or Roar, both remain useful even after you have committed to one of the paths; those two powers have great synergy.

PRIMARY ATTACKS

ATTACK 1

ROAR

COST: N/A

DAMAGE: High

RANGE: Medium

SPEED: Slow

Press the **Attack 1** button to unleash a deafening screech!

UPGRADES

LOUDMOUTH

COST: 500 Gold

PREREQUISITE: None

Roar attack does increased damage.

ECHOLOCATION

COST: 1,700 Gold

PREREQUISITE: Siren Griffin Path

Roar attack continues to expand on impact.

EGG SHOCKER

COST: 2,200 Gold

PREREQUISITE: Siren Griffin Path

Roar at eggs to create a big shockwave that pushes enemies back.

MORE BOOM!

COST: 3,000 Gold

PREREQUISITE: Siren Griffin Path

Increase the damage and size of the Roar attack by holding **Attack 1**.

STRATEGY

Sonic Boom's Roar is powerful, even before you upgrade it. While it doesn't have extremely long range, it also doesn't slow Sonic Boom down, allowing her to continue moving and dodging enemies while unleashing Roars. Egg Shocker is a great knockback attack. More Boom! significantly increases the power potential of the attack. In addition, Echolocation creates a sort of chain effect that can help power up Sonic Boom's babies, and increase overall damage.

ATTACK 2

EGG TOSS

COST: N/A

DAMAGE: Very Low

RANGE: Short

SPEED: Very Slow

Press the **Attack 2** button to launch an egg that hatches into a feisty baby!

UPGRADES

RIDE OF THE VALKYRIES

COST: 900 Gold

PREREQUISITE: None

Babies can now fly too. They travel at increased speed while flying.

THREE'S A CROWD

COST: 1,200 Gold

PREREQUISITE: None

Have THREE babies active at once.

SUNNY SIDE UP

COST: 1,700 Gold

PREREQUISITE: Medea Griffin Path

Can throw all eggs at once. Eggs will knock back enemies before hatching.

SIBLING RIVALRY

COST: 2,200 Gold

PREREQUISITE: Medea Griffin Path

Have FOUR babies active at once.

TERRIBLE TWOS

COST: 3,000 Gold

PREREQUISITE: Medea Griffin Path

Babies hatch fully grown and attack faster.

STRATEGY

Sonic Boom fires out an egg and a baby hatches seconds later. Wait a few more seconds, and the baby grows. Soon, several small griffins fight by their mother's side! Keep in mind that the babies take a long time to become effective against enemies, and at first their low-damage attacks may not seem worth it. Keep upgrading the Egg Toss attack, and you will soon find the power to be one of the most fun ways to take down the Skylanders' enemies in the game.

WOW POW POWER

SUPER BABY!

COST: 5,000 Gold

PREREQUISITE: None

Hold **Attack 2** to combine regular babies into one Super Baby!

STRATEGY

The Super Baby is an awesome attacker that chases down and pecks the Skylanders' foes for high damage per hit. It can even take significant damage from enemies. Getting out a Super Baby doesn't require that you have more than one baby out; just hold down **Attack 2** after throwing Sonic Boom's eggs to create one.

ATTACK 3

LET THERE BE FLIGHT

COST: 700 Gold

PREREQUISITE: None

Press **Attack 3** to fly. Sonic Boom gains increased speed and armor while flying.

STRATEGY

Flying allows Sonic Boom to move faster, and makes her tougher. The babies can also fly when their mother flies with this upgrade (and once you purchase the Ride of the Valkyries upgrade).

WHIRLWIND

"TWISTS OF FURY!"

STATS

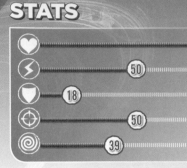

♥	270
⚡	50
🛡	18
◎	50
◎	39

UPGRADE PATHS

ULTIMATE RAINBOWER
Further develop Whirlwind's Rainbow of Doom Attack.

TEMPEST DRAGON
Further develop Whirlwind's Tempest Cloud attack.

SOUL GEM ABILITY

RAINBOW OF HEALING
COST: 4,000 Gold
PREREQUISITE: None
Rainbows HEAL your allies!

STRATEGY

This is a great power to purchase if you are playing Skylanders with a friend in co-op mode. Just shoot a rainbow at a friend to give them some extra health. If you are playing by yourself, it doesn't have any use.

SPECIAL QUEST

WHAT DOES IT MEAN?:
CREATE 50 DOUBLE RAINBOWS.

Once you have unlocked Whirlwind's Duel Rainbows ability, complete this quest by firing a Tempest cloud, and then following up with a Rainbow of Doom. When you hit the cloud, two rainbows will be created. Rainbows made via the Double Dose of Doom power don't count unless they hit a Tempest Cloud. Triple rainbows created via Triple Tempest count as one double rainbow.

Half unicorn and half dragon, Whirlwind's attacks are beautiful and extremely effective. The default Rainbow of Doom attack is a great medium-range area-of-effect attack. Her secondary attack is a dark cloud that acts as a sentry, zapping any enemies that get close to it.

When you upgrade Whirlwind's powers, she gains a great deal of utility that provides extra defense, heals allies, or creates more rainbowy chaos on the battlefield.

PRIMARY ATTACKS

ATTACK 1

RAINBOW OF DOOM

COST: N/A

DAMAGE: Low

RANGE: Medium

SPEED: Average

Press the **Attack 1** button to fire an arced blast of rainbow energy.

UPGRADES

RAINBOW CHAIN

COST: 500 Gold

PREREQUISITE: None

Rainbows do extra damage—shoot a Tempest Cloud and a second rainbow chains off of it.

DOUBLE DOSE OF DOOM

COST: 1,700 Gold

PREREQUISITE: Ultimate Rainbower Path

Shoot two Rainbows of Doom at once.

ATOMIC RAINBOW

COST: 2,200 Gold

PREREQUISITE: Ultimate Rainbower Path

Rainbow of Doom attack does increased damage.

RAINBOW SINGULARITY

COST: 3,000 Gold

PREREQUISITE: Ultimate Rainbower Path

Hold **Attack 1** to charge up a super powerful Rainbow of Doom.

STRATEGY

Rainbow of Doom starts out as a normal ranged attack. It does low damage, but the explosion at the end of the rainbow can hit multiple enemies grouped tightly together. While most of the upgrades for this power are straightforward, Rainbow Singularity stands out. Fully charging Rainbow Singularity takes three seconds, but you can move around (at reduced speed) while charging it. Once the attack is charged, releasing the **Attack 1** button sends out a small black hole. When it hits an enemy, it creates a gigantic rainbow vortex that sucks in and damages all nearby enemies!

ATTACK 2

TEMPEST CLOUD

COST: N/A

DAMAGE: Medium

RANGE: Medium

SPEED: Slow

Press the **Attack 2** button to send forth clouds that electrocute nearby enemies.

UPGRADES

DUEL RAINBOWS

COST: 1,200 Gold

PREREQUISITE: Rainbow Chain

Shoot a Tempest Cloud and two rainbows will chain off of it.

TRIPLE TEMPEST

COST: 700 Gold

PREREQUISITE: None

Have 3 Tempest Clouds active—Tempest Clouds do extra damage.

TEMPEST TANTRUM

COST: 2,200 Gold

PREREQUISITE: Tempest Dragon Path

Bigger Tempest Cloud does increased damage with increased range.

TEMPEST MATRIX

COST: 3,000 Gold

PREREQUISITE: Tempest Dragon Path

Electricity forms between Tempest Clouds that hurts enemies.

TRIPLE RAINBOW, IT'S FULL ON

COST: 1,700 Gold

PREREQUISITE: Tempest Dragon Path

Shoot a Tempest Cloud and three rainbows will chain off of it.

STRATEGY

Send out one of these rain clouds, and it slides to a stop a few feet from Whirlwind. Any enemies near the cloud automatically take damage every few seconds as lightning juts out from the cloud. This is a great power because you can release the cloud, then focus on evading enemies. Initially, you only get one cloud, but Triple Tempest is an early upgrade that allows Whirlwind to shoot out three clouds at once, filling the battlefield with damaging dark clouds.

Improving the damage via Tempest Tantrum transforms Tempest Cloud from a low/medium damage attack to a high damage attack. Once you get Tempest Matrix, you can actually create a wall of Clouds with arcing electrical blasts that serve as a defensive barrier against charging enemies.

WOW POW POWER

CLOUDBURSTING!

COST: 5,000 Gold

PREREQUISITE: None

When clouds disappear, they explode into rainbows.

STRATEGY

This is a great add-on for Tempest Cloud. The clouds fire off arcing rainbow shots. These rainbow shots are the same power as Whirlwind's regular Rainbow of Doom, so if you upgrade Whirlwind's Rainbow of Doom damage, the Cloudbursting damage increases as well.

ATTACK 3

DRAGON FLIGHT

COST: 900 Gold

PREREQUISITE: None

Press **Attack 3** to fly. Whirlwind gains increased speed and armor while flying.

STRATEGY

Dragon Flight can be helpful for avoiding traps and slime on the ground, and also allows Whirlwind to speed through timed puzzles.

LIGHTNING ROD

"ONE STRIKE, AND YOU'RE OUT!"

STATS

♥	290
⚡	43
🛡	18
◎	30
◎	39

UPGRADE PATHS

LORD OF THE LIGHTNING
Further develop Lightning Rod's Grand Lightning attack.

TYPHOON TITAN
Further develop Lightning Rod's defensive clouds.

SOUL GEM ABILITY

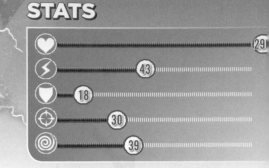

ZAPPER FIELD DELUXE
COST: 4,000 Gold
PREREQUISITE: Zapper Field
Zapper Field and clouds do extra damage.

STRATEGY

This is a straight buff for the Zapper Field ability. Treat it like the final upgrade in the Typhoon Titan Path. If you don't invest in Typhoon Titan, then you can hold off on purchasing this until you have the extra Gold. It won't add much to Lightning Rod's combat prowess.

Lightning Rod is a moving storm cloud, full of electrical potential that he just can't wait to unleash on his foes. While he is a Storm Giant, he isn't related to the Skylanders Giants (they are much bigger).

His two upgrade paths are Lord of the Lightning and Typhoon Titan. Lord of the Lightning dramatically increases his damage potential by super-enhancing his Grand Lightning attack. Typhoon Titan grants a new power that increases Lightning Rod's defense against close-range enemies. Since Lightning Rod is a natural at range, Lord of the Lightning is a stronger path to follow. The defensive clouds just don't provide enough benefit.

SPECIAL QUEST

CURRENT EVENT: DEFEAT 10 ENEMIES WITH ONE GRAND LIGHTNING STRIKE.

You need to find a group of 10 Chompies in one area and use the Grand Lightning to blast them all. This is easiest if you decide to commit to the Lord of Lightning Path since the Grand Lightning attack lasts longer.

PRIMARY ATTACKS

ATTACK 1

LIGHTNING BOLT

COST: N/A
DAMAGE: Low
RANGE: Long
SPEED: Average

Press the **Attack 1** button to throw a lightning bolt at enemies.

UPGRADES

LIGHTNING LANCER

COST: 500 Gold
PREREQUISITE: None

Lightning Bolt does increased damage.

LIGHTNING HARPOON

COST: 1,200 Gold
PREREQUISITE: Lightning Lancer

Lightning Bolts stick into enemies and continue to damage them.

STRATEGY

Lightning Rod's primary attack is a lightning blast directed at nearby enemies. While he doesn't fire these blasts extremely fast, this is a good ranged attack that can clear out enemies from long range. Increasing the damage with Lightning Lancer should be your first purchase as this is Lightning Rod's most dependable attack. After most enemies are hit by Lightning Bolt, they are stunned for one second. When you get the Lightning Harpoon ability, all bolt attacks stick in your enemies and do a few points of extra damage.

ATTACK 3

ZAPPER FIELD

COST: 900 Gold
PREREQUISITE: None
DAMAGE: Very Low
RANGE: Very Short
SPEED: Average

Press **Attack 3** to create an electrical storm that damages enemies.

UPGRADES

CLOUD ZAPPER SATELLITE

COST: 1,700 Gold
PREREQUISITE: Typhoon Titan Path

A protective cloud follows you and zaps any enemies that come near.

ZAPPER SATELLITE DEFENSE

COST: 3,000 Gold
PREREQUISITE: Typhoon Titan Path, Cloud Zapper Satellite

A THIRD protective cloud joins you.

ZAPPIER SATS

COST: 2,200 Gold
PREREQUISITE: Typhoon Titan Path, Cloud Zapper Satellite

Protective zapper clouds do increased damage.

STRATEGY

Zapper Satellite is a passive defensive ability that creates up to three clouds that circle Lightning Rod and defend him from melee attackers. The clouds don't do much damage, but they can help defend him while he nails enemies with his lightning attacks. If you do decide to invest in the Typhoon Titan Path for Lightning Rod, you should purchase Zapper Field Deluxe as soon as possible.

ATTACK 2

GRAND LIGHTNING SUMMONING

COST: N/A
DAMAGE: Low
RANGE: Long
SPEED: Very Slow

Press the **Attack 2** button to bring lightning down from the sky and control where it moves.

UPGRADES

THUNDURATION

COST: 700 Gold
PREREQUISITE: None

Grand Lightning attack lasts longer and does increased damage.

FASTER CASTER

COST: 1,700 Gold
PREREQUISITE: Lord of the Lightning Path

Summon the Grand Lightning attack much faster.

ELECTRICITY CITY

COST: 2,200 Gold
PREREQUISITE: Lord of the Lightning Path

Grand Lightning attack has even more power and does more damage.

LIGHTNING AVATAR

COST: 3,000 Gold
PREREQUISITE: Lord of the Lightning Path, Electricity City

Summon the most powerful Grand Lightning attack ever!

STRATEGY

When you hold down **Attack 2** to use Grand Lightning Summoning, it takes Lightning Rod a few seconds to charge the blast. While it is charging, Lightning Rod is defenseless, so initially this attack has limited usage.

Once the lightning has been summoned, a powerful charge is directed in the ground. You can control where the blast goes as long as you keep holding down the **Attack 2** button. The disadvantage of Grand Lightning Summoning is that Lightning Rod is relatively helpless while using it. He needs to use the power defensively to keep advancing enemies from getting too close.

WOW POW POWER

BIG BOLT!

COST: 5,000 Gold
PREREQUISITE: None

Hold **Attack 1** to throw the biggest bolt of lightning known to man!

STRATEGY

This may be the biggest bolt of lightning known to Skylands, but it only does a fair amount of damage compared to upgraded Lightning Bolt and Grand Lightning Strikes. When Lightning Rod uses BIG Bolt!, a blast of lightning shoots straight out of his fingertips for about three seconds. He can control the lightning and direct it at enemies.

WARNADO

"FOR THE WIND!"

STATS

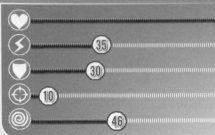

♥	310
⚡	35
🛡	30
◎	10
◎	46

UPGRADE PATHS

EYE OF THE STORM
Further develop Warnado's flying and Spin Attack powers.

WIND MASTER
Further develop Warnado's Tornado attacks.

SOUL GEM ABILITY

THICK SHELLED
COST: 4,000 Gold

PREREQUISITE: None

This ability gives Warnado a thicker shell, reducing damage he takes from enemies.

STRATEGY
This upgrade increases Warnado's Armor (from 30 to 70). This increased damage resistance is well worth the gold spent purchasing the power.

SPECIAL QUEST

CHOMPY CATCHER:
CATCH 100 CHOMPIES IN TORNADOES.

The best place to do this is in the Arena Challenges. Head to any of the early challenges and there are plenty of Chompies. Use Summon Tornado on the Chompies to rack up points towards this quest. High Winds also helps gather up more Chompies at once.

Warnado is a really fun turtle that just can't stop spinning. He has a fantastic dash power that allows him to retreat or attack enemies without putting himself at risk. He can also increase his armor significantly with his Soul Gem upgrade.

The highlights to Warnado's offensive arsenal are his Tornado attacks. The Tornadoes are vicious and sweep through the battlefield, crushing anything smaller than they are. The Eye of the Storm path slightly increases Warnado's spin attack and provides some difficult-to-use upgrades to his tornado flight ability.

PRIMARY ATTACKS

ATTACK 1

SPIN ATTACK

COST: N/A
DAMAGE: Low
RANGE: Short
SPEED: Average

Press the **Attack 1** button to spin Warnado's shell and take out enemies.

UPGRADES

SHARP SHELL

COST: 500 Gold
PREREQUISITE: None

Spin attack does increased damage.

LOW FRICTION SHELL

COST: 1,700 Gold
PREREQUISITE: Eye of the Storm Path

Spin attack strikes farther and faster.

STRATEGY

Spin Attack is a great dash ability that is ideal for hit-and-run situations against big creatures. Since Summon Tornado isn't effective against big bosses, this should be the power you use against them even if you invest in the Wind Master Path. Dash in and out of enemy range with this attack; you won't kill them quickly, but you also won't put Warnado at risk.

ATTACK 2

SUMMON TORNADO

COST: N/A
DAMAGE: High
RANGE: Medium
SPEED: Very Slow

Press the **Attack 2** button to execute a high velocity spin that generates a tornado to pick up enemies.

UPGRADES

EXTEND TORNADO

COST: 700 Gold
PREREQUISITE: None

Hold **Attack 2** to extend the range of the Tornado attack.

HIGH WINDS

COST: 900 Gold
PREREQUISITE: None

Tornadoes can damage multiple enemies.

GUIDED TWISTER

COST: 1,700 Gold
PREREQUISITE: Wind Master Path

Hold **Attack 2** to manually control the direction of your Tornado attack.

SUMMON CYCLONE

COST: 2,200 Gold
PREREQUISITE: Wind Master Path

Tornadoes are super-sized and do increased damage.

WIND ELEMENTAL

COST: 3,000 Gold
PREREQUISITE: Wind Master Path, Summon Cyclone

Tornadoes will attack enemies on their own.

STRATEGY

Summon Tornado is one of the coolest powers in the game. It starts as a simple whirlwind attack that can suck up small enemies, and each upgrade makes it more and more powerful. In the end, it becomes sentient and can attack on its own!

Tornadoes damage any enemies they hit, and Warnado can summon them quickly, ensuring there's always one wreaking havoc somewhere on the battlefield. If there's one disadvantage to Summon Tornado, it's that it dissipates if it hits a larger enemy, such as Blaze Brewers. You need to be ready for that and have Warnado quickly summon a follow-up tornado until the enemy falls.

ATTACK 3

WHIRLWIND FLIGHT

COST: 1,200 Gold
PREREQUISITE: None

Press **Attack 3** to fly. Warnado gains increased speed and armor while flying.

UPGRADES

FLYING MINI TURTLES

COST: 2,200 Gold
PREREQUISITE: Eye of the Storm Path

Mini-Warnados fly with you. Press **Attack 1** to launch them at your enemies.

TURTLE SLAM

COST: 3,000 Gold
PREREQUISITE: Eye of the Storm Path

While flying, hold **Attack 1** to slam down on your enemies.

STRATEGY

Warnado has a unique flying style (he rides a tornado). While he's flying, he can't use his Spin Attack but he can Summon Tornadoes. Warnado gets two powerful upgrades for his attacks if you invest in the Eye of the Storm path. With Flying Mini Turtles, Warnado can rapidly tap the attack button to fire turtle shells at nearby enemies. These turtle shells do about 15 points of damage a hit. Turtle Slam is a slow, powerful area-of-effect attack that dishes out damage to nearby enemies, but cancels Warnado's flight.

SHROOMBOOM

"HE SHOOTS! HE SPORES!"

STATS

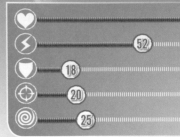

♥	26
⚡	52
🛡	18
⊕	20
◎	25

UPGRADE PATHS

BARRIER BOOST
Upgrades Mushroom Ring for better protection.

PARAMUSHROOM PROMOTION
Provides more upgrades for the Paratrooper and Slingshot attacks.

SOUL GEM ABILITY

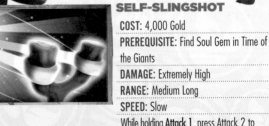

SELF-SLINGSHOT
COST: 4,000 Gold
PREREQUISITE: Find Soul Gem in Time of the Giants
DAMAGE: Extremely High
RANGE: Medium Long
SPEED: Slow
While holding **Attack 1**, press Attack 2 to slingshot Shroomboom towards enemies.

Shroomboom is a crazed mushroom man who uses his fungal brethren to both directly and indirectly attack the Skylanders' foes. The Slingshot and Launch Paratroopers attacks are both deadly and can knock any enemy down to size. Mushroom Ring is an excellent defensive power. It works to protect Shroomboom and buy him enough time to let loose with his deadly slingshot.

Both of Shroomboom's upgrade paths provide viable options, and you have plenty of time to decide which path to follow while working on unlocking Shroomboom's initial skills. If you want to take a more defensive route, pick Barrier Boost, which unlocks an upgrade that makes Shroomboom temporarily invulnerable. Paramushroom Promotion greatly enhances Shroomboom's offensive capabilities, making both of his mushroom attacks significantly deadlier.

STRATEGY

To deploy this attack, you must first activate a mushroom wall by pressing **Attack 2**; this puts up a great defense while Shroomboom winds himself up in the giant slingshot. You then have to hold **Attack 1** and press **Attack 2**. Once you hit **Attack 2**, it takes Shroomboom about three seconds to pull himself back. Aim the attack, then release to inflict massice damage on Shroomboom's foes.

SPECIAL QUEST

LUNCHING LAUNCH: EAT A WATERMELON WHILE PERFORMING A SELF-SLINGSHOT!

Once you have found the Self-Slingshot gem in Chapter 1: Time of Giants, keep your eye out for a watermelon food item. When you find one, blast Shroomboom through the watermelon with the Self-Slingshot power to complete the quest. If you haven't found one by the time you reach Chapter 16: Bringing Order to Kaos!, there are a ton of watermelons located throughout the level.

PRIMARY ATTACKS

ATTACK 1

SLINGSHOT

COST: N/A
DAMAGE: Medium
RANGE: Long
SPEED: Fast

Press the **Attack 1** button to shoot exploding mushrooms.

UPGRADES

BIGGER BOOMSHROOMS

COST: 900 Gold
PREREQUISITE: None

Press and hold **Attack 1** to charge up a giant exploding mushroom.

LOCK 'N' LOAD

COST: 1,700 Gold
PREREQUISITE: Paramushroom Promotion Path

Can fire exploding mushrooms faster that do increased damage.

BOUNCING BOOMSHROOMS

COST: 1200 Gold
PREREQUISITE: None

Exploding mushrooms bounce on the ground and do increased damage.

STRATEGY

Shroomboom's signature slingshot mushroom attack flings mushrooms at enemies in an arc. Shroomboom has the ability to rapidly deploy his poisonous mushrooms, inflicting concentrated damage wherever he's aiming. Bouncing Boomshrooms ensures more mushrooms hit your enemies, while Lock 'N' Load and Bigger Boomshrooms significantly increase the damage of the attack.

ATTACK 2

MUSHROOM RING

COST: N/A
DAMAGE: Medium
RANGE: Short
SPEED: Slow

Press the **Attack 2** button to spawn a ring of mushrooms that damage enemies.

UPGRADES

SUPER SHROOMS

COST: 700 Gold
PREREQUISITE: None

Mushroom Ring gets bigger.

ULTIMATE RING

COST: 2,200 Gold
PREREQUISITE: Barrier Boost Path

Mushroom Ring is the biggest it gets.

SPORE POWER

COST: 1,700 Gold
PREREQUISITE: Barrier Boost Path

Mushroom Ring creates a damaging spore cloud.

BACK TO THE BEGINNING

COST: 3,000 Gold
PREREQUISITE: Barrier Boost Path

Hold **Attack 2** to remain underground, where you can move around freely.

STRATEGY

When you activate this power, Shroomboom quickly erects a wall of mushrooms that surround and protect him. The mushrooms retract if Shroomboom moves to walk through the wall. While the default Slingshot attack does not fire over the mushroom wall, the Slingshot can still fire through gaps in the mushroom wall. Launch Paratroopers works very well in conjunction with the ring, since Shrooomboom launches the mushrooms straight into the air.

If you choose to upgrade the ring via the Barrier Boost Path, the ring quickly becomes one of the best defensive powers in the game. Ultimate Ring makes the ring bigger, and Spore Power makes the ring poisonous. Follow that up with Back to the Beginning and Shroomboom is invincible as long as he is underground. Let the enemies run into his poisonous mushrooms and you can defeat them without ever putting Shroomboom at risk!

ATTACK 3

LAUNCH PARATROOPERS

COST: 500 Gold
PREREQUISITE: None
DAMAGE: Medium/Low
RANGE: Long
SPEED: Slow

Press **Attack 3** to shoot mushroom paratroopers who drop down from the sky.

UPGRADES

FUNGAL INFESTATION

COST: 2,200 Gold
PREREQUISITE: Paramushroom Promotion Path

Mushroom Paratroopers stick to enemies and do damage over time.

PARATROOPER INVASION

COST: 3,000 Gold
PREREQUISITE: Paramushroom Promotion Path

Shoot three Mushroom Paratroopers at once.

STRATEGY

This attack allows Shroomboom to fire mushrooms rapidly straight up into the air. Moments later, the mushrooms float down on nearby targets, exploding for moderate damage. At first you can't have too many paratroopers landing at one time, but if you invest in the Paramushroom Promotion Path, Shroomboom starts tossing them up three at a time, and can fill the sky with deadly spores.

CAMO

"FRUIT PUNCH!"

♥	30
⚡	50
🛡	24
⊕	30
◎	32

UPGRADE PATHS

VINE VIRTUOSO
Further develop Camo's Firecracker vines.

MELON MASTER
Further develop Camo's Melon Fountain abilities.

SOUL GEM ABILITY

ORBITING SUN SHIELD

COST: 4,000 Gold

PREREQUISITE: None

Hold **Attack 1** to create a Sun Blast Shield.

STRATEGY

This is a fairly ineffective power for Camo. The shield only hits an enemy once and does the same amount of damage as one regular sunburst. Save your gold for other upgrades, saving this one for last.

SPECIAL QUEST

GARDEN GORGER: EAT 10 WATERMELONS.

Watermelons are random food items found throughout the game. Chests and enemies can both drop them. If you aren't playing actively as Camo, and you see a watermelon drop, you can quickly switch to him to grab the watermelon. There are also plenty of watermelons in Chapters 1 and 2.

Camo is a colorful Life Element dragon who uses gigantic plants to attack his foes. Camo's standard attack, Sun Blast, is a straightforward ranged blast. Things become more interesting with his Firecracker and Melon Fountain skills.

Firecracker is a difficult-to-control, but deadly, power with many upgrades. Melon Fountain starts off as a straightforward area-of-effect attack, but upgrades turn it into one of the best boss-crushing powers in the Skylands.

PRIMARY ATTACKS

ATTACK 1

SUN BLAST

COST: N/A

DAMAGE: Low

RANGE: Long

SPEED: Very Fast

Press **Attack 1** to blast enemies with concentrated life energy.

UPGRADES

SEARING SUN BLAST

COST: 500 Gold

PREREQUISITE: None

Sun Blast does increased damage.

STRATEGY

Despite the fact that it has a single upgrade, Sun Blast still stands as a fantastic ranged attack. It doesn't get any easier; rapidly press the **Attack 1** button to nail enemies at range. Each blast has a chance to knock back enemies.

All Portal Masters should purchase Searing Sun Blast as Camo's first upgrade. It makes him much more effective, regardless of which upgrade path (Vine Virtuoso or Melon Master) you choose later in his development.

ATTACK 3

MELON FOUNTAIN

COST: 700 Gold

PREREQUISITE: None

DAMAGE: Very High

RANGE: Medium

SPEED: Very Slow

Press **Attack 3** to send melons flying everywhere.

UPGRADES

ATTACK 2

FIRECRACKER VINES

COST: N/A

DAMAGE: Very Low

RANGE: Medium

SPEED: Slow

Press the **Attack 2** button to conjure up a fast-growing vine of explosive melons.

UPGRADES

FIRECRACKER FOOD

COST: 900 Gold

PREREQUISITE: None

Firecracker Vines do increased damage.

VIGOROUS VINES

COST: 1,200 Gold

PREREQUISITE: None

Firecracker Vines move quicker and further.

MARTIAL BOUNTY

COST: 1,700 Gold

PREREQUISITE: Vine Virtuoso Path

Firecracker Vines create more exploding melons.

PEPPERS OF POTENCY

COST: 2,200 Gold

PREREQUISITE: Vine Virtuoso Path

Firecracker Vines do even more increased damage.

PROLIFERATION

COST: 3,000 Gold

PREREQUISITE: Vine Virtuoso Path

Create two Firecracker Vines at once!

STRATEGY

Initially, Firecracker Vines are difficult to use effectively. They don't have great range, are hard to aim, and their explosions are extremely low damage. Once you purchase a few upgrades, however, their effectiveness improves. Despite these improvements, the power remains unpredictable and chaotic.

One of the drawbacks of Firecracker Vines is that it doesn't hold back enemies. Camo lacks a dash ability. This allows melee enemies to move in close while Camo is using Firecracker Vines. Melon Fountain is an effective power, especially when you compare it side-by-side with Firecracker Vines. For that reason, stick with upgrading Melon Fountain.

RING OF MIGHT

COST: 1,700 Gold

PREREQUISITE: Melon Master Path

The Melon Fountain blasts out more melons.

MELON GMO

COST: 2,200 Gold

PREREQUISITE: Melon Master Path

The Melon Fountain does increased damage.

MELON FORTRESS

COST: 3,000 Gold

PREREQUISITE: Melon Master Path

Hold **Attack 3** to hide in the Melon Fountain—release to send the melons flying.

STRATEGY

When you use Melon Fountain, Camo jumps into the ground and a ring of giant watermelons form around him. You might not think melons are too dangerous, but then you aren't a Troll! Camo's melons are tremendously powerful and each one can hit the same enemy multiple times. Even without damage upgrade, Melon Fountain can really dish out the damage.

Once you get Melon GMO, Melon Fountain turns into a tremendously effective attack to use against bosses and large enemies. The trick is to plant the Melon Fountain right next to your target. When the melons explode, they can hit the boss multiple times. With some luck, Camo can dish out 200 damage in one attack!

To use Melon Fortress, you need to tap **Attack 3** once and then HOLD **Attack 3**. This way, Camo stays in the melons and uses them defensively. When you release **Attack 3**, the melons go flying in all directions. You can use this to compensate for Melon Fountain's slow attack speed. Wait for an enemy's opening before releasing.

STUMP SMASH

"DROP THE HAMMER!"

STATS

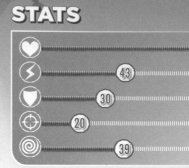

♥		34
⚡	43	
🛡	30	
⊕	20	
◎	39	

UPGRADE PATHS

SMASH 'N BASH
Further develop Stump Smash's Stumpfist and Meganut attacks.

NUT CRAFTER
Further develop Stump Smash's Acorn ability.

SOUL GEM ABILITY

WATERLOGGED
COST: 4,000 Gold
PREREQUISITE: None
Stump Smash can now float and regain health in water.

STRATEGY
Unfortunately, there isn't much water to be found in the Skylands that you explore in *Skylanders: Giants*. The only water is behind Water Element Gates. As such, there's no need to buy this power until you're swimming in gold.

SPECIAL QUEST

MEGANUT BOWLING:
DEFEAT FIVE ENEMIES WITH ONE MEGANUT.

Meganuts are powerful, and bowling over five Chompies with one is no problem. Just roll it around, repeatedly squashing them until this quest pops. The upgrade Acorn Croquet makes this much easier to achieve, since you can wack the acorn directly at enemies.

First and foremost, Stump Smash is a formidable melee combatant. He dishes out high damage at a rapid speed with Petrified Pummel. Additionally, Stump Smash has excellent Health and respectable Armor. This allows him to stand toe-to-toe with most enemies without a problem.

Because Stump Smash is so naturally good at melee, it's hard to turn down the Smash 'n Bash Path. It gives him a few great combos, and allows him to use Meganut to go bowling with enemies as pins!

PRIMARY ATTACKS

ATTACK 1

PULVERIZE

COST: N/A
DAMAGE: High
RANGE: Short
SPEED: Fast

Press **Attack 1** to smash. Press **Attack 1**, **Attack 1**, HOLD **Attack 1** to perform a combo.

UPGRADES

PETRIFIED PUMMEL

COST: 500 Gold
PREREQUISITE: None

Stumpfist attacks do increased damage.

THORNBARK

COST: 1,200 Gold
PREREQUISITE: None

Thorns shoot out when you are hit, damaging all nearby enemies.

STUMP CRUSHER COMBOS

COST: 1,700 Gold
PREREQUISITE: Smash 'n Bash Path

Press **Attack 1**, **Attack 1**, HOLD **Attack 2** for Stumpfist Charge.

Press **Attack 1**, **Attack 1**, HOLD **Attack 3** for Stumpfist Spin.

STRATEGY

Pulverize is fast and deals high damage, which is a rare combination. The drawback of the attack is that Stump Smash has limited maneuverability while using it, which leaves him vulnerable to enemy attacks. If you choose to go down the Smash 'n Bash Path, Stump Smash gets two fantastic combos. Stumpfist Charge allows Stump Smash to rapidly hammer foes with his fists and dishes out knockback on small and medium enemies. Stumpfist Spin is a standard, short-range area-of-effect combo.

ATTACK 2

WHEN ACORNS ATTACK

COST: N/A
DAMAGE: Very Low
RANGE: Long
SPEED: Very Slow

Press the **Attack 2** button to spit acorns at your foes to slow them down.

UPGRADES

SPINY ACORNS

COST: 700 Gold
PREREQUISITE: None

Acorns are spiny and do increased damage.

DOUBLE NUT

COST: 3,000 Gold
PREREQUISITE: Nut Crafter

Press **Attack 2** to spit two acorns at once.

POLLEN PLUME

COST: 1,700 Gold
PREREQUISITE: Nut Crafter

Acorns explode, growing plants on all nearby enemies.

STRATEGY

Initially, Stump Smash's acorn attack isn't very good. It does slow enemies down, but it inflicts low damage, is extremely slow, and is hard to aim. With some upgrades, the power does improve, but not to the point where Nut Crafter is a better choice than Smash 'n Bash. If you have a Series 2 Stump Smash, the power gets a huge improvement via the Auto-Nuts! upgrade.

ATTACK 3

MEGANUT

COST: 900 Gold
PREREQUISITE: None
DAMAGE: High
RANGE: Short
SPEED: Average

Press **Attack 3** to create a Meganut that damages any enemy it touches.

UPGRADES

MEGANUT PROPAGATION

COST: 2,200 Gold
PREREQUISITE: Nut Crafter

Press **Attack 3** when facing a Meganut to make it burst into acorns.

ACORN CROQUET

COST: 2,200 Gold
PREREQUISITE: Smash 'n Bash Path

Press **Attack 3** when facing a Meganut to send it flying at your enemies.

SMASH MEGANUT

COST: 3,000 Gold
PREREQUISITE: Smash 'n Bash Path

Press **Attack 1** when facing a Meganut to make it explode, damaging enemies.

STRATEGY

After Stump Smash spits the Meganut out, push it into enemies to inflict high damage. The drawback to Meganut is that it's hard to control. Enhancing the power with Acorn Croquet and Smash Meganut makes it much more effective. Meganut Propagation is okay, but only when surrounded by enemies. The acorns the Meganut fires out go in random directions and may bounce over small creatures. One interesting note about Meganut is that enemies will attack it.

WOW POW POWER

AUTO-NUTS!

COST: 5,000 Gold
PREREQUISITE: None

Hold **Attack 2** to rapidly spit out a series of nuts.

STRATEGY

Auto-Nuts! automatically fires five giant green nuts. These nuts do moderate damage, and have good range. These nuts get all the benefits of the acorns in the When Acorns Attack power. This power is an absolute must-purchase if you take Stump Smash down the Nut Crafter Path.

ZOOK

STATS

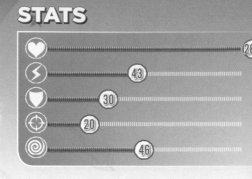

❤	26
⚡	43
🛡	30
◎	20
◉	46

UPGRADE PATHS

ARTILLERYMAN
Further develop Zook's bazooka attacks.

FLORAL DEFENDER
Further develop Zook's Barrier and Cactus abilities.

SOUL GEM ABILITY

MIRV MORTAR
COST: 4,000 Gold

PREREQUISITE: Mortar Attack

Mortar shells explode into three smaller shells.

STRATEGY

This is a fantastic power that not only increases the damage output of Mortar Attack, but with the Floral Defender Path also increases the cactus output! If you like Zook's mortar attack, you should invest in this one as soon as possible.

SPECIAL QUEST

SPORE IT ON: ABSORB 1,000 POINTS OF DAMAGE WITH A FOLIAGE BARRIER.

You will earn this quest very quickly by simply using Foliage Barrier. Just use it a lot around tough enemies, and it will unlock in no time.

Zook is a mortar expert. He's mastered the art of tossing fruit at his enemies. Explosive fruit that is. Zook's Mortar Attack is devastating. Combined with his excellent defensive foliage abilities, he can keep his enemies perpetually distracted while he pelts them with all manner of explosives.

Most players should pursue the Floral Defender Path. However, the foliage defensive ability really doesn't get too great until you unlock the cacti and second mortar upgrade. The Artilleryman path focuses entirely on Zook's weaker bazooka attacks.

PRIMARY ATTACKS

ATTACK 1

BAZOOKA ATTACK

COST: N/A

DAMAGE: Medium

RANGE: Long

SPEED: Average

Press **Attack 1** to fire bazooka shells that explode into shrapnel—hold **Attack 1** to extend the range.

UPGRADES

HARDWOOD SHELLS

COST: 500 Gold

PREREQUISITE: None

Bazooka shells and shrapnel do increased damage.

FULL SPLINTER JACKET

COST: 1,200 Gold

PREREQUISITE: None

Bazooka shells create more shrapnel.

HIGH VELOCITY SHRAPNEL

COST: 1,700 Gold

PREREQUISITE: Artilleryman Path

Bazooka shrapnel has longer range.

OLD GROWTH BAZOOKA

COST: 2,200 Gold

PREREQUISITE: Artilleryman Path

Bazooka shells and shrapnel do even more increased damage.

EXPLODING SHRAPNEL

COST: 3,000 Gold

PREREQUISITE: Artilleryman

Bazooka shrapnel explodes on contact, damaging nearby enemies.

STRATEGY

Unfortunately, even with upgrades, Bazooka Attack remains a relatively slow and low damage ranged weapon. Sure it has shrapnel and long range, but the shrapnel does a relatively insignificant amount of damage, and long range is rarely very useful in Skylanders.

It's a decent power, but not as exciting as the Mortar Attack/Foliage Barrier combo. If you do like the Bazooka attack, you should invest in the Artilleryman Path. The extra damage and shrapnel improves the power significantly.

WOW POW POWER

TARGET LOCK!

COST: 5,000 Gold

PREREQUISITE: Mortar Attack

Hold **Attack 3** to bring up a targeting reticle, and press **Attack 1** to hit that target with a fruit mortar.

STRATEGY

Target Lock! allows Zook to fire pineapple mortars rapidly wherever he likes. This is a huge upgrade because it allows Zook to spread cacti all over the battle field, keeping enemies diverted while he pelts them with even more pineapple mortars!

ATTACK 2

FOLIAGE BARRIER

COST: N/A

DAMAGE: N/A

RANGE: Short

SPEED: Fast

Press the **Attack 2** button to grow a barricade made of plants to protect yourself.

UPGRADES

FUNGAL BLOOM

COST: 700 Gold

PREREQUISITE: None

Barrier is stronger and takes longer for enemies to destroy.

CACTUS BARRIER

COST: 1,700 Gold

PREREQUISITE: Floral Defender

Barrier does damage to any enemy that touches it.

FIGHTIN' FOLIAGE

COST: 3,000 Gold

PREREQUISITE: Floral Defender

Barriers and Cacti knock enemies back and do damage.

STRATEGY

Foliage Barrier starts off as a 100% defensive power. However, if you stick to it, Foliage Barrier becomes a huge defensive boon that can even damage enemies. It's the perfect combination with Mortar Attack. Use barriers to buy time to target and defeat enemies with mortars.

Enemies always attack a Foliage Barrier that gets in their way. This is a great diversionary tactic that buys Zook even more time. You can use Foliage Barrier twice. Always lay down two barriers to create a greater defensive wall from enemy attacks.

ATTACK 3

MORTAR ATTACK

COST: 900 Gold

PREREQUISITE: None

DAMAGE: High

RANGE: Short/Medium

SPEED: Slow

Press **Attack 3** to launch a Mortar attack.

UPGRADES

MORTAR OF LIFE

COST: 2,200 Gold

PREREQUISITE: Floral Defender

Mortar attacks grows a cactus where the shell explodes.

STRATEGY

Mortar Attack starts out as a Zook's stand-out ability. It's slow, but it's easy to aim, and inflicts high damage. Stick with the Floral Defender Path and you get the awesome Mortar of Life upgrade. This pops cacti up all over the battlefield. Most enemies will attack a cactus before they attack Zook, so this causes more battlefield chaos and lets Zook keep firing mortars from a safe area.

STEALTH ELF

"SILENT, BUT DEADLY!"

STATS

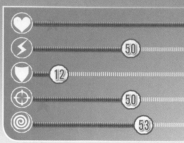

- ♥ ——————————————— 27
- ⚡ ————————— 50 ———————
- 🛡 —— 12 ————————————————
- ◎ ————————— 50 ———————
- ◉ ————————————— 53 ——

UPGRADE PATHS

POOK BLADE SAINT
Further develop Stealth Elf's blade attacks.

FOREST NINJA
Further develop Stealth Elf's Scarecrow skills.

SOUL GEM ABILITY

SYLVAN REGENERATION
COST: 4,000 Gold
PREREQUISITE: None
Regenerate health over time. ✓

STRATEGY

Approximately every five seconds, Stealth Elf automatically regains five health. This isn't huge health restoration, but every bit helps. If you're low on health, try to find a quiet spot in the level and let your health build back up.

SPECIAL QUEST

STEALTH HEALTH:
GAIN 1,000 HP WHILE STEALTHED.

You need to purchase Stealth Elf's Soul Gem power, Sylvan Regeneration, first. Once you do, you will get credit towards the 1,000 HP every time you heal while Stealth Elf is in the Stealthier Decoy mode.

Stealth Elf is a difficult Skylander to master. She has low armor and low health, and most of her attacks are melee. Her advantage comes from the speed of her attacks and her movement. She can dart in and out of combat, striking enemies with deadly knives, or enter stealth mode and catch her enemies unaware for a special back stab attack.

It's hard to pick between the Forest Ninja and Pook Blade Saint paths. Pook Blade Saint is a more straightforward choice, and increases Stealth Elf's damage potential. However, Forest Ninja with her array of Scarecrows is an effective technique, especially after you take some time to practice it.

PRIMARY ATTACKS

ATTACK 1

BLADE SLASH

COST: N/A
DAMAGE: Low
RANGE: Very Short
SPEED: Very Fast

Press **Attack 1** to slice Stealth Elf's enemies up with a pair of sharp blades.

UPGRADES

DRAGONFANG DAGGER

COST: 700 Gold
PREREQUISITE: None
Blades do increased damage.

ELF JITSU

COST: 1,700 Gold
PREREQUISITE: Pook Blade Saint Path
Press **Attack 1**, **Attack 1**, HOLD **Attack 2** for Poison Spores.

Press **Attack 1**, **Attack 1**, HOLD **Attack 3** for Blade Flurry.

ELVEN SUNBLADE

COST: 2,200 Gold
PREREQUISITE: Pook Blade Saint Path
Blade attack does even MORE increased damage.

SHADOWSBANE BLADE DANCE

COST: 3,000 Gold
PREREQUISITE: Pook Blade Saint Path
Magical Blades fight alongside you.

STRATEGY

Stealth Elf's base melee attack is a powerful one. She attacks with blinding speed while moving in and out of range to avoid counterattacks. The Elf Jitsu upgrade adds two combos to the base attack. Poison Spores sprays enemies in front her with a poison cloud. Blade Flurry temporarily turns her into a blinding ball of blades, hitting her enemies even more rapidly. Shadowsbane Blade Dance is an interesting power. It's completely passive. Whenever Stealth Elf attacks, the blades automatically attack her target as well. Additionally, the blades make her Arboreal Acrobatics dish out a small amount of damage.

ATTACK 2

STEALTHIER DECOY

COST: N/A
DAMAGE: Very High
RANGE: Very Short
SPEED: Slow

Press the **Attack 2** button to have Stealth Elf disappear completely but leave behind a decoy image that enemies are drawn to.

UPGRADES

STRAW POOK SCARECROW

COST: 500 Gold
PREREQUISITE: None
A Scarecrow appears in place of your decoy and distracts enemies.

STURDY SCARECROW

COST: 900 Gold
PREREQUISITE: Straw Pook Scarecrow
Scarecrows last longer and take more damage to destroy.

SCARE-CRIO TRIO

COST: 1,700 Gold
PREREQUISITE: Forest Ninja Path
Three scarecrows are created in place of your decoy

SCARECROW BOOBY TRAP

COST: 2,200 Gold
PREREQUISITE: Forest Ninja Path
Scarecrows explode and damage enemies.

SCARECROW SPIN SLICER

COST: 3,000 Gold
PREREQUISITE: Forest Ninja Path
Scarecrows have axes and do extra damage to enemies.

STRATEGY

Stealthier Decoy can be confusing at first. Stealth Elf appears to keep running in place, but if you look closely, you can see her green eyes running around as you move her about. Stealthier Decoy has two benefits. First, once you upgrade it to leave Scarecrows, it creates major distractions for enemies. Later, if you choose the Forest Ninja Path, these Scarecrows can cause serious damage to attacking enemies. Second, Stealth Elf's attack does increased damage when first leaving Stealthier Decoy.

ATTACK 3

ARBOREAL ACROBATICS

COST: 1,200 Gold
PREREQUISITE: None
Press **Attack 3** to perform a quick acrobatic move.

STRATEGY

Consider this Stealth Elf's dash ability. Use Arboreal Acrobatics to jump out of or into the action quickly. Since Stealth Elf often needs to get close to her enemies, you will probably use it more often to dash into combat than dash out.

WOW POW POWER

KNIFE BLENDER!

COST: 5,000 Gold
PREREQUISITE: None
Hold **Attack 1** to unleash a mega 360-degree knife slash attack.

STRATEGY

Knife Blender takes a while to charge and only deals the same amount of damage as a regular blade attack. You don't need to prioritize purchasing this power, wait until you've completed either (or both) of Stealth Elf's upgrade paths.

FRIGHT RIDER

"FEAR THE SPEAR!"

STATS

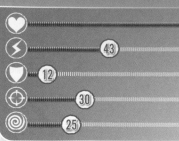

♥ 27
⚡ 43
🛡 12
🎯 30
◎ 25

UPGRADE PATHS

SIR LANCE A LOT
Further develop Fright Rider's melee combat skills.

JOUST JOCKEY
Further develop Jousting Charge abilities.

SOUL GEM ABILITY

A REAL DRAG
COST: 4,000 Gold
PREREQUISITE: Find Soul Gem in the level Aerial Attack!
PREREQUISITE: None
DAMAGE: Very High
RANGE: Long
SPEED: Fast
While burrowing, the spear can drag enemies underground.

Fright Rider never fights alone. He always has his trusty skeletal steed to aid him in battle. This undead warrior has two main modes of attack: a flurry of short-range combos and fierce melee attacks, and a jousting charge that inflicts serious damage while making Fright Rider extremely difficult for enemies to hit.

Fright Rider's Jousting Charge is a unique skill set. It bestows excellent maneuverability that more than makes up for his low armor and average health. For that reason, Joust Jockey is the preferred upgrade path. That said, if you are in need of a competent melee Skylander, Fright Rider can fill that role nicely with the Sir Lance A Lot upgrades. Of particular interest is the Flock of Fury attack which grants an effective medium-range area-of-effect attack.

STRATEGY

When you have this upgrade, any enemies along the burrow trail get picked up by Fright Rider's pike and take damage as he drags them to the pop-out point on the trail. This power greatly enhances Burrow Bomber, allowing you to move enemies around the screen while inflicting massive damage. This does work on most enemies, but Fright Rider isn't able to move giant enemies; they simply take damage as the pike passes through them.

SPECIAL QUEST

DELVING THROW:
TOSS 50 ENEMIES INTO THE AIR

The power to use for this quest is Burrow Bomber. Hit any medium or small enemy with the attack to pop them up in the air and register a "toss."

PRIMARY ATTACKS

ATTACK 1

MELEE ATTACKS

COST: N/A
DAMAGE: Low
RANGE: Short
SPEED: Fast

Press the **Attack 1** button to perform melee attacks with the ostrich and spear. Press **Attack 1**, **Attack 1**, and HOLD **Attack 1** for a special combo.

UPGRADES

GHOUL GLAIVE

COST: 500 Gold
PREREQUISITE: None
Melee attacks do increased damage.

HALBERD OF HORROR

COST: 1,200 Gold
PREREQUISITE: Ghoul Glaive
Melee attacks do even more increased damage.

FRIGHT RIDER COMBOS

COST: 1,700 Gold
PREREQUISITE: Sir Lance A Lot Path
Press **Attack 1**, **Attack 1**, and then HOLD **Attack 2** for Spear Vault.

Press **Attack 1**, **Attack 1**, and then HOLD **Attack 3** for Skull Slam.

FLOCK OF FURY

COST: 2,200 Gold
PREREQUISITE: Sir Lance A Lot Path
Hold **Attack 1** to unleash a fury of multiple ostrich heads.

SUPREME SPEAR

COST: 3,000 Gold
PREREQUISITE: Sir Lance A Lot Path
Melee Attacks do maximum damage.

STRATEGY

Fright Rider is a formidable melee combatant, and if melee is the way you want to develop him, then there are many options in the Sir Lance A Lot path. Fright Rider's normal attacks are short-range, but his combos include medium- and long-range attacks. Spear Vault is a particularly effective combo that deals massive damage in a straight line ahead of Fright Rider (over 100 damage per hit!). Flock of Fury is the highlight of the Sir Lance A Lot Path. When you charge **Attack 1**, Fright Rider's mount splits into eight heads that spread out and attack across the battlefield. The timing on this attack is a bit tricky. You know the mount is ready to attack when Fright Rider starts sparkling.

ATTACK 2

JOUSTING CHARGE

COST: N/A
DAMAGE: Medium
RANGE: Medium
SPEED: Fast

Press and hold the **Attack 2** button to charge towards enemies with spear extended.

UPGRADES

PHANTASM STRIKE

COST: 900 Gold
PREREQUISITE: None
Jousting Charge does increased damage.

JOUST JUICE

COST: 1,700 Gold
PREREQUISITE: Joust Jockey Path
Jousting Charge is faster and does increased damage.

ENTOMBMENT STRIKE

COST: 2,200 Gold
PREREQUISITE: Joust Jockey Path
While charging, press **Attack 3** to perform a powerful, downward strike.

360 DEGREES OF SPEAR

COST: 3,000 Gold
PREREQUISITE: Joust Jockey Path
While charging, press **Attack 1** to swing the spear around in a 360-degree attack.

STRATEGY

This speedy attack starts off as a simple charge. Use it to help Fright Rider get through a level quickly. It's an excellent way to complete a speed run on a level to reach the Time to Beat Dare. Once you spend some hard-earned coin to upgrade the Jousting Charge, Fright Rider gets two extra attacks and damage upgrades, making it a fantastic hit-and-run attack. Speaking of the extra jousting attacks, the most impressive one is Entombment Strike, which causes Fright Rider to jump in the air and slam down on his opponents for serious damage. 360 Degrees of Spear is a less effective tactic that lets you hit enemies while charging (even if you miss them). It is relatively low damage, and hitting them directly with the Joust is usually a better option. Defer buying 360 Degrees of Spear until you have some extra money.

ATTACK 3

BURROW BOMBER

COST: 700 Gold
PREREQUISITE: None
DAMAGE: Medium
RANGE: Long
SPEED: Fast

Hold **Attack 3** to burrow and steer the ostrich's head underground. Release **Attack 3** to teleport to that location.

STRATEGY

This interesting power allows Fright Rider's mount to stretch its neck out underground. You can control where the head goes. When you release the attack button, Fright Rider burrows to the spot and hits the enemy multiple times. This power is particularly useful for attacking enemies around corners. While this attack does not have any standard upgrades, you can earn the Soul Gem Ability, A Real Drag, for some extra attacks while burrowing.

CYNDER

"BOLTS AND LIGHTNING!"

STATS

♥		26
⚡	43	
🛡	18	
⊕	30	
◎	25	

UPGRADE PATHS

NETHER WELDER
Further develop Cynder's Spectral Lightning attack.

SHADOWDANCER
Further develop Cynder's abilities with Ghosts and Shadow Dash.

SOUL GEM ABILITY

HAUNTED ALLY
COST: 4,000 Gold
PREREQUISITE: None
A ghost ally travels with you and damages enemies.

STRATEGY

When you unlock this power, a small purple ghost constantly floats beside Cynder. Whenever enemies get in close range, the Ghost automatically attacks them. The damage and speed of the attack isn't high, but it's automatic, so there's no drawback to using it.

SPECIAL QUEST

ON THE HAUNT:
DEFEAT 50 ENEMIES WITH YOUR GHOST ALLY.

The Ghost Ally does not inflict much damage (only about 6 damage per hit) so you must focus on saving low-health enemies, like Chompies, for the Ghost to attack. The Ghost attacks while Cynder is flying, so flying around an area with Chompies is a good way to rack up points for On the Haunt.

Of all the Undead Skylanders, Cynder is the least creepy. If witches, necromancers, skeletons, and ghouls aren't your thing, then you should consider adding Cynder to your Skylander team!

This violet dragon specializes in taking on large, tough groups of enemies. Her Spectral Lightning attack is great at cutting through enemy health bars, while her Shadow Dash ability can get her out of sticky situations, all the while leaving behind a group of deadly ghosts!

PRIMARY ATTACKS

ATTACK 1

SPECTRAL LIGHTNING

COST: N/A
DAMAGE: Low
RANGE: Medium
SPEED: Fast

Press and hold **Attack 1** to shock enemies with bolts of lightning.

ATTACK 2

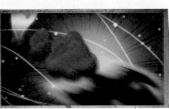

SHADOW DASH

COST: N/A
DAMAGE: Very Low
RANGE: Short
SPEED: Fast

Press **Attack 2** to dash forward in shadow mode, leaving ghostly allies in Cynder's wake.

UPGRADES

BLACK LIGHTNING

COST: 700 Gold
PREREQUISITE: None

Spectral Lightning does increased damage.

BREATH CONTROL

COST: 2,200 Gold
PREREQUISITE: Nether Welder Path

Spectral Lightning hold duration is increased.

UNSTABLE FORCES

COST: 1,700 Gold
PREREQUISITE: Nether Welder Path

Hitting a ghost with Spectral Lightning makes it explode, damaging enemies.

BREATH OF POWER

COST: 3,000 Gold
PREREQUISITE: Nether Welder Path

Spectral Lightning damages enemies in a larger area.

UPGRADES

DOUBLE SPOOKY!

COST: 900 Gold
PREREQUISITE: None

Ghosts do increased damage.

GHOST HAUNTER

COST: 2,200 Gold
PREREQUISITE: Shadowdancer Path

Ghosts last longer and have a greater attack range.

SHADOW REACH

COST: 1,200 Gold
PREREQUISITE: None

Shadow Dash range is increased.

SHADOW STRIKE

COST: 3,000 Gold
PREREQUISITE: Shadowdancer Path

Shadow Dash does damage to enemies.

DEATH BOUND

COST: 1,700 Gold
PREREQUISITE: Shadowdancer Path

Enemies hit by ghosts move slower.

STRATEGY

Spectral Lightning is a powerful ranged attack that has a good spread and good range and hits any enemies in front of Cynder. You can press the **Attack 1** button when using this power, or press and hold it. Cynder suffers reduced movement while the button is held.

This power works well with Shadow Dash once you invest in the Unstable Forces power. Hitting Ghosts causes them to blow up, which then knocks back enemies. This is good for interrupting enemy attacks, but a straight lightning attack actually does more damage.

STRATEGY

Cynder's Shadow Dash doesn't directly damage enemies as she dashes into them. Instead, she leaves behind a trail of ghosts that hurt any nearby enemies. This effect is automatic, and is a great bonus to the powerful inherent defensive nature of dash attacks (it's hard for enemies to hit a Skylander that is dashing). The cool thing about this power is that Cynder can dash right through enemies. While this doesn't affect the enemies at all, if you invest in Shadow Strike further down the line, it deals a moderate amount of damage on enemies without putting her at risk. The Shadowdancer Path has additional options for Shadow Dash. With a fully upgraded Shadow Dash, the ghosts aggressively attack enemies, slow them down, and do moderate damage. This isn't a great power to use against bosses (except as a defensive maneuver), but it's fantastic against large groups of enemies and in arena fights.

WOW POW POWER

LIGHTNING RAIN!

COST: 5,000 Gold
PREREQUISITE: Cynder Flight

While flying, press **Attack 2** to bring a great lightning blast down from the sky.

ATTACK 3

CYNDER FLIGHT

COST: 500 Gold
PREREQUISITE: None

Press **Attack 3** to fly. Increased speed and armor while flying.

STRATEGY

Lightning Rain! is a great addition to Cynder's arsenal. The lightning attack is a medium range area-of-effect and inflicts high damage to everything in the area. This is a great power to use when faced with many smaller enemies, or when fighting enemies while flying.

STRATEGY

Like most other dragons, Cynder has this standard flight ability. Flight is great for increasing speed to help hit level time dares, as well as for avoiding level hazards.

CHOP CHOP

"SLICE AND DICE!"

STATS

♥	30
⚡	50
🛡	24
✛	10
◎	39

UPGRADE PATHS

VAMPIRIC WARRIOR
Further develop Chop Chop's Sword attacks.

UNDEAD DEFENDER
Further develop Chop Chop's Shield abilities.

SOUL GEM ABILITY

CURSED BONE BRAMBLER
COST: 4,000 Gold

PREREQUISITE: Bone Brambler

The Bone Brambles attack (**Attack 3**) does extra damage.

STRATEGY

Cursed Bone Brambler increases Chop Chop's Bone Bramble damage by approximately 20%.

SPECIAL QUEST

STALWART DEFENDER: ABSORB 1,000 DAMAGE WITH YOUR SHIELD.

Enemies can dish out a lot of damage, especially on the harder difficulties. You can complete this quest quickly by simply using Chop Chop's Arkeyan Shield (even before he gets any upgrades for it).

This Undead melee powerhouse is a remnant of the Arkeyan Elite Guard. When the Arkeyan Empire fell, Chop Chop set out in search for an Arkeyan leader to give him orders. That was when Master Eon recruited him to become a Skylander.

Chop Chop values speed and defense over raw damage output. While it's true that you can focus on the Vampiric Warrior Path to increase Chop Chop's damage output, in the end, Arkeyan Shield, with Undead Defender upgrades, is his stand-out ability.

PRIMARY ATTACKS

ATTACK 1

ARKEYAN BLADE

COST: N/A
DAMAGE: High
RANGE: Short
SPEED: Very Fast

Press the **Attack 1** button to slash away at your enemies with this ancient blade.

UPGRADES

VAMPIRIC AURA

COST: 700 Gold
PREREQUISITE: None

The Arkeyan Blade does extra damage and you regain health by defeating enemies.

ARKEYAN COMBAT MASTER

COST: 1,700 Gold
PREREQUISITE: Vampiric Warrior Path

Press **Attack 1**, **Attack 1**, and then HOLD **Attack 2** for Arkeyan Cyclone.

Press **Attack 1**, **Attack 1**, and then HOLD **Attack 3** for Arkeyan Leap.

ARKEYAN VORPAL BLADE

COST: 2,200 Gold
PREREQUISITE: Vampiric Warrior Path

Sword attacks do even MORE increased damage.

DEMON BLADE OF THE UNDERWORLD

COST: 3,000 Gold
PREREQUISITE: Arkeyan Vorpal Blade

Swords have longer range and do MAXIMUM damage.

STRATEGY

Chop Chop has lightning quick, low-damage sword slashing attacks. Upgrades include the ability to heal Chop Chop whenever he kills an enemy. Unfortunately, this healing ability never gets too strong (expect less than 10 HP per kill).

Once you purchase Chop Chop's combos, you get access to two powerful attacks. Arkeyan Cyclone is a whirling short-range area-of-effect combo. Arkeyan Leap starts with a jump into the air and ends with Bone Brambles being shot out at enemies.

ATTACK 3

BONE BRAMBLER

COST: 1,200 Gold
PREREQUISITE: None
DAMAGE: Low
RANGE: Medium
SPEED: Very Slow

Press **Attack 3** to attack enemies with Bone Brambles.

STRATEGY

Bone Brambler is a great add-on ability for Chop Chop. Having a ranged attack to pull out in tricky combat situations greatly increases his versatility. This will never be Chop Chop's primary power, but it's a great addition to his arsenal.

ATTACK 2

ARKEYAN SHIELD

COST: N/A
DAMAGE: N/A
RANGE: Short
SPEED: N/A

Hold the **Attack 2** to protect yourself from most attacks; also deflects projectiles.

UPGRADES

SPIKED SHIELD BASH

COST: 500 Gold
PREREQUISITE: None

While holding **Attack 2**, press **Attack 1** to Shield Bash an enemy.

SHIELD SPARTAN

COST: 900 Gold
PREREQUISITE: Spiked Shield Bash

Move faster and block more damage while holding **Attack 2**.

ARKEYAN SPECTRAL SHIELD

COST: 1,700 Gold
PREREQUISITE: Undead Defender Path

Hold **Attack 2** to absorb incoming damage—while holding, press **Attack 1** to release absorbed damage on your foes.

SHIELD STUN BASH

COST: 2,200 Gold
PREREQUISITE: Undead Defender Path

Shield Bash attacks stun enemies.

DEMON SHIELD OF THE SHADOWS

COST: 3,000 Gold
PREREQUISITE: Undead Defender Path, Arkeyan Spectral Shield

Shield Bash does extra damage—absorbed damage is automatically released.

STRATEGY

When you first play Chop Chop, you may wonder what's so great about his shield. Even if you block an attack with it, it doesn't reduce all the damage from the attack. The secret is that you need to upgrade Arkeyan Shield and turn it into a powerful weapon. Shield Bash is initially a low-damage counter attack, but once you get Shield Stun Bash, the bash turns into a great crowd control ability.

Purchasing the Arkeyan Spectral Shield and Demon Shield of the Shadows upgrades unleashes the full potential of Arkeyan Shield. With these upgrades, Chop Chop can sit in combat, completely absorb enemy attacks, and then return the damage back to his foes.

WOW POW POWER

SHIELD SKEWER!

COST: 5,000 Gold
PREREQUISITE: Spiked Shield Bash

Hold **Attack 2** and press **Attack 1** to burst forward in a mega shield bash attack.

STRATEGY

This Wow Pow greatly enhances the effectiveness of Spiked Shield Blast. It triples its damage output and increases both the speed and range of the attack.

HEX

"FEAR THE DARK!"

STATS

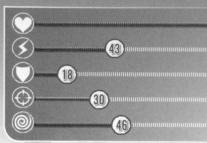

♥	270
⚡	43
🛡	18
◎	30
◎	46

UPGRADE PATHS

SHADE MASTER
Further develop Hex's Phantom Orb attack.

BONE CRAFTER
Further develop Hex's Skull Rain and Wall of Bones abilities.

SOUL GEM ABILITY

SKULL SHIELD
COST: 4,000 Gold
PREREQUISITE: None

Skull Rain knocks away enemies and attacks.

STRATEGY

This upgrade serves to make Skull Rain an even more vicious attack. One of the big problems with Skull Rain is that it can take a long time to fully charge it. With this power, any enemy that tries to hit Hex while she is charging takes damage and gets knocked back.

SPECIAL QUEST

NOGGIN KNOCKER: KNOCK AWAY 100 ENEMIES WITH YOUR SKULL RAIN.

To work on this quest, you need to first purchase Skull Shield. Once you have that, allow enemies to get within melee range while Hex is charging her Skull Shield. If they get too close, they get knocked back, tallying a point for this quest.

Hex is a dark necromancer with two fantastic ranged abilities, and a very powerful defensive wall that gives her time to set off her powerful spells. While Hex can certainly be played as a standard ranged character, her greatest strengths lie in her Bone Crafter Path, which unlocks a unique and powerful necromantic play style.

PRIMARY ATTACKS

ATTACK 1

CONJURE PHANTOM ORB
COST: N/A
DAMAGE: High
RANGE: Short
SPEED: Fast

Press **Attack 1** to launch magic orbs of spectral energy that track Hex's foes.

UPGRADES

TWICE THE ORBAGE
COST: 1,200 Gold
PREREQUISITE: None
Press **Attack 1** to shoot two Phantom Orbs at once.

LONG DISTANCE ORBS
COST: 1,700 Gold
PREREQUISITE: Shade Master Path
Hold **Attack 1** to increase the range of your Phantom Orbs.

CAUSTIC PHANTOM ORBS
COST: 2,200 Gold
PREREQUISITE: Shade Master Path
Phantom Orbs do increased damage.

UNSTABLE PHANTOM ORBS
COST: 3,000 Gold
PREREQUISITE: Shade Master Path
Phantom Orbs explode, damaging nearby enemies.

STRATEGY
Phantom Orbs are ranged attacks. The upgrades provided are fairly straightforward, however Long Distance Orbs is the least useful of the upgrades available on the Shade Master Path. Orbs already have very long range, so increasing the range isn't much help. To use Long Distance Orbs, hold **Attack 1** after firing your orbs.

ATTACK 2

RAIN OF SKULLS
COST: N/A
DAMAGE: High
RANGE: Long
SPEED: Very Slow

Hold **Attack 2** to begin casting this spell. When fully charged, release and ghostly skulls rain down on Hex's enemies.

UPGRADES

STORM OF SKULLS
COST: 700 Gold
PREREQUISITE: None
Conjure up to four skulls with your Skull Rain attack.

MASTER CASTER
COST: 2,200 Gold
PREREQUISITE: Bone Crafter Path
Takes much less time to cast Skull Rain and Wall of Bones.

TROLL SKULLS
COST: 3,000 Gold
PREREQUISITE: Bone Crafter Path
Skull Rain does increased damage.

STRATEGY
Rain of Skulls is a chargeable attack; Hex surrounds herself with giant skulls and flings them into the air, crashing them down on her opponents moments later. The challenge of Rain of Skulls is that it takes about 5 seconds to charge. While Hex can still move during this charge, her movements are slower, leaving her vulnerable. The solution to this is to erect a Wall of Bones between Hex and her enemies before starting to charge the Rain.

ATTACK 3

WALL OF BONES
COST: 500 Gold
PREREQUISITE: None
Press **Attack 3** to create a Wall of Bones to protect Hex.

UPGRADES

BONE FORTRESS
COST: 900 Gold
PREREQUISITE: Wall of Bones
The Wall of Bones is larger and takes more damage to destroy.

COMPOUND FRACTURE
COST: 1,700 Gold
PREREQUISITE: Bone Crafter Path
Wall of Bones damages any enemy that touches it.

STRATEGY
Wall of Bones creates a semi-circle of bones in the direction Hex is facing. The Bones automatically retract if Hex moves towards them, allowing her to pass freely. The wall can be partially destroyed by enemy attacks, but can be replaced at any time by having Hex recast it.

This is one of those powers that may seem pointless when you first unlock it, but gets better and better with upgrades. Initially, Wall of Bones doesn't provide Hex with much defense, but with upgrades it can take huge amounts of punishment and inflict massive damage on any enemies dumb enough to charge into it.

WOW POW POWER

SKULL BUDDY!
COST: 5,000 Gold
PREREQUISITE: None
DAMAGE: High
RANGE: Short
SPEED: Very Slow

Hold **Attack 2** to charge up the Skull Storm, then press **Attack 1** to conjure a giant skull pal.

STRATEGY
Skull Buddy! transforms currently summoned skulls into a gigantic skull that rotates over Hex's head. Whenever an enemy gets within short range, the giant skull fires a hex skull, which inflicts good damage. Unfortunately, even with an upgraded Rain of Skulls, Skull Buddy! takes a very long time to cast, and does not last very long. Purchase this power last; it's difficult to use and has limited range.

GHOST ROASTER

"NO CHAIN, NO GAIN!"

STATS

❤️	28
⚡	43
🛡️	24
🎯	20
🌀	53

UPGRADE PATHS

FEAR EATER
Further develop Ghost Roaster's Ectoplasmic abilities.

SKULL MASTER
Further develop Ghost Roaster's Skull Charge attack.

SOUL GEM ABILITY

LINGERING CURSE

COST: 4,000 Gold
PREREQUISITE: Haunt
Ghosts have a bigger attack range and knock enemies away.

Ghost Roaster may seem like one of the scariest Skylanders, but don't let his creepy face fool you. He's just as loyal to his Portal Master as any of his fellow Skylanders! Ghost Roaster has two high-damage attacks, invulnerability, as well as an effective method to heal himself in combat.

When considering upgrade paths, strongly consider Skull Master. Skull Charge has it all: healing, speed, and at higher levels, high damage. Stick to the Skull Master Path to get the most out of the attack.

STRATEGY

This is a great passive bonus for Ghost Roaster. The Ghosts seek out any enemies close by and inflict about 12 points of damage per hit. They also hit fairly regularly. Whichever path you take, this is definitely a power you want to save up for.

SPECIAL QUEST

GRAVE CIRCUMSTANCES:
DEFEAT 100 ENEMIES WITH SKULL CHARGE.

Skull Charge is a great power, and that makes this quest particularly manageable. Just repeatedly use the Charge to attack enemies and you should complete this in no time.

PRIMARY ATTACKS

ATTACK 1

CHAIN WHIP

COST: N/A
DAMAGE: High
RANGE: Short
SPEED: Average

Press **Attack 1** to swing Ghost Roaster's whip tail at enemies.

UPGRADES

PAIN CHAIN

COST: 500 Gold
PREREQUISITE: None

Chain Whip attacks do increased damage.

HAUNT

COST: 1,200 Gold
PREREQUISITE: None

Defeating an enemy with the Chain Whip turns them into a ghost that attacks other enemies.

STRATEGY

Chain Whip is Ghost Roaster's primary melee attack, and you get its upgrades before you pick a specialization path. Chain Whip is a quick, high-damage attack. When you get Haunt, you can use it to create Ghosts, which offer different enhancements as you improve Skull Charge and Ectoplasm Mode.

ATTACK 2

SKULL CHARGE

COST: N/A
DAMAGE: Low
RANGE: Short

Press **Attack 2** to transform into a ghostly skull that barrels through enemies.

UPGRADES

METALHEAD

COST: 700 Gold
PREREQUISITE: None

The Skull Charge attack lasts longer.

FRIGHT BITE

COST: 1,700 Gold
PREREQUISITE: Skull Master Path

Skull Charge does increased damage.

UNFINISHED BUSINESS

COST: 2,200 Gold
PREREQUISITE: Skull Master Path

Defeating an enemy with Skull Charge creates a ghost.

LIFE TRANSFER

COST: 3,000 Gold
PREREQUISITE: Skull Master Path

Devouring a ghost while doing a Skull Charge heals you.

STRATEGY

This is Ghost Roaster's coolest attack. When in the Skull Charge mode, Ghost Roaster is moving so fast that he's almost impossible for enemies to hit. The speed is a double-edged sword, however. You need to be careful not to run into enemy attacks while using the power. Always try to attack enemies from behind.

The Ghost upgrades on the Skull Master Path are fantastic. They make Ghost Roaster one of the few Skylanders that can heal himself without any help from fruit or items.

ATTACK 3

ECTOPLASM MODE

COST: 900 Gold
PREREQUISITE: None

Press **Attack 3** to enter Ectoplasm Mode. This makes Ghost Roaster immune to all attacks, but he loses health over time.

UPGRADES

PHASE SHIFT BURST

COST: 1,700 Gold
PREREQUISITE: Fear Eater Path

All nearby enemies take damage when Ghost Roaster enters Ectoplasm Mode.

ECTO-FRIENDLY

COST: 2,200 Gold
PREREQUISITE: Fear Eater Path

While in Ectoplasm Mode, Ghost Roaster moves faster and loses less health over time.

NIGHTMARE TOUCH

COST: 3,000 Gold
PREREQUISITE: Fear Eater Path

Touching a ghost while in Ectoplasm Mode creates a powerful explosion.

STRATEGY

Invincibility is an amazing power, but it has a price. Ghost Roaster's unique ability allows him to survive almost anything, as long as you don't overuse it. Ectoplasm Mode is the only attack in the game where a Skylander can hurt themselves. This makes it one power that requires some effective strategy to use. If you aren't careful, you could even knock out Ghost Roaster!

The upgrades provided by the Fear Eater Path are not as strong as those in the Skull Master Path. Specifically, Phase Shift Burst does not do much damage at all to enemies when you enter the mode. It's only good for clearing out Chompies, and there are plenty of other powers that do that equally as well. Ecto-Friendly is nice, but you still lose a bit of health (about 7 points per second). Nightmare Touch is difficult to use because you must create Ghosts first (which happens only when you defeat enemies with Chain Whip).

FLASHWING

"BLINDED BY THE LIGHT!"

STATS

♥	26
⚡	43
🛡	24
⊕	10
◎	25

UPGRADE PATHS

SUPER SHARDS
Further develop Flashwing's Crystal Shard attacks.

SUPER SPINNER
Further develop Flashwing's Shimmering Spin ability.

SOUL GEM ABILITY

CRYSTAL LIGHTHOUSE
COST: 4,000 Gold
PREREQUISITE: Find Flashwing's Soul Gem in the level Bringing Order to Kaos!
DAMAGE: Very High
RANGE: Very Long
SPEED: Very Slow

Hold **Attack 3** to create a Crystal Lighthouse that fires laser light beams.

STRATEGY
This is an astoundingly awesome addition to Flashwing's arsenal. Crystal Lighthouse requires Flashwing to be stationary, but once it's set up it flashes the battlefield in a huge arc, damaging enemies within the light's radius every few seconds. Even after other powers are upgraded, this is Flashwing's highest-damage attack.

SPECIAL QUEST

LET IT SHINE: DEFEAT 20 ENEMIES WITH ONE CRYSTAL LIGHTHOUSE.

Since Crystal Lighthouse is stationary, this is a tricky quest. You need to find an area with 20 low-level enemies. The best candidate for this is one of the arena maps. Go to Arena 3 (Kaos' Royal Flush), and select the second challenge, Birthday Bash. Set up the Lighthouse in the middle of the birthday cake. You should get 20 kills before the D. Riveters (who are just outside of the Lighthouse's range) show up.

Flashwing is one of the most versatile Skylanders in the game. She has an amazing, ultra-wide-range area-of-effect attack and a stunning defensive spin ability that dramatically increases the damage she can dish out.

On top of that, Flashwing has a superb ranged attack that not only has knockback, but you can also purchase Healing Crystals, an upgrade on the Super Shards Path, that allows her to heal herself!

PRIMARY ATTACKS

ATTACK 1

CRYSTAL SHARDS

COST: N/A
DAMAGE: Low
RANGE: Long
SPEED: Fast

Press **Attack 1** to fire Crystal Shards.

ATTACK 2

SHIMMERING SPIN

COST: N/A
DAMAGE: Very Low
RANGE: Short
SPEED: Fast

Hold **Attack 2** to spin around and damage anything in Flashwing's path.

UPGRADES

LUMINOUS LASERS

COST: 700 Gold
PREREQUISITE: None

Hold **Attack 1** to charge up a powerful laser shot.

LIGHT SPEED SHARDS

COST: 900 Gold
PREREQUISITE: None

Shoot Crystal Shards much faster and deal extra damage.

ARMORED AURA

COST: 1,200 Gold
PREREQUISITE: None

Condensed light increases your armor.

SHOOTING SHARDS

COST: 1,700 Gold
PREREQUISITE: Super Shards Path

Crystal Shards stick in walls and shoot their own crystals when **Attack 1** is pressed again.

CRYSTAL CRAZINESS

COST: 2,200 Gold
PREREQUISITE: Super Shards Path, Shooting Shards

Up to three crystals stick in walls and shoot their own crystals when **Attack 1** is pressed again.

HEALING CRYSTALS

COST: 3,000 Gold
PREREQUISITE: Super Shards Path

Crystals embedded in a wall heal Flashwing when she is close.

UPGRADES

EXTRA RADIANT ROTATION

COST: 1,700 Gold
PREREQUISITE: Super Spinner Path

Shimmering Spin lasts longer and does increased damage.

REFLECTION DEFLECTION

COST: 2,200 Gold
PREREQUISITE: Super Spinner Path

Gain extra armor and deflect enemies' shots back at them while spinning.

LIGHTS, CRYSTAL, ACTION!

COST: 3,000 Gold
PREREQUISITE: Super Spinner Path

While spinning, press **Attack 1** to shoot beams of laser light.

STRATEGY

Shimmering Spin is a deadly dash attack that can be used both offensively and defensively. When you get Reflection Deflection, Flashwing's base armor goes over 100 while spinning!

The last upgrade in the Super Spinner path, Lights, Crystal, Action!, doesn't add too much to Shimmer Spin. The damage output from the laser is low, and you can't aim it. Definitely purchase Crystal Lighthouse first.

STRATEGY

This is a great long-range attack. Not only does the Crystal Shard inflict above average damage for a rapid fire attack, but it also provides significant knockback against charging enemies. Once Flashwing unlocks the ability to stick Crystal Shards into nearby walls, this power becomes interesting. Use the crystal embedding to hit tough enemies from behind (Inhuman Shields don't stand a chance!). Unlock Healing Crystals and you can get some extra health whenever you need it (provided you are patient enough; each shard only heals 5 HP every few seconds).

Armored Aura increases Flashwing's base armor by 40.

ATTACK 3

SURROUNDED BY SHARDS

COST: 500 Gold
PREREQUISITE: None
DAMAGE: Low
RANGE: Long
SPEED: Average

Press **Attack 3** to fire Crystal Shards in all directions but forward.

STRATEGY

The best part about this power is that it's cheap. While hitting enemies behind Flashwing can come in handy, Surrounded by Shards is not a power you will use often.

BASH

"ROCK AND ROLL!"

STATS

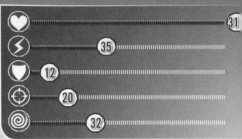

♥	31
⚡	35
🛡	12
◎	20
◉	32

UPGRADE PATHS

GRANITE DRAGON
Further develop Bash's Tail Swipe & Summoning attacks.

PULVER DRAGON
Further develop Bash's Roll attack.

SOUL GEM ABILITY

TRICERATOPS HONOR GUARD
COST: 4,000 Gold
PREREQUISITE: None
This power gives Bash new armor that makes him harder to hit.

STRATEGY
One of Bash's weaknesses is his low armor. When you purchase this ability, Bash's base Armor stat goes from 12 to 52! That's a huge improvement and lets him hang in tough close-range combat situations for longer.

SPECIAL QUEST

ON A ROLL:
DEFEAT 10 ENEMIES WITH ONE ROLL ATTACK.

Look for a group of Chompies; the roll attack does enough damage to knock out a Chompy even before upgrades. If you are having trouble with this quest, consider the Pulver Dragon path. It makes this quest much easier.

Bash is a fantastic Earth Skylander who packs a serious wallop at close-range and a fantastic dash attack that makes him a difficult target for his enemies.

It's a toss up between the Granite Dragon and Pulver Dragon upgrade paths. If you choose Granite Dragon, you get one of the most powerful single attacks in the game. Bash's tail is absolutely brutal and knocks out even huge enemies in one hit. Pulver Dragon increases Bash's overall survivability, ensuring he stays in the fight longer by making him a hard target, all the while dishing out major rolling damage on anything unfortunate enough to get in his way.

PRIMARY ATTACKS

ATTACK 1

TAIL SWIPE

COST: N/A
DAMAGE: Very High
RANGE: Short
SPEED: Slow

Press the **Attack 1** button to swing your tail around to attack 360 degrees of enemies.

UPGRADES

TENNIS TAIL

COST: 500 Gold
PREREQUISITE: None
Deflect incoming objects with your Tail Swipe.

IRON TAIL

COST: 700 Gold
PREREQUISITE: None
Tail Swipe does increased damage.

MACE OF DESTRUCTION

COST: 1,700 Gold
PREREQUISITE: Granite Dragon Path
Tail Swipe does MORE increased damage.

GAIA HAMMER

COST: 3,000 Gold
PREREQUISITE: Mace of Destruction
Hold **Attack 1** to charge up the Tail Swipe and do extra damage.

STRATEGY

Bash's mace tail is his strongest feature. This powerful swipe inflicts massive damage; only some of the Giants inflict as much damage right out the gate. It's so good, that the Granite Dragon Path isn't really even necessary.

If you do choose the Granite Dragon Path, Gaia Hammer is one of the highest-damage attacks in the game. It can dish out over 200 damage! The charge takes a moment, but against bosses, it should be your primary attack.

ATTACK 2

ROCK AND ROLL

COST: N/A
DAMAGE: Medium
RANGE: Short
SPEED: Average

Press and hold the **Attack 2** button to roll into a ball and then over your enemies.

UPGRADES

DOUBLE ROLL

COST: 1,200 Gold
PREREQUISITE: None
Use the Roll attack for twice as long.

PULVER ROLL

COST: 1,700 Gold
PREREQUISITE: Pulver Dragon Path
Roll attack does increased damage.

EARTHEN FORCE ROLL

COST: 2,200 Gold
PREREQUISITE: Pulver Dragon Path
Roll does MORE damage and can roll right through enemy attacks.

CONTINENTAL BOULDER

COST: 3,000 Gold
PREREQUISITE: Pulver Roll
Becomes a giant ball while rolling—roll faster and do even MORE damage.

STRATEGY

For a dash-type attack, Rock and Roll dishes out serious damage. While it's not as fast as other dash attacks, the extra damage more than makes up for it. The end result after buying all the upgrades is a dash-type attack that does more damage than the base mace tail attack, has excellent range (Bash turns into a giant ball once he gets Continental Boulder), and dramatically increases Bash's defense.

ATTACK 3

SUMMONING: STONE PROJECTION

COST: 900 Gold
PREREQUISITE: None
DAMAGE: High
RANGE: Medium
SPEED: Very Slow

Press **Attack 3** to summon a rock wall—hit it with your Tail Swipe to launch rocks.

UPGRADES

SUMMONING: STONE UPPERCUT

COST: 2,200 Gold
PREREQUISITE: Granite Dragon Path
Stone Projection does increased damage.

STRATEGY

Stone Projection is an interesting power that gives Bash some range. It does a high amount of damage whether you use the projection as a mid-range area-of-effect attack, or smash the stone to launch a ranged stone. One difficulty of Stone Projection is that it's difficult to aim the ranged attack. It's long range, but it doesn't have much utility since it's so hard to aim correctly.

WOW POW POWER

ROLLING THUNDER!

COST: 5,000 Gold
PREREQUISITE:
Summoning: Stone Projection
While rolling, press **Attack 3** to launch into the air and slam down.

STRATEGY

When you activate this ability, Bash uses his stone projection to create a ramp, and moments later he slams into the ground with a very wide-range area-of-effect attack. Enemies caught directly in the blast take a lot of damage (approximately double a normal roll attack).

DINO-RANG

"COME RANG OR SHINE!"

STATS

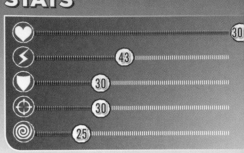

♥	30
⚡	43
🛡	30
◎	30
◉	25

UPGRADE PATHS

GRAND BOOMERANG MASTER
Further develop Dino-Rang's boomerang attacks.

EARTHEN AVENGER
Further develop Dino-Rang's defensive traps and abilities.

SOUL GEM ABILITY

STICKY BOOMERANGS
COST: 4,000 Gold

PREREQUISITE: None

Boomerangs pick up treasure, food, power-ups.

STRATEGY
This power is only good as a novelty or for pursuing Dino-Rang's special quest. Only purchase this power once you have extra gold, or if you really want to unlock all the quests for Dino-Rang.

SPECIAL QUEST

FOODERANG: PICK UP 20 FOOD ITEMS WITH BOOMERANGS.

Once you purchase the Sticky Boomerangs power, you can use his **Attack 1** ability to grab any food lying around the level. 20 food items won't take long, especially if you switch Dino-Rang in on your portal whenever you see a piece of food drop.

An easy way to get this is to go through a few Arena Challenges with Brock. Between each round, the audience throws food items into the arena. Grab them all with your boomerangs to get points towards this quest.

Dino-Rang is an expert trapper and boomerang thrower. His boomerang attacks have two variations. Stone Boomerangs is a rapid-fire, low-damage boomerang attack at his enemies that can bounce off walls or hit enemies on their return trip. His secondary attack allows him to attack with a higher-damage, but slower close-range boomerang attack.

Where Dino-Rang really shines, however, is with his Stonefist Trap abilities. These traps inflict massive damage and can be used strategically to allow Dino-Rang to control any battlefield situation. As such, we strongly recommend players pursue the Earthen Avenger Path with Dino-Rang.

PRIMARY ATTACKS

ATTACK 1

STONE BOOMERANGS

COST: N/A

DAMAGE: Low

RANGE: Long

SPEED: Very Fast

Press the **Attack 1** button to throw boomerangs at your enemies.

UPGRADES

BASALT BOOMERANGS

COST: 500 Gold

PREREQUISITE: None

Boomerangs do increased damage.

BOOMERANG FINESSE

COST: 700 Gold

PREREQUISITE: None

Hold **Attack 1** to control boomerangs in the air.

VOLCANIC GLASS BOOMERANGS

COST: 1,700 Gold

PREREQUISITE: Grand Boomerang Master Path

Boomerangs do even MORE increased damage.

DANCING BOOMERANGS

COST: 2,200 Gold

PREREQUISITE: Grand Boomerang Master Path

Boomerangs bounce off of walls and enemies.

STRATEGY

Stone Boomerangs are a straightforward ranged attack that Dino-Rang can throw rapid-fire at his enemies. If you miss with your initial boomerang throw, the boomerang can still hit an enemy on its way back to Dino-Rang.

The upgrades for Stone Boomerangs are mostly damage-related, but Boomerang Finesse allows Dino-Rang to control a boomerang's path. This can be useful to hit enemies around corners, but generally regular attacks are more effective.

ATTACK 2

BOOMERANG SHIELD

COST: N/A

DAMAGE: High

RANGE: Medium

SPEED: Slow

Press the **Attack 2** button to throw both boomerangs around you in a circle for a close-ranged attack.

UPGRADES

DERVISH SHIELD

COST: 1,200 Gold

PREREQUISITE: None

Boomerang Shield does extra damage and blocks enemies' shots.

IT'S ALL IN THE WRIST

COST: 3,000 Gold

PREREQUISITE: Grand Boomerang Master Path

Boomerang Shield lasts longer and does extra damage.

STRATEGY

Boomerang Shield is a decent close-range area-of-effect attack. Use it when Dino-Rang is surrounded by enemies. It is less effective when paired with upgraded Stonefist Traps since having enemies close by isn't an ideal situation for a trapper Dino-Rang build. However, they can still be useful in overwhelming situations.

Boomerang Shield is much slower than Stone Boomerangs, but it inflicts about 50% more damage. Don't let the name fool you, Boomerang Shield isn't much of a defensive power. In fact, it doesn't hit enemies at very close range, only those at medium/close range. This means if you try to use them against an enemy at melee range, they will likely completely miss.

ATTACK 3

STONEFIST TRAPS

COST: 900 Gold

PREREQUISITE: None

DAMAGE: Very High

RANGE: Short

SPEED: Very Slow

Press **Attack 3** to summon two Stonefist Traps from beneath the earth.

QUAD STONEFIST TRAP

COST: 1,700 Gold

PREREQUISITE: Earthen Avenger Path

Summon 4 Stonefist Traps at once.

OBSIDIAN ARMOR

COST: 2,200 Gold

PREREQUISITE: Earthen Avenger Path

Improved armor makes it harder for enemies to hit you.

FIST TRAP FUNERAL

COST: 3,000 Gold

PREREQUISITE: Earthen Avenger Path

Enemies defeated by Boomerangs spawn Stonefist Traps.

STRATEGY

This is a unique trapping power that can be used defensively to provide cover while attacking at range with boomerangs. When you press **Attack 3** Dino-Rang quickly sets up the stones in the ground directly in front of where he is standing. As soon as an enemy comes within range, the fist pops up inflicting heavy damage.

If you decide to take Dino-Rang down the Earthen Avenger path, then his Stonefists get significantly better. The Quad Stonefist Trap forms a line of Quadfists that he can use defensively to defend against enemies from different angles. Fist Trap Funeral sows chaos on the battlefield; use your Stone Boomerangs effectively, and Stonefists will be popping up all over the place!

Obsidian Armor is a great upgrade that improves Dino-Rang's armor from 30 to 70 points. Add on a high armor hat, and Dino-Rang can have one of the toughest hides in the game!

PRISM BREAK

"THE BEAM IS SUPREME."

STATS

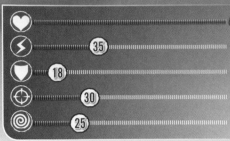

♥	290
⚡	35
🛡	18
◎	30
🌀	25

UPGRADE PATHS

CRYSTALEER
Further develop Prism Break's defensive Crystal abilities.

PRISMANCER
Further develop Prism Break's Energy Beam attacks.

SOUL GEM ABILITY

SHARD SOUL PRISON
COST: 4,000 Gold
PREREQUISITE: None

Crystal Gems form at defeated enemies.

STRATEGY

Whenever you defeat an enemy, a Crystal Shard appears where the enemy goes down. These shards don't do any damage on their own, but they can be used to refract the Prism Break's lasers. This is a great power because it increases the number of Crystal Shards in the field, allowing Prism Break to use his laser more effectively and take out enemies rapidly.

SPECIAL QUEST

BIFURCATION SENSATION: DEFEAT 100 ENEMIES WITH DOUBLE REFRACTION.

To defeat an enemy with double refraction, you first need to unlock the Chained Refractions upgrade. Once you have that, place plenty of Crystal Shards and fire your Energy Beam through them to indirectly take out nearby enemies. A beam has to pass through two Shards before hitting an enemy to count for this quest. The more you upgrade Prism Break's powers, the easier this quest becomes.

Prism Break's secondary attack allows him to summon crystals from the sky. Then he can use his primary attack to shoot the beam into the crystals and spread its damage across the battlefield.

Initially, Prism Break is a difficult Skylander to master. Predicting which direction his refracted lasers will go can be difficult. But, if you invest in the Prismancer path, the increased refraction and effectiveness of the laser make it much easier since the laser refracts multiple times and has excellent range.

PRIMARY ATTACKS

ATTACK 1

ENERGY BEAM

COST: N/A

DAMAGE: Low

RANGE: Medium

SPEED: Fast

Press and hold the **Attack 1** button to fire a powerful energy beam.

UPGRADES

EMERALD ENERGY BEAM

COST: 900 Gold

PREREQUISITE: None

Energy Beam attack does extra damage.

CHAINED REFRACTIONS

COST: 1,200 Gold

PREREQUISITE: None

Split Energy Beams split again if they pass through another Crystal Shard.

GOLDEN DIAMOND ENERGY BEAM

COST: 1,700 Gold

PREREQUISITE: Prismancer Path

Energy Beam attack does even MORE increased damage.

TRIPLE REFRACTED BEAM

COST: 2,200 Gold

PREREQUISITE: Prismancer Path

Energy Beam splits into three beams when refracted through a Crystal Gem.

FOCUSED ENERGY

COST: 3,000 Gold

PREREQUISITE: Prismancer Path

Energy Beam attack has increased range.

STRATEGY

Energy Beam is a powerful mid-range attack. If you direct the Energy Beam into a Crystal Shard, the beam splits into new directions. Aiming this split can be difficult, so this is only a tactic you should use when there are multiple enemies on the field.

Energy Beam has a limited duration, and there are no upgrades to increase it. This isn't much of a problem as long as you remember to pulse the attack rather than constantly hold down the button. Even without Crystals to refract into, Energy Beam is a solid ranged attack. The damage starts out low, but with the Emerald and Golden upgrades, it effectively doubles.

WOW POW POWER

PULSE POWER!

COST: 5,000 Gold

PREREQUISITE: None

While holding **Attack 1**, press **Attack 2** to send a powerful pulse down the beam.

STRATEGY

The pulse you send down does approximately triple the damage of the regular Energy Beam attack! This makes for a great power to use against bosses or other high-HP enemies.

ATTACK 2

SUMMON CRYSTAL SHARD

COST: N/A

DAMAGE: Medium

RANGE: Medium

SPEED: Very Slow

Press the **Attack 2** button to summon crystal shards to smash enemies and refract your Energy Beam.

UPGRADES

SUPER CRYSTAL SHARD

COST: 500 Gold

PREREQUISITE: None

Summoned Crystal Shards do increased damage.

TRIPLE CRYSTAL SHARD

COST: 2,200 Gold

PREREQUISITE: Crystaleer Path

Summon three Crystal Shards at once.

CRYSTALLINE ARMOR

COST: 3,000 Gold

PREREQUISITE: Crystaleer Path

Crystalline armor makes it harder for enemies to hit you.

STRATEGY

Summon Crystal Shard is an interesting power. Beyond its interaction with Energy Beam, it also is a heavily damaging attack on its own. Any enemy caught under a crystal takes a significant amount of damage, particularly after you purchase Super Crystal Shard.

The disadvantage of this power is that it's hard to predict where the crystals will drop, and sometimes it can be extremely frustrating to hit a moving target. One cool bonus you get from Crystal Shards is that enemies get distracted by them. Melee enemies will run up to and attack the shards, diverting them from attacking Prism Break.

ATTACK 3

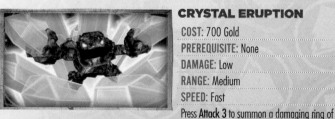

CRYSTAL ERUPTION

COST: 700 Gold

PREREQUISITE: None

DAMAGE: Low

RANGE: Medium

SPEED: Fast

Press **Attack 3** to summon a damaging ring of crystals around Prism Break.

UPGRADES

MASSIVE CRYSTAL ERUPTION

COST: 1,700 Gold

PREREQUISITE: Crystaleer Path

Crystal Eruption attack does increased damage and covers a larger area.

STRATEGY

Crystal Eruption is a great attack to employ if Prism Break is surrounded by enemies. Not only does the attack inflict strong damage, but it also knocks back enemies, giving Prism Break some room to breathe. Don't overlook the potential of Massive Crystal Eruption. The base attack damage is increased by about 30% and the range of the attack increases from short to medium.

TERRAFIN

"IT'S BEATIN' TIME!"

STATS

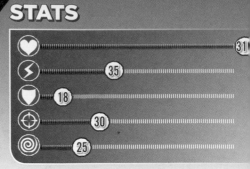

♥	31
⚡	35
🛡	18
◎	30
🌀	25

UPGRADE PATHS

SANDHOG
Further develop Terrafin's burrowing abilities.

BRAWLER
Further develop Terrafin's punching abilities.

SOUL GEM ABILITY

SURFACE FEEDER
COST: 4,000 Gold
PREREQUISITE: None
Collect power-ups while burrowed.

STRATEGY

This is a nice little addition to Terrafin's arsenal, but you can hold off buying it until other upgrades have been purchased. Surface Feeder gives Terrafin immunity from enemy attacks while he is underground.

SPECIAL QUEST

LAND LUBBER:
EAT 20 FOOD ITEMS WHILE BURROWING.

For this quest, you need to first purchase Surface Feeder. Once you have the power, simply stay underground and collect Food Items as they drop. It should only take one or two chapters to reach the target.

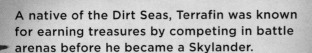

A native of the Dirt Seas, Terrafin was known for earning treasures by competing in battle arenas before he became a Skylander.

Terrafin is a powerful brawler who likes to spend some time underground. Terrafin fights best up close. You should learn how to use Earth Swim to move safely through enemy attacks and get in close enough to attack with Terrafin's fists.

PRIMARY ATTACKS

ATTACK 1

PUNCH

COST: N/A
DAMAGE: High
RANGE: Short
SPEED: Fast

Press the **Attack 1** button to punch the enemy. Press **Attack 1**, **Attack 1**, and HOLD **Attack 1** to perform a combo.

UPGRADES

BRASS KNUCKLES

COST: 500 Gold
PREREQUISITE: None

Punch attacks do increased damage.

MULTI TARGET PUNCHES

COST: 1,200 Gold
PREREQUISITE: None

Punch attack hits multiple enemies.

PUGILIST

COST: 1,700 Gold
PREREQUISITE: Brawler Path

Press **Attack 1**, **Attack 1**, HOLD **Attack 2** for Body Slam.

Press **Attack 1**, **Attack 1**, HOLD **Attack 3** for Uppercut.

SPIKED KNUCKLES

COST: 2,200 Gold
PREREQUISITE: Brawler Path

All punch attacks do even MORE damage!

STRATEGY

Don't mistake a lack of complexity for lack of effectiveness. Punch is deadly at close range, and comes out faster than attacks from other melee Skylanders. In addition, his punches have a slight knockback effect that can temporarily stun enemies, breaking up their attacks.

Terrafin's Body Slam combo has him drop right on his face, shocking any enemies in close range around him. He performs a jumping, spinning upper cut attack when you pull off the **Attack 3** combo.

ATTACK 2

EARTH SWIM

COST: N/A
DAMAGE: Medium
RANGE: Medium
SPEED: Slow

Press the **Attack 2** button to burrow. While underground, press the **Attack 1** button to perform a bellyflop.

UPGRADES

MEGA BELLYFLOP

COST: 700 Gold
PREREQUISITE: None

Bellyflop does increased damage and affects a larger area.

MASTER EARTH SWIMMER

COST: 1,700 Gold
PREREQUISITE: Sandhog Path

Increased speed while burrowing.

RAZORFIN

COST: 3,000 Gold
PREREQUISITE: Sandhog Path

While burrowed, your dorsal fin does damage to enemies.

STRATEGY

Initially, Terrafin doesn't get any extra speed from burrowing, but he is immune to enemy attacks. This allows him to sneak up on enemies and splash them with high damage. He can even use the power to completely evade level hazards. The biggest weakness of Earth Swim is the Bellyflop Attack. It does high damage, but to use it effectively you must flop close to enemies. He also can't move for a moment after the attack, leaving him open to attack.

WOW POW POWER

DIVE BURROW

COST: 5,000 Gold
PREREQUISITE: None

While in the air for a bellyflop, press **Attack 2** to immediately dive back underground.

STRATEGY

Dive Burrow effectively takes care of Terrafin's major weakness, his exposure after executing a bellyflop. If you're using the Sandhog Path, you should purchase this Wow Pow to get it before some of Terrafin's other Earth Swim Powers.

ATTACK 3

FEEDING FRENZY

COST: 900 Gold
PREREQUISITE: None
DAMAGE: Extremely Low
RANGE: Short
SPEED: Extremely Slow

Press **Attack 3** to spawn mini-sharks that burrow and latch onto enemies.

HOMING FRENZY

COST: 2,200 Gold
PREREQUISITE: Sandhog Path

Mini-sharks home in on enemies and do extra damage.

FRENZY SHIELD

COST: 3,000 Gold
PREREQUISITE: Brawler Path

You launch mini-sharks at enemies who damage you.

STRATEGY

No matter how you look at it, Feeding Frenzy is a novelty power that is ineffective in combat. Even most of the upgrades do little to help against tough enemies. Hold off on purchasing the upgrades in this tree until you have extra gold. You do, however, need to purchase the base Feeding Frenzy power to unlock the option to choose a power path.

HOT DOG

"SEE SPOT BURN!"

STATS

❤️	25
⚡	43
🛡️	6
🎯	60
🌀	25

UPGRADE PATHS

BURNING BOW-WOW
Further develop Hot Dog's Firebark and Comet Slam attacks.

PYRO POOCH
Further develop Hot Dog's Wall of Fire attacks.

SOUL GEM ABILITY

DING DONG DITCH
COST: 4,000 Gold

PREREQUISITE: Find Hot Dog's Soul Gem in the Rumbletown level

After a Comet Slam, leave a burning bag that explodes when stepped on.

STRATEGY
Ding Dong Ditch is a nice addition to the Comet Slam, allowing Hot Dog to leave special "traps" around the area for enemies to run into. Each bag does a moderate amount of damage, and is set automatically, so it's essentially just a worry-free add on to Comet Slam.

SPECIAL QUEST

ANIMAL AGGRAVATOR:
SCARE AWAY 20 BIRDS.

Throughout many levels, there are several small little birds pecking at the ground. These birds are the ones you need to scare with Hot Dog for this achievement. A good level to do this on is Chapter 13: The Oracle or Chapter 1: Time of Giants, both have plenty of birds.

Hot Dog's attacks are ranged, but he has the unusual ability to use combos with his ranged primary attack. His short-range area-of-effect attack, Comet Slam, has a few upgrades, but the real upgrade highlights on this Skylander are Firebark and Wall of Fire. Firebark is a fantastic ranged attack that can rapidly take down enemies from a good distance. Wall of Fire is a powerful ranged attack that burns any foe foolish enough to stand in Hot Dog's way.

When you start playing with Hot Dog, try out both Firebark and Wall of Fire and see which turns into your favorite. Wall of Fire is one of the best powers in the game, but ultimately the choice is yours, Portal Master.

PRIMARY ATTACKS

ATTACK 1

FIREBARK
COST: N/A
DAMAGE: Low
RANGE: Long
SPEED: Fast

Press **Attack 1** to spit fireballs. Press **Attack 1**, **Attack 1**, HOLD **Attack 1** for a special combo!

UPGRADES

PYRO PIERCERS
COST: 500 Gold
PREREQUISITE: None
Fireballs pierce multiple enemies and do increased damage.

BARK BOMBS
COST: 2,200 Gold
PREREQUISITE: Burning Bow-Wow Path
Fireballs explode on impact and do increased damage.

HOT DOG COMBOS
COST: 1,700 Gold
PREREQUISITE: Burning Bow-Wow Path
Press **Attack 1**, **Attack 1**, HOLD **Attack 2** for Burnin' Bees.

Press **Attack 1**, **Attack 1**, HOLD **Attack 3** for Comet Dash.

STRATEGY

Hot Dog's primary attack is Firebark, a long-range, low-damage attack. Firebark can be spewed at a rapid rate against enemies at all ranges, and the tiny fireballs have some minor tracking to make it a bit easier to hit enemies. The interesting thing about Firebark is that unlike other Skylanders' ranged Primary Attacks, Firebark has a combos system that allows you to mix up the attacks to be more effective in a variety of combat situations. Burnin' Bees sees Hot Dog vomit up some angry bees that fly forward and attack enemies. Comet Dash is a blazing dash that Hot Dog can use to get in close range of weak enemies.

ATTACK 2

WALL OF FIRE
COST: N/A
DAMAGE: Medium
RANGE: Short
SPEED: Slow

Press **Attack 2** to summon a wall of fire, which can be pushed towards enemies.

UPGRADES

WALL OF MORE FIRE
COST: 900 Gold
PREREQUISITE: None
Walls of Fire do increased damage.

GREAT WALLS OF FIRE
COST: 2,200 Gold
PREREQUISITE: Pyro Pooch Path
Walls of Fire are bigger and do even more increased damage.

BLAZING WILDFIRE
COST: 1,700 Gold
PREREQUISITE: Pyro Pooch Path
Walls of Fire travel faster and do even more increased damage.

MAGMUTT BATTALION
COST: 3,000 Gold
PREREQUISITE: Pyro Pooch Path, Great Walls of Fire
Walls are now made up of fiery dogs that do maximum damage and shoot fireballs.

STRATEGY

Wall of Fire allows the crazed pooch to send endless waves of burning doom at his enemies. Wall of Fire is a solid ability, even before purchasing any upgrades. The flames do a good amount of damage and sweep through enemies, knocking them back, buying Hot Dog time to send out even more waves of flame. Once you have upgraded Wall of Flame, particularly if you commit to the Pyro Pooch path, it becomes one of the best attacks in the game. An upgraded Wall of Flame does tremendous damage, has extremely wide length and can be rapidly sent towards enemies from any distance.

ATTACK 3

COMET SLAM
COST: 700 Gold
PREREQUISITE: None
DAMAGE: Medium
RANGE: Short
SPEED: Slow

Press **Attack 3** to flip into the air and slam down on the ground like a comet.

UPGRADES

SUPER COMET
COST: 1,200 Gold
PREREQUISITE: Comet Slam
Hold **Attack 3** to charge up the Comet Slam and release to do increased damage.

PYRO PINWHEEL
COST: 3,000 Gold
PREREQUISITE: Burning Bow-Wow Path
While holding **Attack 3** to charge up the Comet Slam, Hot Dog shoots fireballs from all angles.

STRATEGY

Hot Dog's Comet Slams blast enemies at short to medium range with an area-of-effect blast that does moderate damage. The slam is a straightforward attack, but it can also be a decent defensive maneuver. Repeatedly Slam to stay above your enemies, and avoid their attacks, just be careful where you land. When you unlock the Pyro Pinwheel upgrade, Hot Dog tosses fireballs out in all directions while you are charging the attack. This is effective against melee-type creatures; they hardly get a shot at Hot Dog since he is almost always hovering in the air, charging the attack.

IGNITOR

"SLASH AND BURN!"

STATS

♥		24
⚡	43	
🛡	12	
◎	40	
◉	25	

UPGRADE PATHS

SOUL OF THE FLAME
Further develop Ignitor's Flame Form abilities.

BLADEMASTER
Further develop Ignitor's skills with the Flame Blade, as well as the Mega Slam attack.

SOUL GEM ABILITY

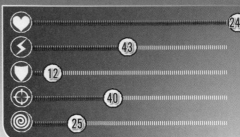

FIRE FORGED ARMOR
COST: 4,000 Gold
PREREQUISITE: None
Better armor makes it harder for enemies to hit you.

STRATEGY
One of Ignitor's weaknesses is his low armor score. If you purchase this power, his base armor stat goes from 12 to 52. This dramatically improves Ignitor's survivability in melee combat.

SPECIAL QUEST

TINDER TREKKER:
TRAVEL 26,000 FEET IN FLAME FORM.

26,000 feet isn't quite as long as it sounds. If you use the power often, this number will accumulate quickly. Just remember to use Flame Form as much as possible.

Ignitor's basic attack is a flaming blade melee swing. He also has a slam variant, which can hit more enemies, but takes more time to charge. Ignitor's abilities include the Flame Form tree of powers. Initially a simple mortar attack, Flame Form Mortar quickly turns into a powerful, but difficult-to-use power once you purchase some upgrades.

Ultimately Ignitor's high Critical Hit and Speed stats (not to mention a buffable Armor Stat), make him a strong melee Skylander. Most Portal Masters should stick to the Blademaster Path and keep him on deck for melee combat situations.

PRIMARY ATTACKS

ATTACK 1

FLAME BLADE

COST: N/A
DAMAGE: Medium
RANGE: Average
SPEED: Slow

Press the **Attack 1** button to swing Ignitor's sword.

Press **Attack 1**, **Attack 1**, Hold **Attack 1** to perform a combo.

UPGRADES

SCORCHING BLADE

COST: 500 Gold
PREREQUISITE: None

Sword attack does increased damage.

INFERNO BLADE

COST: 3,000 Gold
PREREQUISITE: Blademaster Path

Sword gets larger and does even MORE increased damage.

ORDER OF THE BURNING BLADE

COST: 1,700 Gold
PREREQUISITE: Blademaster Path

Press **Attack 1**, **Attack 1**, HOLD **Attack 2** for Fiery Burst.

Press **Attack 1**, **Attack 1**, HOLD **Attack 3** for Fire Slam.

STRATEGY

Ignitor's sword attack is slow, but has some good range. If you decide to pursue the Blademaster Path and improve the sword, you get two extra combos. Fiery Burst is a quick, short-range area-of-effect attack. Fire Slam is similar to the regular Mega Slam attack, but doesn't require any time to charge. When you purchase the two damage upgrades, Flame Blade's damage increases dramatically.

ATTACK 3

MEGA SLAM

COST: 900 Gold
PREREQUISITE: None
DAMAGE: High
RANGE: Medium/Long
SPEED: Slow

Press **Attack 3** to perform a massive, Mega Slam. Hold **Attack 3** to delay the slam.

STRATEGY

When you use Mega Slam, Ignitor charges an overhead swing. Its damage is focused and variable, so it only hits enemies that are very close to the sword, and the exact amount of damage can change hit to hit. When you charge Mega Slam with the Double Mega Slam upgrade, Ignitor's sword turns from blue to red. When you hit a foe with the red sword it does double the damage.

UPGRADES

DOUBLE MEGA SLAM

COST: 2,200 Gold
PREREQUISITE: Blademaster Path

Hold the Mega Slam attack long enough to do increased damage.

ATTACK 2

FLAME FORM MORTAR

COST: N/A
DAMAGE: High
RANGE: Medium/Long
SPEED: Average

Press the **Attack 2** button to launch your flame spirt in an arc at foes.

UPGRADES

FLAME FORM

COST: 700 Gold
PREREQUISITE: None

Control your Flame Form after launching it.

FIRE AND BRIMSTONE

COST: 1,200 Gold
PREREQUISITE: None

Flame Form Mortar does increased damage to a larger area.

DANCES WITH FIRE

COST: 1,700 Gold
PREREQUISITE: Soul of the Flame Path

Flame Form moves faster and does increased damage.

INCINERATE

COST: 2,200 Gold
PREREQUISITE: Soul of the Flame Path

While in Flame Form, press **Attack 1** to trigger a massive explosion.

FIRE FORM SALVO

COST: 3,000 Gold
PREREQUISITE: Soul of the Flame Path

Fire two additional Flame Form Mortars that do extra damage.

STRATEGY

Initially, Flame Form Mortar is a straightforward, high-damage lob attack. Once you unlock the Flame Form upgrade, things change quite a bit. After lobbing the mortar, you can run around in the flame form, automatically setting nearby enemies on fire. If you decide to pursue the Soul of the Flame Path, Flame Form gets more complicated. When you get Fire Form Salvo, Ignitor shoots out three mortars, and Flame Form spawns randomly at one of the mortar positions. Incinerate gives you the ability to hit **Attack 1** to instantly end the Flame Form attack and damage nearby enemies. Leaving Ignitor's body behind safely takes planning and practice.

WOW POW POWER

BLUE FLAME!

COST: 5,000 Gold
PREREQUISITE: None

After executing Flame Form or Mega Slam attacks, Ignitor leaves a trail of blue fire.

STRATEGY

Blue Flame! Leaves behind areas of blue flame that burn for about five seconds. Any enemy that walks into the flame takes some damage. This isn't a game-changer, but it's a nice add on to both Mega Slam and Flame Form, so it's useful no matter which path you pursue with Ignitor.

SUNBURN

"ROAST AND TOAST!"

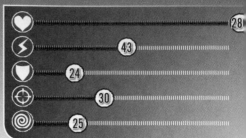

♥	28
⚡	43
🛡	24
◎	30
🌀	25

UPGRADE PATHS

BLAZE DRAGON
Further develop Sunburn's Flamethrower attacks.

FLAME LORD
Further develop Sunburn's Teleportation skills.

SOUL GEM ABILITY

FLIGHT OF THE PHOENIX
COST: 4,000 Gold
PREREQUISITE: Phoenix Dash
Phoenix Dash is longer, does more damage and ends with a blast.

STRATEGY

This is a fantastic upgrade for Phoenix Dash. Not only does it double the damage the dash attack normally does, but the explosion at the end tacks on extra damage on top of the dash. So if you use the dash against a tough enemy, you can hit them twice with each dash.

SPECIAL QUEST

IMMOLATION ITINERANT:
TRAVEL 1 MILE USING IMMOLATION TELEPORT.

Use Immolation Teleport regularly to tally up the distance towards one full mile. The quickest way to complete this quest is to unlock the Guided Teleportation upgrade.

Born of flames, Sunburn is half fierce phoenix, and half savage dragon. He defends the Skylands with Flamethrower Breath and magical teleportation attacks. Both of these powers become more effective after you purchase a significant number of upgrades for them.

Be patient while developing him. It's hard to see how good each power will be until you purchase the upgrades, but strongly consider the Blaze Dragon path. The Flamethrower attack is easier to use and easier to control. Once you get the ability to supercharge it, it cuts through heavy enemies in no time.

PRIMARY ATTACKS

ATTACK 1

FLAMETHROWER BREATH

COST: N/A
DAMAGE: Very Low
RANGE: Medium
SPEED: Slow

Press and hold the **Attack 1** button for a stream of flame breath.

UPGRADES

BLAZETHROWER

COST: 700 Gold
PREREQUISITE: None

Flamethrower Breath does increased damage.

INFINITE FLAME

COST: 1,700 Gold
PREREQUISITE: Blaze Dragon Path

Endlessly use the Flamethrower Breath attack.

INTENSE HEAT

COST: 2,200 Gold
PREREQUISITE: Blaze Dragon Path

Hold the Flamethrower Breath attack longer for extra damage.

PHOENIX GRAND BLAZE

COST: 3,000 Gold
PREREQUISITE: Blaze Dragon Path, Intense Heat

Hold Flamethrower Breath long enough to be surrounded by flame and do extra damage.

STRATEGY

Flamethrower Breath starts out as a decent, medium-range attack. Hold down the attack to fire a continuous stream on nearby enemies. To realize its full potential, you need to upgrade it and use the Blaze Dragon Path. When you have fully upgraded Flamethrower Breath, Sunburn goes through three stages. Each time he increases his stage he gains 100% extra damage per second from Flamethrower Breath. Another nice advantage to Flamethrower Breath is that Sunburn can still move around while using it.

ATTACK 3

PHOENIX DASH

COST: 900 Gold
PREREQUISITE: None
DAMAGE: Medium-Low
RANGE: Medium
SPEED: Average

Press **Attack 3** to perform a Phoenix Dash.

STRATEGY

While there are no upgrades for Phoenix Dash here, you do get an upgrade via the Soul Gem ability. Phoenix Dash is a good attack that makes Sunburn hard to hit. It also does good damage compared to his other attacks.

ATTACK 2

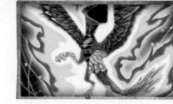

IMMOLATION TELEPORT

COST: N/A
DAMAGE: Low
RANGE: Medium
SPEED: Very Slow

Press the **Attack 2** button to teleport to another location leaving a damaging flame behind.

UPGRADES

GUIDED TELEPORTATION

COST: 500 Gold
PREREQUISITE: None

You can now control the direction of Sunbeam's teleport. Hold **Attack 2** to delay the teleport.

IMMOLATION INFLAMMATION

COST: 1,200 Gold
PREREQUISITE: None

Flames left behind after teleporting do increased damage.

IMMOLATION DESTRUCTION

COST: 1,700 Gold
PREREQUISITE: Flame Lord Path

Flames left behind after teleporting are larger and do extra damage.

FLAME STREAKS

COST: 2,200 Gold
PREREQUISITE: Flame Lord Path

Teleporting creates streaks of flames that damage enemies.

BURNING TRAIL

COST: 3,000 Gold
PREREQUISITE: Flame Lord Path, Flame Streaks

Streaks of flames do increased damage.

STRATEGY

Initially Immolation Teleport is a difficult power to use effectively. It's difficult to aim against larger enemies, and even if you hit, it does low damage. The key to this attack is the vast number of upgrades available for it. The first important upgrade, Guided Teleportation, automatically shoots 4 lava bursts out in different directions. Select which one you want Sunburn to teleport to and then release **Attack 2**. Each subsequent upgrade increases the amount of secondary damage the attack does.

Eventually, the way you should be using this power is to set up a surprise attack against a nearby enemy by dashing right into them. However, that still leaves that upgrade path inferior to Blaze Dragon. Even with all the upgrades, Immolation Teleport remains hard to use effectively.

ERUPTOR

"BORN TO BURN!"

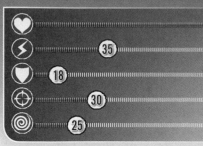

STATS

♥	29
⚡	35
🛡	18
◎	30
◉	25

UPGRADE PATHS

MAGMANTOR
Further develop Eruptor's Lava Blobs and Magma Balls.

VOLCANOR
Further develop Eruptor's Eruption attacks.

SOUL GEM ABILITY

MEGA MAGMA BALLS

COST: 4,000 Gold
PREREQUISITE: Magma Ball
Shoot up to three Magma Balls at a time that do extra damage.

STRATEGY

Mega Magma Balls dramatically improves Eruptor's regular Magma Balls attack. The balls are about twice the size and do about 25% more damage. They're still slow and hard to aim, but since the balls are bigger it's easier to hit enemies.

SPECIAL QUEST

PIZZA BURP: EAT 10 PIZZAS.

Pizzas randomly drop when you defeat monsters throughout the game. If you want to have a greater chance of encountering a pizza, equip Lucky Wheel of Health in the Luck-O-Tron.

Born in a volcano, Eruptor is made of magma and uses his natural abilities to combat the Skylanders' foes. Strategically, Eruptor is an interesting and challenging Skylander to master. His Lava Lob is a fast, high-damage ability with short-range. He also has an excellent melee-range area-of-effect ability, but his low health and armor require him to avoid too much melee combat.

Whether you decide to take him down the Magmantor Path or the Volcanor Path, expect to employ stick-and-move tactics with Eruptor. Keep moving, avoiding enemy attacks and return fire when it's safe to attack.

PRIMARY ATTACKS

ATTACK 1

LAVA LOB

COST: N/A

DAMAGE: Low

RANGE: Short/Medium

SPEED: Fast

Press the **Attack 1** button to lob blobs of lava at your enemies.

UPGRADES

BIG BLOB LAVA THROW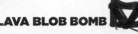

COST: 500 Gold

PREREQUISITE: None

Lava Blob attack gets bigger and does increased damage.

FIERY REMAINS

COST: 700 Gold

PREREQUISITE: None

Lava Blobs leave behind pools of flame when they hit the ground.

HEAVY DUTY PLASMA

COST: 1,700 Gold

PREREQUISITE: Magmantor Path

Lava Blobs bounce and travel further.

LAVA BLOB BOMB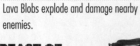

COST: 2,200 Gold

PREREQUISITE: Magmantor Path

Lava Blobs explode and damage nearby enemies.

BEAST OF CONFLAGRATION

COST: 3,000 Gold

PREREQUISITE: Magmantor Path, Heavy Duty Plasma

Lava Blobs do increased damage in the form of a fiery beast.

STRATEGY

Eruptor's Lava Lob attack is fast, but has a short range for a ranged attack. One advantage with the attack is that it's easier to hit enemies standing on ledges above Eruptor. If you decide to pursue the Magmantor Path, the Lava Lob gets much better. Of particular note is Heavy Duty Plasma, which increases the range of the attack, making it more viable as a long-range tactic. Once you unlock Beast of Conflagration, the damage of the power is increased by about 60%.

ATTACK 2

ERUPTION

COST: N/A

DAMAGE: Medium

RANGE: Short

SPEED: Very Slow

Press the **Attack 2** button to erupt into a pool of lava damaging enemies all around you.

UPGRADES

ERUPTION— FLYING TEPHRA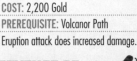

COST: 900 Gold

PREREQUISITE: None

Lava balls shoot out while performing the Eruption attack.

QUICK ERUPTION

COST: 1,700 Gold

PREREQUISITE: Volcanor Path

It takes much less time to perform an Eruption attack.

PYROXYSMAL SUPER ERUPTION

COST: 2,200 Gold

PREREQUISITE: Volcanor Path

Eruption attack does increased damage.

REVENGE OF PROMETHEUS

COST: 3,000 Gold

PREREQUISITE: Volcanor Path, Pyroxysmal Super Eruption

Eruption causes small volcanoes to form, doing extra damage.

STRATEGY

Eruption is a tricky power to master. It requires you to charge the attack for a second or two, which leaves Eruptor vulnerable. Once the magma has erupted, it can hit enemies within range multiple times. The most important upgrade for Eruption is Quick Eruption. Quick Eruption makes the power much more useful since Eruptor barely needs to slow down to release a powerful eruption full of seeping magma, volcanos, and magma balls.

ATTACK 3

MAGMA BALL

COST: 1,200 Gold

PREREQUISITE: None

DAMAGE: High

RANGE: Short

SPEED: Very Slow

Press **Attack 3** to spit out Magma Balls.

STRATEGY

Magma Balls move slowly and are fairly hard to aim at enemies. Hold off on purchasing this power until after you've upgraded Eruptor and Lava Lob a few times.

WOW POW POWER

LAVA BARF!

COST: 5,000 Gold

PREREQUISITE: Magma Ball

Hold **Attack 3** to charge up a powerful stream of projectile lava barf.

STRATEGY

After holding **Attack 3** for a few seconds, Eruptor belches out lava that you can aim by turning him in place. The belch lasts about three seconds and does high damage. Ultimately, this is Eruptor's most damaging attack and is great for boss fights.

FLAMESLINGER

"LET THE FLAMES BEGIN!"

STATS

♥		25
⚡	50	
🛡	24	
⊕	40	
◎	25	

UPGRADE PATHS

MARKSMAN
Further develop Flameslinger's Fire Arrow attacks.

PYROMANCER
Flameslinger learns new fire-based abilities.

SOUL GEM ABILITY

SUPER VOLLEY SHOT
COST: 4,000 Gold
PREREQUISITE: Volley Shot
Flaming Arrow Rain shoots more arrows that cover more area.

STRATEGY
This upgrade slightly improves Volley Shot, but still doesn't help make it a more viable power. Hold off on purchasing this until you have plenty of extra gold.

SPECIAL QUEST

CIRCULAR COMBUSTION:
DEFEAT 10 ENEMIES WITH ONE COLUMN OF FIRE FLAME DASH.

There are two upgrades you can get to help you on this quest. The first is Column of Fire. The second is in the Pyromancer Path and is called Supernova. Once you have one or two of these upgrades, use the column attack on any group of enemies by making a circle with the flaming path. Defeating 10 with one column is a challenge, but keep at it and you'll get it eventually!

Flameslinger is a ranged attack and dash specialist. His Fire Arrows are versatile attacks that allow him to pelt enemies from a long distance. If enemies get too close, use his Flame Dash to evade damage and reposition him on the battlefield.

Of the two upgrade paths, Marksman edges out Pyromancer. Pyromancer extends Flameslinger's bag of tricks, but in practice, they aren't as effective as the added damage output provided by the Marksman Path.

PRIMARY ATTACKS

ATTACK 1

FIRE ARROW

COST: N/A
DAMAGE: Low
RANGE: Long
SPEED: Average

Press the **Attack 1** button to shoot flaming arrows at your enemies.

UPGRADES

SEARING ARROWS

COST: 500 Gold
PREREQUISITE: None

Fire Arrows do increased damage.

HYPER SHOT

COST: 1,200 Gold
PREREQUISITE: None

Shoot Fire Arrows much faster.

HELLFIRE ARROWS

COST: 1,700 Gold
PREREQUISITE: Marksman Path

Fire Arrows and Flaming Arrow Rain do even MORE increased damage.

EXPLOSIVE ARROWS

COST: 2,200 Gold
PREREQUISITE: Marksman Path

Fire Arrows explode, doing damage to anything nearby.

TRIPLE SHOT ARROWS

COST: 3,000 Gold
PREREQUISITE: Marksman Path

Shoot three Fire Arrows at a time.

NAPALM TIPPED ARROWS

COST: 1,700 Gold
PREREQUISITE: Pyromancer Path

Fire Arrows leave behind a burning patch damaging enemies that touch it.

INFERNO BLAST

COST: 2,200 Gold
PREREQUISITE: Pyromancer Path

Hold **Attack 1** to charge a flaming inferno blast attack — release to fire.

STRATEGY

Whether you pick Pyromancer or Marksman, Fire Arrow is Flameslinger's bread and butter ability. Marksman provides more standard upgrades, increasing the damage potential of Fire Arrows and the number of arrows Flameslinger shoots at once. The Pyromancer path changes the nature of the arrows, allowing for a charged attack. It also works well with Flame Dash. Napalm Tipped Arrows causes the arrows to leave behind a trail similar to Flame Dash, and Inferno Blast allows you to double the damage from Explosive Arrows.

One of Fire Arrows' most important features is knockback, which can knock enemies off ledges or interrupt their attacks. Keep in mind that Fire Arrows is not an ideal attack against high-HP enemies. Even fully upgraded, their damage is relatively low, and speed of attack is only average.

WOW POW POWER

SPEED DEMON!

COST: 5,000 Gold
PREREQUISITE: None

While dashing, press **Attack 1** to run even faster and leave a new flame trail.

ATTACK 2

FLAME DASH

COST: N/A
DAMAGE: Very Low
RANGE: Short
SPEED: Fast

Hold **Attack 2** to dash forward, leaving a flaming path of destruction behind.

UPGRADES

COLUMN OF FIRE

COST: 700 Gold
PREREQUISITE: None

Draw a circle with the Flame Dash to create a fire column; Flame Dash does extra damage.

SUPERNOVA

COST: 3,000 Gold
PREREQUISITE: Pyromancer Path

Drawing a circle with the Flame Dash causes fire to spread out, doing more damage.

STRATEGY

Flame Dash is a fun power that allows Flameslinger to run circles around his enemies. Wall off enemies to break up the battlefield and use the power to evade dangerous situations quickly.

This evasive ability is key to Flameslinger's overall combat approach. Whenever a melee enemy gets in range, Flameslinger's low health necessitates that he create space between himself and the enemy as quickly as possible. The ability to inflict damage on the way out is a nice perk. Column of Fire and Supernova both inflict great damage; however, the enemies in Skylands are mobile, so it's difficult to use them consistently. The circle you must draw is fairly tight, and keeping enemies within range without putting Flameslinger at risk is difficult.

ATTACK 3

VOLLEY SHOT

COST: 900 Gold
PREREQUISITE: None
DAMAGE: Medium
RANGE: Medium
SPEED: Very Slow

Press **Attack 3** to fire Flaming Arrow Rain down on your enemies.

STRATEGY

The base Volley Shot is difficult to aim and use effectively. The attack is only useful for picking off enemies at a higher level than Flameslinger. Prioritize purchasing other skills before this one.

STRATEGY

If you like Flameslinger's Flame Dash, then you should really enjoy Speed Demon! This upgrade extends the dash and increases the level of flames left behind. This power is great for general dashing, but not so great for forming Columns of Fire or Supernovas. It's hard to turn Flameslinger while he is dashing with this power. While making circles isn't impossible, it becomes rather difficult.

CHILL

"STAY COOL!"

STATS

❤️	260
⚡	43
🛡️	24
🎯	10
🌀	25

UPGRADE PATHS

ICE LANCER
Further develop Chill's
Ice Javelin attacks.

FROZEN FURY
Further develop Chill's Ice Wall and
Glacial Bash abilities.

SOUL GEM ABILITY

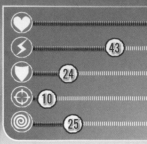

CALL THE NARWHAL!

COST: 4,000 Gold
PREREQUISITE: Find Chill's Soul Gem in
the Lost City of Arkus
DAMAGE: Extremely High
RANGE: Long
SPEED: Extremely Slow

Hold **Attack 1** to charge and release to
summon a narwhal friend!

Chill is a Skylander whose powers work
together wonderfully. Even after you pick the
Ice Lancer or Frozen Fury paths, you should
continue to use all Chill's powers, depending
on the situation.

Chill's Javelin makes for a fantastic ranged
attack that can cut through enemies at
long distance. Ice Wall can act as either a
defensive ability or, with Glacial Bash, be
turned on your enemies by smashing them
with chaotic, sliding ice blocks.

STRATEGY

This long-range, high-damage attack has two drawbacks: charge
time and accuracy. The charge time is about five seconds. After
that, Chill can move around a bit, but very slowly. You can release
before the power is fully charged, but the whale does not do nearly
as much damage.

Whenever you take the time to charge this attack, also take the
time to aim it! The whale flies forward in the direction Chill is
currently facing, so she must be facing the right direction before
you release **Attack 1**.

SPECIAL QUEST

ICE SORE: DEFEAT SIX ENEMIES WITH ONE
ICE NARWHAL ATTACK.

The Narwhal can take out any enemy with less than 100 health,
so damage isn't the issue. Try to find six enemies that are
grouped together at a medium distance to use the Narwhal
attack on. The arenas are a good place to earn this quickly.

PRIMARY ATTACKS

ATTACK 1

ICE JAVELIN

COST: N/A

DAMAGE: Medium

RANGE: Long

SPEED: Fast

Press **Attack 1** to throw a spinning ice javelin.

UPGRADES

IMPERIAL ARMOR

COST: 900 Gold

PREREQUISITE: None

New armor provides increased protection.

BRRRR BLADE

COST: 1,700 Gold

PREREQUISITE: Ice Lancer Path

New ice javelin does increased damage.

SHATTERSPEAR

COST: 2,200 Gold

PREREQUISITE: Ice Lancer Path

Javelins now split into separate ice spears when passing through an Ice Wall.

TRIPLE JAVELINS

COST: 3,000 Gold

PREREQUISITE: Ice Lancer Path

Throw three ice javelins at once.

STRATEGY

Ice Javelin is a straightforward ranged attack. The Ice Lancer Path provides similarly straightforward upgrades for the attack, increasing damage and allowing for the javelins to split and hit more enemies.

Once you get the Shatterspear Upgrade, a great tactic is to lay out an Ice Wall, then stand behind it shooting Javelins into the wall. This creates a huge spread of javelin splinters, dishing out serious damage on any enemies charging Chill.

ATTACK 2

ICE WALL

COST: N/A

DAMAGE: Low

RANGE: Medium-Long

SPEED: Average

Press **Attack 2** to summon a wall of ice blocks. Can use for protection or to knock back enemies.

UPGRADES

THE GREAT WALL

COST: 500 Gold

PREREQUISITE: None

Hold **Attack 2** to extend the length of an ice wall.

ICE BREAKER

COST: 1,700 Gold

PREREQUISITE: Frozen Fury Path

Ice Wall blocks explode when struck by an ice javelin or by an enemy.

ON THE ROCKS

COST: 3,000 Gold

PREREQUISITE: Frozen Fury Path

Exploding ice blocks freeze enemies into ice cubes of their own.

STRATEGY

Ice Wall is a unique ability with great versatility in combat. The Ice Walls absorb attacks and are particularly effective at interrupting enemies who normally stop attacking once they hit a Skylander. Two enemies with such attacks are Mohawk Cyclops and Jawbreaker. If one of these enemies hits an Ice Wall, they think they hit a Skylander, stopping their attack and opening them up for Chill to move in and hit them with her javelins.

If you take Ice Walls to the next level with the Frozen Fury Path, the power becomes a game-changer. As you lay down Ice Walls and enemies run into them, they explode, causing more Ice Blocks to form. Knock the ice blocks around, and you have frozen enemies colliding into unsuspecting enemies focused on trying to attack Chill. This is a fantastically fun power that becomes amazing in arena type combat situations.

ATTACK 3

GLACIAL BASH

COST: 700 Gold

PREREQUISITE: None

DAMAGE: Very Low

RANGE: Very Short

SPEED: Average

Press **Attack 3** to bash enemies and ice wall blocks with your shield.

UPGRADES

COLD FRONT

COST: 1,200 Gold

PREREQUISITE: Glacial Bash

Hold **Attack 3** to keep the shield raised and block attacks from the front.

BETTER BASH

COST: 2,200 Gold

PREREQUISITE: Frozen Fury Path

Glacial Bash hits multiple enemies and Ice Wall blocks in a larger area.

STRATEGY

This is a simple knockback attack that should be used to interrupt enemy attacks or slide ice blocks around the battlefield. As a direct standalone attack, it is not overly effective. When you purchase Cold Front, you get an excellent shield defense. The shield can completely absorb the damage from most attacks. While it is sometimes difficult to face an enemy, it can really help against bosses. Better Bash is a great upgrade for knocking ice blocks around; you can turn the battlefield into a pool table!

ZAP

"RIIIDE THE LIGHTNING!"

STATS

♥	26
⚡	50
🛡	24
◎	30
◉	25

UPGRADE PATHS

TESLA DRAGON
Further develop Zap's Lightning Breath and Wave attacks.

SLIME SERPENT
Further develop Zap's Sea Slime skills.

SOUL GEM ABILITY

LOVE FOR THE SEA
COST: 4,000 Gold
PREREQUISITE: None
Zap regenerates health when swimming in water.

Zap is a fun and fast Skylander who combines water and electricity to shock foes into submission. Zap has a great slide tactic that lets him move quickly through his enemies without putting himself at risk.

While Zap's damage output might seem fairly low at first, once you upgrade either the Sea Slime or Lightning Breath attacks, he quickly becomes a formidable member of your Skylanders team.

STRATEGY

Since there are so few areas with Water in *Skylanders Giants* (mostly behind Elemental Gates), this is an optional purchase. If you want to complete Zap's upgrades, go for it. Otherwise, save the money for unlockables.

SPECIAL QUEST

IN THE SLIMELIGHT: DEFEAT 50 ENEMIES BY ELECTRIFYING THEM IN SEA SLIME.

If you are playing Zap, you should be using Sea Slime to electrify enemies regularly. It only takes 50 to complete this quest, which should be no problem.

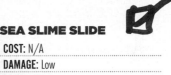

PRIMARY ATTACKS

ATTACK 1

LIGHTNING BREATH

COST: N/A
DAMAGE: Very Low
RANGE: Long
SPEED: Fast

Press the **Attack 1** button to spit out pure electricity.

UPGRADES

MEGAVOLT
COST: 900 Gold
PREREQUISITE: None
Lightning Breath attack does increased damage.

LIGHTNING STRIKES TWICE
COST: 1,700 Gold
PREREQUISITE: Tesla Dragon Path
Lightning Breath bounces off of enemies, objects and walls.

TESLA STORM
COST: 3,000 Gold
PREREQUISITE: Tesla Dragon Path
Lightning Breath attack does even MORE increased damage.

STRATEGY

Lightning Breath is a lightning burst attack. Without upgrades, it does very low damage. However, keep investing in upgrades for it, and soon it becomes Zap's mainstay attack. It is particularly important to use in combination with Sea Slime Slide.

ATTACK 3

WAVE RIDER

COST: 1,200 Gold
PREREQUISITE: None
DAMAGE: Medium
RANGE: Short
SPEED: Average

Press **Attack 3** to summon a great wave to wash away enemies. Hold **Attack 3** to ride the wave.

UPGRADES

ELECTRIC WAVE
COST: 2,200 Gold
PREREQUISITE: Tesla Dragon Path
Wave attack does increased damage.

STRATEGY

Wave Rider is a tricky power to master. It has a slow build up, but once it releases, you can ride it to safely run through and damage enemies. Wave Rider's damage is moderate, but it can be released to hit enemies at a long range. If you stay on the wave once it has started, you can steer its direction.

ATTACK 2

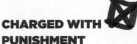

SEA SLIME SLIDE

COST: N/A
DAMAGE: Low
RANGE: Short
SPEED: Fast

Hold **Attack 2** to slide on a trail of sea slime that enemies will become stuck in.

UPGRADES

ELECTRO-SLIME
COST: 500 Gold
PREREQUISITE: None
Shoot Sea Slimes to electrify them and shock enemies.

STAY AWHILE
COST: 700 Gold
PREREQUISITE: None
Sea Slimes stay electrified for much longer.

STRENGTH IN NUMBERS
COST: 1,700 Gold
PREREQUISITE: Slime Serpent Path
Create more Sea Slimes.

CHARGED WITH PUNISHMENT
COST: 2,200 Gold
PREREQUISITE: Slime Serpent Path
Automatically electrify all Sea Slimes.

MORE ELECTRO'D SLIME
COST: 3,000 Gold
PREREQUISITE: Slime Serpent Path
Enemies take MORE damage when stuck in electrified Sea Slimes.

STRATEGY

When you press **Attack 2,** Zap slides forward, leaving a trail of slime behind him. This slime does not damage enemies, but it does cause enemies to get stuck. You can electrify this Sea Slime with Zap's Lightning Breath to hurt enemies trapped by the slime.

Charged with Punishment automatically electrifies the Sea Slime, allowing Zap to weave his way through the enemies creating electrical chaos in their ranks. You can also use Zap to form protective electric walls that keep enemies away while you focus on pounding an enemy with Lightning Breath. Sea Slime is quick, and it can make Zap almost impossible to hit as long as you keep moving.

WOW POW POWER

FOR RILEY!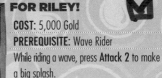

COST: 5,000 Gold
PREREQUISITE: Wave Rider
While riding a wave, press **Attack 2** to make a big splash.

STRATEGY

This is a great addition to the Wave Rider power. It makes Wave Rider much more effective. When you hit the **Attack 2** button, the wave explodes, inflicting solid damage to any enemies nearby.

WHAM-SHELL

"BRACE FOR THE MACE."

STATS

♥	300
⚡	50
🛡	18
◎	30
◎	25

UPGRADE PATHS

CAPTAIN CRUSTACEAN
Further develop Wham-Shell's skills with the mace and Poseidon Strike attack.

COMMANDER CRAB
Further develop Wham-Shell's Starfish attack.

SOUL GEM ABILITY

CARAPACE PLATING
COST: 4,000 Gold

PREREQUISITE: None

New armor makes Wham-Shell harder to hit.

STRATEGY
Purchasing Carapace Plating increases Wham-Shell's armor by 40. This is a big help since he is primarily a melee combatant. This is an incredibly important upgrade for Wham-Shell because his armor starts out relatively low.

SPECIAL QUEST

IRATE INVERTEBRATE: DEFEAT 6 ENEMIES WITH ONE POSEIDON STRIKE.

To get the most out of Poseidon Strike, you need to invest in the Captain Crustacean path. Once you have unlocked Mace of the Deep, go for this quest by finding a group of Chompies and blasting them when they get close enough.

Wham-Shell is one of the best melee Skylanders in the game. Malacostracan Mace is brutal and becomes absolutely unstoppable with upgrades. Poseidon Strike is initially a high-damage, close-range area-of-effect attack. However, if you commit to the Captain Crustacean Path, you get an upgrade for Poseidon Strike that makes it an absolute killer attack.

All of Wham-Shell's attacks include significant knockback, which is an important bonus for arena fights.

PRIMARY ATTACKS

ATTACK 1

MALACOSTRACAN MACE

COST: N/A
DAMAGE: Medium
RANGE: Medium
SPEED: Average

Press the **Attack 1** button to swing Wham-Shell's big mace at enemies.

UPGRADES

KING'S MACE

COST: 700 Gold
PREREQUISITE: None

Mace attack does increased damage.

MEGA TRIDENT

COST: 2,200 Gold
PREREQUISITE: Captain Crustacean Path

Mace attack does MORE increased damage.

CRUSTACEAN COMBOS

COST: 1,700 Gold
PREREQUISITE: Captain Crustacean Path

Press **Attack 1**, **Attack 1**, HOLD **Attack 2** for Mace Master.

Press **Attack 1**, **Attack 1**, HOLD **Attack 3** for Power Slam.

STRATEGY

Most players should stick to using Wham-Shell's mace as their primary attack. If you decide to pursue the Captain Crustacean Path, the mace does more damage and you get a few really cool combos. When you execute Mace Master successfully, Wham-Shell whirls his mace in a circle for a few seconds, grinding up any nearby enemies. Power Slam is a combo that works in a regular Poseidon Strike area-of-effect attack at the end.

ATTACK 3

STRATEGY

Poseidon Strike is a powerful, but short-range area-of-effect attack. It also takes a second to execute, during which time Wham-Shell is open for attack. This is a good power to use against tough enemies like Jawbreakers and Drow Goliaths when they give you an opening. If you upgrade Poseidon Strike, it dramatically improves in both range and damage. The Mace of the Deep upgrade is good enough alone to warrant choosing the Captain Crustacean Path over Commander Crab.

POSEIDON STRIKE

COST: 1,200 Gold
PREREQUISITE: None
DAMAGE: Very High
RANGE: Very Short
SPEED: Slow

Press **Attack 3** to create an electrified field that damages enemies.

UPGRADES

MACE OF THE DEEP

COST: 3,000 Gold
PREREQUISITE: Captain Crustacean Path

Hold **Attack 3** to create a more powerful Poseidon Strike.

ATTACK 2

STARFISH BULLETS

COST: N/A
DAMAGE: Very Low
RANGE: Long
SPEED: Very Slow

Press **Attack 2** to fire starfish bullets from Wham-Shell's mace.

UPGRADES

STARFISHICUS GIGANTICUS

COST: 500 Gold
PREREQUISITE: None

Hold **Attack 2** to charge up your Starfish attack.

STARFISHICUS SUPERIORALIS

COST: 900 Gold
PREREQUISITE: None

Starfish attack does increased damage.

TRIPLICATE STARFISH

COST: 1,700 Gold
PREREQUISITE: Commander Crab Path

Shoot three Starfish at once.

SEMI-ETERNAL PURSUIT

COST: 2,200 Gold
PREREQUISITE: Commander Crab Path

Starfish attack homes in on enemies.

NIGHTMARE HUGGERS

COST: 3,000 Gold
PREREQUISITE: Commander Crab Path

Starfish latch onto enemies doing continuous damage.

STRATEGY

Starfish Bullets would be a decent attack for most other characters, but for Wham-Shell, it's just completely outmatched by the greatness of the mace attacks and Poseidon Strike. If you really want to use Wham-Shell as a ranged character, then you can invest in the Commander Crab Path, which gives the Starfish some extra powers. They become easier to aim and the number of Starfish fired increases to three. Once you have all the upgrades, charged Starfish Bullets are effective against tough enemies. Move in close and unleash a point-blank shot to hit them with all three starfish and inflict triple the damage.

GILL GRUNT

"FEAR THE FISH."

STATS

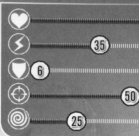

♥		27
⚡	35	
🛡	6	
⊕	50	
◎	25	

UPGRADE PATHS

HARPOONER
Further develop Gill Grunt's Harpoon attack.

WATER WEAVER
Further develop Gill Grunt's Power Hose and Jetpack skills.

SOUL GEM ABILITY

ANCHOR CANNON ☑

COST: 4,000 Gold

PREREQUISITE: None

Hold **Attack 1** to charge Anchor Cannon.

Gill Grunt has two awesome ranged attacks at his disposal. Additionally, he has excellent maneuverability with his Water Jetpack. The Jetpack allows Gill Grunt to quickly escape any hairy situations he might find himself in.

While Harpoon Gun is a decent skill, the really impressive power in Gill Grunt's arsenal is his Power Hose attack. Power Hose does respectable damage while blasting back approaching enemies. This effect and the addition of unlimited Jetpack use make the Water Weaver Path the better pick for this Skylander.

STRATEGY

Anchor Cannon is actually a separate attack from the regular Anchor attack. Hold down the **Attack 1** button and a giant anchor forms in front of Gill. Release to unleash the devastating anchor on any foes standing ahead. Anchor Cannon deals high damage, but requires a good amount of time to charge along with good aim (it doesn't track enemies).

SPECIAL QUEST

ANCHORS AWAY!: DEFEAT SIX ENEMIES WITH ONE ANCHOR ATTACK.

If you have the Series 2 version of Gill Grunt, wait until you purchase Anchor's Away! to make this quest much easier. Otherwise, just line up a group of Chompies with your Anchor Cannon and let loose to complete the quest.

PRIMARY ATTACKS

ATTACK 1

HARPOON GUN

COST: N/A
DAMAGE: High
RANGE: Long
SPEED: Slow

Press the **Attack 1** button to shoot high-velocity harpoons at your enemies.

UPGRADES

BARBED HARPOONS

COST: 500 Gold
PREREQUISITE: None
Harpoons do increased damage.

HARPOON REPEATER

COST: 900 Gold
PREREQUISITE: None
Harpoons reload faster.

QUADENT HARPOONS

COST: 1,700 Gold
PREREQUISITE: Harpooner Path
Harpoons do even MORE increased damage.

PIERCING HARPOONS

COST: 2,200 Gold
PREREQUISITE: Harpooner Path
Harpoons travel straight through enemies and hit new targets.

TRIPLESHOT HARPOON

COST: 3,000 Gold
PREREQUISITE: Harpooner Path
Shoot three Harpoons at once.

STRATEGY

Harpoon Gun starts off a bit slow. Don't overlook it, however. If you are interested in getting Gill Grunt to the highest damage levels possible, then it is the power you should invest in. Harpoons do more damage than Power Hose.

However, Harpoons are a straightforward attack, and the upgrade path has no surprises. Both Piercing Harpoons and Tripleshot Harpoon increase the effectiveness of Gill Grunt's harpoon attacks, allowing them to hit more enemies, more frequently.

ATTACK 2

POWER HOSE

COST: N/A
DAMAGE: Low
RANGE: Short
SPEED: Very Fast

Press and hold **Attack 2** to spray water at your enemies to knock them back.

UPGRADES

HIGH PRESSURE POWER HOSE

COST: 700 Gold
PREREQUISITE: None
Power Hose attack does extra damage and knocks enemies back further.

RESERVE WATER TANK

COST: 1,700 Gold
PREREQUISITE: Water Weaver Path
The Power Hose and Water Jet Pack never run out of water.

BOILING WATER HOSE

COST: 2,200 Gold
PREREQUISITE: Water Weaver Path
Power Hose attack does even MORE increased damage.

NEPTUNE GUN

COST: 3,000 Gold
PREREQUISITE: Water Weaver Path
When using the Power Hose, press **Attack 1** to launch exploding creatures.

STRATEGY

Gill Grunt's Power Hose attack is an awesome ability that knocks back small to large enemies while doing a solid amount of damage in the process. Don't underestimate the knockback portion of this power. Knocking back enemies interrupts their attacks and keeps melee attackers out of range of Gill.

Reserve Water Tank is the most important Water Hose upgrade. It allows for unlimited attacks, and gives Gill Grunt plenty of waterpower to run away with if he finds himself in a bad situation.

ATTACK 3

WATER JETPACK

COST: 1,200 Gold
PREREQUISITE: None
Press **Attack 3** to fly until Water Jetpack runs out. Increased speed and armor while flying.

STRATEGY

Gill Grunt's Water Jetpack is a fantastic way to get around any area. While it does run out of pressure if you use it for too long, you can avoid this by either earning the Reserve Water Tank upgrade or by using it in short bursts.

WOW POW POWER

ANCHOR'S AWAY!

COST: 5,000 Gold
PREREQUISITE: Anchor Cannon
Hold **Attack 1** and release to fire three giant anchors.

STRATEGY

This is a big upgrade for Anchor Cannon. Anchor's Away charges faster and has a wider effect range than the regular cannon. This makes it a fantastic power to use against bosses and high-HP enemies.

SLAM BAM

"ARMED AND DANGEROUS!"

STATS

♥	310
⚡	35
🛡	30
⊕	10
◎	25

UPGRADE PATHS

BLIZZARD BRAWLER
Further develop Slam Bam's close-range combat skills.

GLACIER YETI
Further develop Slam Bam's Ice Prison attacks.

SOUL GEM ABILITY

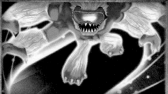

YETI COOLING-FACTOR
COST: 4,000 Gold
PREREQUISITE: None
Slam Bam has increased coolness and can surf faster.

Slam Bam is a master of ice and four-armed fury. This yeti really shines when it comes to melee combat. His attacks are very rapid, inflict massive damage, and have great upgrades. Unlike just about all other melee attackers, Slam Bam has a great slide maneuver that helps him quickly navigate through a level.

Slam Bam's secondary attack, Ice Prison, is difficult to use. Pursuing the Glacier Yeti path is not recommended for most players.

STRATEGY

This upgrade increases the speed of Slam Bam's slide. It also gives him some pretty sweet snow goggles.

SPECIAL QUEST

ICE TO MEET YOU:
TRAP 100 ENEMIES IN YOUR ICE BLOCKS.

Just use the Ice Prison on enemies as you play through a level or arena. You do not need to actually damage or freeze an enemy with the Ice Block; it counts if you just hit them with the Ice Block.

PRIMARY ATTACKS

ATTACK 1

YETI FISTS

COST: N/A
DAMAGE: High
RANGE: Short
SPEED: Fast

Throw powerful punches with all four fists.

UPGRADES

ICE KNUCKLES

COST: 1,200 Gold
PREREQUISITE: None
Punch attacks do increased damage.

BRAWLER COMBOS

COST: 1,700 Gold
PREREQUISITE: Blizzard Brawler Path
Press **Attack 1**, **Attack 1**, HOLD **Attack 2** for Ice Hammer.
Press **Attack 1**, **Attack 1**, HOLD **Attack 3** for Spinning Fist.

ICE MACE

COST: 2,200 Gold
PREREQUISITE: Blizzard Brawler Path
Punch attacks do even MORE increased damage.

BLIZZARD BATTLE ARMOR

COST: 3,000 Gold
PREREQUISITE: Blizzard Brawler Path
Battle Armor makes it harder for enemies to hit you.

STRATEGY

Yeti Fists is a strong melee attack. Slam Bam is a great melee warrior, and Blizzard Brawler is the path most players should choose. Ice Hammer ends with a short-range area-of-effect hammer attack that does double damage. Spinning Fist is another short-range attack, but allows Slam Bam to slide around a bit, dodging incoming attacks. Purchase Blizzard Battle Armor as soon as you can.

ATTACK 2

ICE PRISON

COST: N/A
DAMAGE: Low
RANGE: Short
SPEED: Average

Hold **Attack 2** and then release to summon an ice prison that will trap enemies.

UPGRADES

THREE'S A CHARM

COST: 500 Gold
PREREQUISITE: None
Have up to three Ice Prisons active at once.

ARCTIC EXPLOSION

COST: 700 Gold
PREREQUISITE: None
Ice Prisons explode and damage nearby enemies.

DEEP CHILL ICE COFFIN

COST: 1,700 Gold
PREREQUISITE: Glacier Yeti Path
Ice Prisons damage enemies trapped inside them.

GLACIER TACTICS

COST: 2,200 Gold
PREREQUISITE: Glacier Yeti Path
Ice Prisons travel further and faster. Can Ice Slide for longer too.

WORK OF ICE ART

COST: 3,000 Gold
PREREQUISITE: Glacier Yeti Path
Ice Prisons last longer and are more resistant to attacks.

STRATEGY

Ice Prison is a great secondary power. It can freeze medium and small enemies, keeping the battlefield more manageable. However, taking the Glacier Yeti Path is tough to recommend. Because the Ice Prisons don't work on larger enemies, it lacks versatility in combat. Of all the upgrades, Deep Chill Ice Coffin is the best. It damages enemies even if they don't get directly trapped by the ice cage.

ATTACK 3

YETI ICE SHOE SLIDE

COST: 900 Gold
PREREQUISITE: None
SPEED: Fast
Press **Attack 3** to slide across the ground. Hold **Attack 3** to travel further.

STRATEGY

Most melee characters don't get a great way to travel quickly through levels. Slam Bam is not most melee characters. Ice Shoe Slide is a quick dash that allows him to slide past enemies to escape bad situations, or to strategically place himself in a better position in battle.

WOW POW POWER

SLEIGH ME!

COST: 5,000 Gold
PREREQUISITE: Yeti Ice Shoe Slide
Hold **Attack 3** to take a ride on a powerful ice sleigh.

STRATEGY

Sleigh Me! turns Ice Slide into a high-damage dash attack. This is a fantastic upgrade, and worth every gold you spend to buy it. Remember, dash attacks are great not only for hurting enemies, but also for getting out of harm's way quickly.

POP FIZZ

"THE MOTION OF THE POTION!"

STATS

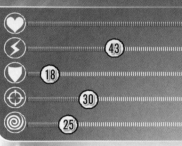

♥		270
⚡	43	
🛡	18	
◎	30	
🌀	25	

UPGRADE PATHS

BEST OF THE BEAST!
Further develop Pop Fizz's Beast Form attacks.

MAD SCIENTIST
Further develop Pop Fizz's potion attacks.

SOUL GEM ABILITY

SHAKE IT!
COST: 4,000 Gold
PREREQUISITE: Find Pop Fizz's Soul Gem in the Wilikin Village level.
Repeatedly press **Attack 3** to shake potion bottle until it explodes.

STRATEGY

Shake It! takes a few seconds to charge (hammer the **Attack 3** button as fast as you can), but when it goes off, it releases a massive explosion that does about 80 damage to all enemies in the area. This is a great power that is tremendously effective against enemies with average health, like Arkeyan Duelists.

SPECIAL QUEST

RAMPAGE: DO 200 HP OF DAMAGE IN A SINGLE RUN IN BEAST FORM.

This challenge is pretty simple since Beast Form dishes out plenty of damage, even before upgrading it. Just transform into Beast Form in a large group of enemies and destroy everything in sight to achieve the quest.

There's a good chance that Pop Fizz is just a little crazy. It doesn't matter, however. You want him as a part of your team of Skylanders.

While Pop Fizz's Beast Form is amazing, it's the variety of potions at his disposal that makes him really shine. Pop Fizz's potion attack makes him one of the most powerful ranged attackers. With some early upgrades, he can toss his potions at enemies at great speed, and his green potion is a fantastic boss-killer.

PRIMARY ATTACKS

ATTACK 1

POTION LOB

COST: N/A
DAMAGE: High
RANGE: Medium
SPEED: Average

Press **Attack 1** to lob Pop Fizz's currently-equipped potion.

UPGRADES

DEXTEROUS DELIVERY

COST: 1,200 Gold
PREREQUISITE: None

Throw potions and grab new ones much faster.

ALL IN

COST: 3,000 Gold
PREREQUISITE: Mad Scientist Path

Hold **Attack 1** to pull up to three potions out and release to throw them all at once.

MASTER CHEMIST

COST: 1,700 Gold
PREREQUISITE: Mad Scientist Path

All potions do increased damage and have improved effects.

STRATEGY

Pop Fizz's default potion attack is a yellow potion that damages enemies at range. As you unlock more powers, use **Attack 3** to change the type of potion Pop Fizz throws. The purple potion drops little potion bottles with feet that walk around and shoot enemies. The green potion creates pools of acid that hurt enemies that step in them.

ATTACK 2

BEAST FORM

COST: N/A
DAMAGE: High
RANGE: Short
SPEED: Very Slow

Press **Attack 2** to drink potion and temporarily change into a beastly form.

UPGRADES

RAGING BEAST

COST: 900 Gold
PREREQUISITE: None

All attacks in Beast Form do additional damage.

BERSERKER BOOST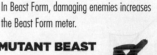

COST: 2,200 Gold
PREREQUISITE: Best of the Beast! Path

In Beast Form, damaging enemies increases the Beast Form meter.

MORE BEAST!

COST: 1,700 Gold
PREREQUISITE: Best of the Beast! Path

Beast Form meter drains more slowly and recharges faster.

MUTANT BEAST

COST: 3,000 Gold
PREREQUISITE: Best of the Beast! Path

In Beast Form, press **Attack 3** to perform a special attack based on which potion is active.

STRATEGY

When you activate Beast Form, a timer appears to the left of the Skylander that counts down. After Pop Fizz resumes his normal form, the timer must refill before the ability is available again. Remember that it takes a moment for the beast potion to kick in, leaving Pop Fizz momentarily vulnerable to attack.

While in Beast form, Pop Fizz's main attack is delivered via **Attack 1**. More Beast! and Berserker Boost both increase the duration of the beast attack. The most interesting upgrade is Mutant Beast. This imbues Beast Form with a special attack based on what potion you have equipped when you enter the form. A green potion results in Pop Fizz nailing any enemy in close range multiple times. With a yellow potion, Pop Fizz belches out a flame thrower attack. Purple potions give Pop Fizz a high-damage lunge attack.

ATTACK 3

NEW CONCOCTIONS

COST: 500 Gold
PREREQUISITE: None

Press **Attack 3** to switch to some new potions, which have different effects when thrown.

UPGRADES

PUDDLE OF PAIN

COST: 700 Gold
PREREQUISITE: New Concoctions

Press **Attack 3** to cycle to a new potion that leaves a damaging puddle of acid when thrown.

MIXOLOGIST

COST: 2,200 Gold
PREREQUISITE: Mad Scientist Path

Mix the effects of different color potions for brand new effects.

STRATEGY

New Concoctions gives Pop Fizz the ability to use different potions to throw at his enemies. When you get Mixologist, you can mix the potions to create new effects. Mix it with purple, and your little purple potion bottles get a poison attack. Throw a yellow potion on a poison pool and it explodes in flames! Pop Fizz's Green Potions are one of the best attacks to use against bosses. Slam an enemy with the potions, and not only does the initial hit do a fair amount of damage, but enemies continue to take damage every second they stay in the poison pool.

SPYRO

"ALL FIRED UP!"

STATS

♥	280
⚡	50
🛡	18
◎	30
◎	25

UPGRADE PATHS

SHEEP BURNER SPYRO
Further develop Spyro's Flameball attacks.

BLITZ SPYRO
Further develop Spyro's Charging attacks.

SOUL GEM ABILITY

SPYRO'S EARTH POUND
COST: 4,000 Gold
PREREQUISITE: Spyro's Flight
DAMAGE: High
RANGE: Medium
SPEED: Slow

This power gives Spyro a new flight attack. Press **Attack 2** while flying to Dive Bomb.

STRATEGY

This dive bomb attack is a great addition to Spyro's arsenal. It's not quite as good as Fireslam, but it's a great area-of-effect attack with excellent range.

SPECIAL QUEST

FULL CHARGE: COLLECT 3 GOLD, EAT 1 FOOD ITEM, AND DEFEAT 2 ENEMIES IN 1 SPRINT CHARGE.

To complete Spyro's unique quest, look for two low health enemies as well as some food and gold on the screen. Chompies are good enemies to attempt this against. Purchase the Sprint Charge upgrade to increase the distance of Spyro's sprint.

Spyro remains a great all-around combatant with fierce ranged and dash attacks. Spyro's primary attack is a burst of fire that he shoots rapidly at his foes. His secondary ability is a great dash attack that sets enemies he passes ablaze.

What really sets Spyro apart from his peers are the excellent knockback effects of his abilities. Both attacks allow Spyro to control the battlefield, push enemies into hazards, and keep them out of melee attack range.

PRIMARY ATTACKS

ATTACK 1

FLAMEBALL

COST: N/A
DAMAGE: Low
RANGE: Long
SPEED: Average

Press the **Attack 1** button to breathe balls of fire at your enemies.

UPGRADES

LONG RANGE RAZE

COST: 500 Gold
PREREQUISITE: None
Flameball attacks travel further.

TRIPLE FLAMEBALLS

COST: 1,200 Gold
PREREQUISITE: None
Shoot three Flameballs at once.

FIRE SHIELD

COST: 1,700 Gold
PREREQUISITE: Sheep Burner Path
A Fire Shield appears when using the Flameball attack.

EXPLODING FIREBLAST

COST: 2,200 Gold
PREREQUISITE: Sheep Burner Path
Flameballs do extra damage and the middle one explodes.

THE DAYBRINGER FLAME

COST: 3,000 Gold
PREREQUISITE: Sheep Burner Path
Hold **Attack 1** to charge up Flameball attack for MAXIMUM damage.

STRATEGY

Flameball is slower than most ranged attacks, but it deals better damage than average and has an excellent knockback. It also has plenty of upgrades, increasing range, damage, and number of fireballs. Daybringer Flame is the upgrade to save for last. Attacking with regular Flameballs actually deals more damage in the amount of time it takes to charge and release Daybringer Flame.

ATTACK 2

CHARGE

COST: N/A
DAMAGE: Very Low
RANGE: Short
SPEED: Fast

Press and hold the **Attack 2** button to lower your horns and charge forward, knocking over anything in your way.

UPGRADES

SPRINT CHARGE

COST: 900 Gold
PREREQUISITE: None
Can perform Charge attack for increased distance.

STUN CHARGE

COST: 1,700 Gold
PREREQUISITE: Blitz Spyro Path
Enemies hit by Charge attack become stunned.

COMET DASH

COST: 2,200 Gold
PREREQUISITE: Blitz Spyro Path
Charge attack does increased damage.

IBEX'S WRATH CHARGE

COST: 3,000 Gold
PREREQUISITE: Blitz Spyro Path, Comet Dash
Charge longer to do extra damage.

STRATEGY

Charge is one of the best dash-type attacks in the game. Once Spyro hits full speed, the damage from the attack more than doubles. Charge also has two great secondary effects. First Stun Charge unlocks a stun effect. Any enemy hit by the Charge cannot move for approximately 3 seconds. The second effect is a huge knockback. Charge is a fantastic power for crowd control and knocking enemies off of ledges. However, due to its low damage, it's tough to unconditionally recommend the Blitz Spyro path over the higher-damage Sheep Burner path.

ATTACK 3

SPYRO'S FLIGHT

COST: 700 Gold
PREREQUISITE: None
Press **Attack 3** to fly. Increased speed and armor while flying.

STRATEGY

Flight increases Spyro's speed and can be helpful when navigating dangerous level hazards. While flying, Spyro can use Flameball, but not Charge attacks.

WOW POW POWER

FIRESLAM!

COST: 5,000 Gold
PREREQUISITE: Earth Pound
DAMAGE: Very High
RANGE: Medium/Long
SPEED: Slow
While flying, press **Attack 2** to shoot fireballs and perform a flaming slam.

STRATEGY

This is a fantastic power that keeps Spyro out of harm's way while slamming enemies with blasts of fire and kinetic energy. This power fundamentally changes how Spyro is played since flight becomes a much more effective tactic. Use Fireslam against large groups of enemies and against single tough monsters alike.

DOUBLE TROUBLE

"BOOM SHAKALAKA!"

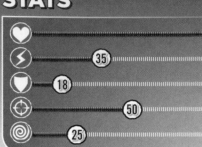

STATS

❤	25
⚡	35
🛡	18
◎	50
◎	25

UPGRADE PATHS

CHANNELER
Further develop Double Trouble's Eldritch Beam and Magic Bombs.

CONJUROR
Further develop Double Trouble's skills with Exploding Doubles.

SOUL GEM ABILITY

WATERWALKER
COST: 4,000 Gold
PREREQUISITE: None
Double Trouble can now fly over water.

STRATEGY

There isn't much water in *Skylanders Giants*, in fact most of the water is found behind Water Elemental Gates. Save the Gold for other upgrades and even store items.

SPECIAL QUEST

BIG BOMB TROUBLE: DEFEAT 10 ENEMIES WITH ONE MAGIC BOMB ATTACK.

This isn't too hard, walk into a group of 10 or more Chompies and set the bomb off. A good place to earn this is any of Brock's Arena Challenges with regular Chompies.

Double Trouble is a crazed Witch doctor that has a power for every situation. Eldritch Beam is a directed attack that can keep enemies from getting too close.

Should any enemies break through the line and surround Double Trouble, switch to his Magic Bomb attack, which explodes for massive damage at close range. His last power, Exploding Double, is great for the times you need to evade attacks. It's a tricky power that hunts down the Skylander's enemies and explodes.

PRIMARY ATTACKS

ATTACK 1

ELDRITCH BEAM

COST: N/A
DAMAGE: Low
RANGE: Medium
SPEED: Fast

Press and hold **Attack 1** to fire a beam of energy that locks onto targets.

UPGRADES

ARCANE ELDRITCH BEAM

COST: 500 Gold
PREREQUISITE: None

Eldritch Beam attack does increased damage.

EXTENDED ELDRITCH BEAM

COST: 1,700 Gold
PREREQUISITE: Channeler Path

Eldritch Beam has longer range and does extra damage.

STRATEGY

What makes Eldritch Beam a stand out ability is that it automatically seeks out any enemy in front of Double Trouble. It's impossible for enemies within range to avoid it. The damage is moderate, but it can cut through the health of your foes quickly.

ATTACK 3

SUMMON MAGIC BOMB

COST: 900 Gold
PREREQUISITE: None
DAMAGE: Very High
RANGE: Short
SPEED: Very Slow

Press **Attack 3** to summon a Magic Bomb.

UPGRADES

MAGICAL CATACLYSM

COST: 2,200 Gold
PREREQUISITE: Channeler Path

Magic Bombs do increased damage.

MAGIC ARMAGEDDON

COST: 3,000 Gold
PREREQUISITE: Channeler Path, Magical Cataclysm

Hold **Attack 3** to fire off repeated Magic Bombs.

STRATEGY

When Double Trouble uses Magic Bomb, it appears directly beneath him and takes a few seconds to charge and explode. This attack deals high damage, and should be the first purchase you make when upgrading him. If you pick the Channeler Path, Magic Bomb turns into a serious boss-killing power. Holding the **Attack 3** button with Magic Armageddon inflicts three rapid high-damage burst attacks at the enemy, inflicting almost 200 points of damage in only a few seconds.

ATTACK 2

CONJURE EXPLODING DOUBLE

COST: N/A
DAMAGE: Average
RANGE: Short
SPEED: Very Slow

Summon a mindless double that seeks enemies and explodes.

UPGRADES

CONJURE UNSTABLE DOUBLE

COST: 700 Gold
PREREQUISITE: None

Exploding Doubles do increased damage.

ADVANCED CONSTRUCT TECHNIQUES

COST: 1,200 Gold
PREREQUISITE: None

Have up to 3 Exploding Doubles active at any given time.

IMBUE CONSTRUCT

COST: 1,700 Gold
PREREQUISITE: Conjuror Path

Shoot an Exploding Double and it increases in size and damage.

ROCKET POWERED DOUBLES

COST: 2,200 Gold
PREREQUISITE: Conjuror Path

Exploding Doubles launch themselves at enemies and do extra damage.

SPIRIT CONSTRUCT

COST: 3,000 Gold
PREREQUISITE: Conjuror Path

Exploding Doubles form automatically when enemies are defeated.

STRATEGY

When you cast Exploding Double, a little Double Trouble pops in and follows Double Trouble. When it senses enemies nearby, the double automatically chases them down. When the foe attacks or Double Trouble gets close enough, it explodes dealing solid damage to any nearby enemies.

The damage upgrades improve the effectiveness of each double significantly, but the upgrade that really shines is Rocket Powered Doubles. This power allows Exploding Doubles to fling themselves into the air to hit enemies in hard to reach places. Imbue Construct is also a great upgrade. Shoot your constructs with your Eldritch Beam, and they double in size and inflict double the damage! Spirit Construct is a strong power, but it only causes new Exploding Doubles to spawn in if you kill the enemies with a power that is not Exploding Double, meaning you need to kill them with Magic Bomb or Eldritch Beam to cause a double to spawn.

WOW POW POWER

TRIPLE TROUBLE!

COST: 5,000 Gold
PREREQUISITE: None

Eldritch Beam splits off into three separate beams when it locks on an enemy.

STRATEGY

This is a great Wow Pow for any Double Trouble invested in the Conjuror Path. Conjurors need to use their Eldritch Beam often to charge their Explosive Doubles, and to quickly spawn more Explosive Doubles. This makes the beam more powerful and also spread its effectiveness, allowing Double Trouble to more quickly imbue his doubles with spirit. Of course, it's also great for any Double Trouble using the Channeler Path; the beam does more damage when it splits.

WRECKING BALL

"WRECK-N-ROLL!"

STATS

♥	27
⚡	43
🛡	24
◎	20
◉	25

UPGRADE PATHS

TOTAL TONGUE
Further develop Wrecking Ball's tongue attack.

ULTIMATE SPINNER
Further develop Wrecking Ball's Force Field attack.

SOUL GEM ABILITY

ENEMY SLURP
COST: 4,000 Gold
PREREQUISITE: None

Can swallow smaller enemies.

STRATEGY

This is an incredible improvement for Wrecking Ball's tongue attack. Wrecking Ball doesn't just eat Chompies, but also mid-sized enemies like Inhuman Shields! He can also eat enemies with more health, like Mace Majors, once they are weak enough. If instantly killing some tough enemies wasn't enough, each time he eats an enemy he gains health!

SPECIAL QUEST

COMPETITIVE EATER:
SWALLOW 100 ENEMIES.

To complete this quest, you first need to purchase the Enemy Slurp upgrade. Once you purchase it, just swallow as many enemies as you can. Any medium sized and smaller enemy can be eaten.

Wrecking Ball was a tiny grub whose voracious appetite once saved him from being the main ingredient in a magic soup! Wrecking Ball didn't stop there. He used his sticky tongue to eat everything in sight. An encounter with Master Eon, who was impressed with Wrecking Ball's abilities, led to Wrecking Ball becoming a Skylander.

Don't let Wrecking Ball's diminutive size fool you, he has the potential to be one of the most powerful Skylanders on your team. From his powerful belches, to his chaotic rolling, to his shocking ability to consume enemies, Wrecking Ball's powers are full of surprises, and well worth a look.

PRIMARY ATTACKS

ATTACK 1

TONGUE WHAP
COST: N/A
DAMAGE: Very Low
RANGE: Medium
SPEED: Slow

Press **Attack 1** to slap enemies with your super-tongue.

UPGRADES

TONGUE EVOLUTION
COST: 900 Gold
PREREQUISITE: None
Wrecking Ball's tongue grows longer and does increased damage.

TONGUE GRABBER
COST: 2,200 Gold
PREREQUISITE: Total Tongue Path
Tongue does extra damage and can pick up food and power-ups.

LIGHTNING TONGUE
COST: 1,700 Gold
PREREQUISITE: Total Tongue Path
Wrecking Ball's tongue can attack quicker than ever.

TONGUE SUPERMAX
COST: 3,000 Gold
PREREQUISITE: Total Tongue Path
Wrecking Ball's tongue grows even longer.

STRATEGY
Tongue Whap starts out as a weak, medium-ranged attack. Wrecking Ball just slaps nearby enemies with his tongue; however, it has a ton of upgrades. The length of the tongue and the damage are all awesome, but the truly sweet upgrade is the Soul Gem. Check out Enemy Slurp for more Information.

ATTACK 2

FORCE FIELD BALL
COST: N/A
DAMAGE: Very High
RANGE: Short
SPEED: Very Slow

Press the **Attack 2** button to summon magic for a spin force field charge.

UPGRADES

MAGIC BALL CONTROL
COST: 500 Gold
PREREQUISITE: None
Force Field Ball can be controlled, and it does increased damage.

SWATH OF TERROR
COST: 2,200 Gold
PREREQUISITE: Ultimate Spinner Path
Force Field Ball is larger and does even MORE increased damage.

FORCE FIELD BLAST
COST: 1,700 Gold
PREREQUISITE: Ultimate Spinner Path
While in your Force Field Ball, press **Attack 2** to create a force field explosion.

IT'S GOTTA GO SOMEWHERE
COST: 3,000 Gold
PREREQUISITE: Ultimate Spinner Path
While in your Force Field Ball, press **Attack 3** to create a powerful burp attack.

STRATEGY
Force Field Ball may seem hard to control at first. The truth is, you don't really need to control it, just let Wrecking Ball bounce around the area and deal as much damage as possible per spin. That's his primary tactic. Once you get the ball upgraded to do more damage, you also get better control. Each time you form the ball, try to hit as many enemies as you can before the spin finishes.

It's Gotta Go Somewhere Is an excellent high-damage area-of-effect attack that has wide range. It's something to look forward to as you save up Gold.

ATTACK 3

POWER BELCH
COST: 700 Gold
PREREQUISITE: None
DAMAGE: High
RANGE: Short
SPEED: Slow

Press **Attack 3** to release a Burp attack.

STRATEGY
Initially, Power Belch attack isn't an impressive power. It's a slow-moving, high-damage attack. That changes when Wrecking Ball unlocks Digestive Detonation. The area-of-effect version of Power Belch does heavy damage in a wide area. A great upgrade considering all Wrecking Balls get it, regardless of their chosen upgrade path.

UPGRADES

DIGESTIVE DETONATION
COST: 1,200 Gold
PREREQUISITE: Power Belch
Hold **Attack 3** to charge up your burp attack.

WOW POW POWER

DISCO BALL!
COST: 5,000 Gold
PREREQUISITE: None
Press **Attack 2** to turn Wrecking Ball's Force Field into a magical disco ball.

STRATEGY
This upgrade permanently converts Wrecking Ball's Force Field Ball into a disco ball! The disco ball doesn't just look cool, it also increases the base damage of the Force Field attack by 30%.

VOODOOD

"AXE FIRST, QUESTIONS LATER!"

STATS

❤	29
⚡	35
🛡	12
◎	30
◉	25

UPGRADE PATHS

ELEMENTALIST
Further develop Voodood's magic abilities.

MARAUDER
Further develop Voodood's skills with the Axe.

SOUL GEM ABILITY

IMPERVIOUS TRIPWIRE
COST: 4,000 Gold
PREREQUISITE: Magic Tripwire Bomb
Voodood's Magic Tripwires now deflect incoming enemy shots.

STRATEGY

Tripwire is already such a great power, why not give it one more upgrade? With this power, Voodood can use Tripwire for cover against attacks, like D. Riveter's gun blasts. This isn't an important upgrade, so you can hold off on purchasing it.

SPECIAL QUEST

TRICKWIRE: DEFEAT SIX ENEMIES AT ONCE WITH YOUR TRIPWIRE.

Tripwire is a great power, so if you get a few upgrades for it, you should have no problems completing this quest. Find a group of six or more low-health enemies, like Bone Chompies, and set the Tripwire up near them. Chapter 1 has several good spots to try for this quest.

Even as a young orc, Voodood collected rare and interesting bones that he used to create weapons and devices. In fact, even today when he's not fighting evil, Voodood continues to search for new and exotic bones to expand his collection.

Voodood often talks about his axe, but his real power is hidden in Tripwire. Tripwire is an incredibly powerful attack that sucks in enemies, slams them around, and damages them. While Voodood could make a formidable melee opponent, his Health and Armor stats mean that most players should focus on his extraordinary trapping ability.

PRIMARY ATTACKS

ATTACK 1

AXE REAVER

COST: N/A
DAMAGE: Medium
RANGE: Short
SPEED: Fast

Press the **Attack 1** button to swing Voodood's axe.

Press **Attack 1**, **Attack 1**, hold **Attack 1** to perform a combo.

UPGRADES

WEIGHTED AXE

COST: 700 Gold
PREREQUISITE: None
Axe attack does increased damage.

SHAMAN STYLE

COST: 1,700 Gold
PREREQUISITE: Marauder Path
Press **Attack 1**, **Attack 1**, hold **Attack 2** for Axe Spin.

Press **Attack 1**, **Attack 1**, hold **Attack 3** for Magic Axe.

LEGENDARY BLADE

COST: 2,200 Gold
PREREQUISITE: Marauder Path
Axe attack does even MORE increased damage.

ELECTRO AXE

COST: 3,000 Gold
PREREQUISITE: Elementalist Path
When Voodood strikes with his Axe, anything nearby gets hurt too.

STRATEGY

Voodood loves his axe, and his axe loves him. Voodood's axe upgrades increase the damage of the attack. The one exception are his combos, which provide a two standard combo attacks. Axe Spin is an area-of-effect attack. Magic Axe is a concentrated damage attack for hitting big enemies and bosses.

ATTACK 2

ZIPLINE AXE

COST: N/A
DAMAGE: Medium
RANGE: Medium/Long
SPEED: Fast

Press the **Attack 2** button to launch the blade of your axe and rapidly reel yourself in.

UPGRADES

EXTENDED BLADE

COST: 1,200 Gold
PREREQUISITE: None
Zipline Axe attack has increased range.

HYPERWIRE

COST: 3,000 Gold
PREREQUISITE: Marauder Path
Zipline Axe travels much faster and does increased damage.

STRATEGY

Zipline Axe is a simple maneuver that shocks a single enemy and quickly moves Voodood into combat range. This power works well in combination with Axe Reaver, and is particularly good for getting close to evasive enemies, such as Grenade Generals and Arkeyan Bombers.

ATTACK 3

MAGICAL TRIPWIRE BOMB

COST: 500 Gold
PREREQUISITE: None
DAMAGE: Very High
RANGE: Short
SPEED: Fast

Press **Attack 3** to summon a Magic Tripwire that collapses on your enemies.

UPGRADES

TRIPWIRE RESERVES

COST: 900 Gold
PREREQUISITE: Magical Tripwire Bomb
Summon up to two Magic Tripwires.

ROADBLOCK TRIPWIRE

COST: 1,700 Gold
PREREQUISITE: Elementalist Path
Magic Tripwires are longer and do increased damage.

ELECTRIC FEEDBACK

COST: 2,200 Gold
PREREQUISITE: Elementalist Path
Magical energy radiates from you when hit, damaging nearby enemies.

STRATEGY

Tripwire is an incredibly powerful trap that Voodood can set for his enemies. Press **Attack 3** to lay down the tripwire and any enemies that cross it set it off. When the trap is set off, it snaps, grabbing all enemies and damaging them heavily.

Tripwire is a fantastic power to use against bosses. One Tripwire can hit the same boss multiple times, each time inflicting massive damage.

SPROCKET

"THE FIX IS IN!"

STATS

♥		24
⚡	43	
🛡	30	
◎	10	
◉	25	

UPGRADE PATHS

OPERATOR
Further develop Sprocket's Wrench and Mine attacks.

GEARHEAD
Further develop Sprocket's Turret and Tank abilities.

SOUL GEM ABILITY

LANDMINE GOLF
COST: 4,000 Gold
PREREQUISITE: Find Sprocket's Soul Gem in Drill-X's Big Rig level.

Facing a mine, press **Attack 1** to send it flying towards enemies.

STRATEGY
This is a great Soul Gem Power, particularly if you pick the Operator Path for Sprocket. She knocks a mine into the direction she is facing. This attack has long range and does increased damage over regular Bouncing Betties. The attack is quick, but difficult to aim.

SPECIAL QUEST

MINED YOUR STEP: DEFEAT 50 ENEMIES USING THE LANDMINE GOLF ATTACK.

Once you unlock the Landmine Golf ability, just use it often. A quick way to complete this quest is to load up one of the easier Arena levels. With good aim, you can even take down multiple enemies with one hit!

Sprocket is all about battlefield strategy. While she always has the option to run up and clobber enemies with her powerful wrench, she has other, and incredibly fun, abilities.

Sprocket has some great Bouncing Betty mines that can be set in enemies' paths, but using them effectively takes some planning and understanding of how enemies move around the battlefield. Where Sprocket really stands out is with her turret abilities. She can deploy multiple automatic turrets on the field, and even get in the turrets and ride them around!

PRIMARY ATTACKS

ATTACK 1

WRENCH WHACK

COST: N/A
DAMAGE: Medium
RANGE: Short
SPEED: Average

Press **Attack 1** to swing the big wrench.

UPGRADES

SPROCKET COMBOS

COST: 1,700 Gold
PREREQUISITE: Operator Path
Press **Attack 1**, **Attack 1**, HOLD **Attack 2** for Power Surge.

Press **Attack 1**, **Attack 1**, HOLD **Attack 3** for Mines O' Plenty.

MONKEY WRENCH

COST: 2,200 Gold
PREREQUISITE: Operator Path
Better wrench does increased damage.

STRATEGY

Wrench Whack is a straightforward melee attack. If you choose the Operator Path you get two combos when you purchase Sprocket Combos. With the Power Surge combo, Sprocket tosses explosives out of her bag. The explosives are a high-damage, short-range area-of-effect attack. When you pull off the Mines O' Plenty combo, Sprocket tosses a set of Bouncing Betties in the air, which creates a defensive minefield around her.

ATTACK 3

STRATEGY

Bouncing Betty Mines are a great trap attack that you can lay out on the battlefield. When any enemy walks near one, it sets off the Betty,

 causing a short-range, high-damage explosion. Sprocket can have about six on the battlefield at once. All Mines just lets her get them out quicker.

BOUNCING BETTY MINES

COST: 700 Gold
PREREQUISITE: None
DAMAGE: High
RANGE: Short
SPEED: Very Slow
Press **Attack 3** to toss mines that explode when enemies are near.

UPGRADES

ALL MINES

COST: 3,000 Gold
PREREQUISITE: Operator Path
Sprocket can now deploy three Bouncing Betty mines at once.

ATTACK 2

TURRET GUN-O-MATIC

COST: N/A
DAMAGE: Very Low
RANGE: Long
SPEED: Very Slow

Press **Attack 2** to build a turret that shoots enemies. Climb inside by facing the turret and pressing **Attack 2**.

UPGRADES

AUTO TURRET V2

COST: 500 Gold
PREREQUISITE: None
Turret Gun-o-Matic does increased damage and has more HP.

2 TIMES THE TURRETS

COST: 900 Gold
PREREQUISITE: None
Can have two active turrets at once.

TANKS A LOT!

COST: 1,200 Gold
PREREQUISITE: Auto Turret V2
When climbing inside a turret, it transforms into a drivable assault tank.

MINE DROP!

COST: 1,700 Gold
PREREQUISITE: Gearhead Path
While driving a tank, press **Attack 3** to drop mines out of the back.

EXPLODING SHELLS

COST: 2,200 Gold
PREREQUISITE: Gearhead Path
Turret and Tank shells now explode on contact, doing extra damage.

SELF DESTRUCT SYSTEM

COST: 3,000 Gold
PREREQUISITE: Gearhead Path
When a Turret or Tank expires, it detonates and damages anything nearby

STRATEGY

Sprocket's automated turrets are a highlight of the character's abilities. While this power will never be high damage enough to destroy bosses in a timely manner, it's still a great tactic for fixed battlefield situations, such as arenas. Even before you commit to the Gearhead Path, you get two cool upgrades for the turrets. The first allows Sprocket to deploy two turrets at once. The second allows Sprocket to jump into a turret, turning it into a controllable tank.

If you decide to pursue the Gearhead path, you get some good, but not breakout, upgrades. The extra damage from Exploding Shells is nice, but don't make a huge difference. Self Destruct System is difficult to use effectively, as it has short range. Even if it hits, it doesn't do much damage. Mine Drop is fun, but no better than just dropping your own mines when Sprocket is outside of the tank. In the end, even if you really like the turrets, the Operator Path is still a good choice to complement your turrets. More effective wrench swings and mines will help you keep your turrets alive longer.

DRILL SERGEANT

"LICENSED TO DRILL!"

STATS

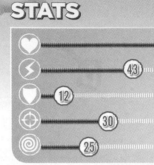

❤		29
⚡	43	
🛡	12	
🎯	30	
◎	25	

UPGRADE PATHS

BATTLEDOZER
Further develop Drill Sergeant's Drill Rocket attack.

MEGADOZER
Further develop Drill Sergeant's Charge and Auto-Blaster attacks.

SOUL GEM ABILITY

ARKEYAN ARMOR
COST: 4,000 Gold
PREREQUISITE: None
New armor makes Drill Sergeant harder to hit.

Drill Sergeant is a nimble and versatile Skylander, but to fully realize his potential, you must upgrade his powers. Drill Sergeant possesses two types of attacks: Ranged and Dashing.

Drill Sergeant isn't a heavy hitter, and he probably won't be your first choice in boss fights. Drill Sergeant fares much better in defensive situations with multiple enemies on the field. He can dash out of dangerous situations while inflicting damage on any enemies that get in his way.

STRATEGY
The extra armor helps, but don't expect Drill Sergeant to be able to tackle enemies at short range; his powers are still best while dashing and firing from range.

SPECIAL QUEST

DRILL SKILL: DEFEAT DRILL-X WITHOUT CHANGING SKYLANDERS.

To complete this quest, Drill Sergeant must defeat Drill-X (the final boss in Chapter 11) solo. You can, however, use Adventure items like Healing Potion to help Drill Sergeant survive the battle. If you find this quest too challenging, try it on the Easy difficulty with a high-level, fully-upgraded Drill Sergeant.

PRIMARY ATTACKS

ATTACK 1

DRILL ROCKET
COST: N/A
DAMAGE: Low
RANGE: Long
SPEED: Very Slow

Press **Attack 1** to shoot homing rockets that chase down enemies for massive damage.

UPGRADES

A SPEEDY RECOVERY
COST: 500 Gold
PREREQUISITE: None
Drill Rockets reload quicker and do increased damage.

A VIEW TO A DRILL
COST: 1,700 Gold
PREREQUISITE: BattleDozer Path
Drill Rockets do even MORE increased damage.

DX3000-DRILL DETONATOR
COST: 2,200 Gold
PREREQUISITE: BattleDozer Path
Drill Rockets explosions are bigger and can damage multiple enemies.

MIRV DRILL ROCKETS
COST: 3,000 Gold
PREREQUISITE: BattleDozer Path, A View to a Drill
Drill Rockets burst into smaller rockets.

STRATEGY

Drill Rockets are a slow, ranged attack. The Drill Rockets do have some heat-seeking properties, so you don't need to aim them perfectly when you fire them. When you upgrade the ability, the damage increases significantly and it becomes much easier to hit enemies with the MIRV upgrade.

The most important upgrade is A Speedy Recovery, which allows Drill Sergeant to fire the rockets much faster. If you attack with Drill Rockets at short range, Drill Sergeant executes a melee attack. This melee attack is slow and does not do as much damage as a full drill attack.

WOW POW POWER

FUTURECANNON!
COST: 5,000 Gold
PREREQUISITE: Auto-Blaster
Hold **Attack 3** to fire energy pulses that haven't even been invented yet.

STRATEGY

This is a major upgrade for the Auto-Blaster power. Drill Sergeant still fires typical Auto-Blaster shots, but he also fires powerful, larger plasma-type shots that do five times the damage of a regular Auto-Blaster shot!

ATTACK 2

BULLDOZE CHARGE
COST: N/A
DAMAGE: Low
RANGE: Short
SPEED: Fast

Hold the **Attack 2** button to have Drill Sergeant dash forward and barrel over enemies.

UPGRADES

DOZER ENDURANCE
COST: 700 Gold
PREREQUISITE: None
Bulldoze Charge lasts longer.

POWER CHARGE
COST: 900 Gold
PREREQUISITE: None
Bulldoze Charge does increased damage.

SPEED DOZER BOOST
COST: 1,700 Gold
PREREQUISITE: MegaDozer Path
Move faster during a Bulldoze Charge.

MEGA DOZER
COST: 3,000 Gold
PREREQUISITE: MegaDozer Path
Bulldoze Charge does extra damage and can charge through some attacks.

STRATEGY

Bulldoze Charge is a fantastic dashing maneuver that hurts enemies even if Drill Sergeant simply grazes them. The speed boost provided by this power helps tremendously and can also help when it's time to solve bomb puzzles or navigate dangerous, trap-filled areas.

All the upgrades provided for Bulldoze Charge are standard damage, speed, and duration increases. Once you have the last improvement, Mega Dozer, it becomes an even better defensive power. You can charge right through most ranged attacks and not take damage.

ATTACK 3

STRATEGY

Auto-Blaster is an interesting power; it's the only power that allows a Skylander to fire while using other powers. Auto-Blaster does not do much damage. It does less damage than any other power in the game!

However, you don't need to worry about aiming and firing it, and it doesn't slow Drill Sergeant down at all. Once you unlock Auto-Blaster, you should always hold down the **Attack 3** button while in combat. Every little bit of damage helps!

AUTO-BLASTER
COST: 1,200 Gold
PREREQUISITE: None
DAMAGE: Extremely Low
RANGE: Medium
SPEED: Average
Press **Attack 3** to activate your Auto-Blaster.

UPGRADES

HAIL STORM
COST: 2,200 Gold
PREREQUISITE: MegaDozer Path
Your Auto-Blaster fires much faster and never runs out of power.

BOOMER

"BRING THE BOOM!"

- ❤ — 23
- ⚡ — 35
- 🛡 — 18
- ◎ — 50
- ◎ — 25

UPGRADE PATHS

DEMOLITION TROLL
Further develop Boomer's Dynamite and Time Bomb attacks.

CLOBBER TROLL
Further develop Boomer's Smash attack.

SOUL GEM ABILITY

TROLL BOMB BOOT
COST: 4,000 Gold

PREREQUISITE: Troll Bomb

Troll Bombs can be kicked at enemies.

STRATEGY

This is an interesting ability, allowing you to direct your bombs at enemies from a distance. Unfortunately, it's difficult to aim the bombs in the direction you want. Troll Bomb Boot can wait until after you've purchased Boomer's other upgrades.

SPECIAL QUEST

ON A TROLL: DEFEAT FIVE ENEMIES WITH ONE KICKED TROLL BOMB.

Once you have Troll Bomb Boot, you need to find a group of tight-knit Chompies. A good place to give this a try is in Chapter 1, where there are several groups of five Chompies. Aiming the kick is difficult, but keep at it and eventually you'll complete the quest.

Boomer is an all-star Troll that's so exceptional he's seen the evil of his people's ways and joined the Skylanders. An explosives expert, Boomer's attacks include throwing dynamite sticks, dropping bombs, and smashing the ground with a mighty two-handed swing.

Dynamite Toss lights up the battlefield with chaotic explosions. Troll Smash, Boomer's secondary attack, is a great area-of-effect attack that can knock back and even stun enemies. This Troll Bomb is a fantastic power to use in just about any combat situation.

PRIMARY ATTACKS

ATTACK 1

DYNAMITE TOSS

COST: N/A
DAMAGE: Medium
RANGE: Medium
SPEED: Slow

Press **Attack 1** to hurl an explosive stick of troll-grade dynamite.

UPGRADES

DYNAMITE FUSE FAKE-OUT

COST: 500 Gold
PREREQUISITE: None

Dynamite does increased damage. Hold **Attack 1** to delay the explosion.

TRIPLE BUNDLE DYNAMITE

COST: 1,200 Gold
PREREQUISITE: Dynamite Fuse Fake-Out

Dynamite does even MORE increased damage.

AN ACCIDENT WAITING TO HAPPEN

COST: 3,000 Gold
PREREQUISITE: Demolition Troll Path

Throw three extra sticks of dynamite at once.

STRATEGY

If you love chaos on the battlefield, then you are going to love Dynamite Toss. Even before you purchase upgrades, rapidly tossing dynamite into the field causes explosions to erupt everywhere since the initial dynamite blast splits off three more dynamite attacks.

When you purchase Triple Bundle Dynamite, Boomer throws one more powerful explosion that does not split off. However, if you continue down the line to An Accident Waiting to Happen, Boomer throws out barrels full of dynamite that split off after exploding again.

ATTACK 2

TROLL SMASH

COST: N/A
DAMAGE: Low
RANGE: Short
SPEED: Very Slow

Press the **Attack 2** button to smash the ground so hard that enemies all around you get knocked back.

UPGRADES

BASH SMASH

COST: 700 Gold
PREREQUISITE: None

Smash does increased damage and knocks enemies back further.

HAVOC SMASH

COST: 1,700 Gold
PREREQUISITE: Clobber Troll Path

Smash does even MORE increased damage.

STUPIFICATION SMASH

COST: 2,200 Gold
PREREQUISITE: Clobber Troll Path

Smash stuns enemies.

MEGATON CHARGED SUPER SMASH

COST: 3,000 Gold
PREREQUISITE: Clobber Troll Path, Havoc Smash

Hold **Attack 2** to charge up the smash attack, release to do MAXIMUM damage.

STRATEGY

Troll Smash does low damage, but has fantastic range and has a great knockback effect. This knockback is particularly useful for knocking enemies off ledges.

If you decide to take the Clobber Troll upgrade path, it allows you to dish out more damage and stun enemies, which is a huge benefit when you're being swarmed by enemies in difficult areas. The stun always hits, and delays enemies for about 3 seconds. It even works against armored enemies.

A fully charged Megaton Super Smash does about four times the damage of a regular smash attack. Unfortunately it does take a few seconds to charge, during which time Boomer is vulnerable to attack. This makes it a bit more situational than the uncharged attack.

ATTACK 3

TROLL BOMB

COST: 900 Gold
PREREQUISITE: None
DAMAGE: High
RANGE: Medium
SPEED: Very Slow

Press **Attack 3** to place a Troll Bomb.

UPGRADES

BOMBLASTIC

COST: 1,700 Gold
PREREQUISITE: Demolition Troll Path
Troll Bombs have bigger explosions and do increased damage.

TROLL BOMBS AWAY

COST: 2,200 Gold
PREREQUISITE: Demolition Troll Path
Boomer can have six Troll Bombs active at once.

STRATEGY

Laying a Troll Bomb down doesn't delay Boomer at all. You're free to keep dropping them as he's running around enemies. Upgrading Troll Bomb means Boomer can lay longer and deadlier trails of bombs. Enemies hit by these bombs are knocked back, and interrupted if they are readying an attack or ability.

When you get Troll Bombs Away on the Demolition Troll Path, this power really shines. You can leave long trails of devastating bombs without the need to stop and attack. You can focus on dodging instead of attacking.

DROBOT

"SEEK AND DESTROY!"

STATS

♥	29
⚡	43
🛡	24
◎	20
◉	25

UPGRADE PATHS

MASTER BLASTER
Further develop Drobot's Blaster attacks.

CLOCKWORK DRAGON
Further develop Drobot's Bladegear attacks.

SOUL GEM ABILITY

AFTERBURNERS ✓
COST: 4,000 Gold
PREREQUISITE: Thruster Flight

Fly faster and afterburners damage enemies.

STRATEGY

It's hard to hit the enemies directly with the Afterburners after you take off, but you can target them before you take off and inflict plenty of damage. This is a great way not only to escape a bad situation, but also to dish out some serious damage on the way out.

SPECIAL QUEST

FEED THE BURN:
DEFEAT 50 ENEMIES WITH AFTERBURNERS.

It's easiest to hit enemies with Afterburners when Drobot first takes off. Try it out in any of Brock's Arena Challenges that have Chompies (even the first level is fine). Once you get the timing and positioning down, you'll complete this quest in no time.

Drobot combines two of the most awesome things in Skylands: robots and dragons! This killer robo-dragon has blisteringly quick eye beams as a primary attack, and deadly buzzsaws as a secondary attack. Drobot is a bit difficult to master at first, but if you are patient and invest in either the Master Blaster or Clockwork Dragon upgrade powers, you will be rewarded with the ability to take out large groups of enemies in a hurry.

Drobot doesn't have any concentrated damage abilities, so he's not the best Skylander to use against bosses. However, he has the ability to cause massive chaos on the battlefield, flying in circles around his enemies while pelting them with eye lasers or grinding them up with buzzsaws.

PRIMARY ATTACKS

ATTACK 1

MEGA BLASTERS

COST: N/A
DAMAGE: Very Low
RANGE: Long
SPEED: Very Fast

Press **Attack 1** to shoot rapid fire laser blasts out of your eyes.

UPGRADES

AXON FOCUS CRYSTALS
COST: 900 Gold
PREREQUISITE: None
Eye Blasters do increased damage.

DENDRITE FOCUS CRYSTALS
COST: 1,700 Gold
PREREQUISITE: Master Blaster Path
Eye Blasters do even MORE increased damage.

ANTIMATTER CHARGES
COST: 2,200 Gold
PREREQUISITE: Master Blaster Path
Eye Blaster beams explode on contact, doing damage to enemies.

QUADRATIC BLASTERS
COST: 3,000 Gold
PREREQUISITE: Master Blaster Path
Press **Attack 1** to shoot lasers out of your wings as well.

STRATEGY

These eye blasts do low damage, but fire quickly and auto-target nearby enemies. This isn't a great power to use against bosses or large enemies, but it is effective against most normal enemies. Don't worry; the blasts you begin with bear little resemblance to the strength they reach along the fully upgraded Master Blaster Path. At that point, Drobot shoots four lasers at a time. Each shot explodes, resulting in minor damage to any surrounding enemies.

ATTACK 2

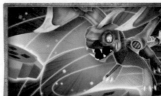

TACTICAL BLADEGEARS

COST: N/A
DAMAGE: Low
RANGE: Long
SPEED: Slow

Press the **Attack 2** button to deploy Bladegears that ricochet off of walls and pummel enemies.

UPGRADES

GALVANIZED BLADEGEARS
COST: 900 Gold
PREREQUISITE: None
Bladegears do increased damage.

DEPLETED URANIUM BLADEGEARS
COST: 1,700 Gold
PREREQUISITE: Clockwork Dragon Path
Bladegears do even MORE increased damage.

EXPLOSIVE BLADEGEARS
COST: 2,200 Gold
PREREQUISITE: Clockwork Dragon Path
Bladegears explode on contact, doing damage to nearby enemies.

TRI-SPREAD BLADEGEARS
COST: 3,000 Gold
PREREQUISITE: Clockwork Dragon Path
Press **Attack 2** to shoot three Bladegears at once.

STRATEGY

Initially, Bladegears may not seem like an impressive power. While the blades do bounce off walls to hit enemies, it's hard to aim them since they don't fire directly ahead of Drobot. However, the power improves with each upgrade purchased.

The most important one is the last step of the Clockwork Dragon Path: Tri-spread Bladegears. With Tri-spread Bladegears, Drobot fires three Bladegears, which make it much easier for you to aim them and hit enemies more often.

ATTACK 3

THRUSTER FLIGHT
COST: 500 Gold
PREREQUISITE: None
Press **Attack 3** to have Drobot fly. Drobot gets increased speed and armor while flying.

UPGRADES

HOVER MODE
COST: 1,200 Gold
PREREQUISITE: Thruster Flight
Hold **Attack 3** to have Drobot hover.

STRATEGY

Drobot's flight increases his speed and allows him to navigate through level hazards quickly. Unlike most other dragons, Drobot's flight gets some pretty enhancements. He has a hover mode, and if you save up enough for Afterburners, he gets a special attack while flying.

WOW POW POWER

SUPREME BLADEGEAR!
COST: 5,000 Gold
PREREQUISITE: None
Hold **Attack 2** to combine Bladegears into one controllable Super Bladegear!

STRATEGY

Instead of pressing **Attack 2** to fire Bladegears, hold it down and the three Bladegears are combined into giant Bladegear. This Bladegear is controllable with the Skylander movement analog stick. Run it back and forth over tough enemies to inflict major damage. This power scales with Bladegear upgrades, so upgrading the damage dealt by Bladegear also increases Supreme Bladegear's damage as well.

TRIGGER HAPPY

"NO GOLD, NO GLORY!"

STATS

♥	20
⚡	50
🛡	30
◎	50
◉	25

UPGRADE PATHS

GOLDEN FRENZY
Further develop Trigger Happy's Golden Gun attacks.

GOLDEN MONEY BAGS
Further develop Trigger Happy's throwing skills.

SOUL GEM ABILITY

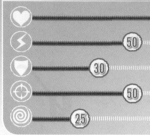

INFINITE AMMO

COST: 4,000 Gold

PREREQUISITE: Golden Machine Gun
The Golden Machine Gun (**Attack 3**) has unlimited ammo.

STRATEGY
Infinite Ammo is a great enhancement for the Golden Machine Gun. Unlimited ammo allows Trigger Happy to more easily hold strategic positions and mow down advancing enemies.

SPECIAL QUEST

HOLDING GOLD:
SAVE UP 50,000 GOLD.

This is one of the hardest quests any character has in the game. Not because it's difficult, but because it will take some time to collect 50,000 Gold. Keep it at and you'll get it eventually.

Trigger Happy is a straightforward ranged expert, who has three excellent ranged attacks. His primary attack, Golden Pistols, is a low damage power, but it can be upgraded and transformed into a chargeable boss-killing attack.

You could also focus on Trigger Happy's lobbing attacks. Trigger Happy throws giant objects at his enemies at medium range. Whichever path you choose, Trigger Happy has a great mini-gun attack that can be improved via his Soul Gem and Wow Pow upgrades.

PRIMARY ATTACKS

ATTACK 1

GOLDEN PISTOLS

COST: N/A
DAMAGE: Very Low
RANGE: Long
SPEED: Fast

Press the **Attack 1** button to shoot rapidfire coins out of both golden guns.

UPGRADES

GOLDEN SUPER CHARGE

COST: 500 Gold
PREREQUISITE: None

Hold the **Attack 1** button to charge up your Golden Gun, release to fire a bullet that does extra damage.

GOLDEN MEGA CHARGE

COST: 900 Gold
PREREQUISITE: Golden Super Charge

Charge up your Golden Gun longer to do even MORE damage.

HAPPINESS IS A GOLDEN GUN

COST: 1,700 Gold
PREREQUISITE: Golden Frenzy Path

Golden Gun does increased damage.

BOUNCING BULLETS

COST: 2,200 Gold
PREREQUISITE: Golden Frenzy Path

Golden Gun's bullets bounce off walls.

GOLDEN YAMATO BLAST

COST: 3,000 Gold
PREREQUISITE: Happiness is a Golden Gun

Charge up your Golden Gun even longer to do MAXIMUM damage.

STRATEGY

Golden Gun starts off as a weak, long-range attack. It may even seem pointless since he has great lob and mini-gun attacks. The trick to this power is the charge upgrades. Golden Mega Charge is pretty good, but Golden Yamato Blast is amazing. Charge the attack for about 5 seconds to launch a beam that inflicts over 150 damage to everything in its path. The amount of time required for charging is the major deterrent to this power, and why you should stick to the Golden Money Bags path.

WOW POW POWER

MEGABLAST!

COST: 5,000 Gold
PREREQUISITE: Golden Machine Gun

While using the mini-gun, press **Attack 1** for a super blast.

STRATEGY

This is a pretty cool add-on to the Golden Machine Gun. While firing, just tap **Attack 1** to send out a wide blast that hurts all enemies within range. The attack does about three times the damage of the normal mini-gun and affects an area instead of a single target.

ATTACK 2

LOB GOLDEN SAFE

COST: N/A
DAMAGE: High
RANGE: Medium
SPEED: Slow

Press the **Attack 2** button to lob golden safes at your enemies.

UPGRADES

POT O'GOLD

COST: 700 Gold
PREREQUISITE: None

Press the **Attack 2** button to throw a Pot of Gold which does increased damage.

JUST THROWING MONEY AWAY

COST: 1,700 Gold
PREREQUISITE: Golden Money Bags Path

Attack 2 has longer range.

COINSPLOSION

COST: 2,200 Gold
PREREQUISITE: Golden Money Bags Path

Attack 2 explodes in a shower of damaging coins.

HEADS OR TAILS

COST: 3,000 Gold
PREREQUISITE: Golden Money Bags Path

Attack 2 tosses a coin that does extra damage — if it lands on heads, it does even MORE damage.

STRATEGY

Lob Golden Safe is a fantastic medium-range area-of-effect blast. Not only is it high damage and easy to aim, but it also doesn't slow down Trigger Happy at all, which keeps him out of trouble. Heads or Tails, the last upgrade in the Golden Money Path, is the highlight of this power. Not only does the initial attack do a ton of damage, but also if the coin lands heads, it becomes a mine, blasting off as soon as an enemy approaches.

ATTACK 3

GOLDEN MACHINE GUN

COST: 1,200 Gold
PREREQUISITE: None
DAMAGE: Low
RANGE: Medium
SPEED: Extremely Fast

Hold **Attack 3** to activate Golden Machine Gun.

STRATEGY

Setting up the Golden Machine Gun takes a second, but the damage output is spectacular and Trigger Happy can quickly adjust the aim to meet attacking enemies. The drawback to this power is that it forces Trigger Happy to remain stationary. Don't start this up while surrounded by enemies.

IMPROVING YOUR SKYLANDERS

As a Portal Master, one of your primary tasks is improving your Skylanders so they can stand up to their enemies throughout Skylands. This chapter covers the many facets and methods of improving and customizing your Skylanders.

Leveling

Whenever you defeat an enemy, they leave behind tiny XP orbs. When your Skylanders absorb these orbs, they gain experience and get closer to leveling up. You can see how close your Skylander is to leveling up by examining the XP Bar just below their health.

Stats

Each Skylander has five Stats: Max Health, Speed, Armor, Critical Hit, and Elemental Power. Max Health is the only stat that increases when you level up your Skylander. Completing Cali's Heroic Challenges awards a permanent boost to a Skylander's stat, while the stat boost conveyed by wearing a hat lasts only as long as your Skylander wears the hat.

MAX HEALTH

This is your Skylander's most important statistic. Whenever their health reaches zero, they are knocked out and you must place another Skylander on the portal.

SPEED

This is how fast your Skylander can move around.

ARMOR

Whenever a Skylander is hit by an enemy attack, it has a chance to be completely deflected by their armor. This stat reflects that chance. For every six points of armor your Skylander has, they have a 1% chance of deflecting an enemy attack. So, a Skylander with 90 Armor has a 15% chance to deflect an attack.

CRITICAL HIT

This stat determines the chance a Skylander will score a Critical Hit or "crit." A crit scores 150% regular damage of an attack. For every five points in Critical Hit, the chance to score a crit increases by 1%. So a Skylander with 50 Critical Hit has a 10% chance of scoring a crit.

ELEMENTAL POWER

Throughout the Skylands, certain zones have favored elements. If you are using a Skylander of that element in one of these zones, they get bonus damage based on how high their Elemental Power is. Each point adds 1% to the bonus damage, so a Skylander with 100 Elemental Power will get 100% bonus damage in their favored zone.

Powers & Upgrades

Each Skylander starts out with two Powers. For more details on what powers your Skylanders start out with, check out the chapter entitled The Skylanders. In addition to these two basic powers, each Skylander can also unlock a third power, but it will cost some gold.

The extra Power and Power Upgrades are all purchased from Persephone, who is found on Flynn's ship the Dread Yacht after Chapter 2.

UPGRADE PATHS

Each Skylander must also choose a Path. This Path is a specialty the Skylander takes in choosing to develop one power over another. Most Skylanders must permanently commit to one path once they have unlocked their first four power upgrades.

The exceptions to this rule are the new Series 2 figures that have been released for *Skylanders Giants*. These Skylanders may switch paths after committing to one.

SOUL GEM POWERS

There are 16 new Skylanders released with *Skylanders Giants*, each of these characters's Soul Gem are found in one of the 16 Chapters of the game. The walkthrough contains more information on where to find each Soul Gem, or check out The Skylanders section of the guide.

Skylanders from the previous game can still purchase their Soul Gem Power in *Skylanders Giants*, but they don't need to find the Soul Gem, they can just purchase the ability outright from Persephone.

WOW-POW POWERS

Series 2 figures have new Wow-Pow powers that cost a ton of gold, but usually significantly improve an existing power. For more details on Series 2 Wow Pows check out the Skylanders' individual chapters.

Hats

Each Skylander can wear one magic hat. Hats are available for purchase from Auric's store, and found throughout Skylands. Most of the best Hats are hidden behind Elemental Gates.

Hats provide bonuses to your stats, and each hat confers a unique bonus. Use Hats to supplement your Skylander's weaker Stats. For instance, if your Skylander has low armor, look for a hat that provides additional armor! You can change your Skylander's Hat at any time via the Skylanders menu. Once you find a Hat, you can put it on as many Skylanders as you like.

Quests

In *Skylanders Giants*, all Skylanders have 9 Quests you can choose to complete. You can check your Skylander's progress on any of these quests at any time by entering the Skylander menu and selecting Quests. Completing these quests improves their rank. Improving a Skylander's rank gives them a medal next to their name and also unlocks special hats that confer bonuses to three stats. Normal hats only give two stats.

Every Skylander has one unique quest, six universal quests, and two elemental quests.

Bronze Rank	Complete 3 Quests
Silver Rank	Complete 6 Quests
Gold Rank	Complete 9 Quests

UNIQUE QUESTS

Each Skylander has their own unique quest. For more information on how to tackle that quest, check out that Skylander's page in The Skylanders section of the guide.

UNIVERSAL QUESTS

Monster Masher: Defeat 1,000 enemies

Defeating 1,000 enemies will take a while. Even if you use the same Skylander through the entire adventure, you may not quite reach this target. A good way to work torwards completing this quest is to play Brock's Arena Challenges.

Battle Champ: Win 10 PvP matches

PvP stands for "Player Versus Player." Work on this quest by battling your friends in the game's Battle Mode. You can also unlock this by entering Battle Mode and fighting your own Skylanders!

Chow Hound: Eat 50 pieces of food

Food is available throughout the Skylands. It can drop randomly from conquered foes, or appear floating in a level. Finding 50 isn't too hard, and will happen naturally as you progress through the game.

Heroic Challenger: Complete a challenge level without taking any damage.

Each Skylander has their own challenge level, but you can also purchase a few extra from Auric's store. Only Series 2 Skylanders, new Skylanders, and Giant Skylanders have Heroic Challenges in *Skylanders Giants*. This quest can be very easy, or very hard depending on which Heroic Challenges you've unlocked. Some challenges like Wrecking Ball's "Jump For It!" do not even require you to fight enemies or face level hazards.

Arena Artist: Complete an arena without taking any damage.

Arena Challenges are the special missions assigned by Brock on Flynn's ship. The best challenge to complete this on is the last contest in Brock's Rump Roaster Ruckus. That arena challenge requires you not take any damage to win, so it works well with this quest.

Elementalist: Cause 7,500 elemental bonus damage.

Your Skylander gets elemental bonus damage when they are in a zone that matches their element. The higher the Skylander's Elemental score, the higher their Elemental damage will go on each hit.

AIR QUESTS

From Above: Defeat 25 enemies while falling.

The best way to complete this quest is to attack enemies while bouncing on a bounce pad. If you defeat the enemy while falling from the bounce pad, you get credit for this quest!

Skylooter: Collect 500 gold in mid-air

If your Skylander has flying, this quest is relatively simple. Just collect gold while using the flying ability. The only Air Skylander that doesn't have flying is Lightning Rod. To complete the quest with him, you must collect Gold via bounce pads or when falling from the edges of cliffs.

LIFE QUESTS

Fully Stocked: Defeat 250 enemies while at full health.

That's a large number of enemies, but you'll make good progress on this quest just by playing through the game's adventure. Of course, avoiding getting hit helps.

Melon Maestro: Hit targets 200 times while in a turret challenge.

There are several turret sequences in the game. Use Life Skylanders to rack up points towards this quest. You can also play the turret mini-game in the Gun Deck on Flynn's ship to work towards this quest. The best spot to work on this is Chapter 10.

☠ UNDEAD QUESTS

Bossed Around: Let yourself be defeated by bosses three times.

This is a unique quest, your Skylander must fall in combat against a boss to get credit for this! Not every chapter has a boss, the big ones are in Chapters 7, 11 & 16.

By a Thread: Defeat an evil Undead Skylander

This is a unique quest, your Skylander has to defeat an evil Undead Skylander to get credit for this! Not every chapter has an Evil Undead Skyander, but a dark Chop Chop ambushes you in Chapter 14.

⛰ EARTH QUESTS

Wrecker: Destroy 20 brick walls.

Brick walls can include regular walls that are punchable, or tougher brick walls that require a Giant or bomb to smash. These are spread out throughout the game. While playing through, switch to your Earth Skylander whenever you see one.

Stonesmith: Defeat 25 enemies with push blocks.

Push blocks are located in every chapter throughout the game. If you push one onto an enemy, they are instantly defeated. It can be tricky to find enemies near push blocks, but if you see a good opportunity, switch in your Earth Skylander.

🔥 FIRE QUESTS

Bombadier: Defeat 30 enemies with bombs.

Almost every level has a bomb puzzle sequence that requires you to throw a bomb to blow up a wall or mission objective. These bombs can also be used to destroy other enemies, those knockouts count towards this quest. You can also get bombs from the enemies called Bag O' Booms, which start to appear in the latter half of the game.

Steamer: Defeat an evil water minion.

There are two chapter with evil water minions: Chapter 8 & Chapter 13, for more information on where these water minions are, check the ambush sections in those two Chapters.

💧 WATER QUESTS

Extinguisher: Defeat an evil fire minion.

There are two chapters with evil fire minions: Chapter 5 & Chapter 13, for more information on where these fire minions are, check the ambush sections in those two chapters.

Waterfall: Knock 25 enemies off the edge of the world

To pursue this quest, you need to find your Skylander's best knockback power. For instance, Gill Grunt's Power Hose power is a great knockback ability. A good level to quickly score this is quest is Brock's Rump Roaster Ruckus, the outer area of that arena counts towards this quest.

✦ MAGIC QUESTS

Puzzle Power: Defeat 25 enemies with light puzzle beams.

Many chapters have light puzzle beams. These beams can be turned on enemies and deal serious damage. The best chapter to work on this quest is Chapter 14: Autogyro Adventure. There are several light puzzles placed near enemies.

Warp Whomper: Defeat 1 enemy within 10 seconds of using a teleporter.

This is one of the easiest quests. You will probably get this accidently while playing through the game. Simply use any teleporter near enemies, then defeat an enemy within 10 seconds to earn the quest.

⚙ TECH QUESTS

Magic Isn't Might: Defeat 50 elemental mages.

"Elemental mage" refers to the enemy Life Spell Punks. There are plenty of punks scattered throughout the various challenges, and you can also find them on several chapters during the playthrough.

Cracker: Unlock 25 locked doors with keys.

Almost every chapter has a section that requires you to place keys in a lock to unlock a gate. Switch to your Tech Skylander whenever you must unlock a gate to work on this quest. There are also several Heroic Challenges that involve finding keys. Ignitor's Heroic Challenge is a good example, it awards several points towards this quest on each playthrough.

MASTERING THE PORTAL

If you own the Skylander, make sure it's part of your collection. To view your collection at any time, pause the game and select Collections. If one of your Skylanders is missing from your *Skylanders Giants* collection, enter the Skylanders menu and select the Manage option. Why bother? Because you earn Accolades based on the number and types of Skylanders in your collection.

ACCOLADES

There are two types of Accolades: Ownership Accolades, which are related to your collection of Skylanders, and Achievement Accolades, which are related to your accomplishments in the game. Ownership Accolades award with bonus XP that makes it much easier to level up your characters. Many Accolades refer to "Orange Base" Skylanders. These are Giant Skylanders, the eight new Skylanders, and Series 2 Skylanders that were specially released for *Skylanders Giants*. There are 54 total Orange Base Skylanders.

OWNERSHIP ACCOLADES

CAPTAIN		Add any non-starter pack Skylander to your collection.
FAITHFUL TRIO		Add Spyro, Trigger Happy, and Gill Grunt to your collection (can be Series 1 versions of the characters).
AMBASSADOR		Add at least one Orange Base Skylander of each elemental type to your collection.
GIGANTIC HERO		Add all 8 Giant Skylanders to your collection.
SERGEANT MAJOR		Add 8 Orange Base Skylanders to your collection.
COLONEL		Add 12 Orange Base Skylanders to your collection.
COMMANDER		Add 16 Orange Base Skylanders to your collection.
GENERAL		Add 24 Orange Base Skylanders to your collection.
FIELD MARSHAL		Add 32 Orange Base Skylanders to your collection.
MASTER OF SKYLANDS		Add 40 Orange Base Skylanders to your collection.

ACHIEVEMENT ACCOLADES

TO THE MAX		Level up any Skylander to Level 15.
HINT SCHOLAR		Collect 10 Story Scrolls.
CHIEF SCHOLAR		Collect all 16 Story Scrolls.
SEEKER ADEPT		Collect 10 Legendary Ship Parts.
TREASURE HUNTER		Collect all 16 Legendary Ship Parts.
SOUL WARDEN		Collect 16 Soul Gems.
FASHION ELITE		Collect 10 Hats.
WARDROBE SAINT		Collect 85 Hats.
ELITE AGENT		Complete 20 Heroic Challenges with one Skylander.
GREAT GLADIATOR		Complete all 21 Arena Challenges.
SAVIOR OF SKYLANDS		Complete the Story mode by recovering the Iron Fist of Arkus and defeating Kaos on any difficulty.
ULTIMATE COMPLETIONIST		Earn 3 stars on all Story mode Chapters.
GRAND ADMIRAL		Earn all Portal Master accolades.

ADVENTURE PACKS

The four Adventure Packs available for *Skylanders Spyro's Adventure* also work in *Skylanders Giants*. Putting one of these Adventure Pack toys on the Portal unlocks the level for play. Additionally, you can use the Adventure Packs during your regular play to execute a special attack. When you put the Pack on the Portal, a huge effect goes out and destroys every normal enemy on the screen. This can be a fantastic help on the Arena Challenges!

ADVENTURE ITEMS

When you purchased an Adventure Pack it also came with a Skylander and two Adventure Items. In total, there are eight Adventure Items that can be used in the game. These are special items that can help your Skylanders by healing them, inflicting damage on your enemies, or causing other special effects.

Most Adventure Items have a timer. The timer resets whenever you start a new level. So if you use up your Healing Potion, you can't use it again until you start a new level or chapter in the game.

ANVIL RAIN

When you put this item on the Portal, anvils fall from the sky randomly hitting enemies in the area. Enemies take about 12 damage with each hit. The anvils can hit your Skylander too, knocking them back, but does not damage them

TIME TWIST HOURGLASS

This Hourglass slows down time, putting the game into slow motion for the duration of the spell. The catch is, your Skylander doesn't slow down!

HIDDEN TREASURE

When you use Hidden Treasure on a normal game Chapter or one of the Adventure Pack levels, a bonus treasure chest is randomly generated. Use the radar at the bottom of the screen to help locate the chest.

SPARX THE DRAGONFLY

Sparx is a Skylander friend who buzzes around the area blasting enemies with his insect breath. He can only stay around for about a minute, but can really help in tough fights. Sparx has a rapid-fire shot that does about 10 damage per hit.

SKY-IRON SHIELD

This Adventure Item causes two rotating shields to protect your Skylander for its duration. This item doesn't make your Skylander invulnerable, but it does make them a lot tougher.

GHOST PIRATE SWORDS

This Adventure Item spawns in two swords that float around the screen attacking the Skylander's foes. These swords only hit for about 4 damage, but there are two of them, and they rapidly attack.

WINGED BOOTS

With this Adventure Item, your Skylander can run much faster than normal. This item is tremendously helpful for hitting time dares and passing lethal level hazards.

HEALING ELIXIR

This awesome item quickly heals your Skylanders while they wander around. Your Skylanders regain 30 health every second. Be forewarned, Healing Elixir has a short duration!

LEVEL MASTERY & COLLECTIBLES

It's impossible to get everything in one playthrough of *Skylanders Giants*. You must play through the adventure many times to see everything and achieve every accomplishment. This chapter summarizes the extra stuff you can find and do throughout your adventure.

Cooperative Play

If you have some friends or family that love the game as much as you do, invite them to bring their Skylanders over so you can adventure together. To play co-op, simply drop an extra Skylander onto the portal, and your friend can adventure with you!

How to Three Star a Level

There are three stars to earn for each Chapter in the Adventure: Story Goals, Dares, and Collections.

STORY GOALS STAR

The first star is automatically earned when you complete the level; you get it for finishing all story goals.

DARES STAR

To earn the Dares star you need to complete the following:

- Finish the chapter in under the par time.
- Defeat the number of enemies given in the enemy goal.
- Find all the level's areas.
- Finish the level without having any Skylanders get knocked out.

It's not possible to complete the level in under par time and get all of the chapter's collectibles and find all areas. To complete in the par time, you need to rush for the end of the level in the most direct path, often avoiding enemies and side areas when possible.

If you reach a boss and haven't yet met the Enemy Goal, you can focus on defeating the boss' minions until you reach the goal.

All Areas are listed and detailed in the Chapter walkthroughs. If you find yourself missing an area, check the walkthrough for details.

COLLECTIONS STAR

This star requires that you find all secret hidden collectibles on a level. This guide's walkthrough has details on how to find every collectible, so earning this star should be no trouble for you!

Skystones

During Chapter Four, you learn how to play the hottest game in Skylands: Skystones. Skystones is a strategy game where you and your opponent take turns placing special stones on the board.

There are nine squares on the board. If you place a Skystone adjacent to an opponent's Skystone, then you have a chance to capture their stone. To do so, you need to have more arrows pointing in the direction of the tile than they have pointing out. When you capture a tile, it changes to your color and counts towards your score. Tiles can be captured multiple times. Whoever has the most tiles at the end of the game wins!

You collect Skystones to improve your deck by defeating Skystones players in the chapters found throughout the world. A good source of extra Skystones for your deck is Captain Dreadbeard, who hangs out in the Game Room on Flynn's ship.

If you have extra Gold, you can also purchase Skystones from Auric's stores. In fact, some of the best Skystones can only be purchased from Auric.

Collectibles

There are a ton of collectibles in *Skylanders Giants*. Each chapter contains at least 11 collectibles to find. Not all collectibles are hidden in hard-to-find places, but most of them are. Here's an explanation of each type of collectible and what it does.

TREASURE CHESTS

Treasure Chests are the most common collectible; each chapter has four. When you shake open a chest, treasure bursts out in all directions. The higher the chapter you are on, the more treasure you are rewarded.

STORY SCROLLS

These ancient scrolls contain some background on the Skylands. They can also contain hints as to the location of rare collectibles like Luck-O-Tron Wheels.

SOUL GEMS

Soul Gems unlock powers for Skylanders. Each chapter contains one new Soul Gem for each of the new Skylanders (eight regular Skylanders, and eight Giant Skylanders).

Getting a Soul Gem bestows the ability to purchase a power, but you still need to come up with the hefty amount of Gold to unlock it for your Skylanders.

LEGENDARY TREASURE

Each level contains one Legendary Treasure. These treasures allow you to customize the appearance of Flynn's Ship, the Dread-Yacht.

WINGED SAPPHIRES

Each level contains a Winged Sapphire. These floating gem butterflies give you a 2% discount in Persephone's power upgrade shop. Unfortunately, they do not provide a discount in Auric's shop. In addition to the 16 found in the story, there are also four Winged Sapphires to be found on Flynn's ship between levels.

HATS

Each chapter contains at least two magic hats to be found. These are normally found behind Elemental Gates, and often require a puzzle to be solved to unlock.

LUCK-O-TRON WHEELS

The trickiest collectible to find are the Luck-O-Tron Wheels. Each level contains one Luck-O-Tron that is usually well-hidden and requires a special action to uncover. For more details on how the Luck-O-Tron Wheels work, check out the chapter on Flynn's Ship.

Auric's Store

After the first chapter, you can find Auric on each level. His main shop is on Flynn's ship, but his best items are often only found in a specific chapter's store.

SINGLE USE ITEMS

These single use items all provide a special benefit. These items can be expensive, and you should wait until you buy all of your Skylander's Powers before you invest in any of these one use power-ups.

FAIRY DUST

COST: 50 Gold
AVAILABILITY: Any Mid-Level Auric Store

This power-up allows you to summon the Upgrade Fairy to purchase any powers you have enough Gold for. Unless you're overloaded with Gold, wait until the end of the level since upgrading your Skylander on Flynn's ship doesn't cost anything extra. Additionally, this purchase only allows you to upgrade the currently active Skylanders. The rest of your crew must wait until you get back to Flynn's ship.

LOCK PUZZLE KEY

COST: 500 Gold
AVAILABILITY: Any Store

Use these keys to bypass one touch lock puzzles you run into on your adventures. To use the key, pause the game on a puzzle, and select the "Use Key" option.

REGENERATION POWER UP

COST: 200 – 650 Gold
AVAILABILITY: Chapter 3, 5, 9, 10, 11, 14 & 16 Stores

Once you purchase this power-up, an 80 second timer starts at the bottom of your screen. While this timer is up, the Skylanders you have in play will be healed for 10 health every few seconds. If you have some injured Skylanders and some extra money, this is a good way to heal them up for the fights in the latter part of the level.

INVINCIBILITY POWER UP

COST: 250 Gold
AVAILABILITY: Chapters 4, 7, & 15 Stores

This power-up gives your Skylanders 60 seconds of complete invulnerability. Since the timer starts as soon as you buy it in Auric's shop, save it up for a big fight in the immediate future before spending hard earned Gold on this power-up!

SKYSTONE CHEAT

COST: 500 Gold
AVAILABILITY: Chapters 5, 7, 9, 12, 13, & 15 Stores

This item allows you to skip any Skystone battle. If you use it, the game treats you exactly the same way as if you won the battle. This means you will get any Skystones or Gold you would normally receive from the battle. To use the cheat, pause the game while in the middle of the Skystone battle and select the Skystone Cheat option.

DAMAGE POWER UP

COST: 250-350 Gold
AVAILABILITY: Chapter 12 Store

This power-up doubles your Skylander's damage for 90 seconds. The power-up activates immediately, so only consider purchasing this right before heading into a big battle.

CHARMS

Charms are a permanent bonus that benefits all your Skylanders. These are great purchases if you have some extra coin, and in some cases, it's worth going out of your way to earn the funds to purchase these charms. They can help you out of tough and annoying situations.

ELEMENTAL ELIXIR CHARM

COST: 400 Gold
AVAILABILITY: Chapter 3 Store

When you enter an Elemental Gate area, the area slowly heals your Skylander. With this charm, the amount of healing in these areas is improved.

BRAWNY BARBELL CHARM

COST: 900 Gold
AVAILABILITY: Flynn's Ship after Chapter 5

This charm allows all of your Giant Skylanders to lift boulders much more quickly. Without the Charm, it takes several button presses for a Giant to lift a boulder. With the Charm, it only takes one or two presses.

SUDSY SOAP CHARM

COST: 5,000 Gold
AVAILABILITY: Chapter 8 Store

This Charm helps Skylanders battle enemy Trolls.

UNERRING ARROW CHARM

COST: 25,000 Gold
AVAILABILITY: Chapter 11 Store

A charm that helps Skylanders battle large enemies.

ROBOT REPELLANT CHARM

COST: 8,000 Gold
AVAILABILITY: Chapter 14 Store

This Charm helps Skylanders battle enemy robots.

HATS

While there are plenty of hats found throughout the levels of Skylands, some can only be purchased from Auric.

COWBOY HAT

COST: 125 Gold
+2 CRITICAL HIT
+2 ARMOR
AVAILABILITY: Chapter 2 Store

PLUNGER HEAD

COST: 125 Gold
+2 CRITICAL HIT
+2 ELEMENTAL POWER
AVAILABILITY: Chapter 2 Store

KUFI HAT

COST: 125 Gold
+2 CRITICAL HIT
+2 ELEMENTAL POWER
AVAILABILITY: Chapter 2 Store

BOWLER HAT

COST: 120 Gold
+2 CRITICAL HIT
+2 ARMOR
AVAILABILITY: Flynn's Ship after Chapter 2

BALLOON HAT

COST: 120 Gold
+2 CRITICAL HIT
+2 ARMOR
AVAILABILITY: Flynn's Ship after Chapter 2

HAPPY BIRTHDAY!

COST: 120 Gold
+2 CRITICAL HIT
+2 ARMOR
AVAILABILITY: Flynn's Ship after Chapter 2

TOP HAT

COST: 450 Gold
+5 CRITICAL HIT
+5 ARMOR
AVAILABILITY: Chapter 5 Store

BIRTHDAY HAT

COST: 250 Gold
+2 CRITICAL HIT
+1 SPEED
AVAILABILITY: Chapter 3 Store

SPY GEAR

COST: 500 Gold
+5 CRITICAL HIT
+2 SPEED
AVAILABILITY: Chapter 6 Store

ELF HAT

COST: 250 Gold
+2 SPEED
+5 ELEMENTAL POWER
AVAILABILITY: Chapter 3 Store

TROPICAL TURBAN

COST: 550 Gold
+2 SPEED
+5 ELEMENTAL POWER
AVAILABILITY: Chapter 6 Store

FANCY HAT

COST: 250 Gold
+2 ARMOR
+1 SPEED
AVAILABILITY: Chapter 3 Store

ROCKER HAIR

COST: 600 Gold
+7 CRITICAL HIT
+3 SPEED
AVAILABILITY: Chapter 7 Store

VIKING HELMET

COST: 350 Gold
+5 CRITICAL HIT
AVAILABILITY: Chapter 4 Store

EYE HAT

COST: 600 Gold
+5 CRITICAL HIT
+5 ELEMENTAL POWER
AVAILABILITY: Chapter 7 Store

FEZ

COST: 320 Gold
+5 ELEMENTAL POWER
AVAILABILITY: Chapter 4 Store

MOOSE HAT

COST: 850 Gold
+5 ARMOR
+2 SPEED
AVAILABILITY: Chapter 8 Store

PROPELLER CAP

COST: 400 Gold
+3 SPEED
AVAILABILITY: Chapter 5 Store

TROJAN HELMET

COST: 850 Gold
+10 ARMOR
AVAILABILITY: Chapter 8 Store

DANCER HAT

COST: 900 Gold
+6 SPEED
AVAILABILITY: Chapter 9 Store

GENERAL'S HAT

COST: 1,000 Gold
+7 CRITICAL HIT
+7 ELEMENTAL POWER
AVAILABILITY: Chapter 10 Store

SPIKED HAT

COST: 1,000 Gold
+7 CRITICAL HIT
+7 ARMOR
AVAILABILITY: Chapter 10 Store

COMBAT HAT

COST: 1,000 Gold
+15 ELEMENTAL POWER
AVAILABILITY: Chapter 11 Store

BERET

COST: 1,000 Gold
+15 CRITICAL HIT
AVAILABILITY: Chapter 11 Store

DANGLING CARROT HAT

COST: 1,300 Gold
+4 SPEED
+10 ELEMENTAL POWER
AVAILABILITY: Chapter 12 Store

ROCKET HAT

COST: 1,100 Gold
+6 SPEED
AVAILABILITY: Chapter 12 Store

CROWN OF LIGHT

COST: 1,200 Gold
+15 ARMOR
AVAILABILITY: Chapter 13 Store

TIKI HAT

COST: 800 Gold
+10 ELEMENTAL POWER
AVAILABILITY: Chapter 13 Store

ANVIL HAT

COST: 1,200 Gold
+5 ARMOR
AVAILABILITY: Chapter 14 Store

NAPOLEON HAT

COST: 1,000 Gold
+5 ARMOR
+5 ELEMENTAL POWER
AVAILABILITY: Chapter 15 Store

WABBIT EARS

COST: 1,200 Gold
+12 ARMOR
+5 SPEED
AVAILABILITY: Chapter 15 Store

CAESAR HAT

COST: 1,800 Gold
+20 ELEMENTAL POWER
AVAILABILITY: Chapter 16 Store

UNICORN HAT

COST: 2,500 Gold
+12 CRITICAL HIT
+12 ARMOR
AVAILABILITY: Chapter 16 Store

WIZARD HAT

COST: 2,000 Gold
+25 ELEMENTAL POWER
AVAILABILITY: Chapter 16 Store

HEROIC CHALLENGES

These super Heroic Challenges can be used to power-up any of your Skylanders with a special trait. Talk to Cali to start the challenge after you've unlocked it.

FLIP THE SCRIPT

DESCRIPTION: A Heroic Challenge that grants extra Speed.
COST: 1,000 Gold
AVAILABILITY: Flynn's Ship after Chapter 4

CHARM HUNT

DESCRIPTION: A Heroic Challenge that grants extra Armor.
COST: 3,000 Gold
AVAILABILITY: Chapter 4 Store

THIS BOMB'S FOR YOU

DESCRIPTION: A Heroic Challenge that grants extra Critical Hit.
COST: 10,000 Gold
AVAILABILITY: Chapter 8 Store

CHOMPY CHOMP-DOWN

DESCRIPTION: A Heroic Challenge that grants extra Elemental Power.
COST: 5,000 Gold
AVAILABILITY: Chapter 10 Store

BATTLE MODE ARENAS

These are arenas for Battle Mode. They are the four Arenas from *Skylanders Spyro's Adventure*.

CYCLOPS SQUARE

COST: 1,000 Gold
AVAILABILITY: Flynn's Ship after Chapter 1

AQUEDUCT

COST: 2,500 Gold
AVAILABILITY: Chapter 6 Store

MUSHROOM GROVE

COST: 2,000 Gold
AVAILABILITY: Chapter 9 Store

TROLL FACTORY

COST: 3,000 Gold
AVAILABILITY: Chapter 12 Store

LUCK-O-TRON BULBS

These bulbs allow you to keep one more Luck-O-Tron gear active on the Luck-O-Tron on Flynn's Ship. Gears can be found on the levels, and provide bonuses to treasure and health, along with other awesome benefits. The Bulbs vary on price based on which level you purchase them.

LUCK-O-TRON BULB #2

COST: 200 Gold
AVAILABILITY: Flynn's Ship after Chapter 2

LUCK-O-TRON BULB #3

COST: 2,500 Gold
AVAILABILITY: Chapter 7 Store

LUCK-O-TRON BULB #4

COST: 5,000 Gold
AVAILABILITY: Chapter 12 Store

FLYNN'S SHIP

Things to Do

Flynn's Ship is your base and you visit it between Chapters of the adventure. This wondrous vessel is full of activities and includes many exciting extras for you to explore and uncover.

Luck-O-Tron Machine

Look for the Luck-O-Tron machine in Cali's room (the door near Cali). During the adventure, you obtain special Luck-O-Tron wheels. These wheels provide bonuses to your Skylanders. There are four kinds of Luck-O-Tron Wheels: Experience, Health, Power, and Wealth. Each type of Wheel provides bonus rewards or a boost to your Skylander's abilities.

There is room for four bulbs on the Luck-O-Tron. The first one is free, but the other three must be purchased from Auric's store. For more information on their locations, please refer to the Collectibles chapter.

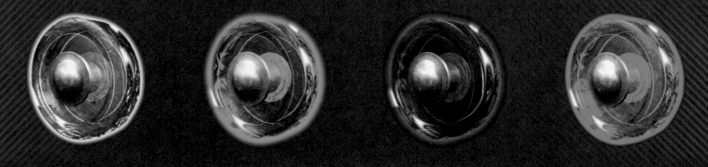

Visiagram

The Visiagram is located in Flynn's room—the door to the right of Cali's room on the main deck. The Visiagram allows you to customize the Dread-Yacht's appearance based on the Legendary Treasures you have collected throughout the main game's adventure. For more details on where these Legendary Treasures are hidden, check out the walkthrough.

Persephone's Cabin

Whenever you want to purchase upgrades for your Skylanders, head over to Persephone's cabin. To get a discount on Persephone's upgrades, find some **Winged Sapphires**. Each one gets you a 2% discount. There are 20 to find, for a total discount of 40%! For more information on Winged Sapphire locations, check the walkthrough.

LOOK FOR TREASURE

There are a few different places you can find Treasure during every visit to Flynn's ship. In the main starting area, look for a vibrating panel or pressure valve. If you see one, hit it with your Skylander's attacks to blow it open and score a free gem!

Between every level, you should visit the Crane Deck. It is located at the absolute rear of the ship. It's the door just above the Game Room where Dreadbeard and Auric hang out. There will almost always be at least one gem out there for you to collect. After completing the game, there will be a 5,500 Gold Treasure on the Crane Deck. It appears once per game.

GAME ROOM ELEMENTAL TREASURE

Right next to Auric's shop are the doors to secret elemental treasure! You can access these doors by switching through the Skylanders to clear all security doors and score the prize.

To get all the treasure, you do need one Skylander of each of the eight element types. The amount of treasure you receive is between 200 and 1,000 Gold after each level. This can be instrumental in getting enough Gold to buy some of the more expensive Skylander powers.

Skystones

After Chapter 4, you unlock the game known as Skystones by defeating Dreadbeard in the Pirate Carnival. Dreadbeard wants a rematch, so he comes to the ship to battle you some more in Skystones. You can play Dreadbeard as many times as you like. Each time you win, you receive a random reward.

SKYSTONE CHALLENGER: DREADBEARD

DREADBEARD'S SKYSTONE DECK	
Spiderlings 1	
Mace Major 2	
Drow Lance Master 2	
Mohawk Cyclops 3	
Drow Archer 2	

The random rewards for defeating Dreadbeard include 75–350 Gold and the following Skystones.

Jawbreaker 1	Mohawk Cyclops 1	Inhuman Shield 2
Jawbreaker 2	Mohawk Cyclops 2	Mace Major 3
Arkeyan Jouster 2	Frigid Chompy 1	Blaster Troll 3
Drow Archer 3	En Fuego Chompy 2	Spiderlings 1
D. Riveter 1	Chompy 2	Spiderlings 2
D. Riveter 2	Chompy 3	Spiderlings 3

Gun Deck Mini-Game

The Gun Deck is unlocked after Chapter 7. Look for it beneath the ship under the red hatch, on the left of the starting point. There are a variety of shooting mini-games on the deck that award small amounts of Gold. These games include shooting sheep, shooting missiles, shooting down Arkeyan Ships, and shooting barrels. You can use Adventure Pack items in these shooting mini-games to make them easier. (Try the Hour Glass!)

Brock's Arena Challenges

Brock has a set of challenges available on the main deck of Flynn's Ship. The challenges becomes available after you beat him in Chapter 3: Rumbletown. These Arena Challenges are the best way to earn money quickly. Become good at his arenas and you can use the Challenges to level up your Skylanders, earn Gold, and work on Skylander Quests all at the same time.

ARENA 1: BROCK'S RUMP ROASTER RUCKUS

This is the Rumbletown Arena. Its main feature is the large pit around the outside of the main fighting area. You can use this in your favor. Use Skylanders with strong knockback effects to knock enemies off the side and score easy and quick kills.

The Perfect Game

1 STOP THE SPELL

INITIAL REWARD: 200 GOLD

REPEAT REWARD: 100 GOLD

Difficulty: Easy

Strategy: For this challenge, try to keep the enemies from entering the magic circle in the middle of the arena. As long as there are less than eight enemies in the circle, you should be fine. If there are more than eight, you lose instantly. Chompies are the top concern here since they often enter the circle in large numbers. Take them out quickly with area-of-effect attacks.

Stage 1: Bone Chompies, Drow Lance Masters, Mace Majors

Stage 2: Bone Chompies, Drow Lance Masters, Mace Majors, Drow Archers

Stage 3: Bark Demons, Bone Chompies, Drow Archers

2 SMOKE SCREEN

INITIAL REWARD: 300 GOLD

REPEAT REWARD: 150 GOLD

Difficulty: Easy

Strategy: During this challenge, smoke bombs that drop down every few seconds and make it harder to see and fight the enemies. However, in practice it's easy to destroy the smoke bombs before they can cloud up the arena. Use area-of-effect attacks to clear them out without interrupting your attacks on the enemies in the arena.

Use the bombs from the Bag O' Booms to take down the Blaze Brewers in the later stages.

Stage 1: Bag O' Booms, Mohawk Cyclops, En Fuego Chompies

Stage 2: Bag O' Booms, Mohawk Cyclops, En Fuego Chompies, Blaze Brewer

Stage 3: Bag O' Booms, Mohawk Cyclops, En Fuego Chompies, Blaze Brewers

③ CLOUDY CURSE

INITIAL REWARD: 300 GOLD

REPEAT REWARD: 150 GOLD

Difficulty: Moderate

Strategy: For this challenge, you must constantly eat food to stay alive. Each piece of food heals you 40 points, and every downed enemy drops a food item. An electrical cloud hovers over your Skylander, dealing 5 damage every second.

The best Skylanders for this challenge have a good knockback attack. Knockbacks equal easy kills, since you can knock enemies off of the sides of the arena. Killing enemies quickly means more food, and keeping your Skylander's health up is pivotal to making it to the end of Round 3.

Watch out for the Crystal Golem finale! He's very, very tough.

Stage 1: Inhuman Shield, Drow Archers, Life Spell Punks

Stage 2: Inhuman Shield, Drow Archers, Life Spell Punks

Stage 3: Inhuman Shield, Drow Archers, Crystal Golem

④ PRESENT PROTECTOR

INITIAL REWARD: 400 GOLD

REPEAT REWARD: 200 GOLD

Difficulty: Moderate

Strategy: To win this challenge, you must keep the stack of presents safe from attacking enemies. The enemies aren't focused on your Skylander, but instead they are trying to hit the presents. Each present can absorb a certain amount of damage before collapsing. Stand near the gift stack and use your best area-of-effect powers to win.

Stage 1: Bone Chompies, Chompies

Stage 2: En Fuego Chompies, Arkeyan Jousters, D. Riveters

Stage 3: Bone Chompies, En Fuego Chompies, D. Riveters, Arkeyan Jousters, Chompy Bot 9000

⑤ SPELL DODGER

INITIAL REWARD: 450 GOLD

REPEAT REWARD: 200 GOLD

Difficulty: Moderate

Strategy: Between each stage of enemies, you must dodge around the red blobs to avoid taking damage. This is similar to both the Chompy Mage and Kaos fights, if you have played through the story. Try to anticipate the patterns and move into the gaps to avoid taking damage. Having a quick, small Skylander, like Stealth Elf, is a big help.

In the last stage, you must dodge two rounds of spells between enemy waves. You know you're at the end when two Troll Stompers attack. Defeat them for a win.

Stage 1: Inhuman Shields, Mace Majors, Grenade Generals

Stage 2: Inhuman Shields, Mace Majors, Grenade Generals, D. Riveters

Stage 3: Inhuman Shields, Mace Majors, Grenade Generals, D. Riveters, Troll Stomper M5s

6 FORCE FIELD FRENZY

INITIAL REWARD: 500 GOLD

REPEAT REWARD: 250 GOLD

Difficulty: Hard

Strategy: For this challenge, all the enemies are invulnerable to damage. To defeat them, you need to knock them off the sides of the arena. While the force fields protect the enemies, they also increase how susceptible they are to knockback effects. The knockback effect of most powers is increased by a significant amount.

Gill Grunt and Spyro are both good Skylanders for this challenge. For the Goliath Drows, you need to trick them off the side. Stand near the edge of the arena and wait for them to start to charge. As soon as they do, dash out of the way. These foes are too slow to turn to prevent falling off the sides.

Stage 1: Chompies, Arkeyan Jousters, Mace Majors, Drow Goliaths

Stage 2: Chompies, Arkeyan Jousters, Mace Majors, Drow Goliaths, Bag O' Booms, Blaze Brewer

Stage 3: Chompies, Arkeyan Jousters, Mace Majors, Drow Goliaths, Bag O' Booms, Blaze Brewers

7 THE PERFECT GAME

INITIAL REWARD: CLEVER CLOVER CHARM (INCREASE DODGE CHANCE OF SKYLANDERS WITH LOW HEALTH)

REPEAT REWARD: 300 GOLD

Difficulty: Very Hard

Strategy: In this challenge, your Skylander's health is reduced to one. This means you can't take any damage at all! You also can't fall off the side of the arena or it's an instant fail.

Do not attempt this until you have fully upgraded and mastered at least one of your Skylanders.

Stage 1: En Fuego Chompies, Drow Archers, Mohawk Cyclops

Stage 2: En Fuego Chompies, Drow Archers, Mohawk Cyclops, Bag O' Booms

Stage 3: En Fuego Chompies, Drow Archers, Mohawk Cyclops, Bag O' Boom, Giant Trog Pincher

ARENA 2: KAOS' ROYAL FLUSH

This is the arena from Chapter 9: Kaos' Kastle. Throughout these fights, pieces of the floor break away and drop into the pit below. Any Skylanders that fall take some damage, but you can use this to your advantage by tricking or knocking enemies into the breakaway floors.

Fog of War

1 DON'T BEAM ME UP

INITIAL REWARD: 600 GOLD

REPEAT REWARD: 300 GOLD

Difficulty: Easy

Strategy: In this challenge, you need to prevent the Trog Wanderers from beaming up via the teleporter rings around the level. You only need to prevent 10 Trogs from going up, and there aren't that many Trogs trying to get up the side. Trogs can be tricky to defeat, so you really need to pour the damage on to take them down because they heal themselves at regular intervals.

Stage 1: Trogs, Armored Chompies, Inhuman Shields, Drow Lance Master, Armored Drow Lance Master

Stage 2: Trogs, Grenade Generals, Drow Lance Master, Jawbreakers

Stage 3: Trogs, Armored Lance Masters, Armored Chompies

2 NO CHOMPIES ALLOWED!

INITIAL REWARD: 800 GOLD

REPEAT REWARD: 300 GOLD

Difficulty: Moderate

Strategy: In this challenge, you need to keep the Chompies out of the center ring. Just focus on using area-of-effect attacks to wipe out the Chompies before eight can make it into the center.

Stage 1: Armored Chompies, Chompies, Mace Majors, Inhuman Shields

Stage 2: Armored Chompies, Chompies, Mace Majors, Inhuman Shields, Goliath Drow, Life Spell Punks

Stage 3: Armored Chompies, Chompies, Mace Majors, Inhuman Shields, Goliath Drow, Life Spell Punks, Chompy Bot 9000,

3 FOG OF WAR

INITIAL REWARD: 900 GOLD

REPEAT REWARD: 400 GOLD

Difficulty: Very Hard

Strategy: This is another smoke challenge. Just keep destroying the smoke bombs to keep your view clear. The bigger thing to worry about is the Crystal Golem in Stage 3. When you defeat him, don't think the challenge is over! You must still beat a bunch of reinforcements and another Crystal Golem!

Stage 1: Spiderlings, Arkeyan Jousters, Grenade Generals

Stage 2: Inhuman Shields, Arkeyan Jouster, Arkeyan Duelist, Grenade Generals

Stage 3: Crystal Golems, Arkeyan Duelist, Grenade Generals, Inhuman Shields

4 AN EARLY FALL

INITIAL REWARD: 1,000 GOLD

REPEAT REWARD: 400 GOLD

Difficulty: Moderate

Strategy: This scenario is similar to the Force Field Frenzy challenge in the previous arena. Enemies don't take damage, but they do suffer increased knockback from your attacks. Use Skylanders with good knockback abilities, like Wham-Shell or Spyro, to more easily knock enemies off the sides. Focus on Drow Archers first, they are the easiest to knock off. Trick the Jawbreakers into diving into open gaps to score easy kills.

Stage 1: Chompies, Drow Archers, Jawbreakers

Stage 2: Chompies, Drow Archers, Jawbreakers, Arkeyan Shield Juggernauts

Stage 3: Chompies, Drow Archers, Jawbreakers, Arkeyan Shield Juggernauts

5 LOSING GROUND

INITIAL REWARD: 1,100 GOLD

REPEAT REWARD: 500 GOLD

Difficulty: Hard

Strategy: In this challenge you face a floor that gets smaller and smaller. Luckily, you can fall in and only take some damage. If your enemies fall, they get knocked out instantly.

Stage 1: Mace Majors, D. Riveters

Stage 2: Mace Majors, D. Riveters, Drow Archers, Blaze Brewer

Stage 3: Crystal Golem, Mace Majors, Blaze Brewer

6 SKY LASERS

INITIAL REWARD: 1,300 GOLD

REPEAT REWARD: 500 GOLD

Difficulty: Moderate

Strategy: In this challenge, a laser blasts down from the sky every few seconds. While this laser can also hit enemies, it always starts targeted on your Skylander. The laser only does about 50 points of damage, so the enemies are much more of a threat on this level.

Even with armor, these enemies can still fall into pits. Use knockback attacks to kick them into this area's many holes. The Life Spell Punks can be difficult to hit because they hang out on isolated tiles. Bring Skylanders with good ranged abilities to this fight.

Stage 1: Armored Mohawks, Armored Chompies, Armored Lance Masters, Armored Archers

Stage 2: Armored Lance Masters, Armored Archers, Armored Drow Master, Armored Life Spell Punk

Stage 3: Armored Mohawks, Armored Lance Masters, Armored Archers, Armored Drow Master, Armored Life Spell Punk, Chompy Bot 9000

7 ONE SHOT THRILL

INITIAL REWARD: SPARKING SPRINKLES CHARM (SKYLANDERS REGAIN MORE HEALTH FROM EATING FOOD.)

REPEAT REWARD: 600 GOLD

Difficulty: High

Strategy: Ready to survive three stages without getting hit? Luckily, Brock tones down the enemy difficulty on this challenge. You only need to take on average difficulty enemies. The most dangerous, besides the Troll Stompers, are the D. Riveters because of their quick ranged attacks. (Watch out for their mines.)

Troll Stomper starts with his stomp attack first, then shoots. Stand far away enough from him when he stomps, then get in close to smack its legs while it is shooting. You must be careful not to fall into the pit. If you do, you must start over.

Stage 1: Arkeyan Jousters, Spiderlings, Arkeyan Bombers

Stage 2: Spiderlings, Arkeyan Bombers, Inhuman Shield, D. Riveters, Arkeyan Jousters

Stage 3: Arkeyan Bombers, Inhuman Shield, D. Riveters, Arkeyan Jousters, Troll Stomper M5

ARENA 3: PIPSQUEAK'S MINCEMEAT MAYHEM

This is the arena from the end of Molekin Village. Depending on the challenge, you must contend with buzz saws on the exterior ring and, occasionally, the interior ring. Knock enemies into the buzz saws for easy kills.

Bubble Buster

1 STICKY SITUATION

INITIAL REWARD: 1,200 GOLD

REPEAT REWARD: 600 GOLD

Difficulty: Easy

Strategy: In this arena, an off-screen Slobbering Mutticus drops slime regularly into the arena. This doesn't hurt your Skylander, but can make it more difficult to fight back against the incoming enemies. The fight ends when you defeat a duo of Blaze Brewers.

Stage 1: En Fuego Chompy, D. Riveters, Armored Cyclops

Stage 2: En Fuego Chompy, D. Riveters, Armored Cyclops, Grenade Generals, Blaze Brewer

Stage 3: En Fuego Chompy, D. Riveters, Armored Cyclops, Grenade Generals, Blaze Brewers

2 BIRTHDAY BASH

INITIAL REWARD: 1,500 GOLD

REPEAT REWARD: 700 GOLD

Difficulty: Moderate

Strategy: This is another defense level. Enemies won't attack your Skylander at all. You need to focus on defeating them before they can reach the cakes and attack them. Knockback attacks are the most effective for this battle. Take special care of the late-arriving Shadow Duke. He can really ruin your party.

Stage 1: Spiderlings, Chompies, Drow Lance Masters, Armored Lance Masters, D. Riveters

Stage 2: Spiderlings, Chompies, Drow Lance Masters, Armored Lance Masters, D. Riveters, Trog Wanderers

Stage 3: Spiderlings, Armored Lance Masters, D. Riveters, Trog Wanderers, Shadow Dukes

3 TROG TROUBLE

INITIAL REWARD: 1,600 GOLD

REPEAT REWARD: 800 GOLD

Difficulty: Easy

Strategy: You should be familiar with this type of arena challenge by now. If not, check out Don't Beam Me Up in Arena 2. Use the Arkeyan Bombers' bombs to destroy the Trog Wanderers quickly.

Stage 1: Mace Majors, Arkeyan Bombers, Trog Wanderers, Trog Pinchers

Stage 2: Mace Majors, Arkeyan Bombers, Trog Wanderers, Trog Pinchers, Trogmanders

Stage 3: Mace Majors, Arkeyan Bombers, Trog Wanderers, Trog Pinchers, Giant Trog Pincher, Crystal Golem

4 BAAAAAAAD IDEA!

INITIAL REWARD: 1,800 GOLD

REPEAT REWARD: 900 GOLD

Difficulty: Easy

Strategy: Throughout this challenge, your Skylander is chased by electric sheep. These sheep inflict 5 damage every second. In order to stay alive, you need to eat food dropped from enemies. For the finale, it is important to remember that you can shoot the Chompy Bot's Chompies for extra food.

Stage 1: Chompies, Frigid Chompies, Mace Majors, Bark Demon

Stage 2: Inhuman Shield, Frigid Chompies, Bark Demons, Mace Majors

Stage 3: Inhuman Shield, Frigid Chompies, Bark Demons, Mace Majors

Stage 4: Inhuman Shields, Mace Majors, Chompy Bot 9000

⑤ BUBBLE BUSTER

INITIAL REWARD: 2,200 GOLD

REPEAT REWARD: 1,000 GOLD

Difficulty: Extreme

Strategy: This is another challenge with protected enemies. This time, you need to push the enemies onto the whirring outer blades. You can make this task a bit easier by luring the enemies to stand on the edge of the arena by moving your Skylander there. When the enemies get close, dash along the edge to avoid the blades, and the enemies will follow; right into the buzz saws.

The best Skylanders for this challenge are those with good knockback and good dash attacks like Spyro. Stun attacks help, too (and Spyro has that as well).

Stage 1: Chompies, Armored Chompies, Drow Lance Masters, Arkeyan Bombers, Arkeyan Duelist, Arkeyan Juggernaut

⑥ ICY BLAST

INITIAL REWARD: 2,300 GOLD

REPEAT REWARD: 1,100 GOLD

Difficulty: Extreme

Strategy: In this challenge, blue balls drop from the sky and explode into ice crystals that can damage your Skylander (but not your foes.) The crystals are actually not the biggest worry on this map. The biggest worry is the difficult enemies you must survive to make it to the end. Use a Skylander that's good at confusing enemies or one that can take them out with massive area-of-effect attacks.

Stage 1: Armored Mohawk, En Fuego Chompies, D. Riveters

Stage 2: Arkeyan Bombers, Slobbering Mutticus, Armored Mohawk, En Fuego Chompies, D. Riveters

Stage 3: D. Riveter, Blaze Brewer, Armored Mohawk, Slobbering Mutticus

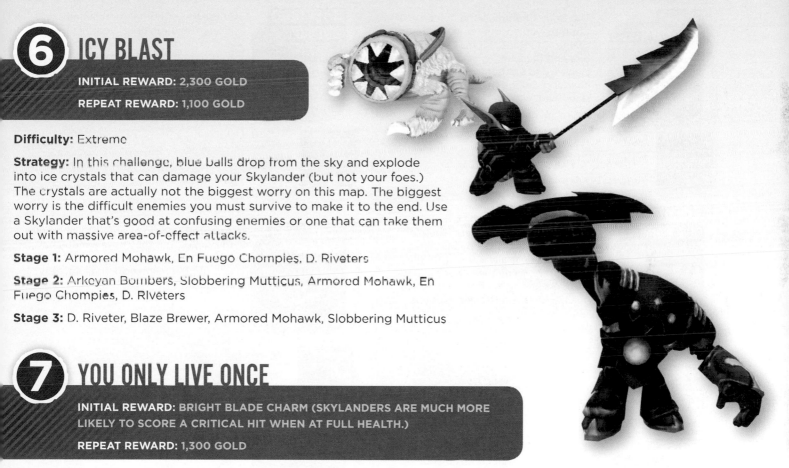

⑦ YOU ONLY LIVE ONCE

INITIAL REWARD: BRIGHT BLADE CHARM (SKYLANDERS ARE MUCH MORE LIKELY TO SCORE A CRITICAL HIT WHEN AT FULL HEALTH.)

REPEAT REWARD: 1,300 GOLD

Difficulty: Extreme

Strategy: You must survive the arena without getting hit. The first two rounds are straightforward enough. Stick to ranged attacks and take the Crystal Golem and Trogmanders out from the safety of the edge of the ring.

The last stage is when it gets serious. First En Fuego Chompies by the bucketful drop from above into the ring. Unless you have a really fast attack, just avoid them when they start to explode. When they're down, two Crystal Golems arrive. Just stay on the opposite side of the ring from them and pick off their shields with your best ranged attacks. Beat them both, and you are declared Arena Master!

Stage 1: En Fuego Chompies, Armored Archer, Crystal Golem

Stage 2: Armored Archer, Trogmander

Stage 3: En Fuego Chompies, Crystal Golems

BESTIARY

Chompies

Chompies come in a variety of species. They are nasty little ball-shaped critters full of big, nasty teeth. Despite their horrid appearance, they are rarely much of a threat to your Skylanders. Consider them battlefield fodder.

BONE CHOMPY

The Bone Chompy is the first type of Chompy you encounter in *Skylanders Giants*. The Bone Chompy charges a bite and then lunges at your Skylander. Don't try to hit them while they are charging. Dodge their attack first, then slam them with a melee attack.

Threat	Very Low
Health	Very Low
XP Rewarded	Very Low

EN FUEGO CHOMPY

These fiery Chompies are kamikaze killers. They run up to your Skylanders and explode. If you don't manage to dispatch them first, they dish out major damage.

Threat	Low
Health	Very Low
XP Rewarded	Very Low

CHOMPY

The regular Chompies are healthier than their Bone Chompy buddies, but are never really a threat for your Skylanders. Since they attack in large numbers, use area effect attacks to quickly wipe out attacking groups.

Threat	Very Low
Health	Very Low
XP Rewarded	Very Low

ARMORED CHOMPY

Armored Chompies are just like regular Chompies, but they have a metal hat which deflects incoming attacks. Once you get the helmet off, they are easy to squash!

Threat	Very Low
Health	Very Low
XP Rewarded	Very Low

FRIGID CHOMPY

These Chompies have a freezing breath attack that can stop your Skylander cold. Avoid getting hit by the blast by quickly disposing of the Chompies when they get in range. If you get caught by their ice breath hammer the Activate button (or shake your Wii Remote) to break free.

Threat	Very Low
Health	Very Low
XP Rewarded	Very Low

CHOMPY BOT 9000

The Chompy Bot 9000 is what you get when Chompies and Trolls hang out too much. The giant robot is heavily armored and can take a massive amounts of damage. The Chompy Bot's primary attack is to rapid-fire Chompies at Skylanders. This attack causes the Chompy Bot to overheat. Giving you an opening for attack. If you get too close to the Chompy Bot 9000, it starts a stomp attack.

Threat	High
Health	EXTREME
XP Rewarded	High

The best way to fight a Chompy Bot is at mid-range. Try to find the sweet spot that causes the Chompies to fly over your head, but still keeps your Skylander out of range of the foot stomp.

Drow

Drow are the dark elves of Skylands. While they come in many colors and sizes they are all angry, and almost universally hate the Skylanders.

DROW LANCE MASTER

The Drow Lance Master is the basic Drow unit. They have one simple twirling attack with their lances, but be wary, the lance dishes out major damage if it connects. Wait until the Lance Master swings. When they miss they shake their head in disapproval. That's your opening! Move in for the kill.

Threat	Medium
Health	Medium
XP Rewarded	Low

DROW ARCHER

Drow Archers have astounding range and accuracy with their arcing arrows. Luckily, you have an advantage: they shoot their arrows so high into the sky, it gives you plenty of time to dodge out of the way of the attack.

When an Archer fires at your Skylander, red circles appear on the ground to indicate where the arrows will fall. Quickly move out of the red circles to avoid taking damage.

Threat	Low
Health	Low
XP Rewarded	Low

ARMORED LANCE MASTER

These Drow have a set of armor that completely defends them from incoming attacks. Hammer them with attacks to knock their armor off. Without their armor, they are no different than regular Drow Lance Masters.

Threat	Medium
Health	Medium
XP Rewarded	Medium

GOLIATH DROW

Goliath Drow don't look much like the Lancers or the Archers. They are giant, armored, over-muscled elves. Brock is the most famous Goliath Drow. To defeat a Goliath Drow, focus on dodging out of the way of their charging attack. When they miss, you get a few seconds to focus attacks on their exposed backs.

Threat	High
Health	Medium
XP Rewarded	Medium

ARMORED ARCHER

These archers can take twice the licking normal Drow Archers can, but if you knock their armor off they are identical to regular archers.

Threat	Low
Health	Medium
XP Rewarded	Low

ARMORED GOLIATH

This Drow Goliath variant is covered in tough armor that effectively doubles the amount of damage they can take. The same strategies you use on regular Drow Goliaths apply, you just need to continue them for a longer period of time.

Threat	High
Health	High
XP Rewarded	Medium

Arkeyans

Arkeyan enemies include a variety of robotic high-tech attackers. Arkeyans are masters of both Magic and Tech, so it can be tough to predict the tactics they will employ.

ARKEYAN JOUSTER

The Arkeyan Jouster is the first of many Arkeyan enemies you must defeat on your journeys. The jouster is a straightforward melee fighter. It only has one attack, a large overhead swing of its pike. The attack does major damage if it connects, so fight from range if possible!

When you encounter Jousters later in the game (after Chapter 1), their maces are charged with electricity. This makes their attacks much harder to dodge, and they possess an electric shield which blocks attacks.

Threat	High
Health	Medium
XP Rewarded	Medium

ARKEYAN BOMBER

These robotic ranged attackers have a tricky attack. They toss a plasmoid bomb at your Skylanders that sticks to their heads. In order to evade the bomb, you have to quickly hit the Activate button.

Toss the bomb back at the Arkeyan bomber to give him a taste of his own medicine, and score a quick KO.

Threat	Medium
Health	Low
XP Rewarded	Low

ARKEYAN SHIELD JUGGERNAUT

These enemies have strong shields that completely protect them from attack while raised. Every few seconds, the Juggernaut puts its shields together to let loose a laser blast. It's hard to avoid this blast, and quick Skylanders have a better chance of dodging.

A trick to avoiding the laser is to get in close to the Juggernaut, and circle around him. It won't be able to turn its laser fast enough to hit you. Watch out though, it has a close-range melee attack that can really hurt!

Threat	High
Health	EXTREME
XP Rewarded	High

ARKEYAN CRACKLER

Master illusionists, Arkeyan Cracklers can materialize identical shades that can absorb damage for them. Interestingly Arkeyan Cracklers don't attack directly. If you hit a shade, it emits an electrical burst that damages your Skylander. For this reason, always try to take on Arkeyan Cracklers with a ranged Skylander. You can tell which shade is the actual Arkeyan Crackler by its distinct animation. The real Crackler moves its arms more and clenches its fists.

Threat	Low
Health	Medium
XP Rewarded	High

BLAZE BREWER

Blaze Brewers are super-tough flame thrower enemies. They can shrug off most attacks, and slowly trudge towards your Skylanders with hopes of lighting them aflame. Blaze Brewers are most deadly if they get too close to your Skylander, so it's best to use long range attacks against them. If you have a fast melee warrior, you can circle a Blaze Brewer's back. It can't turn its flame thrower quickly. If you do get caught by the flame thrower, stop attacking and retreat immediately. The attack can knock out a Skylander in seconds.

Threat	High
Health	High
XP Rewarded	EXTREME

ARKEYAN DUELISTS

These giant knights have devastating melee attacks, but they can also drive their swords in the ground to inflict even more damage. And it also generates a force field that allows the Knight to take a few hits without sustaining damage. You can interrupt this charging by hitting them with a knockback attack.

Keep at range, or better yet, use the bombs their Arkeyan Bomber allies often toss around to take them out quickly. These Duelists don't have many hit points. Three or four high damage attacks are enough to take them down.

Threat	High
Health	Medium
XP Rewarded	High

ARKEYAN SNIPER

Arkeyan Snipers are only found in Arkeyan cities, as they fight from specially-designed tunnels that allow them to pop up and attack from multiple points. Snipers train their beam on their targets and unleash a deadly ranged attack. Move around and use cover to avoid their targeting beams.

To defeat a Sniper, you need to sneak up on them while they are trying to track you with their beam. Hit their hidey hole with a strong attack to take them out.

Threat	EXTREME
Health	Low
XP Rewarded	High

Cyclopes & Ogres

The Skylands are full of these weird creatures. Cyclops are a race of small one-eyed creatures. Ogres are giant and have two eyes, but they're not in the order you'd expect.

MOHAWK CYCLOPS

These ugly little warriors are single-minded, and a bit clumsy. A Mohawk Cyclops' main attack is to swing an axe in a dizzying circle. The attack can do a surprising amount of damage if they catch you unaware. Either take them out with ranged attacks or wait for your opening when they dizzy themselves with the axe attack.

Threat	Medium
Health	Low
XP Rewarded	Low

AXECUTIONER

Axecutioners are tough Ogres that have two fierce attacks. If you are at range, the Axecutioner tosses an axe, an attack which can dish out serious damage. If you get too close, it swings the axe in a semicircle, which deals even more damage! Surprisingly, Axecutioners can also teleport to get the drop on you with a short-range axe attack.

To defeat the Axecutioner, stay at medium range and wait until it throws an axe. Dodge out of the way. With the axe gone, the Axecutioner is open to attack! Move in, and get in a few attacks, but retreat as soon as the axe returns to the Axecutioner.

Threat	Medium
Health	Medium
XP Rewarded	Medium

BAG O' BOOM

These Cyclops love bombs more than anything, and love tossing them at your Skylanders. Avoid their initial bomb blast, and you can pick up the bomb left behind. These bombs are useful for solving puzzles, and defeating tough enemies.

Threat	Medium
Health	Low
XP Rewarded	Medium

D. RIVETER

D. Riveter is a ranged troll enemy. Their primary attack is a rapid fire blast with their plasma guns. This attack does not do much damage, so you don't have to worry about it. If you get too close, D. Riveter unleashes a troll mine that explodes, damaging everything in the area. These mines are deadly, so listen for their distinctive beeping sound.

Threat	Medium
Health	Medium
XP Rewarded	Medium

ARMORED MOHAWK

These upgraded Mohawks have helmets that make them a bit tougher to take down. Armored Mohawks also do a bit more damage to Skylanders. Knock their helmets off with quick attacks, then move in to finish them.

Threat	Low
Health	Medium
XP Rewarded	Low

TROLL STOMPER M5

The Troll Stomper M5 is a powerful, but very slow Troll-driven mech warrior with two primary attacks. The first is what it's named after, a short jump into the air. This stomp doesn't do too much damage, but does knock your Skylander back. The second attack is a rapid fire rocket attack. This attack is highly damaging and should be avoided at all costs. You can either dodge (if you're already at short range), or move into short range to avoid the attack. It's extremely difficult for Giants to avoid this attack, so stick with regular Skylanders when fighting the Stomper. Watch out, when you defeat a Troll Stomper! A Mace Major ejects from the cockpit and continues the attack!

Threat	High
Health	High
XP Rewarded	EXTREME

Trolls

Trolls are found causing trouble throughout the Skylands. While many of their race are masters of technology and explosives, some just like to hit things with maces.

MACE MAJOR

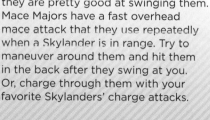

These ugly trolls love their maces, and they are pretty good at swinging them. Mace Majors have a fast overhead mace attack that they use repeatedly when a Skylander is in range. Try to maneuver around them and hit them in the back after they swing at you. Or, charge through them with your favorite Skylanders' charge attacks.

Threat	Medium
Health	Medium
XP Rewarded	Medium

Trogs

Trogs are ugly, blueish-green creatures that are rare in the Skylands. Each variant has unique powers that require some strategy.

TROG WANDERER

Trog Wanders are mysterious, slow-moving creatures. As you hit the Trog Wanderer, it shrinks. When it gets to half size, it starts running towards your Skylander. If you don't keep up the attack, the Trog Wanderer automatically heals itself and regrows to normal size. Trog Wanderers only have one attack, a simple melee chomp. Because of this, it's best to use high-damage ranged attacks against them, but melee fighters with good defensive skills are also useful.

Threat	EXTREME
Health	High
XP Rewarded	Medium

GRENADE GENERAL

Grenade Generals are tricky ranged attackers. They toss timed grenades into at your Skylanders that blow up after a few seconds. The grenades can be hard to see on a chaotic battlefield, so it's always a good idea focus on taking these guys down first.

Threat	Medium
Health	Low
XP Rewarded	Medium

TROG PINCHER

These little guys aren't any tougher than Chompies, but they can dish out some damaging bite attacks. Of course, if one of these guys gets transmogrified by a Trogmander, that's a different story. These guys turn into gigantic, super strong bruisers. Defeat the Trogmander to knock them back to size.

Threat	Low
Health	Very Low
XP Rewarded	Very Low

TROGMANDER

Trogmanders are tough little wizards that transform Trog Pinchers into Giant Trog Pinchers. These guys prefer to stay out of the action directly, and will dodge your Skylanders attacks by quickly moving around the area.

These wizards don't have any attacks of their own, but they can spawn new Trogs. This makes for an endless stream of deadly giant Trog Pinchers. Defeating a Trogmander dispels their growth spell, returning Trog Pinchers to their normal size.

Threat	Medium
Health	High
XP Rewarded	EXTREME

CRYSTAL GOLEM

Another formidable enemy, the Crystal Golem is surrounded by a crystal shield that provides extensive protection from your Skylanders' attacks. The shield reduces even the strongest attacks to practically nothing.

To defeat the Golem, you must first take down its crystal shield. Do this by slamming it with ranged attacks. Watch out for its crystal burrow attack. This is a slow moving attack, but it's hard to avoid if you're right on top of the Crystal Golem. Stick to ranged Skylanders while battling these enemies.

Threat	High
Health	High
XP Rewarded	EXTREME

Other Enemies

ROOT RUNNER

Root Runners are giant plants that regularly spit out Chompies. They have a good deal of health, so use your strongest ranged attacks to take them out as quickly as possible.

Threat	Low
Health	Medium
XP Rewarded	Medium

BARK DEMON

Watch out, these powerful and gigantic trees eat Chompies to heal themselves! These demons have two attacks:

At range, a burrowing root follows your Skylander. If it catches your Skylander, a gigantic tree erupts from the ground inflicting serious damage.

Up close, Bark Demons have a slow double-fisted crush attack.

Taking on one Bark Demon isn't much of a problem, but they can quickly overwhelm a Skylander with numbers. Move in and out of range to avoid their attacks and keep them confused.

Threat	Medium
Health	Medium
XP Rewarded	Medium

LIFE SPELL PUNK

Don't underestimate these goofy characters because of their dimunitive size. Life Spell Punks can dish out major heals to any of their nearby allies. They fire off an area effect healing spell every few seconds. Because they are so good at keeping their friends alive, you should always focus on killing them first when they are encountered as part of a group.

Threat	High
Health	Very Low
XP Rewarded	Low

INHUMAN SHIELD

Inhuman Shields are completely immune from damage from the front. They slowly move towards your Skylanders and perform a powerful spinning attack if they get close. The secret to beating these shield enemies is to wait for them to attack, then move behind them and let loose with a quick attack.

Threat	Low
Health	Low
XP Rewarded	Medium

JAWBREAKER

Jawbreakers are ugly bruisers that excel at pugilism. To defeat the Jawbreaker, wait until it makes a move to lunge at your Skylander. When it does, get out of the way. When it misses, it falls on its face and is open to attack. Jawbreakers have plenty of health, so you usually need to perform this juke maneuver a few times to take one down.

Threat	EXTREME
Health	High
XP Rewarded	High

SLOBBERING MUTTICUS

The Slobbering Mutticus is a monstrous mount piloted by a crazed Cyclops. Mutticus fires giant globs of slime that slow down your Skylanders, and make it impossible to dodge incoming attacks. Mutticus also has some nasty stomping attacks, but they're easy to avoid as long as you don't get hit by the slime.

Threat	EXTREME
Health	EXTREME
XP Rewarded	High

SPIDERLINGS

Spiderlings are the spider equivalent of Chompies. They attack in numbers, but aren't much of a threat unless you completely ignore them. Giants automatically stomp them. Normally Spiderlings pop out of spider eggs. To stop them, you must first destroy the spider eggs.

Threat	Low
Health	Low
XP Rewarded	Very Low

SHADOW DUKE

Shadow Dukes are frightening suits of armor that slowly stalk your Skylanders. Because they move so slow, they aren't much of a threat one-on-one. They have a considerable amount of health, and if you don't see them coming when they are attacking with large groups, they can sneak up and take down a Skylander in one hit! Focus on avoiding the sword attack, then hitting them in the back.

Threat	EXTREME
Health	High
XP Rewarded	High

GARGANTULA

These gigantic mama spiders have a ranged web attack that can temporarily freeze your Skylander until it breaks out. The best way to take down a Gargantula is to charge in and attack it at close range. Keep moving around in a circle, attacking it's green back side. The Gargantula will have trouble counterattacking, making it an easy target.

Threat	EXTREME
Health	EXTREME
XP Rewarded	EXTREME

ABOUT THE WALKTHROUGH

Use the following pages anytime you need help in your new adventure through Skylands. The maps that appear at the start of each Chapter show not only the fastest route through each level, but they also show the side paths that lead to collectible items, such as hats and Soul Gems, as well as the locations of Auric and Skystone Challengers.

WHAT DO I NEED TO SEE EVERYTHING?

In order to access every secret area, you need at least the following:

- **One Skylander of each of the eight elements.**

- **One Skylander Giant, although the Giant can overlap with the element. So, if you have Thumpback, you don't need another Water Skylander.**

- **One fast Skylander. You need a Skylander that can dash or fly to complete some bomb puzzles and to make it safely through some of the traps.**

While you could clear the main story of *Skylanders Giants* with only one Skylander figure, the more Skylanders you have, the less trouble you will run into while playing through the game. Skylanders cannot be revived once they fall in battle, and you must to restart the level if you run out of healthy Skylanders.

WHAT IF I DON'T HAVE A GIANT SKYLANDER?

You can still clear the main story, but you will miss out on many secret areas and bonus events that only the Giants can take part in. Getting through bomb gates, and some puzzles, are easier if you have access to a Giant, but the walkthrough always includes information on how to get past a main story area even without a Giant.

The legend shows you what the callouts on each map mean. The numbers inside orange circles that appear on the maps show connections between two points on the map where you move to a different area, such as a hidden cave or drop underground. It's important to keep in mind that the trips between connectors may be one-way. The walkthrough has more information about getting around each Chapter of the adventure.

KEEPING TRACK OF SOUL GEMS FOR THE GIANTS

You can use the sticker sheet included in this guide to help track your progress with Skylander Giants Soul Gems! In each Chapter where you can collect a Giant's Soul Gem, there's a spot to place that Giant's sticker.

THE MOST IMPORTANT STRATEGY

The most important strategy you can employ in *Skylanders Giants* is to take your time. Never rush into battle against an enemy you've never encountered before. Always hang back and note the enemy's attacks before returning your own attacks. Many of the enemies have very difficult attack patterns, observing their patterns gives you a leg up on the Skylanders' foes. There is a Dare for completing a Chapter within a certain time limit, but you should go for the timed Dare after you've cleared everything else in the Chapter.

CHAPTER 1

TIME OF THE GIANTS

STORY GOALS

- ✓ Meet Norticus
- ◯ Free the Mabu Slaves

ELEMENTAL GATES

- Life
- Undead
- Air

DARES	
Time To Beat	4:20
Enemies to Defeat	40

AREAS TO FIND

- ◯ Forgotten Path
- ◯ Mountain Peak
- ◯ Turtle Falls
- ◯ Hungry Plateau
- ◯ Ancient Mines
- ◯ The Broken Bottom
- ◯ The Hungry Depths
- ◯ Zucchini Grotto
- ◯ Arkeyan Work Site
- ◯ Windy Work Site
- ◯ The Planks
- ◯ Cursed Construction

COLLECTIBLES & ENEMIES

Soul Gem		Self-Slingshot (Shroomboom)
Legendary Treasure		Starry Night Paint Job
Hats		Flower Fairy Hat, Turban, Paper Fast Food Hat
Story Scroll		Avalanche Anticipation
Luck-O-Tron Wheel		Lucky Wheel of Experience
Treasure Chests		4 to collect
Winged Sapphire		1 to collect

Bone Chompy

Arkeyan Jouster

Root Runner

MAP LEGEND

Direct Path	
Optional Path	
Feat of Strength	
Auric (Vendor)	
Hat Box	
Legendary Treasure	
Luck-O-Tron Wheel	
Soul Gem	
Story Scroll	
Treasure Chest	
Winged Sapphire	

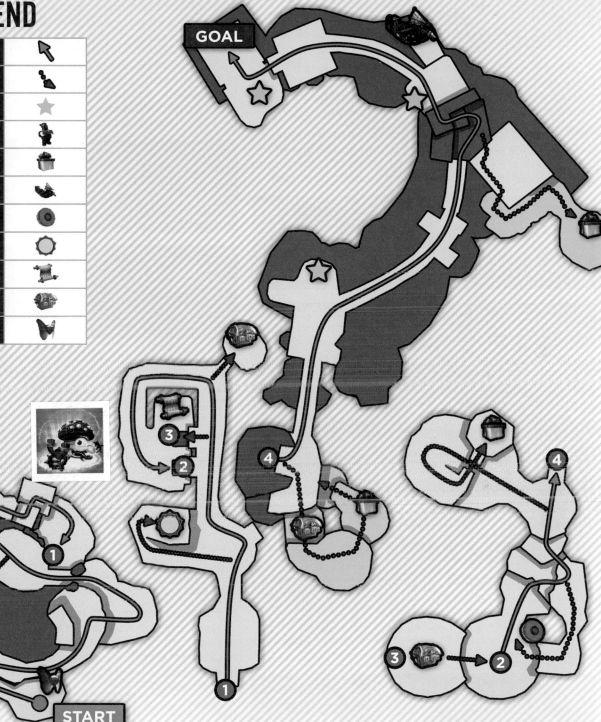

GOAL

START

THE FORGOTTEN PATH & MOUNTAIN PEAK

Welcome to Skylands, Portal Master!

This level takes place tens of thousands of years in the past. In a time when the Arkeyan machine race ruled the Skylands. After you place your favorite Skylander, you start in an area called Forgotten Path. To move on, proceed along the path and up the side of the mountain. To get the **Winged Sapphire** at the start of this level, switch to a Giant Skylander. Pick up the nearby boulder and smash the gate to reveal the Winged Sapphire and a pile of treasure!

When you reach the top of the spiral path, switch to a Giant Skylander (if you haven't already) and pick up the boulder here to discover a secret bounce pad. Use the pad to reach a bridge above and gather some extra treasure. Follow the coin trail down to the lower area and press the Action button to fire the cannon at the rock wall.

TURTLE FALLS & HUNGRY PLATEAU

Push the gigantic turtle out of the way and cross the bridge to the plateau. To get to the **Treasure Chest** on the far plateau, push the turtles into the ravine. This forms a natural bridge; cross it to collect the treasure.

Push the right turtle into the ravine to create a bridge to the downward path. Drop from the path to the bamboo platforms to the next area. At the bottom of the path, you meet Norticus, but he's surrounded by Bone Chompies!

ANCIENT MINES & THE BROKEN BOTTOM

When you enter the mines, Gigantus shows you some of the powers Giant Skylanders get over normal Skylanders. Don't follow Gigantus immediately; use a Giant Skylander to remove the two rocks blocking the path on the left. Follow the path around to grab Shroomboom's **Soul Gem** along with a few piles of gold.

Follow Gigantus through to the other side of the mines and watch as he demonstrates the Giant leap ability. Don't jump just yet! Follow the path down to the lower area and switch to a Giant if you aren't using one already. On the way down the path, look for the boulder at the upper right corner. Remove it with your Giant Skylander to discover a secret room and a **Treasure Chest**. The **Story Scroll: Avalanche Anticipation** is also in the area, behind a wooden wall.

If this isn't your first time through the level, drop down the hole Gigantus opened to continue to the next area. If it is your first time, switch to a Giant, go back up to the ledge, and hop down from the indicated spot. The hole created by your Giant leap leads to a **Treasure Chest** in the Hungry Depths.

THE HUNGRY DEPTHS

The Hungry Depths is a Chompy arena. You must defeat all the enemies here to move on. You can tell you are in an area that requires you to defeat enemies by the crossed swords. These swords can appear on gates and over some bounce pads. After defeating all the enemies in the arena, go into the back of the cavern until Norticus calls out.

Before you bounce up to meet Norticus, switch to a Giant Skylander. Use the Skylander to remove the boulder on the right after the second bounce pad. This path leads back into the Chompy arena. Defeat two more waves of Chompies to earn this level's coveted **Luck-O-Tron Wheel**. Use the bounce pads to hop up to Norticus' perch above. When you get to the top, Norticus exits to the next area.

LIFE ELEMENT GATE:
ZUCCHINI GROTTO

Before following Norticus, switch to a Life Skylander to access this special area on the left. Push the turtle out of the way to access the Chompy-filled garden. When you make it inside the garden, clear out the Chompies and push the turtle back into place. Follow the upward path around to the wrapped present, the **Fairy Flower Hat**.

If your Skylander has some good ranged attacks, you can try to take out the Root Runner, but it is in a spot that is difficult to hit. Don't be afraid to switch to a different Skylander (the Life Skylander is only needed to gain initial access to the area).

ARKEYAN WORK SITE

Outside the cave, Norticus introduces you to the Arkeyan Conquertron. An ultra-tough giant robot. Your next goal is to break the three chains suspending the Conquertron. You can also use a Giant to pull up the Conquertron's chains instead of attacking them.

AIR ELEMENT GATE:
WINDY WORK SITE

Head in the opposite direction of the Conquertron to discover this elemental gate. You can't miss the first **Treasure Chest**; it's at the first drop down of the Windy Worksite area.

Use the bounce pad to jump between levels and avoid the rotating jet stream. The Turban is on the plateau just past the rotating jet stream. When you reach the end of the plateaus, use the bounce pad to return to Arkeyan Work Site.

Cross the bridge over to Norticus and he points out one of the Conquertron's suspension chains. Either destroy the first chain with attacks, or use a Giant to rip them from the ground.

THE PLANKS

Ignore the Conquertron's threats and continue around the wooden walkway. Push the blocks out of your way and continue to the bamboo platforms. Defeat the two Arkeyan Jousters to reveal a bounce pad up to the next area. Before you use the uncovered bounce pad, walk in the opposite direction to discover an Undead elemental gate.

UNDEAD ELEMENT AREA:
CURSED CONSTRUCTION

On the other side of the gate, there is a spear trap. Wait for the spears to retract, and cross over. The **Paper Fast Food Hat** is on the other side of the trap.

Bounce back up to The Planks and drop back down to the Conquertron's second chain point. Move towards the camera after destroying the second of Conquertron's chains. Move to the right of the screen to drop down into a secret area containing the **Legendary Treasure: Starry Night Paint Job**.

Continue around the planks and defeat the large group of Jousters and Chompies waiting for you. When they are all gone, the next gate opens. One final piece of the chain remains. Watch out, Conquertron recovers enough to start using his eye beams on you. Avoid the beams and attack the chain to complete the level.

BURNING QUESTIONS!

The creators of *Skylanders Giants* have taken the time to answer some questions. These questions and their answers have been included at the end of each level so there are no spoilers!

Q: Are the Mabu you meet in Time of the Giants the ancestors of Nort, Rizzo, Snuckles, and Blobbers?

A: Yes! But not the same Nort, Rizzo, Snuckles, and Blobbers you met on Shattered Island in *Skylanders Spyro's Adventure*. These are ancestors of a totally different Nort, Rizzo, Snuckles, and Blobbers. The weird thing is none of those names are particularly common in Mabu culture either! We suppose it's just one of those amazing Skylands coincidences.

STORY GOALS

- ✓ Find the Music Box
- ◯ Buy the Engine
- ◯ Find the Compass

ELEMENTAL GATES

- Earth
- Fire

DARES	
Time To Beat	5:30
Enemies to Defeat	60

AREAS TO FIND

- ◯ Dread-Yacht
- ◯ Persephone's Cabin
- ◯ Rotten Moorings
- ◯ Walled Ruins
- ◯ Rotten Bottom
- ◯ The Cave
- ◯ Crumbling Remains
- ◯ Hephaestus' Chain
- ◯ Lonesome Drow Landing
- ◯ Barker's Knob
- ◯ Forger's Basement

- ◯ Bottleneck's Keep
- ◯ Soda Square
- ◯ Bottleneck's Soda Shop
- ◯ Bottle Top Inn
- ◯ Forgotten Reach
- ◯ Long Walk Pier
- ◯ Stone Stronghold
- ◯ Under Mines
- ◯ Boiling Cavern
- ◯ The Last Stand

COLLECTIBLES & ENEMIES

Soul Gem	⬤	Hot Rod (Hot Head)
Legendary Treasure		Propeller Pilot House Roof
Hats		Police Siren Hat, Biter Hat
Story Scroll		Chompy Pits
Luck-O-Tron Wheel	⬤	Lucky Wheel of Health
Treasure Chests		4 to collect
Winged Sapphire		1 to collect

Bone Chompy

Drow Lance Master

 Root Runner

Bark Demon

 Drow Archer

MAP LEGEND

Direct Path	
Optional Path	
Feat of Strength	
Auric (Vendor)	
Hat Box	
Legendary Treasure	
Luck-O-Tron Wheel	
Skystones Challenger	
Soul Gem	
Story Scroll	
Treasure Chest	
Winged Sapphire	

DREAD-YACHT & PERSEPHONE'S CABIN

You start this level on Flynn's new (well, relatively new) ship. Talk to Flynn and he gives you your mission. You need to pass through the ruins and retrieve the "thingamawhatsit."

Right at the level start, head through the door on the left to find Persephone's Cabin. Persephone is the fairy your Skylanders use to purchase new powers and upgrades. Leave the ship when you're ready to begin your quest.

Flynn: —Then go pick up the thingamawhatsit over there and then it's BOOM! GREATNESS!

Persephone: I am also here to grant you amazing upgrades.

ROTTEN MOORINGS & WALLED RUINS

Outside the ship is a field filled with Bone Chompies and Root Runners. Clear the area, and when it is safe, break through the brick wall to access the next area. Keep in mind that Earth Skylanders have a special quest to break through these brick walls. Whenever you encounter one of these walls, switch to an Earth Skylander to work on the quest.

To smash the wall, pick up the nearby bomb and press the Activate button to toss it towards the wall. Alternatively, you can switch to a Giant Skylander and smash the wall apart!

The next area has two Root Runners. Defeat them and their Chompies, then destroy the second brick wall. One more brick wall stands in your way. Bomb it or crush it, and follow the path to Crumbling Remains.

ROTTEN BOTTOM & THE CAVE

Before breaking through the third wall in Walled Ruins, look for a cliff edge on the left side of the screen. Drop down to access the secret Rotten Bottom area; this in turn leads to the secret cave. Inside The Cave is a **Treasure Chest** behind a large door you can open with either a Giant Skylander, or head back up to Walled Ruins to get a bomb. Getting a bomb all the way down to The Cave requires a speedy Skylander. Use a power like Drill Sergeant's Charge ability to make it before the bomb explodes.

CRUMBLING REMAINS & HEPHAESTUS' CHAIN

Favored Element: Undead

This is the first of many areas of the game that have a "favored element." When the area element and your current Skylander's element match, you get bonus elemental damage with every hit. All Skylanders have a quest called Elementalist. This requires that your Skylander do damage to enemies in areas of their element. After defeating the few Chompies here, move the push blocks on your right to reveal a path up to a bomb and some treasure.

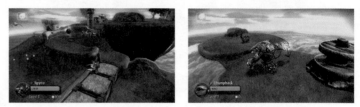

Use the bomb to destroy the two brick walls blocking the path up to the next area. Up top, there are two Drow Lance Masters. Defeat them to reveal a protected bounce pad. Before hopping up the bounce pad, switch to a Giant Skylander and throw the rock on the left. This gives your Giant access to the first Feat of Strength. To pass the Feat, you need to hit the Activate button as fast as you can! Success reveals the second **Treasure Chest**.

Use the bounce pad to pop up to the last plateau to retrieve the Octophonic Music Player. You automatically head back to Flynn's ship and he lets you in on your next quest, which is to buy an engine from a nearby seller.

LONESOME DROW LANDING, BARKER'S KNOB, FORGER'S BASEMENT & BOTTLENECK'S KEEP

Favored Element: Earth

It's time to retire the angry raccoons running Flynn's ship. Exit the Dread-Yacht onto the next floating plateau. Defeat the Bark Demon, and a nearby gate will open to reveal a key. Move to the key to automatically pick it up. Now, bring the key to the locked gate to open the way to the next zone.

You first encounter a Mabu surrounded by a trio of Drow Lancers. Make quick work of the Lancers, and then move on to the Bark Demon and Root Runner near the back of the area.

The key for the next zone is behind a brick wall on the right. You can smash it down with a Giant, or grab a bomb from inside the nearby hut. The hut also has a friendly Mabu paint forger, and the **Legendary Treasure: Propeller Pilot House Roof** behind a wall.

After you unlock the gate, cross over to the next plateau to enter this zone. This area is filled with Chompies, and a new enemy: Drow Archer. The Archer isn't alone; plenty of Drow Lancer reinforcements arrive to make the fight a bit more difficult. Retreat back the way you came to draw the Archer off of his perch, making him a more vulnerable target. More Archers arrive as reinforcements. Use the same strategy, draw them off the ledge, then move in for the beatdown.

SKYSTONE CHALLENGER: BERT	
Reward For Winning First Game: Mohawk Cyclops 4	
BERT'S SKYSTONE DECK	
Spiderlings	
Bark Demon	
Mohawk Cyclops 4	

Back in Soda Square, some serious enemy reinforcements have arrived: a Bark Demon and Bone Chompies flanked by Drow Archers and a Drow Lance Master. Defeat the Bark Demon and the Lancer to unlock the bounce pad. Bounce up to finish off the Archer back line. The second door key is located on the highest plateau with the last two Drow Archers.

After collecting the second key, switch to a Giant to complete the level's second Feat of Strength. This time you need to hammer on the Activate button to make a natural bridge out to a **Treasure Chest**. Use the Soda Square bounce pads to bounce on the floating platforms. Nail two landings to the right to find the **Story Scroll: Chompy Pits**.

SODA SQUARE, BOTTLENECK'S SODA SHOP & BOTTLE TOP INN

Favored Element: Life

When you first enter this area, you see another harassed Mabu, this time his tormenters are Chompies. Defeat the Chompies and head onto the planks toward the Mabu houses. The first house is Bottleneck's Soda Shop; it has small amounts of treasure, but nothing important.

The second house is Bottle Top Inn. Bert runs the inn, and he loves a game called Skystones. If this is your first time through the level, you must come back later to challenge him. The Bottle Top Inn also has the key to the next area. Grab it, and head back outside to Soda Square.

Now that you have both keys you can exit the area via the locked gate. Cross the bridge to meet Auric, a Mabu merchant, and someone you'll be seeing a lot of in the future!

Talk to Auric again to access three rare hats in his store. If you don't have enough coins at the moment, don't worry, you can always come back here later in the game via the Replay Chapter option.

	AURIC'S INVENTORY	
	ITEM	**COST**
	Cowboy Hat	125 Gold
	Plunger Head	125 Gold
	Kufi Hat	125 Gold

Grab the outboard motor and you are automatically teleported back to Flynn's Ship for a second time.

LONG WALK PIER & STONE STRONGHOLD

Favored Element: Tech

Next up is the Drow compass! Stop by Persephone's cabin if you have enough Gold to purchase an upgrade, then cross the bridge to confront the pair of Bark Demons guarding the end of Long Walk Pier. This is a tough fight because the Bark Demons feed off the Chompies the Root Runner keeps spitting out. To make matters worse, if you get too close, the Drow Archers fire a volley of arrows at you. Stick to a ranged Skylander (preferably one of the Tech Skylanders), and pick off the Bark Demons from range before moving in to finish off the Root Runner.

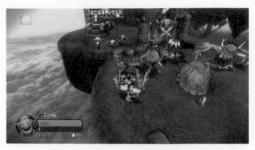

When you've taken out all the enemies, the gate opens automatically and a group of Drow Lancers charges you. Hang back and take them out safely. When the Lancers are down, charge forward to finish off the Drow Archers. A turret opens up, but don't hop into it just yet!

EARTH ELEMENT GATE:
UNDER MINES

Before jumping on the turret, switch to an Earth Skylander and drop down to the lower plateau across from the turret. Walk inside the cave to discover this secret area. Grab the pick on the left, and start chipping away at the rock formations to fully explore the cave. You need to use bombs to destroy the large crystal formations. Note that Crusher (the Earth Giant Skylander) doesn't need to use either the pick or the bombs to clear out the crystals.

The **Treasure Chest** is behind two gigantic crystals at the back right of the cavern. If you don't have Crusher available, you need a fast Skylander that can carry the bomb all the way from the lower right corner of the cavern up to where the treasure chest is. Break the rocks through the straight path to reveal a floating key. Grab the

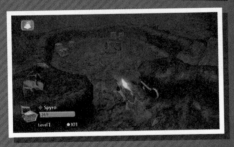

key and then return back to the entrance. Now follow the left path to the locked gate. After gathering the Police Siren Hat and treasure, don't forget the treasure room at the back left of the cavern. Clear the crystal formations to claim your rewards.

Back in the Stone Stronghold area, jump in the turret by hitting the Activate button when standing near. Shoot the locks off the door to complete the sequence and move on to the next zone.

FIRE ELEMENT GATE:
BOILING CAVERN

Drop down the cliff edge just beyond the door opened with the turret and switch to a Fire Skylander to access this secret area. Walk across the lava lake in Boiling Cavern to collect the **Biter Hat**.

THE LAST STAND

Favored Element: Tech

Back on the main path to the compass, you encounter Persephone who explains how Winged Sapphires work (and points out the location of a **Winged Sapphire**). Note that the Winged Sapphires do not provide discounts in Auric's store. Push one of the blocks out of the way. Before moving on, push that block back into place (to keep the higher walkway intact). Switch to a Giant Skylander to knock down the brick wall on the right. Hot Head's **Soul Gem** floats just on the other side.

Follow the walkway above to access another turret. Get in the turret, and several Drow Archers emerge from the wagon on the left. Shoot

the wagon to stop the Archers from spawning and finish them off before destroying the windmill to reveal the hidden **Luck-O-Tron Wheel**. Take out the locks next; claim the **Luck-O-Tron Wheel** before grabbing the Compass and ending the level.

BACK ON FLYNN'S SHIP

Once you get back on Flynn's Ship, it's time to explore a bit! As you play through the game, you unlock more and more special activities to do on the ship. For more details on where everything is on the ship, check out the chapter on Flynn's Ship found earlier in this guide.

Talk to Flynn when you're ready for the next mission. But before you go, check out the following locations for extra goodies. There is a **Winged Sapphire** just behind the cockpit. Explore around the edge to the left and smash the barrels to reveal it.

Always check Auric's Shop after a mission. There are usually new items in his inventory. You need to pass a lock puzzle to get to the store initially.

🔒 **Perfect Lock Puzzle Solution: 8 moves**
Right, Left, Left, Right, Right, Right, Left, Right

While you're talking with Auric, purchase the Luck-O-Tron Bulb #2 for 200 Gold. Cali's Room has the Luck-O-Tron, which uses the Bulb and any Luck-O-Tron Wheels you've found up to this point. Visit Persephone's Cabin if any of your Skylanders earned 500 Gold or more on the previous two missions and buy their first power upgrade.

BURNING QUESTIONS!

Q: Just how did a family of raccoons manage to function, at least temporarily, as an engine for the Dread-Yacht?

A: The key is that they were angry raccoons and also a family. Had you thrown just some ordinary, unrelated group of relatively calm raccoons into the engine room, there is no way they would have been able to get that ship to go anywhere. But the combination of the family bond and their anger created enough heat to power the ship. I wish I could tell you more, but to be honest, it doesn't make a whole lot of sense to me either.

Q: What did Flynn do to get banned from setting foot on the Junkyard Islands?

A: Like he said, it is a long story. Too long to tell here, we're afraid. But, what we can tell you is that the islands didn't used to be islands, and the only fruit that will grow there now is something called clamberries.

CHAPTER 3

RUMBLETOWN

STORY GOALS

- ✓ Locate the Hermit
- ◯ Win the Arena

ELEMENTAL GATES

- Life (x2)
- Undead

DARES

Time To Beat	8:40
Enemies to Defeat	185

AREAS TO FIND

◯ Sky Drifter's Jetty	◯ Weed Whisper Home
◯ Toebiter's Ascent	◯ Flap Jack Inn
◯ Moldy Retreat	◯ Guarded Tower
◯ Stink Breeze Point	◯ Watching Tower
◯ Cavern of Echoing Nibbles	◯ Sky Docks
◯ Quigley's Grotto	◯ Bridge Belly Dumps
◯ Shadow Grove	◯ Loglifter's Secret Place
◯ The Practice Pit	◯ Sour Sink Lodge
◯ Noggin-knock Village	◯ Toebiter's Keep
◯ Toebiter's House	◯ Lost Well

COLLECTIBLES & ENEMIES

Soul Gem	⬡	Ding Dong Ditch (Hot Dog)
Legendary Treasure		Eagle Pilot House Roof
Hats		Pilgrim Hat, Carrot Hat
Story Scroll		Mole Drop
Luck-O-Tron Wheel	⬤	Wheel of Power
Treasure Chests		4 to collect
Winged Sapphire		1 to collect

Chompies

Root Runners

Armored Lance Masters

Drow Archers

Life Spell Punk

MAP LEGEND

Direct Path	
Optional Path	
Feat of Strength	
Auric (Vendor)	
Hat Box	
Legendary Treasure	
Luck-O-Tron Wheel	
Skystones Challenger	
Soul Gem	
Story Scroll	
Treasure Chest	
Winged Sapphire	

SKY DRIFTER'S JETTY, TOEBITER'S ASCENT & MOLDY RETREAT

Favored Element: Air

Cross over into Sky Drifter's Jetty where a Chompy rushes to greet you. This is the standard breed of Chompy; you'll be seeing them often throughout your adventure. Move further into the area and a larger group of Chompies and a new type of enemy (Armored Lance Masters) are waiting for you.

Defeat the Chompies at the base of the mountain and approach the stacked stone blocks with faces etched in their side. Push these pillars to the right, then drop down to the left and collect the gold and a watermelon.

Bounce back up and follow the trail uphill. At the top, defeat the Armored Lance Masters and Root Runner to open the sealed gate. Continue up the path, but drop off the edge just before you reach the locked gate. Push the top stone block once to create a staircase that leads to the Moldy Retreat entrance.

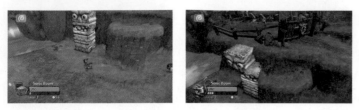

Inside there are three Root Runners and a Life Spell Punk defending a sealed gate. Maneuver around the Root Runners and take out the Punk first. After the gate drops, collect the **Luck-O-Tron Wheel** behind it.

Now, return outside to the locked gate. Go back up to the area near the Undead Element Gate. If you dropped down to grab the key, you can still enter Stink Breeze Point through the lower gate.

CAVERN OF ECHOING NIBBLES

Favored Element: Air

Now that you have the key, continue up Toebiter's Ascent and unlock the door. On the other side, a large group of enemies has assembled, including a Life Spell Punk. These guys heal their friends, so you should always defeat them first. Defeat the Punk and his Drow buddies and talk to the small Mabu for a hint on how to get to the Life area above.

At the top of Toebiter's Ascent is an encounter with several Drow Archers and Lancers. To access the Cavern of Echoing Nibbles, push the stone block nearest the edge of the path at the top of Toebiter's Ascent down to the level below and drop down on top of it. Inside the cave is a large group of Chompies and two Root Runners. Defeat them to recover the **Treasure Chest** at the back of the cave.

If you have an Air Skylander, this Cavern is a great spot to work on the "From Above" quest. Use the bounce pad on the left to keep bouncing while firing with a ranged attack to kill Chompies while falling.

UNDEAD ELEMENT GATE:
STINK BREEZE POINT

This is a small area with one hat, and Spoooooky, a Skystones challenger. Look for the **Pilgrim Hat** behind a brick wall. Bust down the wall with a Giant, or use the bomb at the top of Toebiter's Ascent to blow it open.

SKYSTONE CHALLENGER: SPOOOOKY
Reward For Winning First Game: Frigid Chompy 3

SPOOOOKY'S SKYSTONE DECK	
Mace Major	
Mohawk Cyclops 2	
Drow Archer	
Frigid Chompy 3	
Drow Lancemaster	

LIFE ELEMENT GATE:
QUIGLEY'S GROTTO & SHADOW GROVE

Go up to the Life Gate and defeat the Root Runner and minions that greet you on the other side. Use one of the push blocks near the entrance of the area to bridge the gap to the **Story Scroll: Mole Drop**. Drop down to the next lower level, and a vine bridge appears to allow you to cross to the next area, but watch out for the Ambush!

AMBUSH
STEALTH ELF

This is the first ambush attack your Skylanders face. Ambush enemies are significantly tougher than regular enemies since they are dark versions of your Skylanders. This Ambush features three evil versions of Stealth Elf.

Dark Stealth Elf has two attacks. The first is a charging dash that ends in a dagger swipe. Get away from this attack as it can inflict over 100 points of damage to your Skylander! If you successfully dodge Stealth Elf's attack, she is momentarily stunned. This is your opening! Attack each Elf until they teleport away. Now, get ready for another dagger swipe.

The trick to winning is to use your fastest Skylander. Prioritize dodging over attacking. You need to defeat all three of these Stealth Elves to pass this Ambush.

After winning the ambush, you can't access the locked door yet. Instead, cross the vine bridge to the right. Run up the walkway and drop down behind the push blocks. Slide the stone blocks to make a bridge to cross a walkway that ends at a bomb.

Toss the bomb across the skyway to the circular switch. The bomb explodes and opens the door north of the Ambush area. Continue through the newly-opened area near where you threw the bomb. Solve the lock puzzle on the left to capture another **Winged Sapphire**.

 Perfect Lock Puzzle Solution: 16 moves
Right, Right, Right, Right, Left, Left, Left, Left, Left, Left, Left, Left, Right, Right, Right, Right

To get to the **Carrot Hat**, you must break through one last brick wall. Getting through the wall is easiest with a Giant, but if you don't have one handy, return to the bomb earlier in the area and toss it over the one-way path. Use the teleporter behind the hat box to warp back to Quigley's Grotto.

THE PRACTICE PIT, NOGGIN-KNOCK VILLAGE & TOEBITER'S HOUSE

Favored Element: Magic

Return to where you originally entered Quigley's Grotto and smash the crates in the next area to uncover a secret bounce pad. Use it to jump up to the castle spire and collect some bonus treasure above. Drop down to the next area to enter The Practice Pit.

Defeat the four Drow Lancers, and the oversized Drow named Brock emerges. Brock plays a bigger role in the future, but for now you just need to defeat a mixed group of Drow minions.

After defeating them, continue into Noggin-knock village. The exit gate for this village is blocked by a double-key lock. One key is down the left path, and one is down the right.

Start by exploring the wooden bridge on the right. This leads to two small houses. The first house is Toebiter's House. It contains one Lancer and one Life Spell Punk. Defeat them to open the gate and collect the first key.

LIFE ELEMENT GATE:
WEED WHISPER HOME

Switch to a Life Skylander to get past the gate inside the second home, farther to the left of Toebiter's House. Defeat the Chompies and the Root Runner past the wall, and then solve the Lock Puzzle to access the **Treasure Chest**.

🔒 **Perfect Lock Puzzle Solution: 5 moves**
Right, Right, Left, Left, Left

FLAP JACK INN & GUARDED TOWER

Favored Element: Magic

When you return to Noggin-knock Village, several Chompies, Lancers, and a Life Spell Punk spawn in the main area. Defeat them and enter the newly-opened

house door next to the lock gate. Eat the stack of pancakes if you need to restore any life, then head back out and prepare for the left path.

The second key is at the top of the spiral building. Before using the keys on the locked gate, drop down to the lower area to find more pancakes, some gold, and the door to Guarded Tower. Quigley is inside, guarded by Drow Archers. This time Quigley wants to challenge you to Skystones.

SKYSTONE CHALLENGER: QUIGLEY
Reward For Winning First Game: Axecutioner

QUIGLEY'S SKYSTONE DECK
Axecutioner (x5)

Quigley's Skystones are serious business. You won't be able to beat him until you manage to get some of the best Skystones in the game.

WATCHING TOWER & SKY DOCKS

Favored Element: Air

Pass through the locked gate to enter the Watching Tower. Ignore the floating ball for now and move down to the landing.

The Sky Docks are accessed by moving the push blocks into place near the timed door. The Sky Docks contain an easy-to-find **Legendary Treasure: Eagle Pilot House Roof**.

Head back to the floating ball and attack it to lower a door in the next area. You have 13 seconds to make it through the door before it closes. Defeat the Drow Archers and Life Spell Punk to drop the gate to the next area. Attempt to cross the bridge, but Brock destroys it before you make it all the way across.

BRIDGE BELLY DUMPS & SOUR SINK LODGE

Favored Element: Undead

After falling from the bridge, move to the stack of push blocks at the top right of the screen. Push the blocks down to form a walkway to the second plateau, and push the blocks there to make a second walkway. The key is on the third plateau.

Before using the key on the exterior gate, check out the house near it. Use the key inside the Sour Sink Lodge to unlock the door. Grab the second key as well as Hot Dog's **Soul Gem** inside.

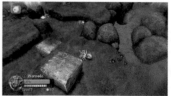

Head outside to unlock the gate. Beyond the gate, there is another set of push blocks. Use these three blocks to make a new path to the final plateau. You may need to drop back down to push one of the old push blocks into place.

Defeat the Root Runners, Chompies, and Drow Archers to unseal the gate up to the castle. Turn around from the castle gate before you enter and look for some items to smash for extra treasure and Auric, who has a few items to sell you.

AURIC'S INVENTORY	
ITEM	COST
Elemental Elixir Charm	400 Gold
Elf Hat	250 Gold
Fancy Hat	250 Gold
Birthday Hat	250 Gold
Regeneration Power Up	100 Gold
Lock Puzzle Key	500 Gold
Fairy Dust	50 Gold

LOST WELL & LOGLIFTER'S SECRET PLACE

Favored Element: Undead

If you have a Giant, there are two additional secret areas to check out before exiting the level. Continue south past Auric, and look for a Giant jumping pad. Jump down to uncover Lost Well, which contains a **Treasure Chest.** Exit Lost Well, and move across the plateau to discover a Giant Feat of Strength Challenge. Successfully toss the logs with your Giant to access Loglifter's secret place. This chapter's last **Treasure Chest** is located inside.

TOEBITER'S KEEP

When you are ready for the final fight, head back up to where Auric's store was. There is a trick door here; hit the triggers on either side of it to open it and begin the showdown with Brock!

BOSS FIGHT
BROCK

Before you fight Brock, you must first take care of the waves of his minions. The first wave is Chompies and Lance Masters. The second wave consists of Chompies, Lance Masters, Drow Archers, and Life Spell Punks. To make things interesting, the center of the arena intermittently catches fire.

The final wave is Brock and Life Spell Punks. Brock is a tough Goliath Drow. He is invincible while charging, so you must focus on dodging. If he misses you, you get an opening and can hit him from behind. Brock gets help from Life Spell Punks, so focus on taking them out when they arrive.

PRO FIGHT TIPS

Since there is no favored element during this battle, use your highest-level Skylander. You can knock enemies off the sides of the arena. This is a great way to handle tougher enemies if your Skylander has a power that can push enemies.

If you haven't yet met the enemy Dare target when you enter the arena, take out as many enemies as possible before finishing off Brock. You can quickly and easily defeat Brock by luring him off the side of the arena. Just stand on the arena edge and wait for him to charge you. Move out of the way at the last second to win the arena fight instantly!

BACK ON FLYNN'S SHIP

Once you get back on Flynn's Ship, you discover Brock isn't such a bad guy. In fact, he's even ready to set up Arena Fights for your Skylanders. For more information on Arena Fights, check out the Flynn's Ship Chapter.

You can now access the Crane Deck area which is in the bow of the ship. There is a big ruby you can collect back there. Check this area after completing every chapter for a free gem.

BURNING QUESTIONS!

Q: Why would a hermit live in a town? Shouldn't hermits live way out in the middle of nowhere, away from the public?

A: That would make sense if Ermit actually was a hermit. But he's not! People just confuse him with one because of his name and paranoid nature. He's really quite a people person, though. Just not a cloud person.

Q: How did Quigley acquire such an incredible deck of Skystones?

A: He constantly bugs his parents to get him the best Skystones the day they come out. Eventually, he just wears them down.

CHAPTER 4
CUTTHROAT CARNIVAL

STORY GOALS

✓ Repair the Ship

ELEMENTAL GATES

Air

Undead

DARES

Time To Beat	8:15
Enemies to Defeat	80

AREAS TO FIND

- Loading Platform 1
- Janitor's Lounge
- Concessions
- The Oar and Plank
- The Batson House
- Loading Platform 2
- House of Cards
- The Promenade
- Loading Platform 3
- The Boat House
- The Galleon
- Swirling Vista
- Pirate Prison
- Pirate Island
- Quartermaster's Cabin
- Batson's Summer House
- Undead Wastes
- The Crow's Nest

COLLECTIBLES & ENEMIES

Soul Gem		Bee is for Butt Stinger (Swarm)
Legendary Treasure		Skull Masthead
Hats		Lampshade Hat, Mariachi Hat
Story Scroll		Forger's Basement
Luck-O-Tron Wheel		Lucky Wheel of Wealth
Treasure Chests		4 to collect
Winged Sapphire		1 to collect

Drow Archer

Mohawk Cyclops

Armored Chompy

Goliath Drow

Axecutioner

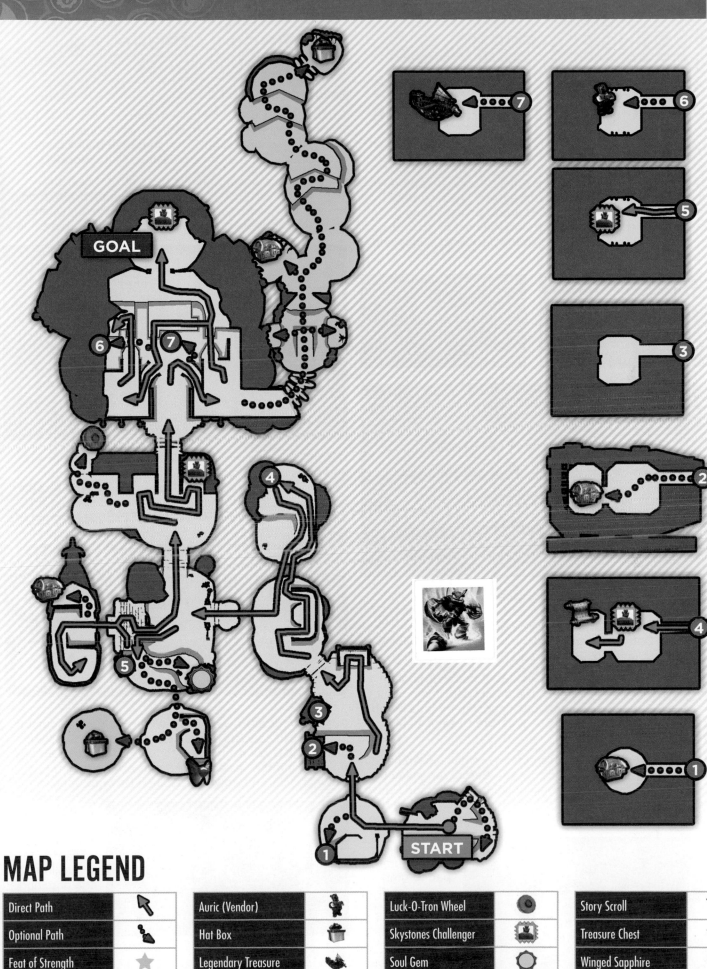

GOAL

START

MAP LEGEND

Direct Path		Auric (Vendor)		Luck-O-Tron Wheel		Story Scroll	
Optional Path		Hat Box		Skystones Challenger		Treasure Chest	
Feat of Strength		Legendary Treasure		Soul Gem		Winged Sapphire	

LOADING PLATFORM 1, JANITOR'S LOUNGE, CONCESSIONS, THE OAR AND PLANK & THE BATSON HOUSE

Favored Element: Tech

Welcome to Cutthroat Island, Skylands' premiere pirate circus! After talking to Bowers, head south to explore the pier and collect the loose treasure. The next deck is called Loading Platform 1. Hold off on activating the steering wheel, and move around the cockpit to find a secret door. This door leads to the Janitor's Lounge and contains a **Treasure Chest**.

Back outside, use the steering wheel to move the platform to the next deck, Concessions. The area is defended by Mohawk Cyclops enemies and Drow Archers. Defeat the enemies and head into the building on the first landing, The Oar and Plank.

The Oar and Plank is a small area that has an iron gate inside. Use a Giant to smash the door open. If you don't have a Giant, you can come back here later with a bomb found in the Batson House. A **Treasure Chest** is behind the gate in here.

Head back outside and finish off any remaining Archers. This reveals a jump pad up to a key. Before retrieving the key, head to the second small building, The Batson House. Inside, there is a bomb and some loose treasure. Use the bomb on the gate in The Oar and Plank if you don't have any Giants. Back outside, use the jump pad to grab the key and enter the next area.

LOADING PLATFORM 2 & HOUSE OF CARDS

Favored Element: Life

On the other side of the locked gate is Loading Platform 2 and your first encounter with Armored Chompies. Don't worry; they're only slightly tougher than their Chompy brothers. Defeat the Chompies and talk to Blobbers.

Use the ship's wheel to move the platform near the shipping crates. Push the crate onto the platform, then move it again with the ship wheel. Push the block into the hole, and Blobbers remembers you need to retrieve a key.

Use the wheel to move the platform to the right again, and cross over. Continue up into the town and enter the door to find the House of Cards and Fangs. The tutorial does a great job introducing the basics to you but for more advanced info, check out the Skystones section of this guide. After defeating Fangs, grab the key and the **Story Scroll: Forger's Basement**.

SKYSTONE CHALLENGER: FANGS

Reward For Winning First Game: Enfuego Chompy 3

FANGS' SKYSTONE DECK

Spiderlings (x5)

Get ready for a Drow ambush, when you're back outside. The ambush consists of a Goliath Drow who keeps you busy while Drow Archers try to hit you with their arrows from behind the sealed gate. Focus on dodging the Drow attacks and down the Goliath Drow to open the gate back to Blobbers. Speak with Blobbers for a reward before unlocking the gate and entering the next area.

THE PROMENADE & LOADING PLATFORM 3

Favored Element: Water

Defeat the Cyclops and Drow Goliaths that drop into the ring to battle you. Defeating the three Goliaths and their archer buddies opens the sealed gate. Cali points out a nearby floating Galleon. To access the Galleon you must either use a Giant to pull the ship closer, or talk to Chance inside the Boat House and beat him at Skystones.

Before doing either, continue past Cali and along the path to grab Swarm's **Soul Gem.** Continue further along to find Loading Platform 3. Move up to where the ship wheel is and drop down to find a **Winged Sapphire.**

AIR ELEMENT GATE:
SWIRLING VISTA

Turn the ship's wheel to move the platform. Cross the platform to reach an Air Gate. Grab the **Lampshade Hat** and head back out to Loading Platform 3.

THE BOAT HOUSE & THE GALLEON

Favored Element: Water

Make sure to play Skystones against Chance before your Giant Skylander pulls the ship in! He leaves town if you beat him to the punch.

SKYSTONE CHALLENGER: CHANCE
Reward For Winning First Game: Drow Lance Master 2

CHANCE'S SKYSTONE DECK	
Spiderlings (x2)	
Drow Lance Master (x2)	
Drow Lance Master 2	

Board The Galleon and look for a **Treasure Chest** at the bow. Use the cannon on the stern of the ship. Return to The Promenade, defeat the Cyclops enemies, and proceed up the path to Woof.

PIRATE PRISON & PIRATE ISLAND

Favored Element: Fire

The first thing to do in the Prison is to push the cannon all the way to the left. Blow the gate to uncover the **Lucky Wheel of Wealth.** Now push the cannon to the next cell to access the track switch. You can also use a Giant to destroy the gates.

Activate the switch and continue pushing the cannon all the way to the right. Blow the gate and challenge Bandit to a game of Skystones. After defeating Bandit, go talk to Woof.

SKYSTONE CHALLENGER: BANDIT
Reward For Winning First Game: Blaster Troll 2

BANDIT'S SKYSTONE DECK	
Chompy (x2)	
Blaster Troll	
Blaster Troll 2 (x2)	

When the gate to the next area opens, defeat the Axecutioner. Cali shows up again to point out the house of the best Skystones player in the carnival. Head up the right ramp and defeat the Axecutioners and Drow Archers to unlock the sealed gate.

UNDEAD ELEMENT GATE:

UNDEAD WASTES

Before exploring more of Pirate Island, head to the right and talk to T-Bone in front of the gate to the Undead Wastes. In the first puzzle block area of the wastes, hit the two switches on either side of the center platform. Use the same push block to form a bridge to the third and fourth switches. After hitting all four switches, use the push block a third time to form a bridge to the next plateau.

The next area contains an iron gate that you need a Giant to break through. Smash the gate to access a **Treasure Chest**. Continue along the bony plateaus, dodging the giant rotating scythes. When you reach the end, you receive the **Mariachi Hat** for your efforts.

QUARTERMASTER'S CABIN & BATSON'S SUMMER HOUSE

Favored Element: Fire

Back on Pirate Island, knock the push block down to form a walkway to the center area. Push a second block down in the center area, and drop down to push it into place in the left walkway.

Walk past Cali up the left walkway. Defeat the Goliath Drow and his Cyclops buddies to open the sealed gate. Continue along the walkway to grab the key. After retrieving the key, drop down to the lower area on your left and enter the door to the Quartermaster's Cabin. Auric is waiting for you inside. Before leaving Auric, smash all the crates to find a special button. This unlocks a gate back in the main courtyard.

AURIC'S INVENTORY	
ITEM	COST
Drow Archer 2 Skystone	100 Gold
Gargantula Skystone	1,200 Gold
Charm Hunt Challenge	3,000 Gold
Viking Helmet	350 Gold
Fez	320 Gold
Invincibility Power Up	250 Gold
Lock Puzzle Key	500 Gold
Fairy Dust	50 Gold

Back in the courtyard, enter the middle door to access the secret Batson's Summer House area. Inside, there is some food, some treasure, and the **Legendary Treasure: Skull Masthead**. Continue to the locked gate at the top of Pirate Island to meet Dreadbeard.

THE CROW'S NEST
Favored Element: Life

BOSS FIGHT
DREADBEARD

Dreadbeard wants to fight more than play Skystones, but he's not one to get his hands dirty. He sends in two waves of minions for you to contend with first. The first wave is Drow Archers, Mohawk Cyclops enemies, and an Axecutioner. The second wave consists of Drow Archers, Armored Chompies, Mohawk Cyclops, and Drow Goliaths.

The enemies here tend to come out in tight groups, so area-of-effect attacks are best. Beat his minions, and Dreadbeard challenges you to a game of Skystones!

SKYSTONE CHALLENGER: DREADBEARD
Reward For Winning First Game: Arkeyan Jouster

DREADBEARD'S SKYSTONE DECK	
Mohawk Cyclops (x3)	
Spiderlings	
Arkeyan Jouster	

BACK ON FLYNN'S SHIP

Back on Flynn's ship, you get the news that you have another member on your crew, Dreadbeard! Dreadbeard is always ready to play Skystones in the Game Room next to Auric.

BURNING QUESTIONS!

Q: What made Blobbers want to work at the Cutthroat Carnival?

A: First off, Blobbers has a history of making bad decisions, so he probably didn't really think this through. What really might have attracted him was that Cutthroat Carnival is the last known place in Skylands where one can purloin a churro. The pirates told Blobbers that if he worked for them, he could eat all the churros he wanted. The instant Blobbers heard that, he hastily signed a contract without first finding out what the job paid (nothing) and what his hours would be (all of them—he got no days off). Thus, another bad decision sealed by Blobbers.

Q: How did Skystones get started?

A: Few people know the origin of Skystones, but we do! It was invented by a group of lazy Molekin workers. They were hired to put tiles down on a floor, but they quickly got bored of this job and tried to make a game out of it. That game became Skystones, and these Molekin became very rich. All for being lazy! That's probably not the best message to send out to the children of Earth, but hey, it's the truth!

CHAPTER 5

GLACIER GULLY

STORY GOALS

☑ Find the Giant Robot

ELEMENTAL GATES

Magic

Fire

DARES	
Time To Beat	7:40
Enemies to Defeat	75

AREAS TO FIND

○ Snow Bump

○ Icy Remains

○ Magical Happening

○ Noodles' Cold Plate

○ Crystal Shards

○ Windy Reach

○ Frozen Cactus Shrine

○ Frozen Toe

○ Fiery Thumb

○ Burnt Depths

○ Phoenix Rising

○ Chilled Bowl

○ Icy Drain

○ Snow Drift Gate

○ Island of Ice

COLLECTIBLES & ENEMIES

Soul Gem	⬡	Blowhard (Thumpback)
Legendary Treasure		Floral Reef Paint Job
Hats		Purple Fedora, Firefighter Helmet
Story Scroll		Arkeyan Memory
Luck-O-Tron Wheel	◉	Lucky Wheel of Experience
Treasure Chests		4 to collect
Winged Sapphire		1 to collect

Frigid Chompy

Mohawk Cyclops

Axecutioner

Bag O' Boom

En Fuego Chompy

Armored Mohawk

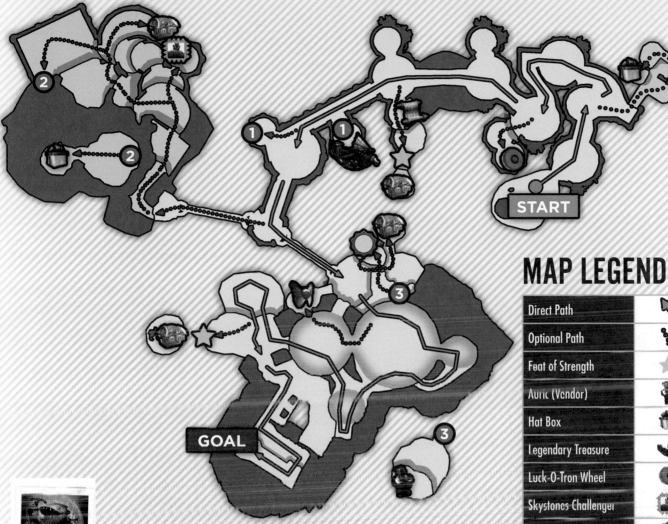

MAP LEGEND

Direct Path	
Optional Path	
Feat of Strength	
Auric (Vendor)	
Hat Box	
Legendary Treasure	
Luck-O-Tron Wheel	
Skystones Challenger	
Soul Gem	
Story Scroll	
Treasure Chest	
Winged Sapphire	

SNOW BUMP & ICY REMAINS

Favored Element: Water

The first thing to do is to take a dive into the secret Snow Bump plateau off the left side of the starting platform. Down there, you find some loose treasure and a bomb. Toss the bomb towards the domed building visible at the top of the screen. This reveals a Luck-O-Tron Wheel that you can collect later.

Head back up via the bounce pad and break down the brick wall to enter Icy Remains and encounter a new enemy type, Frigid Chompies. Watch out for their frozen breath! Talk to Machine Ghost to gain him as a follower.

MAGIC ELEMENT GATE:
MAGICAL HAPPENING

After meeting Machine Ghost, take a right on the icy path and slide your way to this Magic Gate entrance. Slide the blocks into place to form a walkway up to the **Purple Fedora.**

NOODLES' COLD PLATE, CRYSTAL SHARDS & WINDY REACH

Favored Element: Air

In the next area, Machine Ghost shows you how to use a light crystal to melt ice. These crystals are the key to many puzzles in future chapters. They can also hurt enemies! Follow Noodles down the ramp to Noodles' Cold Plate. Destroy the Cyclops and the Snowmen in the area and Noodles returns. Defeat the minions he summons to unlock the gate.

Before passing through the gate, drop down through the broken rail on the left to snag the **Lucky Wheel of Experience** you uncovered earlier in the level. Continue along the path until you find another light crystal. Push the crystal towards the ice block and then activate the switch on the right to turn the light crystal to reflect the beam into the giant ice cube.

Next up is a trickier crystal puzzle. Push the first crystal to melt the ice block on the right. Move this same crystal all the way back to its starting position, then push it southward. Turn the activated crystal to aim at this first crystal to melt the second ice block.

Before leaving the area, smash the wall on the left to gain access to the **Story Scroll: Arkeyan Memory**. Switch to a Giant and rip up the stone on the left. Drop down and complete the Feat of Strength to enter Windy Reach and earn a **Treasure Chest.**

FROZEN CACTUS SHRINE & FROZEN TOE

Favored Element: Water

After clearing out Windy Reach, head back to the main path to discover Frozen Cactus Shrine. Watch out, the cacti here are prickly! When you see the Bag O' Boom enemy, catch one of his bombs and toss it towards the domed building on the left. The first bomb just breaks the stone wall; toss a second to destroy the building. Destroying the building reveals this chapter's Legendary Treasure.

Defeat the short ogres and Mohawk Cyclops in the next area and search for the hidden teleporter on the right platform. This portal takes you up to the domed building you destroyed and the **Legendary Treasure: Floral Reef Paint Job**.

FIRE ELEMENT GATE:

FIERY THUMB, BURNT DEPTHS & PHOENIX RISING

Before exploring further into the Frozen Toe, how about a change of climate? Turn right down the long chain and switch over to a Fire Skylander.

Follow the lava path down to where you encounter En Fuego Chompies for the first time. Defeat the Chompies, and continue falling down the lava platforms. Destroy the fire crystals at the edges of the platforms. Keep dropping to the left until you find the world-class Skystones player, Smoltergeist!

SKYSTONE CHALLENGER: SMOLTERGEIST

Reward For Winning First Game: Boom Fiend

SMOLTERGEIST'S SKYSTONE DECK	
Chompy 2	
Mace Major (x2)	
Mace Major 2	
Boom Fiend	

After defeating Smoltergeist, use the bounce pads to get back up one platform. This time take the right path. Keep dropping to the right and you should come to an area with two push blocks and a crystal. Leave the blocks up here and push the crystal down to the lower level. Drop down after the crystal.

Before solving the big puzzle at the base of the Burnt Depths, use the bounce pad to jump up to the area on the left. Search the back of the area for a **Treasure Chest**.

Back at the puzzle. Push the crystals into the formation as shown in the screenshot to open the gate to the last section.

Teleport to the top, and you face an ambush! After you escape the ambush, collect your reward in the next area, a **Firefighter Helmet**.

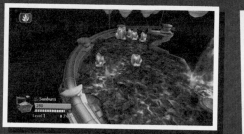 

AMBUSH

SUNBURN

Dark Sunburn has high health and effective and damaging attacks. Don't worry about switching to a non-fire Skylander; the lava won't hurt you here. You need to use a fast Skylander to dodge Sunburn's primary attack, which is hard to avoid and inflicts an impressive amount of damage.

Sunburn's second attack is to teleport to where your Skylander is standing. This can be hard to see because his teleportation circle is magma-colored, and you are fighting in a magma arena. If you do see her doing this, run as fast as you can! When she pops out, she can seriously injure your Skylander. Keep moving and zapping Sunburn; patience and speed are the keys to success.

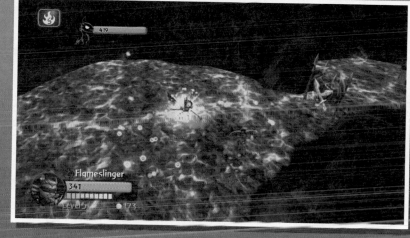

CHILLED BOWL & ICY DRAIN

Favored Element: Water

After dealing with the Fiery Thumb, it's time to return to the Frozen Toe. Slide down the chain to encounter Noodles and his minions. Defeat the Frigid Chompies, Armored Mohawks, Bag O' Booms, and Axecutioners to reveal two hidden bounce pads. To make this fight easier, toss the bombs thrown by the Bag O' Booms back at your foes.

Noodles: So now you're gonna pay for your mistake!

Use the bounce pads to get inside the Chilled Bowl. Traversing its icy surface can be difficult, but it is much easier if you have a Skylander with a dash ability like Slam Bam's Yeti Ice Shoe Slide. The first place you should slide to is the edge of the bowl nearest the screen. Drop down there to find Thumpback's **Soul Gem**. Enter the cave in the same area to find the Icy Drain and Auric.

AURIC'S INVENTORY	
ITEM	COST
Propeller Cap	400 Gold
Top Hat	450 Gold
Frigid Chompy 2	100 Gold
Arkeyan Jouster 4	800 Gold
Regeneration Power Up	175 Gold
Skystone Cheat	500 Gold
Lock Puzzle Key	500 Gold

After talking to Auric, return to the Chilled Bowl. Push the block that you used to cross to the Soul Gem. When you've pushed the block as far as you can go, re-enter the other side of this area via the Chilled Bowl (the same way you originally got to the Soul Gem). This allows you to keep pushing the block until you make a bridge to a **Treasure Chest.**

Head back to the Chilled Bowl again. This time, head to the second (smaller) bowl on your right. Use your momentum to get over the right ledge and land near a **Winged Sapphire**. Next, your goal is to collect the three keys to open a gate. The first key is in the very small bowl in the northwest of the area. Smash the brick wall and then slide over the top to collect it.

The second key is in the miniature bowl at the north of this area. Slide into the bowl and smash the wall to find the key. With the two keys collected, it's time to exit the bowl. Find the exit all the way to the east of the bowl area.

SNOW DRIFT GATE & ISLAND OF ICE

Favored Element: Magic

Snow Drift Gate still requires one more key. To retrieve it, drop down to the lower plateau at the bottom of the screen. Once you have the key, you must escape the plateau; you need to defeat the waves of enemies to reveal a bounce pad.

Before opening Snow Drift Gate, switch to a Giant and complete the Feat of Strength on the right for one last **Treasure Chest** on the Island of Ice.

Take out the Bag O' Boom and then use the nearby switch to melt the far-off ice block. Now, use the push block at the south end of the area, and push the crystal into place. After melting the first ice cube, push the block into the hole and melt the second ice cube. Follow the path around and use the bounce pad up to the giant robot. Turn the beam up top to melt the giant robot's icy cage.

BACK ON FLYNN'S SHIP

Before moving on to Chapter 6, head to the Crow's Nest for a bonus **Winged Sapphire**.

BURNING QUESTIONS!

Q: Noodles...what went wrong?

A: A lot. How long is this book anyway? What? We better be quick.

Okay, well for one, Glacier Gully is known for some pretty incredible hail storms. Big, heavy chunks of ice fall from the sky and most residents know to stay indoors when this happens. Not Noodles, though. Growing up, he loved to run outside during these storms and try to catch ice blocks on his tongue. He never succeeded, but did manage to take many falling ice blocks to the head. Since he would not wear a helmet in these situations, it led to a steep decline in Noodles' general brain functionality.

Q: How did Ermit even get a giant robot in the first place?

A: After trying unsuccessfully to build one for years, Ermit won it in a Skystones game with Freebot 002.

CHAPTER 6
SECRET VAULT OF SECRETS

STORY GOALS

- ✓ Unlock the East Dam
- ◯ Unlock the West Dam
- ◯ Open the Arkeyan Vault

ELEMENTAL GATES

 Tech

DARES

Time To Beat	13:10
Enemies to Defeat	50

AREAS TO FIND

- ◯ Sunrise Canyon
- ◯ East Dam Approach
- ◯ East Dam
- ◯ East Dam Controls
- ◯ Forgotten Caverns
- ◯ Flood Gulch
- ◯ West Dam Approach
- ◯ Logger's Corner
- ◯ West Dam
- ◯ West Dam Cliffside
- ◯ Gorge of the Ancients
- ◯ Vault Approach
- ◯ Vault Inner Workings
- ◯ Vault Control Platform
- ◯ Vault Access Area

COLLECTIBLES & ENEMIES

Soul Gem	◯	Fists of Destruction! (Bouncer)
Legendary Treasure		Stripes Ahoy Paint Job
Hats		Officer Hat, Archer Hat
Story Scroll		Onk and a Totem
Luck-O-Tron Wheel	◉	Lucky Wheel of Health
Treasure Chests		4 to collect
Winged Sapphire		1 to collect

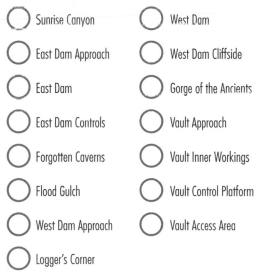

Arkeyan Autogyro

Arkeyan Ultron

Arkeyan Bomber

Arkeyan Jouster

Chompy

Bark Demon

Root Runner

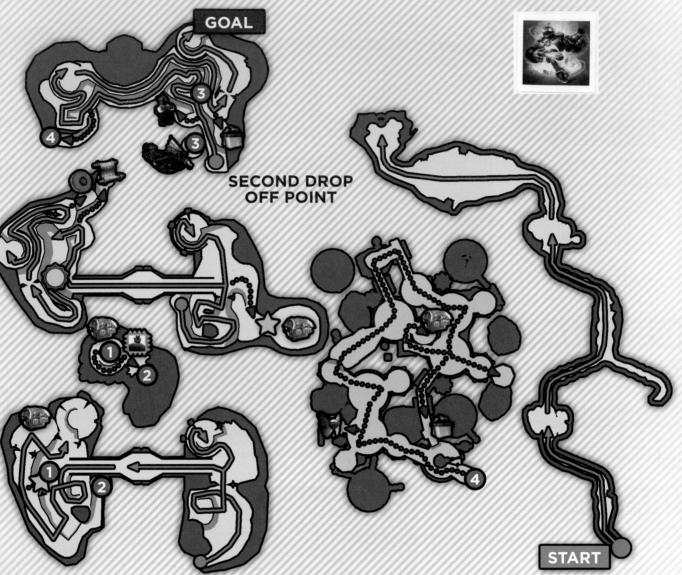

GOAL

3

4

3

SECOND DROP OFF POINT

1

2

1

2

4

START

FIRST DROP OFF POINT

MAP LEGEND

Direct Path	
Optional Path	
Feat of Strength	
Auric (Vendor)	
Hat Box	
Legendary Treasure	
Luck-O-Tron Wheel	
Skystones Challenger	
Soul Gem	
Story Scroll	
Treasure Chest	
Winged Sapphire	

SUNRISE CANYON

You start this level off in Machine Ghost's giant robot. Throughout this section, there's not much to strategize, just blast or punch everything you see!

The Attack 1 button fires the robot's cannons; the Attack 2 button performs a giant robot punch. Whenever you

punch one of the Generators, this charges your super attack. Press Attack 3 to fire the Shockwave attack, wiping out everything on the screen! To see how many Shockwave attacks you have, look for the nuclear sign at the bottom of the screen.

EAST DAM APPROACH & EAST DAM

Favored Element: Earth

Machine Ghost drops you off in East Dam Approach, the first dam you must open. The first group of enemies you encounter are Chompies and a new enemy, the Arkeyan Bomber. Whenever an Arkeyan Bomber hits you with one of their bombs, quickly hit the Activate button to toss it back.

This first switch gate is trickier than the ones encountered previously. You must hit one switch, then the other in under six seconds to open the gate. First hit the switch on the left (use a bomb thrown by the Arkeyan Bomber if you can), then shoot the switch on the right, and make a dash for the door!

Continue to the Dam Generator and follow the onscreen prompts to restore power. Avoid the electricity on the East Dam (using a burrowing Skylander like Terrafin helps). Halfway across the dam you encounter a new Arkeyan enemy, the Arkeyan Jouster. Hang back and wait for their shields to come down before you attack. If you have a melee Skylander, wait until they miss with their attack before you move in to strike.

EAST DAM CONTROLS & FORGOTTEN CAVERNS

Favored Element: Earth

The other side of the bridge is East Dam Controls. Defeat the Arkeyan enemies here to reveal the bounce pad. Before jumping up, grab the key on the path at the bottom of the screen.

Right before you hit the bounce pad to the upper path, hit the nearby switch. Now, you need to keep hitting the switches all the way up the path to open a sealed door with a second key and a **Treasure Chest** behind it.

Bounce back up to the path and switch to a Giant Skylander. Perform a cannonball halfway up the ramp to enter Forgotten Caverns. This secret area contains a **Treasure Chest** and a Skystones Challenger.

SKYSTONE CHALLENGE: WEAPON MASTER
Reward For Winning First Game: Arkeyan Jouster 3

WEAPON MASTER'S SKYSTONE DECK	
Spiderlings 2 (x2)	
Chompy 3 (x2)	
Arkeyan Jouster 3	

Back in the main area, use the keys on the locked door at the top of the controls and solve the Lock Puzzle to gain access to turn on the second dam switch.

🔒 **Perfect Lock Puzzle Solution: 5 moves**
Left, Left, Left, Left, Left

FLOOD GULCH

You return to the giant robot and continue blasting and punching a path through the gulch until you encounter an unmanned Arkeyan robot. To defeat the robot, wait until just before the robot punches to counterpunch. Machine Ghost helps with a prompt that makes this easier. Just wait until you see the prompt before you hit Attack 2.

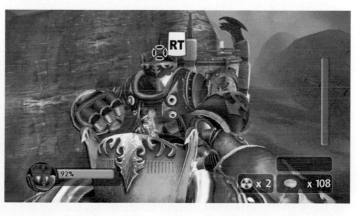

161

WEST DAM APPROACH & LOGGER'S CORNER

Favored Element: Tech

You must now reactivate the West Dam's power. The first area features Arkeyan Jousters, a Bark Demon, and an Arkeyan Bomber. If you are using a melee Skylander, you can use the bombs from the Arkeyan Bomber to blow up all the enemies in the area. To open the switch door, start by attacking the rightmost switch, then hit the two switches on the left.

After you pass through the gate, take a slight U-turn and explore the path on the right. Discover a Feat of Strength. Complete it to enter Logger's Corner and find a **Treasure Chest**.

WEST DAM & WEST DAM CLIFFSIDE

Favored Element: Tech

Return to West Dam Approach and activate the coil. Carefully cross over the West Dam and solve the Lock Puzzle to gain access to Bouncer's **Soul Gem**.

 Perfect Lock Puzzle Solution: 11 moves
Left, Left, Right, Right, Right, Right, Right, Right, Left, Left, Left

Move up West Dam Cliffside until you find an intersection. Continue along the side of the cliff away from the visible enemies to find the **Story Scroll: Onk and a Totem**.

Go back to the intersection and continue up the West Dam Cliffside. The enemies in this area include Bark Demons, a Root Runner, Chompies, and an Arkeyan Bomber off to one side. Use the Arkeyan Bomber's bombs to quickly defeat the demons.

With the first wave of enemies down, a new enemy, the Arkeyan Shield Juggernaut, arrives to give you some trouble. Before taking on the Juggernaut, finish off the Bombers. Their bombs are hard to use against the Juggernaut's shields, and they just make taking it down harder. Focus on dodging while the Juggernaut's laser is up, and get in as many attacks as you can while it recharges between blasts.

After taking care of the enemies, you must hit another set of switches to open a door at the top of the path. Defeat the three Arkeyan Jousters waiting on the path to open the next locked gate. Before passing through the gate, drop down to a small ledge off the path for a **Luck-O-Tron Lucky Wheel of Health.** Bounce back up to the main path and follow it up to the top where you must solve another Lock Puzzle.

 Perfect Lock Puzzle Solution: 7 moves
Right, Left, Left, Right, Right, Left, Left

GORGE OF THE ANCIENTS

You're sent back to the giant robot, and you should stick to your previous strategies. There are more Arkeyan defenses to contend with, but nothing more challenging than what you've already passed through. You must defeat a pair of giant Arkeyan Robots this time.

VAULT APPROACH & VAULT CONTROL PLATFORM

Favored Element: Water

After jumping off the robot a third time, take the left path to meet up with Auric. Buy what you can, then continue up the right path and smash the vases at the end to uncover a secret teleporter. The teleporter sends you to a platform with the **Legendary Treasure: Stripes Ahoy Paint Job.**

AURIC'S INVENTORY

ITEM	COST
Aqueduct	2,500 Gold
Spy Gear	500 Gold
Tropical Turban	550 Gold
Arkeyan Ultron Skystone	1,000 Gold
Regeneration Power Up	200 Gold
Lock Puzzle Key	500 Gold
Fairy Dust	50 Gold

Back to the Vault Approach path, activate the power coil to open the way to the vault walkway. Cross the walkway to reach the Vault Control Platform. Instead of moving straight up to the Vault Control Platform, look for a gap in the fence and drop down to a short path below.

TECH ELEMENT GATE:
VAULT INNER WORKINGS

Ignore the giant key and move through the turning platform to get the first regular-sized key. Return to the big key and turn it to move the platform. Cross over both turning platforms to another big key and activate it.

Use your regular key to open the door with the bounce pad. Before using the bounce pad, turn the nearby giant key to move the platforms back to access the **Winged Sapphire**.

Return to the bounce pad, jump up to the next area and follow the path through more metal platforms, wooden bridges, and a handful of enemies. Look for a raised platform with another large key and a **Treasure Chest**.

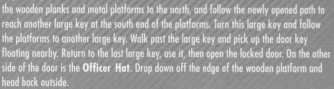

Turn the key and retrace some of your steps back around the wooden planks and metal platforms to the north, and follow the newly opened path to reach another large key at the south end of the platforms. Turn this large key and follow the platforms to another large key. Walk past the large key and pick up the door key floating nearby. Return to the last large key, use it, then open the locked door. On the other side of the door is the **Officer Hat**. Drop down off the edge of the wooden platform and head back outside.

VAULT ACCESS AREA

Favored Element: Water

Follow the path up to the platform, which is guarded by Arkeyan Bombers, Jouster, and a Bark Demon. Go up on the platform and wait for the Bombers to toss bombs. Throw the bombs back at your enemies to clear the area quickly. You must solve the puzzle to open the next walkway.

 Perfect Lock Puzzle Solution: 7 moves
Right, Right, Right, Left, Left, Left, Right

The path leads to the Vault Access Area and a handful of Chompies. Beyond the Chompies, you must deal with another Juggernaut and Arkeyan Bombers. Use the cliff path for cover from the Juggernaut's laser. Stick to ranged attacks; the Juggernaut is just too deadly up close in this spot. When the Juggernaut falls, look to the south for a gap in the gate. Drop down onto a small ledge with a floating hat box. Open the box and claim the **Archer Hat**. Continue further into the Vault Access Area, clear it of Bombers, and solve one last Lock Puzzle to completely unlock the Arkeyan Vault.

Perfect Lock Puzzle Solution: 11 moves
Right, Right, Right, Left, Left, Left, Left, Right, Left, Left, Right

BURNING QUESTIONS!

Q: Why did the Arkeyans stash their map inside the vault? Don't they know where their own city is?

A: They do, but Arkeyans have a tendency to forget things that are underneath them, and the city of Arkus just happens to be buried deep underground. So, they decided to keep a map around just in case anyone ever got lost. But they also keep it locked up in their vault so the Giants couldn't find it. Only problem is, their vault is also underground, and thus, the Arkeyans forgot about it as well.

CHAPTER 7
WILIKIN VILLAGE

STORY GOALS

- ✓ Enter Wilikin World
- ◯ Clear out all the Monsters
- ◯ Beat the Chompy Mage

ELEMENTAL GATES

- 🏔 Earth

DARES	
Time To Beat	11:15
Enemies to Defeat	95

AREAS TO FIND

- ◯ Isle of the Wilikins
- ◯ Facadeville
- ◯ The Abandoned House
- ◯ Doll Day-Care
- ◯ Rutherford's Game Room
- ◯ Stephanie's House
- ◯ Helena's Home
- ◯ Hamilton Landing
- ◯ Carlton's House
- ◯ Catherine's Home
- ◯ The Mud Flats

- ◯ Planer Plateau
- ◯ The Wing Caves
- ◯ The Cliffside Path
- ◯ Roc's Elbow
- ◯ The Perilous Coil
- ◯ Logger's Ascent
- ◯ Lower Facadeville
- ◯ The Wood Shop
- ◯ Kate's Keyroom
- ◯ Evie's Puzzle Place
- ◯ The Green Room

COLLECTIBLES & ENEMIES

Soul Gem	⬡	Shake it! (Pop Fizz)
Legendary Treasure		Eagle Engine
Hats		Toy Soldier Hat, Fishing Hat
Story Scroll		Sky Pirates
Luck-O-Tron Wheel	⬤	Lucky Wheel of Wealth
Treasure Chests		4 to collect
Winged Sapphire		1 to collect

Mace Major

Chompies

Root Runner

Bark Demon

En Fuego Chompies

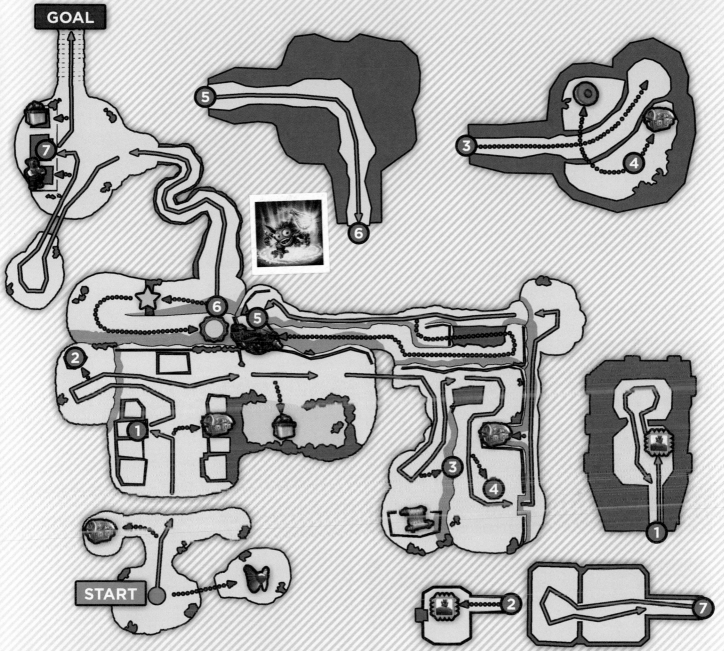

GOAL

START

MAP LEGEND

Direct Path	➤	Luck-O-Tron Wheel	◉	
Optional Path	↘	Skystones Challenger	▦	
Feat of Strength	★	Soul Gem	⬡	
Auric (Vendor)	🧍	Story Scroll	📜	
Hat Box	🎁	Treasure Chest	🏠	
Legendary Treasure	🐟	Winged Sapphire	🦋	

ISLE OF THE WILIKINS & FACADEVILLE

Favored Element: Magic

On the Isle of Wilikins, your first step is to activate the magic switcher to bring the Wilikin village to life. Don't rush into the Wilikin village. Instead, head back to the start point and look for a bridge to an island containing a **Winged Sapphire**.

Head back towards the village and deactivate the magic switcher. Break through the cardboard wall on the left and claim the **Treasure Chest** on the other side. Turn the switch back on again and cross the bridge to Facadeville. A few Mace Majors drop in to attack the village! Defeat them to open up a bounce pad.

THE ABANDONED HOUSE, DOLL DAY-CARE & RUTHERFORD'S GAME ROOM

Favored Element: Magic

There are several houses to explore in Facadeville. The house on the left side nearest the entrance of Facadeville has a creepy ghost Wilikin, but nothing else of interest. Doll Day-Care has three Wilikins to talk to, and Linda has some interesting info about Kaos. Rutherford's Game Room has a key you need to get out of Facadeville. Talk to Rutherford and defeat him in a game of Skystones to earn the key.

SKYSTONE CHALLENGER: RUTHERFORD

Reward For Winning First Game: Life Spell Punk

RUTHERFORD'S SKYSTONE DECK	
En Fuego Chompy 2	
Chompy 2	
Spiderlings 3	
Frigid Chompy 2	
Life Spell Punk	

STEPHANIE'S HOUSE & HELENA'S HOME

Favored Element: Magic

The house directly north of the switch in the center of town has two Wilikins to talk to, and some furniture to smash. The house to the right of the switch has a Lock Puzzle, Hazel, and Helena, a puzzle-loving Wilikin. Solve the Lock Puzzle for a **Treasure Chest**.

Perfect Lock Puzzle Solution: 21 moves

Left, Left, Right, Right, Right, Right, Left, Left, Left, Left, Right, Right, Left, Left, Left, Right, Right, Right, Left, Left, Left

HAMILTON LANDING, CARLTON'S HOUSE & CATHERINE'S HOME

Favored Element: Magic

Hamilton Landing has two Wilikins to talk to, Wellsley and Hamilton. Carlton's House has two more Wilikins (Chamberlin and Carlton). After exploring all the houses, head to the back of Facadeville and use the jump pad.

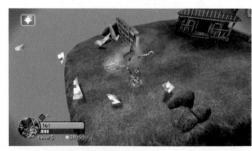

Enter the home found at the top. Talk to Catherine inside to play a game of Skystones.

SKYSTONE CHALLENGER: CATHERINE

Reward For Winning First Game: Mohawk Cyclops

CATHERINE'S SKYSTONE DECK	
Drow Archer 3 (x2)	
Bark Demon (x3)	

After defeating Catherine, drop back into Facadeville and deactivate the magic switcher. Now return to the brick wall outside of her house. Smash it, and retrieve the second key. Reactivate the magic switcher and unlock the double-locked door on the right. Look for an Earth gate beyond the locked gate, with Elizabeth standing near it.

EARTH ELEMENT GATE:
THE MUD FLATS

Use an Earth Skylander to destroy the rocks to get the **Toy Soldier Hat.** You should continue smashing the rocks and collect additional treasure here before you head back outside the Earth Element area.

PLANER PLATEAU

Favored Element: Life

Activate the switcher and smash the brick wall blocking the path. In the "real world" a Bark Demon and Fn Fuego Chompies block your path. If you smash the wall and quickly return things back to Wilikin world, the enemies turn into much weaker Chompies and cardboard trees.

Smash the brick wall in the corner for extra treasure, then reactivate Wilikin world to cross the bridge to Planer Plateau. Explore the end of the plateau for a **Story Scroll: Sky Pirates**.

Use the magic activator to smash the brick wall with the large bomb behind it. Roll the bomb to destroy both sets of doors (the one directly ahead of the bomb and the other nearer the main path), then head into The Wing Caves.

THE WING CAVES, THE CLIFFSIDE PATH & ROC'S ELBOW

Favored Element: Life

Talk with Seraphina inside the cave (if you can't speak with her, use the switcher) to learn about the blobs that appear behind her. Return outside and walk up the path until you encounter Chompies and a Root Runner. Dispatch the enemies, then switch to a Giant Skylander. Pull up the rock in the middle of this area to access a secret part of The Wing Caves and a **Treasure Chest**. Use the jump pad to fly over to the other side of The Wing Caves to collect the **Lucky Wheel of Wealth**.

Return back to the top of Planer Plateau, and take the elevator down to The Cliffside Path. For these crate puzzles, you should pick a Skylander who is small and fast. A Skylander such as Zap or Spyro is a great choice. Move under the crates and grab the **Treasure Chest** in the first alcove.

Next up are Chompies, Mace Majors, and Grenade Generals. Defeat them to reveal a bounce pad up to another timed crate puzzle. While you're running under a long line of crates, watch for the ones that wiggle as that's a warning they're about to descend.

When you get to the other side of the crates, climb on top of the crates to access the upper plateau. Move all the way down the plateau and collect the **Legendary Treasure: Eagle Engine**.

Drop down and enter the cave. After talking to Seraphina, head back outside and hit the activator to make the magic blobs heal you.

THE PERILOUS COIL & LOGGER'S ASCENT

Favored Element: Undead

Roc's Elbow leads outside to The Perilous Coil. Walk up the path on your right to find a Feat of Strength. Use a Giant to win the feat and proceed inside to Logger's Ascent. Follow the path to the end to discover Pop Fizz's **Soul Gem**.

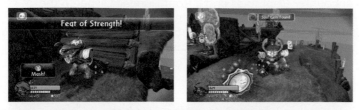

Return to The Perilous Coil and push the giant bomb down the path and use it to crush the Bark Demons and Chompies in your way. At the bottom, use the bomb to blow up the gate and open the way to Lower Facadeville.

LOWER FACADEVILLE & THE WOOD SHOP

Favored Element: Undead

Activate the switcher again. Erickson provides a hint on what to do next. You must gather three keys to unlock the next gate. The first key is floating on the island across a short bridge. Grab it and start entering the houses, starting with the one nearest the bridge. This is The Wood Shop, which contains Auric's Store.

AURIC'S INVENTORY	
ITEM	COST
Luck-O-Tron Bulb #3	2,500 Gold
Rocker Hair	600 Gold
Eye Hat	600 Gold
Bag O' Boom Skystone	500 Gold
Invincibility Power Up	225 Gold
Lock Puzzle Key	500 Gold
Fairy Dust	50 Gold
Skystone Cheat	500 Gold

KATE'S KEYROOM & EVIE'S PUZZLE PLACE

Favored Element: Undead

The next house is Kate's Keyroom. Talk to the little Wilikin here and grab the key at the back of the house. When you go back outside, Trolls appear and attack. After you defeat them, some smart Chompies hit the switch and force you back into the real world where you face Root Runners and Bark Demons. Take out the Bark Demons before tackling the Root Runners. When they are all defeated, the bounce pad opens up, allowing you to grab the key floating above it.

With the area safe again, re-enter Wilikin world and enter the house nearest the locked gate. Solve the lock puzzle inside to obtain the **Fishing Hat**.

Perfect Lock Puzzle Solution: 23 moves

Right, Right, Right, Left, Right ,Left, Left, Left, Left, Right, Right, Left, Right, Right, Left, Left, Left, Left, Right, Right, Right, Right, Right

THE GREEN ROOM

Use the three keys to unlock the gate and cross the bridge to The Green Room. Get ready for a big boss fight!

BOSS FIGHT
GIANT CHOMPY & CHOMPY MAGE

The Giant Chompy runs around in a circle, throwing giant Chompy eggs into the air. These eggs spawn into Chompies to attack you, and inflict damage to any Skylander caught under them.

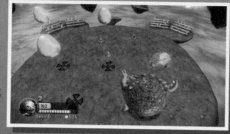

The Giant Chompy also uses a two-stage breath attack when it comes to a stop. First he breathes out, repelling any ranged attacks, then he breathes in to try to suck your Skylander into his waiting jaws.

Stay clear of Giant Chompy when it performs these breath attacks, and wait for him to run in circles before you let loose with your own attacks. Hurt the Giant Chompy enough, and he reveals his true form!

Now, you must dodge the Chompy Mage's magic. Remember, the red blobs damage while the blue ones heal. Run into any blue blobs, and avoid the patterns of red blobs. After dodging a few of the Chompy Mage's attacks, he surrounds you with red blobs. Luckily, Seraphina is nearby and gives you a way to transform the blobs. Hit the Activate button to switch red blobs to blue blobs!

Be careful, though, when you do this; any blue blobs turn to red blobs!

Whenever a wave of red blobs gets too close, hit the Activate button to switch it. Wait until the last possible second each time you do this to avoid turning friendly blue blobs into deadly red blobs.

PRO FIGHT TIPS

Always try to collect as many blue blobs as you can before you hit the Activate button. This makes it easier to dodge the wave when it turns red.

When Chompy Mage transforms back into Giant Chompy, you can switch his Chomples back and forth between En Fuego Chompies and regular Chompies with your world switcher.

Avoid killing the Mage's Chompies, and wait until the Giant Chompy executes his breath attack. When he does, switch worlds to change the Chompies into En Fuego Chompies. When the Giant Chompy accidently sucks them in with his breath, he takes massive damage!

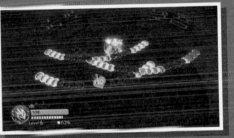

BACK ON FLYNN'S SHIP

The Wilikins have decided to come aboard the ship, and have opened up the new Gun Deck area. Come down to the Gun Deck to play the shooting mini-game and earn some extra prizes.

BURNING QUESTIONS!

Q: What's the deal with those devices that allow the player to shift into different realms?

A: You may have picked up some clues, but we'll put it to rest: Kaos created the Wilikins. They were his toys when he was a young lad. He didn't know he was a Portal Master back then, and was shocked to discover he could bring Wilikins to life. Shocked, and a bit fearful of what his mother would say if she knew he had these powers (she often blamed Portal Masters for the problems in the Skylands), he thought it best to keep the Wilikins secret. He began building a device that would return the Wilikins to their inanimate toy state whenever mother visited his room. Only problem was that these devices caused other things in the world to shift too, not just the Wilikins.

During one of these shifts, Kaos' mom noticed that the radishes she was boiling for dinner suddenly became bombs. Shortly after that, she learned of the Wilikin and her son's Portal Master powers. She wasn't too happy, but agreed to let Kaos keep his Wilikin friends on the condition that he get rid of those crazy switchers. Thus, he dumped a bunch of them on a remote island that would later become Wilikin village.

Q: Why did the Chompy Mage come to Wilikin town anyway?

A: The Chompy Mage actually arrived in the village by accident. He was on his way to the annual Chompy Convention (ChompyCon), but got lost. Then he didn't want to ask for directions, so he pretended like he moved there on purpose. He figured he would stay there for a while, practicing his magic, and then set out for ChompyCon again next year!

CHAPTER 8
TROLL HOME SECURITY

STORY GOALS

- ✓ Trigger the Explosives
- ◯ Take out the Big Cannons
- ◯ Destroy the Shield Gun

ELEMENTAL GATES

- Water

DARES

Time To Beat	7:05
Enemies to Defeat	115

AREAS TO FIND

- ◯ Crumbling Edge
- ◯ Circle Run House
- ◯ Coal Stack
- ◯ Shell Shock Bastion
- ◯ Failing Fields
- ◯ Anchored Island
- ◯ Puzzling Cavern
- ◯ Cheese Cavern
- ◯ Frightful Filtration Pools
- ◯ Secret Cave
- ◯ Tilting Tower
- ◯ The Battlements
- ◯ Cloudy Corner
- ◯ Chaotic Corner

COLLECTIBLES & ENEMIES

Soul Gem		Rockslidin' Out (Crusher)
Legendary Treasure		Fire Sail Paint Job
Hats		Sombrero, Pants Hat
Story Scroll		Those Wacky Arkeyans
Luck-O-Tron Wheel		Lucky Wheel of Power
Treasure Chests		4 to collect
Winged Sapphire		1 to collect

Mace Major

Grenade General

En Fuego Chompies

Inhuman Shield

Chompy Bot 9000

D. Riveter

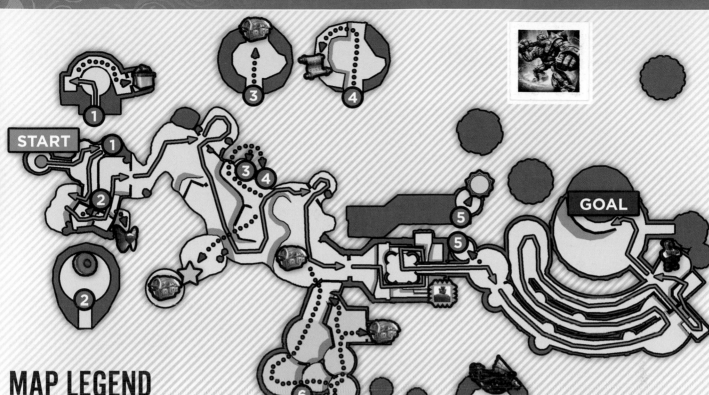

START

GOAL

MAP LEGEND

Direct Path	
Optional Path	
Feat of Strength	
Auric (Vendor)	
Hat Box	
Legendary Treasure	
Luck-O-Tron Wheel	
Skystones Challenger	
Soul Gem	
Story Scroll	
Treasure Chest	
Winged Sapphire	

CRUMBLING EDGE & CIRCLE RUN HOUSE

Favored Element: Life

When you start the chapter, head across the bridge to Crumbling Edge and speak with Flynn. Head into Circle Run House. Defeat the Mace Majors inside to gain access to the exterior circle. Grab the bomb and walk around the edge of the circle until you run into a brick wall. Destroy the wall with your bomb and collect the **Sombrero**.

Grab a second bomb and take it outside to destroy the wall near Flynn. Move through to the drop-down area and defeat the En Fuego Chompies, Grenade Generals, and Mace Majors to reveal a bounce pad.

COAL STACK & SHELL SHOCK BASTION

Favored Element: Fire

Use the second bounce pad to jump into the fiery chimney. The chimney leads to the secret Coal Stack area. Defeat the En Fuego Chompies and claim the **Lucky Wheel of Power**.

Back outside, use the two bounce pads to get on top of the building. Instead of heading towards Cali, drop down on the far edge of the building. This leads to a secret area that contains a **Winged Sapphire**.

After gathering the collectibles, go find Cali. Use Cali's explosives to blow open the gate to Shell Shock Bastion. Shell Shock Bastion is filled with dud bombs. Attack the bombs to reactivate them and take out nearby enemies. Giants automatically blow up these bombs when they walk on them!

Defeat the Trolls and a new enemy, the Chompy Bot 9000, arrives. If you have a Giant, use the blinking red bombs like boulders. The megabombs inflict massive damage, but are a difficult attack to aim.

You must solve the Lock Puzzle to open the next set of gates.

Perfect Lock Puzzle Solution: 10 moves
Left, Right, Right, Left, Left, Left, Left, Right, Right, Left

FAILING FIELDS, ANCHORED ISLAND, PUZZLING CAVERN & CHEESE CAVERN

Favored Element: Earth

Hit the switch on the other side of the Lock Puzzle and walk to the next area, Failing Fields. Move the left push block to clear the way up to the ranged Troll enemies. When the area is clear, return to the push blocks.

Push the double stack of blocks toward the stone wall. Walk around to the top of the stone wall and push the top block down. Now, push the three blocks to form a bridge to the right plateau. Complete the Feat of Strength on the plateau to gain access to Anchored Island and a **Treasure Chest**.

Back in Failing Fields, look for a stack of push blocks in a lower area on the left. Drop down and push the blocks to the left to reveal two caves. The first cave is Puzzling Cavern. Solve the Lock Puzzle for a **Treasure Chest**.

Perfect Lock Puzzle Solution: 15 moves
Right, Right, Left, Right, Left, Left, Right, Right, Right, Left, Left, Left, Left, Right, Right

The second cave is Cheese Cavern. Defeat the Chompies and Grenadiers inside to unseal the back gate and access the bounce pad. Use the bounce pad to get to the **Story Scroll: Those Wacky Arkeyans**.

Exit the north end of Failing Fields to meet up with Cali and Flynn again. Solve the Lock Puzzle here for some treasure and access to a bomb.

Perfect Lock Puzzle Solution: 10 moves
Right, Right, Left, Right, Left, Left, Right, Right, Right, Right

To destroy the cannon blocking your progress, you can either use a Giant to toss a blinking mega bomb at the cannon, or you can have a regular Skylander use a normal bomb. Note the **Treasure Chest** near the stone wall directly across from this cannon.

Before you confront the Inhuman Shield enemies on the other side of the cannon, bounce up to the platform on the right to enter the Water Element gate.

WATER ELEMENT GATE:
FRIGHTFUL FILTRATION POOLS & SECRET CAVE

Push the crystal before entering this gate to start the giant water turbines. Move past the first turbine and drop down to the first crystal puzzle. Configure the crystals and push blocks as shown in the screenshot and bounce back up to the next turbine.

Use the bounce pad near the second turbine to bounce over to the upper area on the left. Defeat the Grenade Generals and D. Riveter to open the gate to the **Treasure Chest**. Head back to the second turbine, bounce up to the high tower, and drop down into the ambush area.

AMBUSH
DARK GILL GRUNT

In this encounter, you must defeat three Dark Gill Grunts. They only have one ability: a three-pronged harpoon attack. If you are playing a melee character, you must attack off to the right or left to avoid getting hit by the anchors.

The better approach here is to hang back with a long-range Skylander and unleash your own attacks while dodging the anchors and incoming volleys.

Fire Skylanders have a special quest here. Defeat the Gill Grunts to complete the Steamer Quest. Since there are three Gill Grunts, you can complete this quest for up to three of your Fire Skylanders.

Defeat the Gill Grunts to earn the fabled **Pants Hat**. This is an astoundingly good Hat, so put it to use immediately. After retrieving the Hat, return to the light puzzle. Move one of the push blocks to the opening midway up the wall. Jump up to the second turbine again, and now drop down onto the block. This gives you access to the super-ultra-secret Secret Cave area and a Skystones Challenger.

Gurglefin has one of the best decks in the game. If you lose, don't worry; you can always come back and face him again when you have a better deck. To beat Gurglefin, play defensively. Put your best Skystones in spots where they can't be captured. Try to force him to place his Mace Major or Drow Lance Master in a square where you can capture it. You only need one capture to win. Beating Gurglefin opens the gate to the **Legendary Treasure: Fire Sail Paint Job**.

SKYSTONE CHALLENGER: GURGLEFIN
Reward For Winning First Game: D. Riveter 3

GURGLEFIN'S SKYSTONE DECK	
Mace Major 2 (x2)	
Drow Lance Master 3 (x2)	
D. Riveter 3	

After all that, head back to where you destroyed the cannon. Ignore the Inhuman Shields and take out the Grenade Generals first. Defeat the Inhuman Shields by waiting for their shield attack, then hitting them from behind. When you've defeated everything, move around the back of the tower and meet up with Fangs for a Skystones rematch. After you defeat Fangs, move back to the front of the tower and use it to bounce up to Tilting Tower.

SKYSTONE CHALLENGER: FANGS

Reward For Winning First Game: Armored Chompy

FANGS' SKYSTONE DECK

En Fuego Chompy 2 (x2)	
D. Riveter (x2)	
Armored Chompy	

TILTING TOWER

Favored Element: Tech

Tilting Tower is equipped with moving platforms that tilt depending on what side your Skylander is standing on. Some platforms also require you to hit a switch before you can jump on them.

Move around the tower, activating switches and bouncing on pads until you reach the top. Cali and Flynn are waiting for you there. (How do they keep getting ahead of you like that?) Follow your friends to The Battlements.

THE BATTLEMENTS & CLOUDY CORNER

Favored Element: Air

Switch to a Giant and pull up the Kaos statue to unveil a secret teleporter to Cloudy Corner and Crusher's **Soul Gem.**

If you have a Giant, throw the nearby blinking mega bomb across the platform to destroy the first cannon. Now solve the Lock Puzzle.

🔒 **Perfect Lock Puzzle Solution: 8 moves**
Left, Right, Right, Right, Right, Right, Left, Left

Grab the regular bomb and use it to destroy the cannons on the walkway. There are two cannons to destroy. Regular Skylanders must run back to retrieve a second regular bomb, but Giants can use the megabomb near the second cannon.

Dodge the far off cannon shots and follow Cali and Flynn to the next section of cover. Use Cali's explosives to break down the next gate, but be ready for a group of En Fuego Chompies and Inhuman Shields.

You must move across the walkway again. This time, note the pattern of the cannon fire. Once you've memorized the pattern of the cannons ahead, move from gap to gap for cover. Use a fast Skylander in this section if you're having trouble getting through it.

For the third walkway, you can't make it all the way across in one run, so use the gap in the rockets at the halfway point. Watch out for the embedded dud rockets in the walkway. You need to hit these so they explode and clear the path ahead.

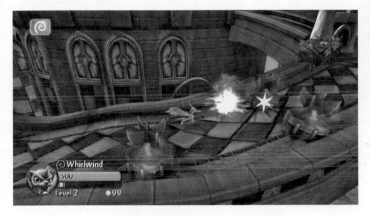

Look for Auric at the end of the third walkway.

AURIC'S INVENTORY	
ITEM	**COST**
Sudsy Soap Charm	5,000 Gold
This Bomb's For You	10,000 Gold
Moose Hat	850 Gold
Trojan Helmet	750 Gold
Chompy Bot 9000 Skystone	150 Gold
Damage Power Up	250 Gold
Fairy Dust	50 Gold

CHAOTIC CORNER

Favored Element: Air

After talking to Auric, use a Giant to smash through the brick wall. If you don't have a Giant, solve the push block puzzle to the south of the area to gain access to a regular bomb. Just be careful not to fall down off the push blocks. If you do, you must replay the entire walkway bomb sequence!

Enter the final area and defeat the Troll enemies hiding inside. The first wave consists of Grenade Generals and Mace Majors. The second wave is Chompy Bot 9000 and Inhuman Shields. Focus on the Chompy Bot 9000 before you go after the Inhuman Shields here. Defeating both waves causes the shield generator to explode.

BURNING QUESTIONS!

Q: Why does the shield generator gun thing seemingly emit no beam or other visible source of energy?

A: This question always comes up when both potential clients and current customers visit the Troll Home Security facilities. The Generator does actually emit a beam, but it is not visible. Nor is it audible. It cannot be touched or tasted either, but some say you can detect a slight cinnamony smell when you get next to it.

The reason for this is that the location of Troll Home Security is supposed to be a secret. If people could see the beams projecting a force field, they could easily follow those beams to the source. Some have tried to track them by following a cinnamony smell, but this usually just leads to Cutthroat Carnival, where churros are baked daily.

Q: Why do the Trolls not bother aiming their cannons at anything? Why do they fire repeatedly in the same direction?

A: That's not the Troll way.

Q: Must the Trolls themselves complete lock puzzles every time they attempt to activate their own switches and gates? That seems pretty inefficient.

A: THAT's not the Troll way.

CHAPTER 9
KAOS' KASTLE

STORY GOALS

✓ Enter the Castle

◯ Remove the 2 Arena Door Locks

◯ Defeat the Arena Master

ELEMENTAL GATES

⚙ Tech

✦ Magic

DARES	
Time To Beat	11:50
Enemies to Defeat	110

AREAS TO FIND

◯ Cliffside Castle Approach

◯ The Raven Court

◯ The Pool

◯ Shackled Island

◯ Game of Chance

◯ Secret Passage

◯ Pushblock Challenge

◯ Forgotten Sepulcher

◯ Mechanized Whirlygig

◯ Cliffside Terrace

◯ Castle Green

◯ Secret Passage: Balcony

◯ The Ethereal Ballroom

◯ The Great Hall

◯ Auric's Overhang

◯ Sodaworks

◯ The Aviary

◯ The Windswept Tower

◯ The Sewing Room

◯ The Man Cave

◯ East Gallery

◯ Needlepoint Nook

◯ Adept's Alcove

◯ The Theatre

COLLECTIBLES & ENEMIES

Soul Gem	⬡	Dazzling Enchantment (Ninjini)
Legendary Treasure	🐉	Dragon Engine
Hats	🎩	Princess Hat, Graduation Hat
Story Scroll	📜	Squirreling vs. Hiding?
Luck-O-Tron Wheel	◉	Lucky Wheel of Experience
Treasure Chests	📦	4 to collect
Winged Sapphire	🦋	1 to collect

Chompies

Armored Chompies

Mace Major

Grenade General

Mohawk Cyclops

Arkeyan Crackler

Troll Stomper M5

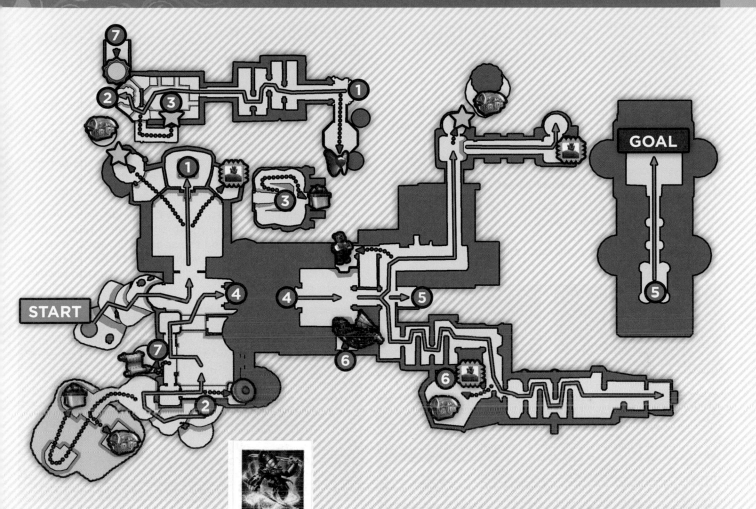

MAP LEGEND

Direct Path	
Optional Path	
Feat of Strength	
Auric (Vendor)	
Hat Box	
Legendary Treasure	
Luck-O-Tron Wheel	
Skystones Challenger	
Soul Gem	
Story Scroll	
Treasure Chest	
Winged Sapphire	

CLIFFSIDE CASTLE APPROACH

Cliffside Castle Approach is a simple bounce pad area. Just jump on the pads to reach The Raven Court.

THE RAVEN COURT

Favored Element: Life

At The Raven Court, deal with the Chompies, Cyclops enemies, and Trolls hanging about in the courtyard. When they are defeated, a new type of enemy arrives, the illusion-using Arkeyan Crackler. Only one of the four images you see takes damage. Carefully examine the mirror images' animations in order

to pick out the real Crackler. After you take down the Crackler, talk to the Wilikin Archibald to get a hint on how to get into Kaos' Kastle.

THE POOL, SHACKLED ISLAND & GAME OF CHANCE

Head into The Pool on the left. There are two moving bounce pad pedestals and three stationary bounce pads. First, press the button to lower the first row of bounce pads, and bounce up to the Feat of Strength on the left. Move the back platform all the way to the left and use the bounce pads to get up on the left platform. Switch to a Giant and complete the Feat of Strength to pull in the Shackled Island and a **Treasure Chest**.

Push the back platform all the way back to the right. Move the middle platform almost all the way to the right and use the bounce pads to jump up to the area called a Game of Chance where you can challenge Kensington, a Wilikin, to Skystones.

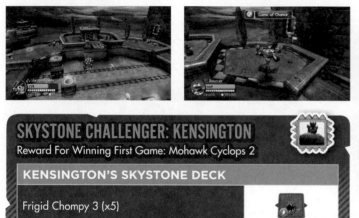

SKYSTONE CHALLENGER: KENSINGTON

Reward For Winning First Game: Mohawk Cyclops 2

KENSINGTON'S SKYSTONE DECK

Frigid Chompy 3 (x5)

SECRET PASSAGE

Favored Element: Undead

After talking to Kensington, push both platforms to the middle to access the middle platform. Use the invisible bounce pad at the back of the building to score the treasure on top of the area exit. Break the brick wall and enter the Secret Passage.

TECH ELEMENT GATE:
MECHANIZED WHIRLYGIG

Look to the left immediately after entering the Secret Passage. There's a Tech gate to an area called Mechanized Whirlygig. A Winged Sapphire is floating on the opposite end of a dangerous path. Carefully avoid the blades and claim the **Winged Sapphire**.

PUSHBLOCK CHALLENGE & FORGOTTEN SEPULCHER

Favored Element: Undead

Back in the Secret Passage, move around the whirling blades to reach the end. Watch out for the Cyclops tossing barrels down the walkway. If possible, switch to a Giant. The barrels (both wood and metal) don't hurt Giants. Instead, the Giants automatically kick the barrels out of the way. You could also use a Skylander with a ranged attack to take out the barrels and the Cyclops.

The ramp leads to the Pushblock Challenge. To solve the challenge, drop down and move all five push blocks into their respective indents on the spear walkway. Use the teleporter to get up on the walkway and hurry all the way around to the floor button. Triggering the button lowers a bounce pad.

Bounce up to the right for some gold, then bounce up to the left and follow the passage around to a Giant jump point, which opens the way to Forgotten Sepulcher and the **Princess Hat**.

CLIFFSIDE TERRACE

Back in the Pushblock Challenge area, hop up and talk to Bancroft on the way out to Cliffside Terrace. There's a Soul Gem visible here, but don't worry about it yet. Jump up the side of the mountain. When you see Wilikin Brewster, check out the element gate on the left.

MAGIC ELEMENT GATE:
THE ETHEREAL BALLROOM

The lower area is full of push blocks. The switch near where you enter raises the push blocks and allows you to walk on them. Grab the **Treasure Chest** on the left. You must move one of the push blocks in the main room to complete the walkway to the chest. Use the bounce pad at the bottom of the screen to jump back up to the switch.

Next up is the hat box. The first step is to create a walkway over to the Trolls across the room. Push the blocks in the main area to create a bridge over the Trolls (the suspended platforms help). Defeat both Trolls to reveal another bounce pad. Push the blocks into two squares to the right. Activate the switch again to cross over to the **Graduation Hat**.

CASTLE GREEN & SECRET PASSAGE: BALCONY

After finishing off The Ethereal Ballroom, return to Cliffside Terrace and use the bounce pad up to Castle Green. Move down the right path for the **Lucky Wheel of Experience**.

Drop down into the center area and defeat the Cyclops enemies, Trolls, and Chompies. When they're out of your way, a new enemy, Troll Stomper M5, arrives. Defeat the Troll Stomper and a new bounce pad appears. Hop up to the upper walkway and drop down to the lower platform. Grab the **Story Scroll: Squirreling vs. Hiding?**

Head inside the doorway near the scroll to find the Secret Passage: Balcony and Ninjini's **Soul Gem.** Jump back up to Castle Green, then hit the big red button to open up the castle.

THE GREAT HALL & AURIC'S OVERHANG

Favored Element: Tech

Head inside the castle to discover The Great Hall, an area full to the brim with Kaos' minions. In the first wave, the big threats are the Grenadiers. Keep an eye out for their grenades as you take out the other enemies in the area. The second wave starts with more Mohawk Cyclops. This wave includes a large number of Cyclops enemies accompanied by Troll Stompers. Use a Skylander with a good ranged ability to avoid getting too close to either type of enemies.

After defeating all the enemies, the gate at the back of the area opens up. Talk to Alistair if you're interested in additional backstory on Kaos. Climb the stairs and turn left at the locked door. Look for a push block on the left corner of the staircase and push it forward twice to form a walkway to Auric's Overhang.

AURIC'S INVENTORY	
ITEM	**COST**
Mushroom Grove	2,000 Gold
Dancer Hat	900 Gold
Shadow Duke Skystone	500 Gold
Regeneration Power Up	275 Gold
Skystone Cheat	500 Gold
Fairy Dust	50 Gold

SODAWORKS, THE AVIARY & THE WINDSWEPT TOWER

Favored Element: Magic

Continue down the left passage of the hall to an area called Sodaworks. Avoid the metal barrels and hop up on the bounce pad. Try to dodge the rolling barrels. You can smash the wooden ones, but avoid the metal barrels. Look for a Feat of Strength at the top of the walkway, on the left side. Use a Giant to pass it and access The Aviary. The small area contains a **Treasure Chest**.

Beat up any surviving barrel-tossing Cyclops enemies to unveil another bounce pad. Continue up the next walkway to reach The Windswept Tower. To unlock the first door lock, you must defeat Butterworth at Skystones.

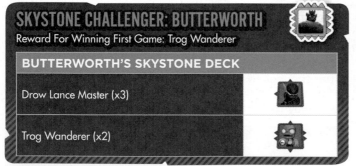

SKYSTONE CHALLENGER: BUTTERWORTH

Reward For Winning First Game: Trog Wanderer

BUTTERWORTH'S SKYSTONE DECK	
Drow Lance Master (x3)	
Trog Wanderer (x2)	

After taking down Butterworth, hit the switch and teleport back to the main area. It's now time to check out the right passage.

THE SEWING ROOM & THE MAN CAVE

Favored Element: Tech

Dodge the buzz saws at the start of this area, and continue down the passage until you see a glowing floor switch. Use the switch to angle your Skylander on the correct side of the first two push blocks. After the second push block, look for a passage on the right that

leads to The Man Cave. The back of this area contains a **Treasure Chest**. Grab it, and then talk to the Wilikin for some more Skystones.

SKYSTONE CHALLENGER: CONLAN

Reward For Winning First Game: Goliath Drow

CONLAN'S SKYSTONE DECK	
Inhuman Shield 2 (x2)	
Goliath Drow	
Drow Archer 2	
Drow Lance Master 2	

EAST GALLERY & NEEDLEPOINT NOOK

Favored Element: Tech

Use the door next to Conlan to discover the East Gallery area and the **Legendary Treasure: Dragon Engine**. Return to the main passage and hit the floor switch a third time to access Needlepoint Nook. Time your movements to dodge the floor spears and the buzz saws.

ADEPT'S ALCOVE

Favored Element: Magic

A simple puzzle stands between you and the second door lock. Hit the floor switch once, then move the push block. Move the crystal forward twice and hit the floor switch a second time. Time to head into the Arena!

THE THEATRE

Run across the collapsing bricks, using the narrow gray blocks as safe spots. It helps to use a Skylander that has an ability that boosts their speed. When you reach the other side, get ready for a big showdown with Kaos!

BOSS FIGHT

BRUTE

The floor you are fighting on intermittently collapses. If your Skylanders fall, they take damage and are teleported back into the center of the ring. The first wave of enemies includes Armored Life Spell Punks, Chompies, Mace Majors, and Mohawk Cyclops enemies. The second wave includes Troll Stomper Mark 5, Grenade Generals, Mace Majors, Mohawk Cyclops enemies, and an Armored Life Spell Punk. The final wave includes Brute (Jawbreaker), Armored Life Spell Punks, Chompies, and Grenade Generals.

PRO FIGHT TIPS

The priority in this fight is always the Life Spell Punks. They keep their allies in the fight. It's vital that you take them out as quickly as possible during Waves 2 & 3 to avoid extending the lifespans of the Troll Stomper and Brute.

Brute is a regular Jawbreaker enemy. The best way to defeat these guys is to wait for their lunging punch. When they miss, they land face first on the ground; move in and wack them as much as you can before they get back up. No use trying to fight him heads up. In Wave 3, the match is over as soon as you defeat Brute. Prioritize hitting him with your most powerful attacks and take him down as quickly as possible.

BACK ON FLYNN'S SHIP

Defeating Brute unlocks a second Arena in Brock's Arena challenges. This arena has much higher rewards for success. Use the challenges to score some extra gold for your Skylanders. Check out the game room for a **Winged Sapphire** hiding in plain sight next to Dreadbeard.

BURNING QUESTIONS!

Q: What's the deal with those pictures of Kaos and Glumshanks where they both have big afros?

A: Those were made a long time ago when Kaos attended his school's Senior Prom. Of course, being Kaos, he was unable to get an actual date for the evening, so he ordered his butler, Glumshanks, to go with him. It was actually quite a magical evening...for both of them.

Q: Does Kaos ever take Brute fishing?

A: To date, no, Kaos has never taken Brute fishing. But who knows?

One day, Kaos actually might do it. Although you know what? We think we can say for certain this is never going to happen. Just don't tell Brute. Let him hang on to his dream a bit longer.

CHAPTER 10

AERIAL ASSAULT

STORY GOALS

- ✓ Survive the Attack
- ◯ Destroy the 2 Turrets
- ◯ Sink the Dreadnaught

ELEMENTAL GATES

- Water
- Air

DARES	
Time To Beat	13:30
Enemies to Defeat	135

AREAS TO FIND

- ◯ Dread-Yacht
- ◯ Gun Deck
- ◯ The Ghost Ship
- ◯ Ghost Ship Bilge
- ◯ Fishy River Rapids
- ◯ Fishy River Cavern
- ◯ Fishy River Grotto
- ◯ The Spectral Dreadnaught
- ◯ Tiger's Citadel
- ◯ Propeller Array
- ◯ Dragon's Tower
- ◯ Freewind Flats
- ◯ Machineworks
- ◯ Phoenix's Maw

COLLECTIBLES & ENEMIES

Soul Gem		A Real Drag (Fright Rider)
Legendary Treasure		Skull Roof
Hats		Sailor Hat, Nefertiti Hat
Story Scroll		A Real Ladies Man
Luck-O-Tron Wheel		Lucky Wheel of Health
Treasure Chests		4 to collect
Winged Sapphire		1 to collect

Armored Archer

Mace Major

Jawbreaker

Armored Goliath

Bag O' Boom

Trog

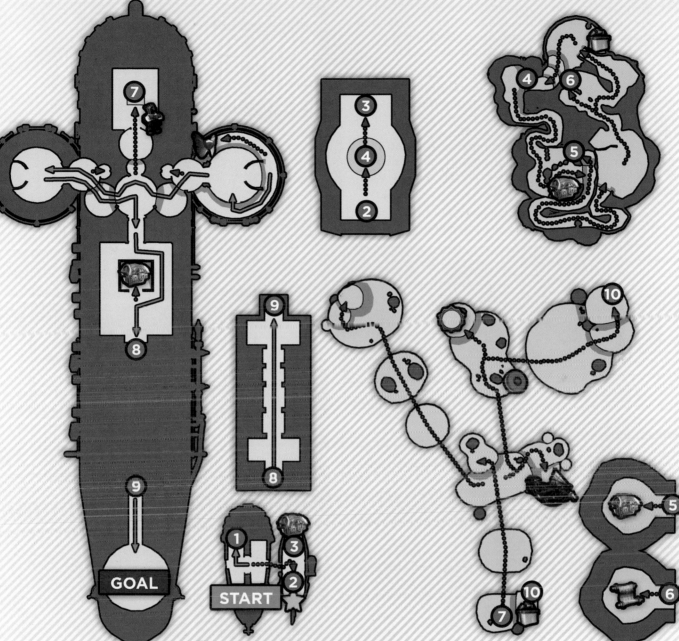

ⓘ **GOES BELOW DECKS**

MAP LEGEND

Direct Path	↗	Legendary Treasure		
Optional Path		Soul Gem	◯	
Feat of Strength	★	Story Scroll		
Auric (Vendor)		Treasure Chest		
Hat Box		Winged Sapphire		

DREAD-YACHT & GUN DECK

Favored Element: Air

You start this level on Flynn's ship when a Ghost Ship suddenly attacks your team! The enemies you encounter throughout this level are ghosts, but they use the same strategies and have the same amount of health as their living counterparts. Throughout this sequence, watch out for pirate strafing ships pelting the deck. They only attack half the ship, so just move to the other side while they are sweeping through. Clear the deck of Mace Majors, and take out the new Armored Archer enemy.

Next, Flynn orders you to man the ship's guns. If you have any Life Skylanders, this is a great time to use them and work on the Melon Maestro quest. Each kill in this sequence counts toward the quest's goal of 200.

Drop down into the Gun Deck. There are three types of enemies on the Gun Deck: Mines, Pirate Strafers, and Cannon Ships. Mines are rarely much of a threat; just shoot them when you have a chance. You want to shoot Pirate Strafers before they turn towards you. If they survive your shots, they will start rapidly attacking your ship. Cannon Ships are the toughest and take multiple hits to bring down. Note that you can shoot down the cannonballs they fire at your ship.

Keep your eye out for floating hearts. Shoot the hearts to heal the ship. Destroy 4 Mines, 20 enemy Pirate Strafers, and 3 Cannon Ships to clear this first sequence.

After the shooting sequence, head back to the top deck and prepare for a fight with a Jawbreaker, Armored Archers, and Mace Majors. Defeating this round of enemies causes a Ghost Ship to pull up alongside the Dread-Yacht. This ship has a new Armored Goliath enemy along with Mace Majors and Bag O' Booms. Use the Bag

O' Booms' bombs to quickly take down the Armored Goliath, then board The Ghost Ship.

THE GHOST SHIP & GHOST SHIP BILGE

Favored Element: Undead

The Ghost Ship has a **Treasure Chest** placed in plain sight on the left of the ship. Now head to the back of the boat and use a Giant on the jump spot to smash down into the Ghost Ship Bilge area. Down below, switch to a Water Skylander to teleport to Fishy River Rapids.

FISHY RIVER RAPIDS, FISHY RIVER CAVERN & FISHY RIVER GROTTO

This is one of the largest Elemental Gate areas and holds many collectible items. Move up the river and push the gigantic cannonball ahead of you. Crush the enemies standing in the river bed on the way down.

Hit the fish fountains to disable them, and continue pushing the cannonball forward. Use a Giant Skylander to lift the boulders on the right at the bottom of the river to open the way to a **Treasure Chest**.

Push the cannonball into the vault gate to blow open the passage into the waterfall and stop! Immediately after dropping down the first waterfall look to the right. The entrance to Fishy River Cavern is hard to find, but worth checking out. There's a **Treasure Chest** waiting for your inside.

Teleport back up from Fishy River Cavern and look for a second cannonball. Push it through the enemies and past the fish fountains to destroy the second vault door. At the bottom of the second waterfall is another group of enemies. Find a third cannonball and use it to crush the Goliath Drow.

When you've cleared the area, push the third cannonball further down stream. At a curvy part of the river, look for a door just past the first fish fountain. Use the door to enter Fishy River Grotto and grab the **Story Scroll: A Real Ladies Man**.

When you reach the sealed gate, you must defeat several waves of Trolls, Ogres, and Drow. When you defeat the Drow Goliath, the gate opens. Push a cannonball all the way to the end of the river and smash the vault door to uncover the **Sailor Hat**.

Congratulations, you've found everything in this large area! Use the jump pads to bound over the waterfall and find the exit teleporter.

THE SPECTRAL DREADNAUGHT & TIGER'S CITADEL

Favored Element: Undead

Back on The Ghost Ship, return to the Gun Deck for round two on the guns. Your goal this time is to shoot down five Cannon Ships. There is a new enemy this time around, giant laser asteroids. Blow up the lasers before they can target your ship. The sequence is much tougher this time. Prioritize destroying the Strafers as they do the most damage if they get in range. Don't go out of your way to get hearts; they're often hard to hit and only open you up to attack.

After successfully completing the second round of gunning, Flynn drops you off on the Dreadnaught. Move around the right side of the circular structure. All the way at the end is a **Winged Sapphire.**

Move back to the left and you automatically take the elevator up to Tiger's Citadel. A boarding ship of Mace Majors led by a Jawbreaker attack you. Focus on the Mace Majors and wait for a Bag O' Boom to arrive. When he does, first use his bomb to defeat the Jawbreaker, then throw a second bomb at the nearby cannon. Finish off the Ogre to unseal the gate to Propeller Array.

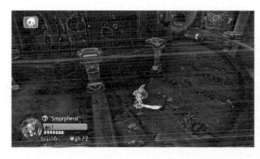

PROPELLER ARRAY

Favored Element: Undead

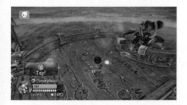

Hit the floor switch near the first propeller, then move all the way to the other side of the propeller deck to a group of enemies in an area called Dragon's Tower.

DRAGON'S TOWER

Favored Element: Tech

Dragon's Tower is defended by Mace Majors and a Goliath Drow. Defeat the Mace Majors and a second Goliath arrives along with two Bag O' Booms. Use the Bag O' Booms' bombs to quickly defeat the Drow, then turn the bombs on the ship's cannon.

With both cannons destroyed, you can now return to Propeller Array. Hit the second floor switch to open the northern gate in the center propeller area. When you make it back to the center propeller, take the left path to Ermit and Auric.

AURIC'S INVENTORY	
ITEM	COST
Chompy Chomp-Down	5,000 Gold
General's Hat	1,000 Gold
Spiked Hat	1,000 Gold
Chompy Bot 9000 2 Skystone	180 Gold
Regeneration Power Up	300 Gold
Fairy Dust	50 Gold

AIR ELEMENT GATE:
FREEWIND FLATS

This is another large Elemental area full of treasure. Move forward on the plateau to be warped to an area occupied by Mace Majors. Defeat the Mace Majors and drop down two levels to find the **Legendary Treasure: Skull Roof.**

Hop back up via the bounce pads, use the floor switch between the two gates, and teleport through the left gate. Continue along the floating islands until you reach the multi-story island with Drow inhabiting it. Defeat the enemies to activate a bounce pad and hit the floor switch to open the right gate back on the main island.

Teleport back to the main island and head through the right gate. Check the bottom corner of this new island to discover the **Luck-O-Tron Wheel.** The plateau at the opposite end of the island contains Fright Rider's **Soul Gem.**

Use the teleporter here to warp to another island. This island has three Armored Goliaths to contend with. Use the Bag O' Booms' bombs to make short work of them. Jump up to the third plateau and use the teleporter to discover the wondrous **Nefertiti Hat.**

MACHINEWORKS

Favored Element: Tech

Now, it's time for the final confrontation with the Ghost Ship crew. Return to Propeller Array and move back across to the Spectral Dreadnought area. Defeat the Drow and Mace Majors on the lower deck, and a secondary Troll raiding party boards to attack you. Defeat the Mace Majors, then take on the Chompy Bot.

One final boarding party arrives. This is a tough one: two Armored Drow Goliaths and a Chompy Bot. The Chompy Bot is a slightly bigger threat, so take it down first. When you've cleared the area, search the left side of the screen for a **Treasure Chest**. Enter the newly-opened exit to Machineworks.

Carefully make your way through the crushers. Use the small rest areas to get the timing of each consecutive set of crushers down.

PHOENIX'S MAW

Favored Element: Tech

When you emerge back outside in the Phoenix's Maw, you've reached your goal: the Dreadnaught's gigantic cannon. To get to the cannon you must defeat several waves of enemies. These enemies should be familiar at this point: Mace Majors, Armored Archers, Armored Goliaths, and Jawbreakers.

Taking on multiple Armored Goliaths and Jawbreakers at once is not easy. Luckily a Bag O' Boom appears on the outskirts of the fight, after defeating some enemies. The bombs that he tosses in the area make your job easier. First, toss a bomb at the Armored Archers on the left side. This means your Skylander won't need to keep moving to avoid arrow volleys. Use the next few bombs to take out the Goliaths and Jawbreakers. The timing can be tricky, but you get unlimited bombs, so just keep at it.

You could also focus on destroying the big cannon. Toss the Bag O' Boom's bombs at the two giant purple energy sources to cause the Dreadnaught to self-destruct!

BURNING QUESTIONS!

Q: What's the deal with the Ghost Ship, and why does it attack you?

A: Just like people, ships can be ghosts, too. This just happens to be a ghost of a ship. And just like people, ghosts need something to sail or fly around on, right? While they could potentially sail or fly a regular ship, it's just a lot better for all parties involved if they use a ghost ship.

The ghosts aren't necessarily after you, per se, they're mainly after Flynn. He borrowed 5 gold pieces from them and never gave them back. So they've attacked the Dread Yacht to get their revenge. Also, because there is little else for ghost ships to do these days. And all the ghosts just happen to be bad guys.

Q: Why is there a gateway to a mystical, water area on board one of the ships?

A: I guess the better question is, "Why ISN'T there a gateway to a mystical, water area on board EVERY ship?" Well, maybe that's not a better question. But, it might be cool if more ships had these. This particular one appeared after a relatively uneventful fishing trip this vessel and crew embarked on.

What they didn't know was that they caught a very special fish that day, one known simply as "Stay-At-Home Fish." Like the name suggests, this fish can never really leave its home, so if you try to take it away, it will find a way to bring its home to you.

In this case, the pool and gateway just magically appeared inside the hull of the ship, and there was nothing the ghost sky pirates could do to make it go away.

CHAPTER 11
DRILL-X'S BIG RIG

STORY GOALS

- ✓ Defeat the Drill
- ◯ Find the Big Drill

ELEMENTAL GATES

- Life
- Earth

DARES

Time To Beat	08:00
Enemies to Defeat	85

AREAS TO FIND

- ◯ Utility Deck
- ◯ Machine Retrofit Assembly
- ◯ Drawworks
- ◯ Aux Hanger
- ◯ Aux Storage Area
- ◯ Riley's Tube
- ◯ Lower Transition Station
- ◯ Spore Works
- ◯ Middle Transition Station
- ◯ Southern Rig Platform
- ◯ Golem's Fortune
- ◯ Ventilation Platform
- ◯ Gas Refinery
- ◯ Rock Works
- ◯ Upper Transition Station
- ◯ Middle Auxiliary Deck
- ◯ Centrifuge
- ◯ Aux Piston Platform
- ◯ Aux Control Room
- ◯ Landing Deck
- ◯ The Apex
- ◯ Triple Piston Trouble

COLLECTIBLES & ENEMIES

Soul Gem	◯	Landmine Golf (Sprocket)
Legendary Treasure		Propeller Engine
Hats		Safari Hat, Traffic Cone Hat
Story Scroll		Nice Try, Kaos
Luck-O-Tron Wheel	●	Lucky Wheel of Power
Treasure Chests		4 to collect
Winged Sapphire		1 to collect

En Fuego Chompy

D. Riveter

Arkeyan Bomber

Inhuman Shield

Blaze Brewer

Crystal Golem

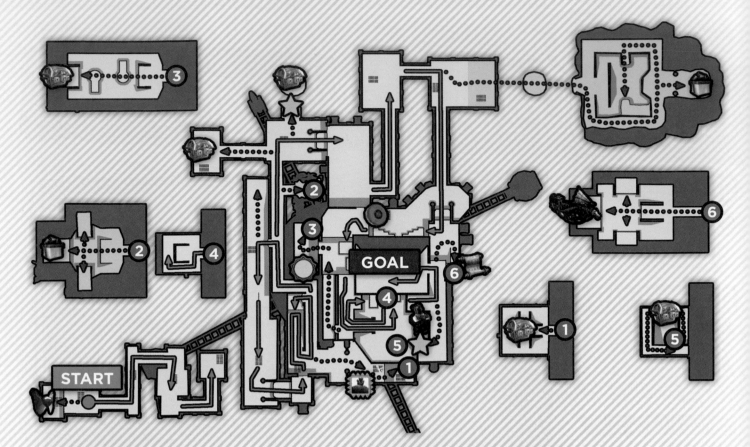

MAP LEGEND

Direct Path	
Optional Path	
Feat of Strength	
Auric (Vendor)	
Hat Box	
Legendary Treasure	
Luck-O-Tron Wheel	
Skystones Challenger	
Soul Gem	
Story Scroll	
Treasure Chest	
Winged Sapphire	

UTILITY DECK, MACHINE RETROFIT ASSEMBLY & DRAWWORKS

Favored Element: Tech

Flynn drops you off on a giant oil rig. From the starting point, move to the ledge at the bottom of the screen to drop down to the Utility Deck. Pick up the **Winged Sapphire** floating nearby.

Hop back to the main deck and proceed to Machine Retrofit Assembly. Defeat the En Fuego Chompies and D. Riveter to unseal the gate to the teleporter. The teleporter sends you to Drawworks. Defeat the En Fuego Chompies, then break through the Giant gate at the top of the screen.

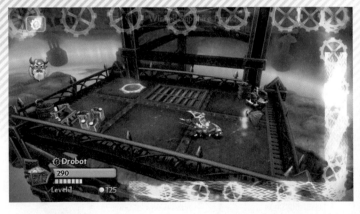

AUX HANGER & AUX STORAGE AREA

Favored Element: Tech

This gate leads to Aux Hanger. Hanging out here is Criggler, a Skystones player.

SKYSTONE CHALLENGER: CRIGGLER
Reward For Winning First Game: Boulder Bowler

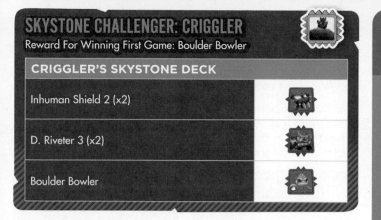

CRIGGLER'S SKYSTONE DECK	
Inhuman Shield 2 (x2)	
D. Riveter 3 (x2)	
Boulder Bowler	

Look behind Criggler for a secret ledge. Drop down and prepare for a Lock Puzzle.

Perfect Lock Puzzle Solution: 23 moves
Left, Left, Left, Left, Left, Left, Left, Right, Left, Left, Left, Left, Left, Left, Right, Right, Right, Right, Left, Right, Right, Right, Right

Step inside the room behind the Lock Puzzle to enter Aux Storage Area and claim the **Treasure Chest**. Back in Drawworks, continue around the left path and confront the Arkeyan Bomber. Wait for the Bomber to throw a bomb, then send it back to destroy the Arkeyan and unseal the gate to the conveyor belt.

Climb the conveyor belt and use it to access the big red button where the Arkeyan Bomber was standing. Make it to the end of the conveyor belt and drop down into Riley's Tube.

RILEY'S TUBE & LOWER TRANSITION STATION

Favored Element: Fire

Riley's Tube is defended by Inhuman Shields and Bombers. Defeat all the enemies to unseal the gate to the next section. Inside is your first encounter with a Blaze Brewer, an enemy you should always take out from a safe range.

Switch to a Skylander with a ranged attack to defeat the Blaze Brewer and uncover a jump pad. The floor switch at the top of the platform opens up the rest of the main conveyor belt. Drop back into Drawworks and follow the conveyor belt.

LIFE ELEMENT GATE:
SPORE WORKS

Just before the end of the conveyor belt, look for a Life Element gate. Hop off and enter the gate to drop into Spore Works. This is a simple area with a rotating platform. Ride the platform to the opposite deck to procure the **Safari Hat**. On the way out, snag the treasure in the alcove underneath the hat.

MIDDLE TRANSITION STATION, SOUTHERN RIG PLATFORM & GOLEM'S FORTUNE

Favored Element: Air

At the end of the conveyor belt, drop down into the Middle Transition Station and take out the D. Riveter enemies to reveal a bounce pad. Instead of jumping up there, check out the left path for a Feat of Strength. Complete the challenge to access Golem's Fortune island and retrieve a **Treasure Chest**. Look for the walkway at the bottom of the screen. It leads to the Southern Rig Platform. There's nothing to collect here, but you need to find it to complete the "All Areas Found" Dare. Head back to the bounce pad and jump up to the Ventilation Platform.

VENTILATION PLATFORM & GAS REFINERY

Favored Element: Fire

Defeat the D. Riveter and Arkeyan Bomber enemies spaced out on top to unlock the sealed gate to the next conveyor belt. Avoid the crushers on the belt to reach the Gas Refinery. The Gas Refinery is defended by a Blaze Brewer and Inhuman Shields. Evade the Inhuman Shields while you take down the Blaze Brewer at range. Take out all the enemies to unlock the belt up to the next level.

EARTH ELEMENT GATE:
ROCK WORKS

At the top of the conveyor belt in Gas Refinery, you will see an Earth Element gate. Cross the earth bridges to reach Rock Works.

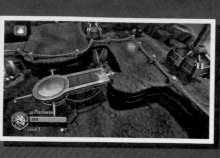

Rock Works is a bit trickier than Spore Works. The first step to solving this puzzle is to take the walkway right around the edge of the area.

Follow it almost all the way around, until you see a big red button. Hit the button to start the rotating platform.

Now, use the bounce pad at the start of the area to jump up on the rotating platform. Ride the platform to access the key. Now, move back around the walkway and use the key to unlock the door at the back of the area and receive the **Traffic Cone Hat**.

UPPER TRANSITION STATION, MIDDLE AUXILIARY DECK & CENTRIFUGE

Favored Element: Magic

After clearing Rock Works, take the second conveyor belt out of the Gas Refinery. This next section has some moving blocks. Follow the moving blocks around the edge of the building, then use the jump pad to clear the gap. There is some treasure in this area, but you can't get to it just yet.

When you turn the first corner of the building, drop down to the lower area to access the Middle Auxiliary Deck. Drop down twice here for Sprocket's **Soul Gem**.

The giant warehouse door leads to the Centrifuge. Keep hitting the floor button on the left until the nearby rotating platform matches the rotating platform a bit farther away. Jump up on the platforms and cross over to claim the **Treasure Chest**.

Head back outside to the Upper Transition Station. Continue following the edge of the building until you reach the next conveyor belt. Before moving down to the Aux Piston Platform, look for the break in the walkway to jump down on the conveyor belt on the left. Ride the conveyor belt to the end and hit the large button.

This button opens the gates to the treasure directly ahead, and it also opens the drill gate to the **Lock-O-Tron Wheel** back in the Upper Transition Station area. Head back there before continuing on to Aux Piston Platform.

AUX PISTON PLATFORM, AUX CONTROL ROOM & LANDING DECK

Favored Element: Tech

Walk back to the walkway and follow the ramp down to the Lock Puzzle. Solving the puzzle leads into the Aux Control Room.

 Perfect Lock Puzzle Solution: 15 moves
Right, Right, Right, Left, Left, Left, Left, Left, Right, Right, Right, Left, Right, Right, Right

Hit the giant floor button to release the upper jump pads. Head outside for an encounter with the rig's defender, a Crystal Golem. These guys are tough! Stick to a Skylander with a strong ranged attack to take down the Golem's crystal shield at range. With the shield down, he's vulnerable to all attacks. You can move in to attack at close-range, but watch out for his double-armed slam attack.

Use the newly erected bounce platforms to get up to the next level of the rig. Up top, explore the lower path until you encounter Auric and his store.

AURIC'S INVENTORY	
ITEM	**COST**
Unerring Arrow Charm	25,000 Gold
Combat Hat	1,000 Gold
Beret	1,000 Gold
Chompy Bot 9000 3	650 Gold
Regeneration Power Up	325 Gold
Fairy Dust	50 Gold
Lock Puzzle Key	500 Gold

Use the Giant jump point near Auric to open the way down to the Landing Deck and a **Treasure Chest**. Bounce back up to where Auric was, but this time take the top path. This leads to The Apex.

THE APEX & TRIPLE PISTON TROUBLE

Favored Element: Magic

When you first enter the Apex, walk straight across to the ledge and drop back down into Upper Transition station. You're now able to claim the **Story Scroll: Nice Try, Kaos** that you spotted earlier.

The doorway here leads to Triple Piston Trouble. Use the bounce pad to reach the moving platforms on the left and right. Hit the floor switches on either side of the room to raise the path to the **Legendary Treasure: Propeller Engine.** After grabbing the last of the level's loot, continue to the main platform in The Apex. Beware! Drill-X awaits!

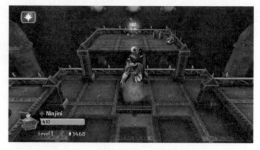

BOSS FIGHT

DRILL-X

Don't let Drill-X's cool rap fool you. This guy has it out for your Skylanders, and you're in for a serious battle.

In phase 1, Drill-X uses a brutal downward drill attack. The red arrows on the ground show you where his attack is going to land. Steer clear of the drill; when it first enters the ground it sprays rocks in all directions. You need to stay at medium range to avoid taking damage. When the screen returns to normal, it's safe to attack Drill-X's drill. However, you must watch out for Drill-X's lasers and his minion reinforcements.

When Drill-X's health bar is depleted by one-third, phase 2 starts. Drill-X sweeps the area with his deadly spinning drill. Luckily, two bounce pads appear at the same time. Use the pads to jump clear of the drill just before it's about to hit your Skylander.

After dodging the drill-sweep tactic, Drill-X's arm overheats. This is your opportunity to hit him some more. For this phase, melee attackers are the best type of Skylander to use; they can dish out more damage at short range to these drill pieces than ranged Skylanders can.

After Drill-X loses another third of his health, he switches tactics again. For phase 3 he slams his broken drill on the ground. When he does, flames are emitted in all directions. Focus on dodging the flame (the bounce pads make this easier), then worry about damaging one of his three drill bits. Any drill bit will do, just hit whichever is closest. Drill-X has more minions and three lasers. Avoid these, but keep your focus on damaging Drill-X.

BURNING QUESTIONS!

Q: So why does a giant drilling machine want to sing?

A: Because he needs to express himself. Who he is, where he came from, etc. Most people have no idea what it's like to be a giant drill and Drill-X wants us to understand his plight.

Q: Why do the Molekin work for a bad guy?

A: Being a friendly race, the Molekin only worked with good guys and turned down all work that came from villains everywhere.

However, a long time ago, the Molekin won a construction bid that covered a large portion of Skylands. This means that any and all construction that takes place in this area is done by them and no one else.

So, against their wishes, the Molekin must accept work from anybody who requests it, be they good, or be they bad.

CHAPTER 12

MOLEKIN MOUNTAIN

STORY GOALS

- ✓ Rid the Village of Bad Guys
- ◯ Overthrow Pipsqueak

ELEMENTAL GATES

- Undead
- Tech (x2)

DARES

Time To Beat	10:40
Enemies to Defeat	140

AREAS TO FIND

- ◯ Sunrock Quarry
- ◯ Allegory Pathway
- ◯ Titan Crossing
- ◯ The Dirt Room
- ◯ Sunrock Village
- ◯ Cogwheel Housing
- ◯ Sunrock Peak
- ◯ The Cleft of Bone
- ◯ Sunrock Overlook
- ◯ Trappe Hut
- ◯ Crystalsong Mines
- ◯ Razor Box
- ◯ Under Mountain Mechanogear
- ◯ The Mechinarium
- ◯ Mincemeat Mayhem Arena

COLLECTIBLES & ENEMIES

Soul Gem		Woodpecker Pal (Tree Rex)
Legendary Treasure		Eagle Masthead
Hats		Battle Helmet, Trucker Hat
Story Scroll		Trial of Wealth
Luck-O-Tron Wheel		Lucky Wheel of Experience
Treasure Chests		4 to collect
Winged Sapphire		1 to collect

En Fuego Chompy

Chompy

Arkeyan Crackler

Blaze Brewer

Grenade General

Slobbering Mutticus

Mohawk Cyclops

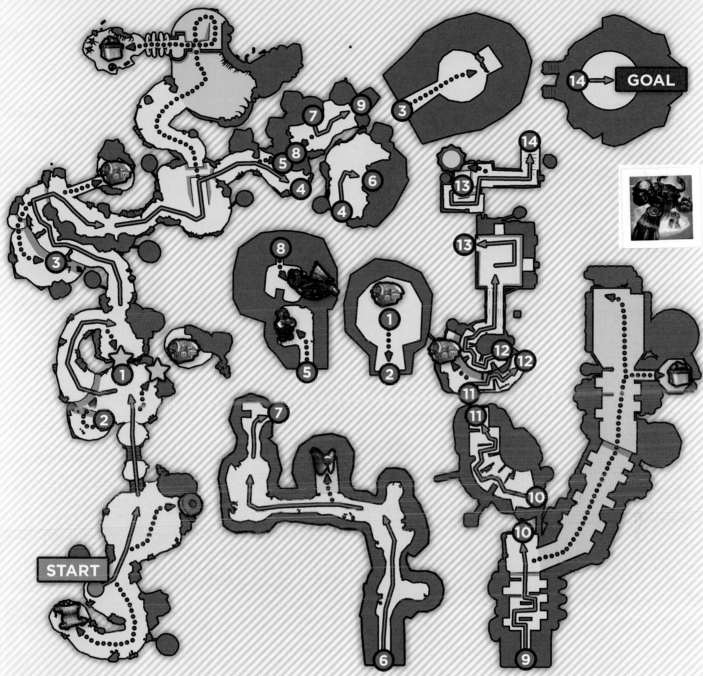

GOAL

START

MAP LEGEND

Direct Path	➤	Luck-O-Tron Wheel	⊙
Optional Path	➤	Soul Gem	⬡
Feat of Strength	★	Story Scroll	📜
Auric (Vendor)	🧍	Treasure Chest	🧰
Hat Box	🎩	Winged Sapphire	🦋
Legendary Treasure	🐟		

SUNROCK QUARRY & ALLEGORY PATHWAY

Favored Element: Fire

You arrive at Sunrock Quarry just outside Molekin Village. After the introduction, move right to enter Allegory Pathway. Charge through the En Fuego Chompies to score the **Story Scroll: Trial of Wealth**.

Head down to the push block area. Move one of the blocks onto the wooden platform on the left side of the crane. This causes it to tilt, revealing the **Luck-O-Tron Wheel**.

Push two more blocks into the gap on the left to form a walkway over to the bounce pad. Bounce to the next plateau where you must fight an army of Arkeyan Cracklers, Mohawk Cyclops enemies, and En Fuego Chompies. Focus on the Chompies and the Mohawks first; the Cracklers don't attack on their own. Beating all these guys reveals a hidden bounce pad.

TITAN CROSSING & THE DIRT ROOM

Favored Element: Earth

Before jumping up, switch to a Giant and complete the Feat of Strength at the back of the area. This leads to Titan Crossing and a **Treasure Chest**.

Follow the path up Sunrock Quarry and defeat the Grenade Generals at the top. When you get up here, a Blaze Brewer emerges from a hut. Many more Grenade Generals are hiding in that house. If you have a Giant, tear up the loose boulder and toss it at the house to reduce the number of reinforcements the Blaze Brewer gets. Defeat all the enemies to open the sealed gate.

Before moving on, check out the right side of the area for a Giant jump point. Crash through to The Dirt Room, which has a **Treasure Chest** and a ton of loose treasure. Head back to Sunrock Quarry and move through the open gate to Sunrock Village.

SUNROCK VILLAGE, COGWHEEL HOUSING & SUNROCK PEAK

Favored Element: Earth

Sunrock Village is overrun with Grenade Generals. Smash anything in your way and quickly make your way across to the left side of the town. When you reach the end of the lower path, head down to discover a secret cave entrance that leads to Cogwheel Housing. Turn the cogs inside, then head back up to Sunrock Village via the bounce pad.

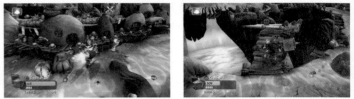

Jump up to the second level of Sunrock Village, then defeat the Cyclops and Troll enemies there. Look for a wooden bridge on the left side of this upper area. This is the bridge that was lowered when you were in Cogwheel Housing. Cross the bridge to enter Sunrock Peak and grab a **Treasure Chest**.

Continue to the top of the road until you find a bunch of push blocks. Push the smaller push blocks into place to create two paths on the wooden walkway. Pushing the two piled blocks southward lowers the stone block that prevents you from pushing one of the push blocks. Follow the left walkway down to the Undead Element Gate.

UNDEAD ELEMENT GATE: THE CLEFT OF BONE

Move the push block aside, then move it back in place to reform the walkway up to the **Battle Helmet**. After grabbing the hat, teleport back to Sunrock Village.

SUNROCK OVERLOOK & TRAPPE HUT

Favored Element: Magic

Back on the split walkway, head right this time. This upper area of the village is called Sunrock Overlook. Talk to the Molekin. Don't worry; Trappe Hut really isn't a trap, unless you consider Auric wanting to take your gold a trap!

AURIC'S INVENTORY

ITEM	COST
Luck-O-Tron Bulb #4	5,000 Gold
Troll Factory	3,000 Gold
Dangling Carrot Hat	1,300 Gold
Rocket Hat	1,100 Gold
Chompy Bot 9000 4 Skystone	1,200 Gold
Blaze Brewer Skystone	1,200 Gold
Fairy Dust	50 Gold
Damage Power Up	350 Gold
Skystone Cheat	500 Gold

CRYSTALSONG MINES

Favored Element: Magic

Use the teleporter ring to warp across to another plateau and a fight against a new enemy, Slobbering Mutticus. Avoid the beast's slime attack, and focus on taking it out first. If you get caught in its slime, it is impossible to dodge the Grenade General reinforcements.

Destroy the huts on either end of the plateau to stop the Grenade Generals from raiding the field. This is most easily done with a Giant tossing

a boulder. When you are victorious, the gate leading to Crystalsong Mines opens up. Don't attack the Cyclops inside! He's a friendly Skystones player. Challenge him for the key. If you aren't a fan of Skystones, you can skip this battle and smash through the wall with a Giant Skylander. Otherwise, use the key that Quick Draw gives you to get access to a side passage that contains a bomb.

SKYSTONE CHALLENGER: QUICK DRAW

Reward For Winning First Game: D. Riveter 4

QUICK DRAW'S SKYSTONE DECK

Blaster Troll	
Jawbreaker (x3)	
D. Riveter 4	

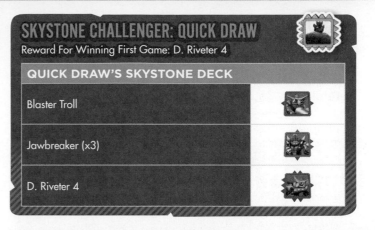

TECH ELEMENT GATE:
RAZOR BOX

However you make it through the brick wall, there's a Tech gate beyond it. Make it past the buzz saws safely to score a **Winged Sapphire**.

The side passage leads to a cavern full of Mohawk Cyclops enemies. Defeat them and some Mutticus arrive. Use the back of the cave to stay out of range of the Mutticus' slime.

Follow the path up to emerge back out in Sunrock Village. Use the chimney on the right to access a secret section of Trappe Hut. This contains the **Legendary Treasure: Eagle Masthead**. You can buy some items from Auric on this side of the hut as well. Smash the brick wall here with either the bomb from the end of Crystalsong Mines, or with a Giant.

UNDER MOUNTAIN MECHANOGEAR

Favored Element: Undead

Carefully navigate through the buzz saws to get to safety on the opposite side of this new zone.

TECH ELEMENT GATE:
THE MECHINARIUM

Just after the first set of buzz saws in Under Mountain Mechanogear, there is another Tech gate on the right side of the path. Dodge through the rotating blades until you get about two-thirds of the way through the area. A small passage juts off to the right. Explore it to find the **Trucker Hat**. Continue to the end of The Mechinarium and use the teleporter, which sends you ahead of the spike traps in the next area. Go back through the spike traps and walk down one level for a **Treasure Chest**.

Use the teleporter to the third spear plateau. These spears shoot out together every few seconds. Use the gap in the spears halfway down the path to make it through unharmed. This plateau leads to a complicated bounce pad / push block puzzle.

The first thing you should do is hit the floor switch on the left side.

Push the right push block forward one square, so it forms a corner with the stationary blocks in the right corner.

Use the jump pad to jump up on the push block and move to hit the switch. Hit the newly revealed floor switch. Move the three push blocks to form a straight line at the north end of this chamber. This provides just enough room to access the last raised floor switch. Bounce up there and hit the switch.

Before jumping down to the next area, push the middle block over the side, down into the next area. With two blocks in the lower area you can make a walkway that opens the way to Tree Rex's **Soul Gem**.

MINCEMEAT MAYHEM ARENA

Follow the walkway around to find an elevator. Get ready for Pipsqueak's Arena Battle!

BOSS FIGHT

PIPSQUEAK

This Arena Battle is similar to the one with Brock. Pipsqueak sends in progressively more difficult waves of enemies for your Skylanders to contend with.

The first wave is made up of En Fuego Chompies, Chompies, Grenade Generals, and Mohawk Cyclops. The Grenade Generals are the biggest threat here. They like to hang at the edge of the arena. Focus on taking them down first, then move on to any of the melee attackers.

The enemies in the second wave include Mohawk Cyclops, En Fuego Chompies, Grenade Generals, and Slobbering Mutticus. At the start of this wave, whirling buzz saws emerge on the sides of the drill pit. These drills can hurt your enemies as much as they hurt you.

The third wave consists of Chompies, Mohawk Cyclops, Grenade Generals, and Blaze Brewers. In this wave, the center island pops up and more whirling blades emerge. The end of this wave is particularly difficult. You must defeat two Blaze Brewers, some armored Cyclops enemies, and En Fuego Chompies all at the same time. Focus on wiping out the Chompies first, then the Cyclops enemies, then the Blaze Brewers. A Skylander with a ranged attack is best for this section.

After completing three waves, Pipsqueak comes out to challenge you! Luckily, Pipsqueak is wimpier than even a normal Mohawk Cyclops. Unluckily, Pipsqueak decides to sick his Shadow Duke on you. A Shadow Duke isn't much to worry about. They are incredibly slow. You must worry more about the reinforcements, which include En Fuego Chompies, Mohawk Cyclops enemies, Grenade Generals, and four Blaze Brewers.

PRO TIPS

Fight from the edge of the arena and dodge out of the way when the spinning blades circle. Most enemies won't move fast enough to avoid getting mowed down by the blades. This is particularly effective against tougher enemies.

Instead of contending with Shadow Duke's reinforcements, just pour on the damage as soon as he enters the arena. The fight is over as soon as you defeat him, so make that the priority.

BACK ON FLYNN'S SHIP

Defeating Pipsqueak unlocks Pipsqueak's Mincemeat Mayhem, a new set of Arena Challenges that you can play by talking to Brock. These arenas have fantastic rewards and are the best way to earn extra money for purchases.

BURNING QUESTIONS!

Q: How did the Molekin and Oracle forge their relationship?

A: It goes back a long ways. The Oracle is not a normal being, as you will see in the next chapter! In fact, he's not from Skylands. He's not from anywhere, necessarily.

To meet him, you have to believe in him. But most people don't. They have heard about an Oracle, but they never see him, so they don't believe. The Molekin, however, can't see anything, so to them, it's quite normal to believe in things you can't see. They do it all the time!

So by believing in the Oracle, they were the first to meet him. The Molekin have had a special relationship with the Oracle ever since.

Q: How did Pipsqueak become the boss of *anything*?

A: Nepotism. Pipsqueak is the nephew of some high-ups in the Cyclops government. Well, "government" might be the wrong word for Cyclops government, but you know what we mean.

CHAPTER 13
THE ORACLE

STORY GOALS

✓ Pass the Oracle's Trials

ELEMENTAL GATES

None

DARES	
Time To Beat	5:25
Enemies to Defeat	50

AREAS TO FIND

- ◯ Octavius' Lair
- ◯ Trial of Courage: Spiders
- ◯ Trial of Courage: Chompies
- ◯ Trial of Heart: Big Fish
- ◯ Trial of Heart: Little Fish
- ◯ Trial of Element: Fire
- ◯ Trial of Element: Water
- ◯ Trial of Valor: Catch
- ◯ Trial of Valor: Princess
- ◯ Trial of Knowledge: Reflection
- ◯ Trial of Knowledge: Puzzle
- ◯ Trial of Strength: Speed
- ◯ Trial of Strength: Power
- ◯ Titan's Digs

COLLECTIBLES & ENEMIES

Soul Gem	🔘	You'll Shoot Your Eye Out (Eye-Brawl)
Legendary Treasure		Dragon Roof
Hats		Bowling Pin Hat, Umbrella Hat
Story Scroll		Arkeyans Before Dressers
Luck-O-Tron Wheel	⚫	Lucky Wheel of Wealth
Treasure Chests		4 to collect
Winged Sapphire		1 to collect

Spiderlings

Gargantula

D. Riveter

Root Runner

Jawbreaker

Chompy

Frigid Chompy

Chompy Bot 9000

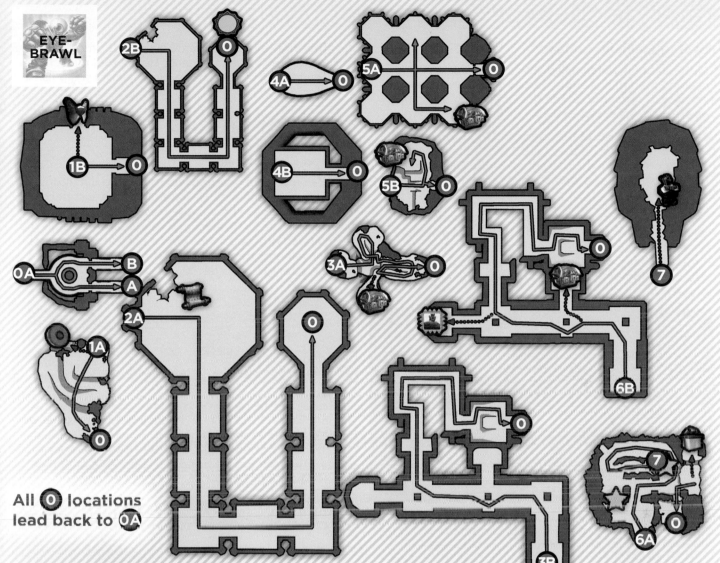

EYE-BRAWL

All **O** locations lead back to **OA**

MAP LEGENDS

Direct Path	
Optional Path	
Feat of Strength	★
Auric (Vendor)	
Hat Box	
Legendary Treasure	
Luck-O-Tron Wheel	●
Skystones Challenger	
Soul Gem	○
Story Scroll	
Treasure Chest	
Winged Sapphire	

1A	Trial of Courage: Chompies
1B	Trial of Courage: Spiders
2A	Trial of Heart: Little Fish
2B	Trial of Heart: Big Fish
3A	Trial of Valor: Princess
3B	Trial of Valor: Catch
4A	Trial of Element: Fire
4B	Trial of Element: Water
5A	Trial of Knowledge: Puzzle
5B	Trial of Knowledge: Reflection
6A	Trial of Strength: Power
6B	Trial of Strength: Speed

BEFORE STARTING IN CHAPTER 13: THE ORACLE

One important note on this Chapter is that unlike all of the other Chapters, you cannot do every thing in one playthrough. Each time you visit the Oracle, you must make a choice between two paths. All the paths have been included here, so you may need to skip around this chapter to find your exact spot.

OCTAVIUS' LAIR #1

The first part of your trial is to pick the path to the monster you fear most: Spiders or Chompies.

Octavius: Provided this Skylander can pass a series of trials. They are for my research. You

TRIAL OF COURAGE: SPIDERS

Favored Element: Undead

This area is completely filled with new spider enemies including Spiderlings and a Gargantula. To make matters even worse, for some reason the Oracle is keeping two Jawbreakers in here as well.

Stay at the outskirts of this room and focus on damaging the Jawbreakers when they fall on their face. When both are down, turn your attention to the Gargantula. The giant spider has a web attack that can trap your Skylander.

To take on the Gargantula, charge in with your best melee Skylander and circle around the spider while constantly attacking the green spot on her back. When Gargantula falls, finish off any spider eggs that remain. Grab the **Winged Sapphire** on the left side of the room before you exit.

TRIAL OF COURAGE: CHOMPIES

Favored Element: Life

Chompies? Really, who is afraid of Chompies? Unfortunately, the area isn't just full of Chompies; it's full of Chompy Bot 9000s and Root Runners. Before you get started on beating up poor Chompies, look for the spot where you can drop down near the level starting area. Fall back on this secret ledge to discover a **Luck-O-Tron Wheel**.

Continue the fight down the hill, blowing up the Chompy Bots and Root Runners. When you've cleared the area of big enemies, your trial is a success! Exit back to Octavius' Lair.

OCTAVIUS' LAIR #2

Now that you've passed your first trial, it's time to choose again. The Oracle has the Trial of Heart. You must choose between being a small fish in a big ocean, or a big fish in a small pond.

TRIAL OF HEART: BIG FISH

Favored Element: Air

In this area you are charged with defeating a multitude of miniaturized enemies. Be careful though, just because they're small, doesn't mean they're any easier. The enemies include D. Riveters and Jawbreakers. Defeat the enemies and proceed to the clamp challenge. Just time your movements through each set of clamps to make it through safely. Using a fast Skylander helps as well.

Further along the path you encounter some miniaturized Gargantulas and D. Riveters defending a sealed gate. Use melee attacks to take down these range-focused enemies quickly. Make it through the next two clamp puzzles to uncover the exit. Before using the teleporter, grab Eye-Brawl's **Soul Gem**.

TRIAL OF HEART: LITTLE FISH

Favored Element: Air

This area is full of gigantic Chompies! Hopefully, Chompies weren't your most feared enemy! Right at the start, grab the **Story Scroll: Arkeyans Before Dressers**.

Defeat the giant Chompies (they aren't any harder than regular Chompies) and proceed through the clamp challenges. At the next corner you must deal with two giant Jawbreakers, who are much more frightening than Chompies! Dodge the Jawbreakers' attacks and finish them off while they are on the ground. Defeating them unseals the next gate. Next up are two more Jawbreakers accompanied by giant D. Riveters. Defeat the D. Riveters first, then finish the Jawbreakers to unseal the final gate in the trial.

OCTAVIUS' LAIR #3

After clearing two trials, the Oracle offers four potential trials to you. Which trials you are offered depends on which choices you made earlier in the path. If you go with Big Fish, you get Trial of Element. If you selected Little Fish, you get Trial of Valor.

The Trial of Element asks you to choose between fire and water. The choices for Trial of Valor are saving the princess and catching the bad guy.

TRIAL OF ELEMENT: FIRE

Favored Element: Fire

AMBUSH
ERUPTOR

You must fight and defeat two Dark Eruptor Skylanders. If you have a Water Skylander, then this is your shot to complete the Extinguisher Quest. It requires that you defeat a fire minion; these guys both count.

These fiery enemies have two attacks. The first is a bouncing fireball ranged attack. They follow that up quickly with a short-range area-of-effect lava attack.

These enemies are fairly easy to defeat if you stay at range. Their fireballs move slowly enough to make them easy to dodge. If you are trying to take them down with melee attacks, you must wait until after their short-range magma attack, when they take a moment to chuckle at you. Move in to get in a few swings before retreating.

TRIAL OF ELEMENT: WATER

Favored Element: Water

AMBUSH
ZAP

In this ambush you must fight and defeat three fast-moving Dark Zaps. If you have a Fire Skylander, then you can complete the Steamer Quest by defeating one of the Zaps in this zone.

Zap has two attacks; one is a ranged lightning breath attack, and the other is a slide attack. This fight is made a bit more difficult by the water on the platform. It slows down the movement of most Skylanders. To circumvent this disadvantage, pick a flying Skylander like Swarm or use a Water Skylander. Of all the Dark Minion ambushes, Zap's is one of the easiest. These Dark Skylanders are particularly susceptible to damaging dash attacks. Just keep dashing in circles around the enemies until they fall.

TRIAL OF VALOR: CATCH

Favored Element: Tech

Follow the flying key and try to catch it before it reaches the end of the maze. Watch out for the flaming apples it drops. Switch to a fast Skylander and you should be able to catch the key quickly. Take the key all the way to the door at the end of the maze to pass the challenge. If you let the key wander off on its own, you will fail the challenge, so you must capture it before exploring the rest of the area.

TRIAL OF VALOR: PRINCESS

Favored Element: Life

This is a short trial. Push the blocks to form a walkway up to the princess. She's on the highest point of this island. Move towards the princess and the exit gate opens. Before you leave, grab the **Treasure Chest**.

OCTAVIUS' LAIR #4

Octavius' next trial is either the Trial of Strength or the Trial of Knowledge. To get the Trial of Knowledge, you must have completed the Trial of Element. To get the Trial of Strength, you must have completed the Trial of Valor.

If you get the Trial of Knowledge, you can choose between Lock Master or Light Beam Perfectionist. If you get the Trial of Strength, you can choose between Built for Power or Built for Speed.

TRIAL OF KNOWLEDGE: REFLECTION

Favored Element: Earth

This level requires you to solve a complicated light puzzle. Before you get started, grab the **Treasure Chest** up on the left hill. Push the crystal on the left hill off the ledge. You must move the push blocks to make room for the crystal's passage. Go back to the lower area. Push the left crystal forward once. Push the right crystal forward, then left.

Puzzle Solved!

TRIAL OF KNOWLEDGE: PUZZLE

Favored Element: Undead

To get in this door, you must first solve a simple Lock Puzzle.

 Perfect Lock Puzzle Solution: 3 moves
Right, Right, Right

This area has three Lock Puzzle doors in the starting area. They're identified here as Left Front, Middle Front, and Right Front.

First solve the Middle Front puzzle. This leads to the middle cell.

 Perfect Lock Puzzle Solution: 3 moves
Right, Right, Right

Solve the puzzle on the left to get the first key.

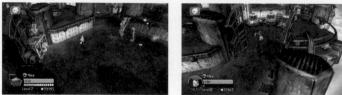

 Perfect Lock Puzzle Solution: 8 moves
Right, Left, Left, Right, Left, Left, Left, Left

Grab the first key then return to the entrance. You now need to solve the Right Front puzzle.

 Perfect Lock Puzzle Solution: 10 moves
Left, Right, Right, Left, Right, Right, Right, Right, Left, Left

Destroy the Root Runners and Chompies in this room. When it's clear, solve the cell's puzzle.

 Perfect Lock Puzzle Solution: 8 moves
Left, Left, Left, Left, Left, Right, Right, Left

Now you can collect the second key as well as the **Treasure Chest**. Use both keys on the back door to exit the trial.

The solution to the Left Front puzzle is presented here just in case you want to solve all the puzzles before moving on.

 Perfect Lock Puzzle Solution: 8 moves
Left, Left, Right, Right, Right, Right, Right, Right

TRIAL OF STRENGTH: SPEED

Favored Element: Tech

For this trial, dodge the rolling, spiked wheels. Pick a fast Skylander, then use dash attacks and good timing to make it through safely. When you get to the first intersection, turn right to claim the **Treasure Chest**. At the next intersection, follow the north path and talk to Clam-Tron 4000 to play a game of Skystones. There's not much else to the trial; just walk carefully to the teleporter at the end of the spiked paths.

SKYSTONE CHALLENGER: CLAM-TRON 4000

Reward For Winning First Game: Arkeyan Bomber

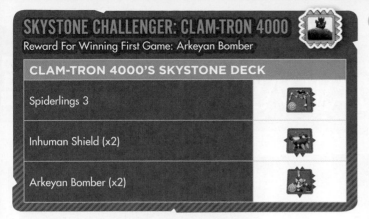

CLAM-TRON 4000'S SKYSTONE DECK	
Spiderlings 3	
Inhuman Shield (x2)	
Arkeyan Bomber (x2)	

TRIAL OF STRENGTH: POWER & TITAN'S DIGS

Favored Element: Earth

When you first enter this area, complete the Feat of Strength on the left with a Giant Skylander. If you don't have a Giant Skylander, you must fight through a winding tunnel on the right. Either way, you end up at a grassy hill with a Giant jump point.

Don't jump just yet. First, hop down to the right and use the teleporter, which sends you to an area with push blocks. Push the near blocks off the edge, and push the far block to make a bridge to the **Umbrella Hat**.

Drop back down. If you have a Giant, climb the hill and use the Giant jump point to smash into an area called Titan's Digs. Otherwise, use the push blocks to make a ramp that leads down to the teleporter below. The cave entrance here leads to the same area as the Giant drop-off, Titan's Digs. Auric has set up shop inside Titan's Digs.

AURIC'S INVENTORY	
ITEM	**COST**
Crown of Light	1,200 Gold
Tiki Hat	800 Gold
Chompy Bot 9000 5 Skystone	1,400 Gold
Fairy Dust	50 Gold
Skystone Cheat	500 Gold

OCTAVIUS' LAIR #5

The Oracle's last challenge isn't really a full challenge. You are essentially picking your reward. If you choose wealth you get a stack of gold bars worth 500 Gold. If you pick knowledge, you get collectibles. For the first reward you receive the **Bowling Pin Hat**. The next time through, you receive **Legendary Treasure: Dragon Roof**. Once you get both rewards, you always get the same reward as choosing the wealth path.

After you've collected your reward, your mission is complete! Plan to revisit this chapter and try the doors you missed the first time around.

BURNING QUESTIONS!

Q: Sprocket designed her turrets to only fire at bad guys. If she assembles one near the Oracle, it fires on him. Is this a bug in her code, or is it telling us something important about Oracle?

A: The answer is quite simple. The Oracle is not a bad guy. Nobody knows what he really is, but his intentions are never evil.

Sprocket, however, is not one to take chances. When she designed her turrets, she designed them so that if they could not detect a foreign entity's evilness or goodness, the turret defaults to evilness. Just in case.

While this could end with some unfortunate accidents, Sprocket takes her job as Tech defender of the Skylands seriously.

Q: What data did the Oracle actually glean by watching me make these choices?

A: He believes that if he can watch enough people make enough choices, he will be able to know what choice anyone will make before they actually make it. So far, he has been able to do this for some things, but not everything.

For instance, he can predict what donut you're going to order before you order it. He can even do that right now through this book. He says the next time you order a donut it will be...a chocolate old-fashioned!

It'll happen. Just you wait.

CHAPTER 14

AUTOGYRO ADVENTURE

STORY GOALS

- ☑ Reach the Machine
- ◯ Unlock the Gate to Arkus
- ◯ Escape the Caverns

ELEMENTAL GATES

- Undead
- Water

DARES

Time To Beat	14:50
Enemies to Defeat	40

AREAS TO FIND

- ◯ The Caverns
- ◯ Forgotten Hollows
- ◯ Hidden Crypt
- ◯ Cold Storage Area Z
- ◯ Neverending Falls
- ◯ Maze of Myth
- ◯ The Source
- ◯ Auric's Hidden Vault
- ◯ Hall of Silence
- ◯ Cold Storage Area A
- ◯ Cold Storage Area B
- ◯ Gear Box
- ◯ The Long Hall
- ◯ The Machine
- ◯ Final Tour of Duty

COLLECTIBLES & ENEMIES

Soul Gem	◯	Eagle-Air Battle Gear (Jet-Vac)
Legendary Treasure		Propeller Masthead
Hats		Future Hat, Bottle Cap Hat
Story Scroll		Wilikin Neighbors?
Luck-O-Tron Wheel	◉	Lucky Wheel of Power
Treasure Chests		4 to collect
Winged Sapphire		1 to collect

Arkeyan Juggernaut
Arkeyan Ultron
Arkeyan Autogyro
Arkeyan Duelist
Blaze Brewer
Trog Pincher
Crystal Golem

MAP LEGEND

Direct Path	↖	Hat Box	
Autogyro Path	↖	Legendary Treasure	
Autogyro Path	↖	Luck-O-Tron Wheel	
Autogyro Path	↖	Skystones Challenger	
Autogyro Path	↖	Soul Gem	
Autogyro Path	↖	Story Scroll	
Optional Path		Story Scroll	
Feat of Strength	★	Treasure Chest	
Auric (Vendor)		Winged Sapphire	

THE CAVERNS

Jump in the Autogyro with Flynn to begin the level. You must steer the ship safely from section to section within the level. Avoid the lasers, Arkeyan beams, giant robots, and other obstacles. If you do blow up the ship, don't worry; you just restart from the last checkpoint; you don't need to replay the entire level.

You can also collect gold in jet mode. Collect the "2x" Symbols to increase the amount of gold you earn. When Flynn switches the Autogyro to hover, shoot with Attack 1. Hit the big circles on the first door to open it up.

Collecting the purple power ups increases the ship's boost. While in jet mode, hold down Attack 1 to kick in overdrive. Save this for when you really need it! Going faster makes it harder to collect coins and avoid obstacles.

When you reach the platform with the Arkeyan Ultron, wait for it to pop out from behind cover and nail it with the ship's blasters. Move the Arkeyan battery into the socket to open the tunnel door. Immediately after getting back into the gyro, turn right to land on the purple platform on the right side of the cave. If you miss the platform, crash the plane on purpose to try again.

UNDEAD ELEMENT GATE:
FORGOTTEN HOLLOWS & HIDDEN CRYPT

This gate is just off this first landing. The Weapon Master gives you the low-down on Forgotten Hollows when you enter. Defeat the crazy Trog Pincher (basically crazy Chompies) and scale the side of the undead cliff. When you see a set of push blocks, move one over the side of the cliff and drop down on it to access a secret area. The cave entrance leads to Hidden Crypt and a **Treasure Chest**.

Bounce back up the side of Forgotten Hollows and drop down into the large arena area.

AMBUSH
CHOP CHOP

For this ambush, you need to defeat two Dark Chop Chops. Use Undead Skylanders against Chop Chop. Not only do you get Elemental bonus because this is an Undead area, but if you succeed in taking down one of the Chop Chops, you can complete the quest By a Thread.

These Chop Chops are completely focused on sword attacks, and don't use their shields much. They use a variety of sword attack combos as they rush to attack. Hang back with Ranged Skylanders and take them down from range. Note that they each have a considerable amount of health, so it will take some time to take them down, even with your best attacks. Patience is key.

Defeat the Chop Chops and bounce up through the spinning blades to reach the final plateau and the **Future Hat**. Take the teleporter back to the Autogyro.

COLD STORAGE AREA Z

Back in the Autogyro, you resume your trip through the Caverns. Fly high and to the right of the screen. Your next stop off will be on another platform on the right side, but this one is much higher. After successfully landing on the second platform, head inside the door to enter Cold Storage Area Z. There are several Arkeyan Duelists inside the area. These guys are tough on their own, but they soon get reinforced by a Blaze Brewer and an Arkeyan Bomber.

This is a tough spot to fight all these tough melee enemies. If you need a breather, retreat back outside. Use the Bomber's plasma bombs on these tough guys and open the sealed gate. Defeat a second Blaze Brewer to unlock the gate blocking the **Legendary Treasure: Propeller Masthead**. Return to your ship and the Caverns.

WATER ELEMENT GATE:
NEVERENDING FALLS

Immediately after boarding the Autogyro, get ready to land on another platform on the left. This leads to a Water Elemental Gate. This is a small room featuring the **Bottle Cap Hat**. Grab it and return to your ship.

MAZE OF MYTH

Favored Element: Magic

When you get back in the jet, continue forward until you reach another platform defended by an Arkeyan Ultron, where Flynn switches the Autogyro to hover mode. This time you must defeat the mole robot. These robots spit out rockets that you can use to destroy Arkeyan Shields and tough Arkeyan enemies. Press Attack 2 to fire the rockets. After defeating the robots, head inside to the Maze of Myth.

Move down the ramp and get ready to take on two Arkeyan Duelists (this is their official introduction). They come at you one at at time. Nail them with ranged attacks, and don't let them get up the ramp towards your position. When you've won, head through the right gate and move the two crystals on the right into position to pull the floating island with the Arkeyan battery closer. Grab the battery and bring it back to the entrance area.

This time, go through the left gate. Place the Arkeyan battery in the socket at the end of the left path. On the way back, some Bombers and a Blaze Brewer show up and attack. You must defeat them all to open the sealed gate. Before returning to Flynn, explore the left path here to talk to the Weapon Master. He's always up for a game of Skystones.

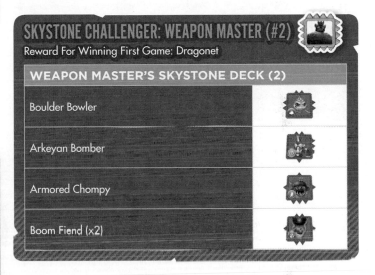

SKYSTONE CHALLENGER: WEAPON MASTER (#2)
Reward For Winning First Game: Dragonet

WEAPON MASTER'S SKYSTONE DECK (2)	
Boulder Bowler	
Arkeyan Bomber	
Armored Chompy	
Boom Fiend (x2)	

This Skystones match takes place on a grid with four elemental squares: Fire, Air, Earth, and Water. If you have any good Skystones of those elements, switch them in before the match. This is an odd fight, because you don't need to capture Skystones to win. Simply force Weapon Master to place his tiles on mismatched elemental squares. If you can get him to destroy two of his own tiles, you win.

THE SOURCE

Back in the Arkeyan Autogyro, follow the floating rings through the robot cavern and into the next passage. When you reach the shielded door at the end, destroy the enemy gyro formations to earn rockets. Use the rockets to blast through the door's shield. Immediately after breaking through the shielded door, watch out for a platform on the right. This doorway leads to Auric's Hidden Vault.

Arkeyan Juggernauts and Arkeyan Bombers arrive to ruin your day after you take a few steps inside. Use the Bomber's bombs to destroy the Juggernaut quickly, then move on to the next section. The next platform up has two Arkeyan Duelists and a Bomber. Defeat them from the safety of the walkway and continue on to the crystal lever on the left. Keep switching the light beam until it intersects the far crystal.

AURIC'S HIDDEN VAULT

Grab the **Treasure Chest** when you first enter this area. Go to the back of the room to check out Auric's store! When you're done, head back to the Autogyro.

![] AURIC'S INVENTORY	
ITEM	**COST**
Robot Repellent Charm	8,000 Gold
Anvil Hat	1,200 Gold
Chompy Bot 9000 6 Skystone	1,350 Gold
Regeneration Power Up	400 Gold
Fairy Dust	50 Gold

HALL OF SILENCE

Favored Element: Air

After clearing out Auric's Hidden Vault, go to the next locked door. Destroy the robots defending the door. After you land, head inside to the Hall of Silence.

Watch out! The Duelists respawn with a Juggernaut. Use the stairs here to avoid the Juggernaut's beam and hit the platform with your Skylander's best ranged attacks.

When the way is clear, move back down to the energy beam's location. Push the second crystal to the left, then grab the Arkeyan battery. Place the battery in the socket (back near where the Duelists were), and exit back to Flynn.

COLD STORAGE AREA A

After returning to Flynn, get ready to make another quick landing. This time it's at a platform on the left. Head inside to discover Cold Storage Area A. Move down the walkway to discover a **Treasure Chest** on the right, and **Story Scroll: Wilikin Neighbors?** on the left. Head back out to the Autogyro.

Right after taking off from the Cold Storage Area A platform, there's a second platform on the left for you to land on. This platform is higher, so steer your gyro up and to the left as soon as you take off.

COLD STORAGE AREA B

This is another simple side room. Pop up to the upper platform and grab Jet-Vac's **Soul Gem**. If you were searching for all the side areas, congrats! That was the last one. For the rest of your trip, you can focus on flying and not worry about finding these difficult to spot side areas. All of the areas you see in the latter part of the level are areas you've already visited.

Back with Flynn, it's not long before you face another sealed door. This one is much more difficult than the previous doors. You need to shoot the waves of Autogyros to get rockets, all while dodging incoming fire from the Ultron robots. Defeat both Ultrons to complete the sequence. Flynn automatically lands the ship.

GEAR BOX

Favored Element: Magic

If you have a Magic Skylander, this is a great place to get the Puzzle Power Quest. You need to kill 25 enemies with light beams. Luckily this area has plenty of beams and weak enemies. Direct the beams to the platform you are standing on and lure the little Trogs into the beam to quickly earn kills towards the quest.

The first thing you should do in Gear Box is rotate the first crystal switch to the platform containing the **Luck-O-Tron Wheel**. This summons the platform to

your area. After you grab the wheel, shift the crystal to blast the beam across to the battery platform.

Next up is the big gear blocking the beam to the Arkeyan battery. Turn the second beam away from the big gear when the beam from the first beam is clear. This causes the Arkeyan battery to move to where the Luck-O-Tron Wheel was. Grab the battery and deposit it in the socket. Watch out! A Crystal Golem spawns at the beginning of the area. Turn the second beam towards the platform and lure the golem into the beam for a quick kill.

THE LONG HALL

Prepare for a long haul through the Long Hall! Collect the treasure in the air as you pass through the area. When you reach the end of the

tunnel, you must blast another shielded door. Shoot the mole Ultrons and the Autogyros for rockets to destroy the door. One last section left! Destroy the Ultrons defending the next platform and Flynn lands the ship.

THE MACHINE

Favored Element: Water

After landing, head up the walkway. Watch out! A bunch of Arkeyan Duelists are waiting to attack. Fighting the Duelists in an enclosed space isn't a good idea. Instead, retreat back down the staircase and pelt them with ranged attacks. Blaze Brewers join the part after the Duelists are downed. Apply the same defensive-minded strategy here to take them down.

With all the enemies defeated, head up the platform and look for an Arkeyan switch. Using the switch causes a strange Arkeyan device to emerge from the ground. You must activate two more of these devices to complete the level. Continue up the walkway and look for a teleporter pad on the right. Use the teleporter to gain access to the secret platform and a **Treasure Chest**.

Back on the main path, the next area you reach includes many push blocks. Configure the blocks as shown in the screenshot, then use the teleporter to get to the top of the grid.

Navigate along the corners of the blocks to reach the **Winged Sapphire**. That's the last collectible of the level! Now you must reach the bounce pad. Configure the blocks as shown in the screenshot.

Traverse the pads diagonally to make it to the bounce pad. At the next bend, a Crystal Golem arrives to challenge you. The Golem is tough to fight in such a small area, so lure him back to the push block room.

Defeat the Golem and continue along the path until you spot the second Arkeyan switch. The next platform has a few Juggernauts to defeat. After you take care of them, follow the walkway up to the higher platform. Up top, another Juggernaut and two Blaze Brewers are defending the area. Use the Lower ramp to avoid the Juggernaut's lasers and take them down with ranged attacks. Hit the last switch and the door to Arkus is finally open!

FINAL TOUR OF DUTY

Now you and Flynn need to escape before the chambers completely collapse! Grab the purple turbo chargers to keep your ship moving. You must use a turbo charge to make it through the final door.
Dodge the closing doors to complete your escape!

BURNING QUESTIONS!

Q: How do the Arkeyans carry those batteries around? They aren't exactly built to be stored in pockets.

A: They might not be built to be stored in *your* pocket, but have you seen Arkeyan pockets? They're huge. And they aren't connected to clothing. But they found that cup holders actually work better for carrying those batteries anyway. Their cup holders are pretty big too. They can get pretty thirsty and there were very few Arkeyan convenience stores back during their reign. Some say this is what really led to the collapse of their society.

Q: How do the giant robots get through the smaller gates that the Autogyro flies through?

A: For the most part, they don't. Due to the aforementioned lack of Arkeyan convenience stores, there was little reason for them to go through the gate. If a convenience store did open up on the other side, they would just give some copters money to pick something up for them. They loved all convenience store food, as long as it was hot and cheap.

CHAPTER (15) LOST CITY OF ARKUS

STORY GOALS

☑ Enter the Palace

ELEMENTAL GATES

💧 Water

✹ Magic

🔥 Fire

DARES	
Time To Beat	6:40
Enemies to Defeat	55

AREAS TO FIND

- ○ The Beginning of the End
- ○ Hidden Slide Entrance
- ○ Azure Slide
- ○ Elliptical Arena
- ○ Water Cliff Terrace
- ○ Hazard Path
- ○ Fractured Ledge
- ○ A Pit With Possibilities
- ○ Pit Puzzler
- ○ Hazard Bridge
- ○ Turquoise Tomb
- ○ Inside the Tomb

- ○ CAUTION: Rolling Hazards Ahead!!
- ○ Hidden Ledge
- ○ Cannon Fodder
- ○ Fire Battle
- ○ Batterson's Stovetop
- ○ Hazard Depository
- ○ Upper Arena
- ○ Downhill Challenge
- ○ Gate Crasher Battle
- ○ Treasure Cave
- ○ Reflection Locking Mechanism

COLLECTIBLES & ENEMIES

Soul Gem	◎	Call the Narwhal! (Chill)
Legendary Treasure	🐦	Skull Engine
Hats	🎩	Funnel Hat, Atom Hat
Story Scroll	📜	Roboto-Ball
Luck-O-Tron Wheel	◉	Lucky Wheel of Wealth
Treasure Chests	⚙	4 to collect
Winged Sapphire	🦋	1 to collect

Trog Wanderer

Trog Pincher

Trogmander

Arkeyan Sniper

Arkeyan Duelist

Arkeyan Juggernaut

MAP LEGEND

Direct Path	↖
Optional Path	↘
Feat of Strength	★
Auric (Vendor)	
Hat Box	
Legendary Treasure	
Luck-O-Tron Wheel	●
Skystones Challenger	
Soul Gem	○
Story Scroll	
Treasure Chest	
Winged Sapphire	

GOAL

START

THE BEGINNING OF THE END, HIDDEN SLIDE ENTRANCE & AZURE SLIDE

Favored Element: Magic

Finally! You've reached the Lost City. Head down the first platform and take out the two Trog Wanderers hanging out. Drop down through the gap on the right to discover the Hidden Slide Entrance. Use a Giant to smash the wall and take the teleporter to Azure Slide. If you don't have a Giant, you can use the bomb in the Elliptical Arena to blow open this door.

Fly or run down the ramp, avoiding the spike traps. At the bottom is the **Story Scroll: Roboto-Ball**. Continue down the path to drop back down to the level start.

ELLIPTICAL ARENA

Favored Element: Magic

Continue around the walkway and drop down to Elliptical Arena. There, you encounter your first Trogmander. Whenever you encounter these guys, focus on defeating them before attacking the Trog Pinchers. Once the Trogmanders go down, their spells of giant growth fade away.

Exit the arena and continue on to the next area, Hazard Path.

WATER ELEMENT GATE:
WATER CLIFF TERRACE

This gate is located at the point where you first drop down into the Elliptical Arena. Smash the crystals for bonus treasure, then bounce up the waterfall on the left to retrieve the **Funnel Hat**.

HAZARD PATH & FRACTURED LEDGE

Favored Element: Magic

The aptly named Hazard Path includes several spear hazards. Before you start tiptoeing down this trail, drop down in the opening at the bottom of the screen. This leads to a secret area: Fractured Ledge. Use a Giant to smash the wall.

Talk to Freebot on the other side of the wall to play Skystones.

SKYSTONE CHALLENGER: FREEBOT

Reward For Winning First Game: Jawbreaker 4

FREEBOT'S SKYSTONE DECK

Chompy 2	
Jawbreaker 4 (x4)	

A PIT WITH POSSIBILITIES & PIT PUZZLER

Favored Element: Earth

Back at Hazard Path, continue along the winding path, dodging the barrels and spiked traps until you reach A Pit With Possibilities. The first thing to do is drop down in the pit to reach the Pit Puzzler area.

Arkeyans are known to use the word "puzzler" loosely. This pit isn't much of a puzzle. Just walk around the edge of the area until you hit the floor switch. Walk back to the center area to grab all the treasure and the **Luck-O-Tron Wheel**.

Now that you've cleared out the Pit Puzzler area, head out the exit (It's at the bottom of the screen) to teleport back up to A Pit With Possibilities.

Note the two push blocks at the bottom of the screen. Push the top one to the right, then walk around the ledge to get in pushing position for the bounce pad push block.

HAZARD RIDGE

Favored Element: Tech

Push the block into the pit and bounce up to Hazard Bridge and retrieve the key. Before you drop back down, smash the two walls on the left to

discover Chill's **Soul Gem**. If you don't have a Giant, get the bomb from the lower area and bring it up here (but you must do it twice). Drop back down and open up the gate to Turquoise Tomb.

TURQUOISE TOMB

Favored Element: Magic

When you drop down into the tomb, you are immediately thrust into battle against a new kind of enemy, the Arkeyan Sniper, along with a large group of Trog Wanderers. The Snipers are a bit tricky. Wait for them to pop up from their hidey holes to attack them, and use the cover of buildings to avoid their sniper shots. Defeat both the snipers and all the Trogs to unseal the gate. Pop up to the upper area to meet Auric. Wabbit Ears are one of the best hats in the game. If you have some extra money, they are a good investment.

AURIC'S INVENTORY	
ITEM	COST
Napoleon Hat	1,000 Gold
Wabbit Ears	1,200 Gold
Arkeyan Sniper Skystone	250 Gold
Invincibility Power Up	425 Gold
Fairy Dust	50 Gold
Skystone Cheat	500 Gold

MAGIC ELEMENT GATE:
INSIDE THE TOMB

Look for this gate in the center of Turquoise Tomb. Push the right block back to make a walkway towards the elevated block. Use a bounce pad to get up top and push that high block down. Push both blocks down to form a path to the second elevated block (on the left of the screen). There is a

secret bounce pad at the back of the plateau near where you pushed the first block. Now push the second high block down and cross over to the **Treasure Chest**.

CAUTION: ROLLING HAZARDS AHEAD!! & HIDDEN LEDGE

Favored Element: Earth

With the tomb cleared out, proceed up the stairs on the right. This leads to the area named CAUTION: Rolling Hazards Ahead!! Instead of heading up the path, drop down to the right (down where the barrels are falling). This leads to Hidden Ledge and the **Legendary Treasure: Skull Engine**.

Take the bounce pad back up top. You need a fast Skylander to make it past the giant rolling barrel without taking damage. Sprint up to the top and take a right to continue along the trail.

FIRE ELEMENT GATE:
CANNON FODDER & FIRE BATTLE

Look for this gate just off the main path of CAUTION: Rolling Hazards Ahead!! Inside, the first thing to do is activate the first cannon. Don't worry, it won't hurt the hat. Now, just past the gate, look for a secret cave entrance below and to the left. This leads to Fire Battle and an ambush.

AMBUSH
FLAMESLINGER

This is a tough fight against three Dark Flameslinger Skylanders. If you bring the bomb in from Cannon Fodder (it's right above the entrance), you can use it to open this fight up with a bang!

These Flameslingers have three attacks. The first is a fire-foot dash that kicks up a wall of high flames. Don't run into these flame trails, they do serious damage.

The second attack is a straightforward bow attack. This attack does more damage than the flame wall, so prepare to dodge it. Each Flameslinger fires four of these flame arrows in a row, but then they stop and laugh. This is a great opening to get in some attacks of your own.

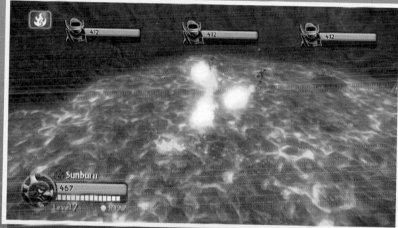

The last attack is a charged bow shot that explodes into a fireball. This attack is easily avoided, so long as you keep an eye out for the charged attack. This is a tough fight. If you're having problems getting past it, use a Skylander with excellent defensive skills such as Hex, Shroomboom, or Terrafin.

BATTERSON'S STOVETOP

Defeating the Flameslingers rewards you with a **Treasure Chest**, but you're not done here. Head back out to Cannon Fodder. Use the bomb at the top of the lava flow to destroy the giant purple crystal. Push the cannon to the left and activate it to blow the second hat pedestal block.

Drop down to the next magma lake and look for a string of coins leading down on the right side of the area. Fall down where the coins are to discover Batterson's Stovetop area and its **Winged Sapphire**.

Hop back up to Cannon Fodder. Bounce up to the area on the right and look for four push blocks. Push the blocks into a straight line, then bring the bomb over to the left area. Use the bounce pad to jump up and smash the purple crystals. Activate the cannon on the other side to smash another pedestal block.

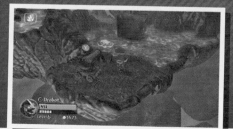

Continue along the magma trail and use the bomb to destroy the purple crystals down below. Drop down to the hat box area, and use the last cannon to blow the last pedestal block. Your reward for all that hard work is the amazing **Atom Hat**.

If you are hungry for some more gold, smash the purple gems in the right section of the hat area to uncover a cache of loose treasure (about 300 Gold). When you're done, take the portal back to the main path.

HAZARD DEPOSITORY

Favored Element: Earth

When you return from Cannon Fodder, look for a secret cave entrance near where the second set of giant barrels drops down from. Enter the cave to enter Hazard Depository. Weave through the hazards to recover the **Treasure Chest** at the other end of the room.

There's one last pathway to clear in the CAUTION: Rolling Hazards Ahead!! area. A Cyclops throws spiked barrels down the path. Use the bounce pads to avoid the barrels. When you make it to the top, you end up in the Upper Arena.

UPPER ARENA

Favored Element: Water

This arena is full of Arkeyan Duelists and also includes an Arkeyan Sniper on the left side. Avoid the Duelists and focus on taking out the Sniper. Your next targets are the Duelists. Keep moving around, and try to interrupt them while they are charging their swords.

After the Duelists are down, Trogmanders arrive with a bunch of Trogs. Wipe out the Tiny Trogs, then wait for the Trogmanders

to jump into the arena, and focus on taking them down. Defeating the giant Trogs is pointless since the Trogmanders can just summon new ones.

DOWNHILL CHALLENGE

Favored Element: Water

When all the enemies have fallen, the gate opens up to Downhill Challenge. Hit the switch to release the Roboto-Ball. This ball is explosive, and if you lose it by accident return to this pedestal for another one.

Use the Roboto-Ball to destroy the Arkeyan Duelists in the next area and reveal a bounce pad. Use the bounce pad to clear the wall and get to the floor switch. The floor switch lowers two barriers. Go back up to where you left the Roboto-Ball and move the push blocks out of the way to continue down the path with the ball. Push the ball onto the lowered barrier, then hit the floor switch to raise it back up. Use the bounce pad to hop up to the ball and push it farther down the path. Smash the gate to enter Gate Crasher Battle!

GATE CRASHER BATTLE

Favored Element: Water

This is a tough fight! Use the hallway back towards where you came to get some space between your Skylanders and these deadly enemies. This battlefield is filled with Giant Trogs, Trogmander, and Arkeyan Snipers. Focus on the sniper first. When he's down, take out the Trogmander to get a two for one (he actually didn't summon two of the Trogs in this area, so they'll still be around).

When you finish off the last Trog, the Arkeyans join the fray. This round includes several Duelists and two Juggernauts. When both the Juggernauts are down, a third joins the fray. Defeat him to unseal the gate.

Before leaving the area, use a Giant to tear up the boulder in the back corner of the arena. This reveals a secret portal to Treasure Cave.

TREASURE CAVE & REFLECTION LOCKING MECHANISM

Favored Element: Water

As you can guess, Treasure Cave contains a **Treasure Chest**. Avoid the simple spear trap to retrieve it and teleport back up to Reflection Locking Mechanism. This is a complicated light puzzle, so follow these steps carefully.

Head up the left ramp and push the crystal back once.

Continue around the side and push the crystal here right once. Use the lever to redirect the light into the crystal you just pushed.

On the right walkway, hit the floor switch to raise the blocks to form a walkway. Cross over and push the block down to complete the path.

Push the stacked block up, and then to the left. When the crystal is on your level, push it once more downward, then retrace your steps to hit the floor switch again. Mission complete!

BACK ON FLYNN'S SHIP

Head to the Crane Deck at the back of the ship for a double bonus. There's both a **Winged Sapphire** and a large stack of gems worth 300 Gold.

BURNING QUESTIONS!

Q: How did the city become lost?

A: As mentioned in the Secret Vault of Secrets chapter, Arkeyans have a strange idiosyncrasy where they have trouble remembering anything that is below them. Above and to the side, no problem, but below...forget about it.

Being deep underground, the City of Arkus posed a particular problem. The Arkeyans tried to rectify this by moving their city high up, but the plans were placed in the basement of the City Hall of Arkus, so they got lost, too!

Q: Were the Arkeyans always bad guys?

A: Not originally.

A very, very, very long time ago, before the Giants even, Skylands was a peaceful place. All species were able to co-exist in harmony. But, the Arkeyans found themselves advancing much faster than the other races.

They were the first to develop the Tech element, and later, were the first to discover a way to merge Magic and Tech together. This discovery made them so ridiculously powerful, some factions wanted to take over Skylands. (It's something to do, right?)

But other Arkeyans, ones less violent and greedy, stood against these rabble-rousers and said that instead their society should focus on music, the arts, and the most popular sport at the time, Roboto-Ball.

The problem was that most of them also played Roboto-Ball and since the roboto-balls themselves had a tendency to explode, well...most peaceful Arkeyans eventually disappeared. The war-like Arkeyans soon outnumbered the peaceful ones and the Arkeyan conquest of Skylands began.

CHAPTER 16
BRINGING ORDER TO KAOS!

STORY GOALS

- ☑ Destroy the Fist of Arkus
- ◯ Find the Arkeyan Throne Room

ELEMENTAL GATES

- 🏔 Earth
- ✦ Magic

DARES	
Time To Beat	8:50
Enemies to Defeat	65

AREAS TO FIND

- ◯ Arc of Faith
- ◯ The Bomb Hole
- ◯ Arkeyan Foyer
- ◯ Secret Alcove
- ◯ The Machinery
- ◯ Arkeyan Vault
- ◯ Observation Platform
- ◯ Arkeyan Well
- ◯ Golem's Retreat
- ◯ Hall of the Ancients
- ◯ Crumbling Vista
- ◯ Hall of Archives
- ◯ Magician's Lighthouse
- ◯ Stone Cutter's Vault
- ◯ The Final Battle

COLLECTIBLES & ENEMIES

Soul Gem	⬡	Crystal Lighthouse (Flashwing)
Legendary Treasure		Dragon Masthead
Hats		Scrumshanks Hat, Rasta Hat
Story Scroll		Classic Pirates
Luck-O-Tron Wheel	◉	Lucky Wheel of Health
Treasure Chests		4 to collect
Winged Sapphire		1 to collect

Chompies

Arkeyan Jouster

Arkeyan Duelist

Arkeyan Bomber

Arkeyan Juggernaut

Arkeyan Sniper

Crystal Golem

Trog Pincher

Trogmander

218

MAP LEGEND

Direct Path	
Optional Path	
Feat of Strengthw	
Auric (Vendor)	
Hat Box	
Legendary Treasure	
Luck-O-Tron Wheel	
Skystones Challenger	
Soul Gem	
Story Scroll	
Treasure Chest	
Winged Sapphire	

GOAL

START

ARC OF FAITH & THE BOMB HOLE

Favored Element: Water

Time to find Kaos! Walk down the path to enter the Arc of Faith. Keep walking and kill the Chompies, then drop down in the hole at the left end of the path to discover The Bomb Hole secret area.

In The Bomb Hole, recover the Winged Sapphire, and head back up top. Return to the entrance of the Arc of Faith area and use the button to materialize a Roboto-Ball. Start it down the path, then use the bounce pad to get ahead of it and stop it right in front of the vault door. Push it into the vault door to open the way to the Arkeyan Foyer

ARKEYAN FOYER & SECRET ALCOVE

Favored Element: Water

In Arkeyan Foyer, there are two Arkeyan Snipers, some Chompies, and an Arkeyan Juggernaut. Defeat the snipers first, then work on the Juggernaut. After clearing the area, head back up to get another Roboto-Ball. Steer this one back to the Foyer and use it on a cracked portion of the far wall.

This leads to the Secret Alcove. Grab the **Treasure Chest** inside. Head up the stairs on the right to enter the conveyor belt area.

THE MACHINERY

Favored Element: Tech

Avoid the intermittent flamethrowers, and use the floor switches on the conveyor belts to open up the gates in this area. The area ends when you reach the first bounce pad. Unlock the last gate and loop around one more time to take the bounce pad back to the Arkeyan Foyer.

Move over the tilting platforms, but before you cross the last set of moving platforms, wait for the Arkeyan Bomber in the next area to toss a bomb. Return it to him to destroy the Bomber and his Jouster buddies.

The moving platforms lead to a large room full of Jousters and Bombers. The Jousters have shields, so the easiest way to take them down is to use the Bomber's plasma bombs.

OBSERVATION PLATFORM & ARKEYAN WELL

Favored Element: Tech

After you've taken down all the enemies in the area, two bounce pads appear. Use the bounce pad on the right to bounce down to the Observation Platform and Flashwing's **Soul Gem**. Step inside the cave door down here to find the Arkeyan Well. Talk to Freebot 001 for another game of Skystones.

SKYSTONE CHALLENGER: FREEBOT 001

Reward For Winning First Game: Arkeyan Crackler

FREEBOT 001'S SKYSTONE DECK	
Life Spell Punk (x3)	
Arkeyan Crackler (x2)	

After defeating Freebot 001, hop up to the second level of the Arkeyan Foyer and smash the breakable objects on the left. This leads to an Earth Gate.

EARTH ELEMENT GATE: GOLEM'S RETREAT

This small area features a Crystal Golem. Instead of taking on the Golem in the standard way, use the button from the upper level of the Arkeyan Foyer to obtain an Arkeyan Roboto-Ball, bring it with you to this area, and roll the Crystal Golem over with it for a quick victory. Use the Roboto-Ball to smash open the brick wall and retrieve the **Scrumshanks Hat**.

HALL OF THE ANCIENTS, ARKEYAN VAULT & CRUMBLING VISTA

Favored Element: Fire

Back in the foyer, roll the Roboto-Ball across the moving platforms and through the vault door. You're not done yet! Go back and spawn in another ball. Roll this one all the way down the hallway to smash a second vault door and retrieve the **Legendary Treasure: Dragon Masthead** in the Arkeyan Vault. Head up the stairs to the Hall of Ancients.

The Hall is defended by a group of Jousters and a Juggernaut. Use the stairs for cover from the Juggernaut's laser. When the Jousters go down, some Duelist reinforcements show.

Keep fighting until there are no more enemies left facing you, then head around the left side of the building here to discover a door to Crumbling Vista. Defeat the Arkeyans inside for a **Treasure Chest**. Exit from this area and hop up to the second level of Hall of the Ancients.

HALL OF ARCHIVES

Favored Element: Fire

Back in the Hall of the Ancients, move to the rotating platform and hit the switch in the middle to prevent getting thrown off into the flamethrowers below. When you make it across, a Juggernaut and two Bombers arrive to attack you. Use the bombs to quickly take care of the Juggernaut, then move through the flamethrowers on to the turnstiles. Finish off the Arkeyan Bombers to unlock a bounce pad on the rotating platform.

Hop up to the second floor and check the back corner for a door that leads to Hall of Archives. Inside the Hall, you meet Freebot 002. Like his brothers, he also wants to play Skystones.

MAGIC ELEMENT GATE:
MAGICIAN'S LIGHTHOUSE

This gate is on the right side of the second level of Hall of the Ancients. Use the teleporter behind the gate to teleport to Magician's Lighthouse. Climb the path on the right and use the switch up top. You first want to rotate the crystal so that the beam reaches the northern crystal past the left side gate, which unlocks the gate behind your Skylander.

Head through this gate to find a **Treasure Chest**. Return to the switch and use it to lower the gate near the hat box. Walk towards the hat box and clear the path of ground turrets. You can use

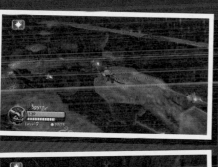
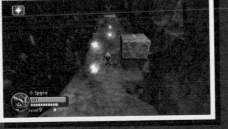

the push blocks for cover, or just charge through the area. When you reach the bounce pad ledges, stick to the bounce pads and avoid the teleporters to make it to the top. Carefully time your movements to cross the retracting spears and reach the **Rasta Hat**.

SKYSTONE CHALLENGER: FREEBOT 002
Reward For Winning First Game: Grenade General

FREEBOT 002'S SKYSTONE DECK	
Grenade General (x2)	
Arkeyan Ultron	
D. Riveter 5	
Axecutioner	

If you can beat Freebot 002's excellent deck, you not only receive the Grenade General, but you also receive the Luck-O-Tron Wheel from the back room.

Back in the Hall of the Ancients, use the bounce pads to make it to the third rotating platform. Hit the rotation switcher to move the barrier blocking the path to the conveyor belt section. Sprint through the conveyor belt traps to land in the Stone Cutter's Vault.

STONE CUTTER'S VAULT

Favored Element: Fire

The vault is defended by a Crystal Golem and two Arkeyan Bombers. Use the Arkeyan plasma bombs to destroy the Golem's crystal shield, then finish off the Bombers. Hop up on the bounce pad and use the tilting platform to reach the **Story Scroll: Classic Pirates** visible in an alcove at the top of the screen.

Getting through the whirling blades requires good timing, but take comfort in the fact that you've almost made it to Kaos! When you reach the top of the next ledge, you encounter Auric. Before talking to him, head down the path on the right to claim a **Treasure Chest**.

AURIC'S INVENTORY	
ITEM	COST
Caesar Hat	1,800 Gold
Unicorn Hat	2,500 Gold
Wizard Hat	2,000 Gold
Conquertron Skystone	6,500 Gold
Regeneration Power Up	650 Gold
Fairy Dust	50 Gold

Note that the Conquertron is the best Skystone in the game. Come back here when you have spare Gold and want to perfect your Skystones deck. Ready for the big fight? Head down the ramp behind Auric.

BOSS FIGHT

KAOS

This fight starts with a chase between your Skylanders and Kaos. Watch out for the red targeted areas; if Kaos manages to catch any Skylanders in one, they are knocked out instantly!

This sequence is easiest to do with a flying or dashing Skylander. Swarm, Spyro, and Drobot are all good choices. When you make it to the end, Kaos slams the red button, causing an avalanche to fall on his head.

STAGE 1

Kaos survives the avalanche and things aren't looking good. Luckily Ermit and Machine Ghost arrive just in time in the Giant Robot to help you with your fight. When Kaos slams the Giant Robot's head into the platform, this exposes his weakness: the Iron Fist of Arkus! Pound the Iron Fist whenever it's exposed.

Kaos also summons Arkeyan guards to help in the fight. Initially these include Jousters and Juggernauts. Focus on taking these guys out quickly, so that you get a better opening on Kaos' hand.

STAGE 2

After beating on Kaos' hand for a while, he brings in a blob-generator. This is similar to the battle with the Chompy Mage, but this time there aren't any blue blobs to heal you. Dodge the spiky blobs and hit the generator whenever you get an opening. The generator has two phases. When you get its health halfway down it switches its patterns.

STAGE 3

After you destroy the generator, Kaos goes back to slamming the Giant Robot's head into the platform. He also summons more Jousters and Juggernauts. Between head slams, he uses his eye beams to blast the area. Just balance hitting the hand with swatting away his reinforcements. When his eye blast starts, stop what you're doing and dodge it.

STAGE 4

For the fourth part of the fight, Kaos has the tables turned. Now his head gets slammed into the plateau. Beat on his head, but watch out for more Arkeyan reinforcements. He can also still use his deadly eye beams from this position.

If you defeat his reinforcements, he summons a second blob generator. Continue to hit both Kaos and the generator when you have openings between dodging the waves of blobs. Once you do enough damage to the fist, Kaos collapses!

PRO TIPS

For fight Stage 2, switch out your Giants. It's much easier for your smaller Skylanders to dodge the blobs. Use Skylanders with great defensive powers like Terrafin, Chop Chop, and Hex to make this fight easier. You can completely avoid most attacks by using defensive powers effectively.

If you have an attack that does massive, concentrated damage, such as Camo's Melon Fountain attack, you can safely ignore Kaos' Arkeyan reinforcements. They are automatically destroyed each time you beat one of Kaos' phases.

BACK ON FLYNN'S SHIP

That's it for this adventure, but there's still a ton more to do! Talk to Cali for Heroic Challenges and Brock for Arena Challenges. If you need help with either, there is plenty of help to be found elsewhere in this guide!

BURNING QUESTIONS

Q: What is the Iron Fist of Arkus, and why is it so important?

A: After the Arkeyans initially took over Skylands, they had a strict policy about what the now-conquered inhabitants were allowed to do and not do. It was often said that they "Ruled with an iron fist."

This got back to the Arkeyan leaders, who were not familiar with this metaphor, and believed that these other races actually expected their leaders to literally have an iron fist.

Not wanting to disappoint or confuse anyone, the Arkeyan robot king had an iron fist constructed. Then, during public appearances, the king kept getting asked what the iron fist actually did. Of course, it didn't do anything, so the king had it forged with a blend of Magic and Tech to bestow superior powers and ultimate authority over his Arkeyan army of robots.

Why didn't he just do that in the first place? Well, it turns out he probably shouldn't have done it at all, because once the other Arkeyans found out that having the Iron Fist of Arkus gave these powers, they tried to steal it from the king when he wasn't looking.

This led to frequent power struggles throughout Arkeyan history.

Q: Why is there a button to trigger that big avalanche? What purpose would that serve?

A: While Arkeyans were not known for having many holidays, one thing they did like to celebrate were birthdays. What better way to throw a surprise birthday party than by dumping a bunch of rocks and pieces of ceiling on them while yelling, "Surprise!"

According to the Arkeyans, there was no better way to celebrate one's birthday, hence the button.

CHAPTER 17

EMPIRE OF ICE

STORY GOALS

☑ Destroy the Wall

◯ Find Catapult Parts

ELEMENTAL GATES

 Undead

DARES	
Time To Beat	10:10
Enemies to Defeat	50

AREAS TO FIND

◯ The Frozen Wastes

◯ The Maze of Obelisks

◯ Ice Crater Lake

◯ Altar of Eyes

◯ The Sunken Garden

◯ The Pits

◯ The Winter Wall

COLLECTIBLES & ENEMIES

Hats		Cossack Hat, Santa Hat
Story Scroll		Empire of Ice
Treasure Chests		4 to collect

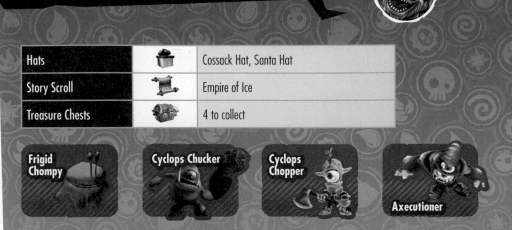

Frigid Chompy

Cyclops Chucker

Cyclops Chopper

Axecutioner

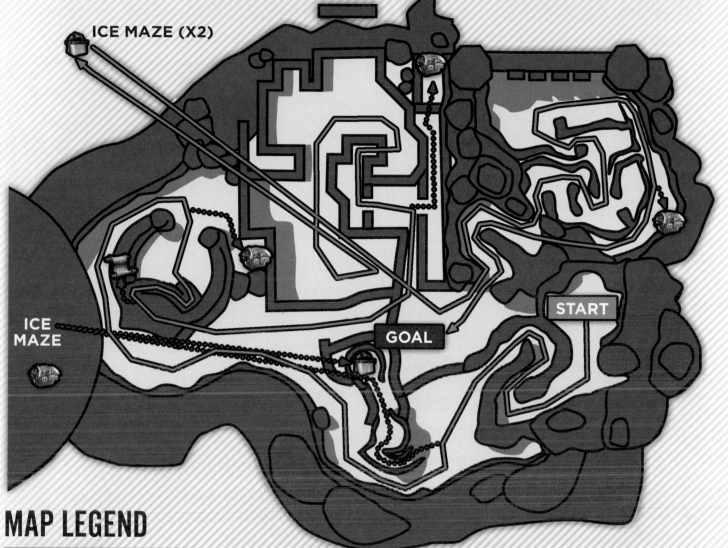

ICE MAZE (X2)

ICE MAZE

START

GOAL

MAP LEGEND

Direct Path	
Optional Path	
Hat Box	
Story Scroll	
Treasure Chest	

THE FROZEN WASTES

Favored Element: Undead

After talking to Haldor and breaking the nearby jars, head down the icy path to take on a few Chompies. Smash the snowman and knock the snowballs down toward the Chompies for a fun way to take them out. Continue along the path, following its curves, and be careful not to hit the frozen cacti, which cause a small amount of damage to Skylanders who touch them.

When the path opens up, there's a fight against a larger group of Chompies and a Cyclops Chucker who throws snowballs. The Chompies can freeze you in place for a few seconds so be careful when they get too close.

MAZE OF OBELISKS

Favored Element: Undead

Head to the left and use the teleporter there, which leads to the Maze of Obelisks. There are several jars to break inside, as well as a **Treasure Chest** to the left.

Head to the back right corner of the maze to reach a switch. Trigger it to open the gate blocking the teleporter. Once you've explored the entire maze, use the teleporter to return to The Frozen Wastes. Defeat the group of Chompies to open the locked gate. Follow the frosty path to reach the Altar of Eyes.

ALTAR OF EYES

Favored Element: Water

A group of five Chompies, backed by an Axecutioner, welcome you to the Altar of Eyes. Take down the Chompies and quickly mash the correct button if your Skylander becomes frozen. Watch out for the axe! Dodge to the side when it gets close. The Axecutioner can also teleport a short distance to get a good shot, so keep a close eye on him. As soon as he throws the axe, use the opening to attack!

UNDEAD ELEMENT GATE:
ICE CRATER LAKE

The only element gate in Empire of Ice leads to Ice Crater Lake. The portal leads to a challenge where you have two minutes to collect 20 skulls inside Ice Crater Lake. Collect all 20 in time and your reward is the **Santa Hat**. The ground is slippery and the shape of Ice Crater Lake makes it tough to get where you want to go. Head towards each skull and let momentum carry you into each before gravity drags you toward the center. Bumping into a snowball changes your trajectory.

After taking down this group, the gate opens. Continue to the left to reach Haldor, who has found a key. The problem is that he doesn't have it, he just found it. Follow the path around, taking on the snowball-throwing Chuckers along the way. Once you clear them out, continue past a group of Chompies and another Chucker to claim the **Treasure Chest**.

Go after the Chompies and Chucker you just passed. Defeating them opens up the path to the key. Grab the **Story Scroll: Empire of Ice**, collect the key, and head back towards the locked gate. Unlock the gate and collect the first **Catapult Part**.

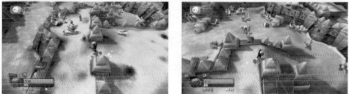

Head to the left of Haldor and down the ramp. At the end of the path, head left and take on the small group of Chompies. Collect the nearby loot and head down the path to face a Cyclops Chopper. Cyclops Choppers aren't tough but they have a dangerous whirlwind attack. Stay out of their way until they finish spinning, then move in to attack.

THE SUNKEN GARDEN

Favored Element: Water

Once you defeat both Chuckers at the bottom of the ramp, step on the pressure switch hidden under breakable objects to open the nearby gated area. Continue down the path to face more Chompies and a Chucker. Clear them out before continuing on to face additional Chompies and an Axecutioner. Once you eliminate these enemies, the gate drops to let you pick up the second **Catapult Part**. Once you have it, use the teleporter to reach The Pits.

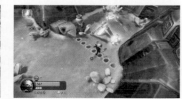

THE PITS

Favored Element: Water

This area looks pretty simple but the slippery ice makes it more troublesome than you suspect. The icy ground makes it difficult to stay out of the deep pits dotting the area. If you fall into a pit, you are teleported back to the beginning of The Pits. Your goal is the switch plate in the front left corner. After you reach it and activate it, return to the back of The Pits to reach the teleporter.

The third **Catapult Part** is in the left side of the area. Directly beyond the part is the pressure switch. Step on it, but then make your way to the far right corner to reach the **Cossack Hat**. Once you've collected the hat, return to the teleporter in back.

THE FROZEN WASTES

Favored Element: Undead

There are two blocked paths nearby, but Haldor has a plan. Pick up the bomb in the right corner and quickly carry it to the blocked gate on the front left of the screen. You only have a short amount of time to reach the gate. Once you are near, throw the bomb to clear the way. Follow the short path down to the left to reach the bounce pad. It boosts you over the short wall where you should claim the **Treasure Chest**.

Retrace your steps, grab another bomb from the same spot and quickly take it to the other blocked gate behind Haldor. Once you breach the gate you are ready to face The Winter Wall.

THE WINTER WALL

Favored Element: Tech

As Haldor warned, The Winter Wall is a dangerous place because the Cyclops inside use live ammunition instead of snowballs! Be on the lookout for the targeting reticule that appears on the ground. It will be yellow when it is near and red if it is close enough to hurt you. Keep moving to avoid the projectiles.

In several spots throughout this area the path is blocked by sturdy metal barricades. These barricades are too sturdy to break through on your own. Use the pesky Cyclops artillery to your advantage. As the targeting reticules follow you, lead them close to the metal barricades blocking the path so that the artillery fire blows them up, clearing the path.

Follow the path and watch out for Chompies and an Axecutioner. Once you clear out the foes, the gate opens and you encounter another metal barricade and a group of breakable jars leading to another **Treasure Chest**. If you fall off at any point, retrace your steps back up the path to reach the final **Catapult Part**. Drop off the ledge and head back to Haldor.

Once Haldor repairs the catapult you are ready to begin the assault on the wall. Your job is to use the catapult to take down the wall and let in the warm sunlight. Launch your fireballs at the wall, moving from right to left to avoid the incoming fire from the Cyclops enemies manning the wall. If you hit the cannons on top of the wall, a 3x Multiplier comes at you. Quickly move to pick it up. This lets you fire three fireballs out of each catapult

on your next shot! As you destroy more of the wall, the desperate defenders begin flinging barrels at you as well.

Sometimes when you destroy a section of the wall, a piece of food comes flying out at you. Move the catapult to catch it to increase your health. Once you've destroyed the wall, the sunlight can once again reach the area and begin thawing the ice. Congratulations! You've brought back the spring!

BURNING QUESTIONS!

Q: Why did the Ice Ogres want to keep everything so cold?

A: As you know, they're called "Ice Ogres," and when they are found anywhere that is not completely frozen over, they face constant questions like, "Hey, if you guys are Ice Ogres, what are you doing out here in the sunshine?" or "Shouldn't Ice Ogres actually live somewhere icy?" And as you can imagine, this got very annoying over time. So they decided to build a wall that would keep warm weather out entirely, and they no longer had to endure this nuisance.

Q: So when the Ice Ogres moved in and kept warm weather out, why didn't Haldor just move?

A: As you probably also know, Haldor is a real curmudgeon. He was born in that valley and he's going to stay there, no matter what. And I think he actually grew to love the cold. Supposedly when the Skylanders took down the wall and spring finally came to the Empire of Ice, he started complaining that it was too hot.

CHAPTER 18
PIRATE SEAS

STORY GOALS

- ✓ Defeat the Pirates
- ◯ Destroy the Island Defenses
- ◯ Defeat Dreadbeard

ELEMENTAL GATES

🌿 Life

DARES	
Time To Beat	5:35
Enemies to Defeat	63

AREAS TO FIND

- ◯ The Docks
- ◯ Shipwright's Square
- ◯ Pirate Training Grounds
- ◯ Fountain Square
- ◯ Mayor's Office
- ◯ Coconut Islands
- ◯ Plunder Island

COLLECTIBLES & ENEMIES

Hats	🎁	Pirate Hat, Pirate Doo Rag
Story Scroll	📜	Pirate Seas
Treasure Chests	🧰	4 to collect

Chompy

Chompy Pod

Life Spell Punk

Seadog Skipper

Seadog Pirate

Captain K9

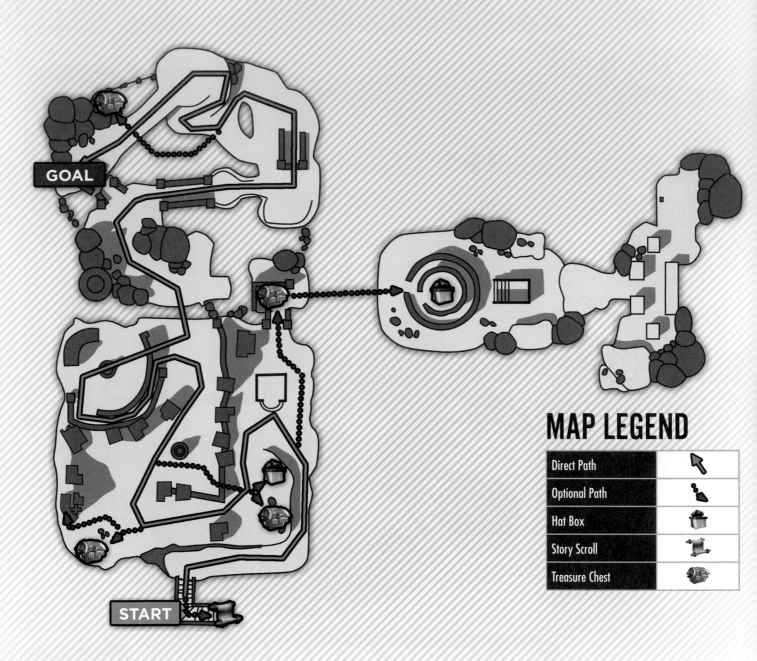

GOAL

START

MAP LEGEND

Direct Path	
Optional Path	
Hat Box	
Story Scroll	
Treasure Chest	

THE DOCKS

Favored Element: Life

After speaking to Jess LeGrand, turn around and head down the dock to the right and collect the **Story Scroll: Pirate Seas**. Go past Jess to enter The Docks. Several small groups of Chompies guard a Chompy Pod, which is spawning hordes of the little monsters. Once the way is clear, continue up the path to face more Red Chompies in Shipwright's Square.

SHIPWRIGHT'S SQUARE

Favored Element: Life

Several Seadog Skippers fire cannons at you as soon as you enter Shipwright's Square. Once you clear them out, look for Fangs, the Seadog Skipper behind the desk, in front of a cage. It's time to play your first hand of Pirate Cards!

Pirate Cards is a matching game. You must match pairs of Pirate Cards before time runs out. Fangs deals out six cards onto the table. There are three types of cards in his Anchor Deck: Swords, Maps, and Schooners. You must first select a card to flip, then another. If the cards match, they are removed from play. If they don't match, they are flipped back over. Remember which cards are where, so you can quickly match the pairs and win the game.

Once you beat Fangs, you free the Shipmaster. He asks for your help rescuing Mayor LeGrand who's being held in the estate at the top of the hill.

LIFE ELEMENT GATE:
PIRATE TRAINING GROUNDS

The Training Grounds are locked, so go around the locked area and look for glowing switches up some steps. Step on both switches to activate the nearby blocks. Jump off of the platform with the switches and push the block to the left and down until it forms a bridge between the platform and the raised grassy ridge to the left. Cross over the blocks and activate the switch there to raise another block near the platform.

Jump down and move the block to the other side, creating the same type of bridge to the grassy ridge on the right. Once there, step on the switch to raise another block. Once again push the moveable block up and to the left so that it forms a bridge between the platform with the two switches and the ridge ahead.

Cross over and use the bounce pad on the left to reach the bounce pad on the right. Watch out for the spike traps, which pop up between the bounce pads. As soon as the spikes drop, step on the bounce pad in the center to reach the raised area on the right. Follow the path to reach a **Treasure Chest**.

Grab the bomb and use the bounce pads to make your way over to the left side of the area. Your time is short, so be careful with your movements. Once you get close enough to the wall, toss the bomb to bring it down, clearing the way to the key. Collect the key and use the teleporter to return to the locked gate. Follow the circular ramp to reach the gift box containing the **Pirate Hat**!

Retrace your steps past where you freed the Shipmaster and follow the path to encounter a Seadog Pirate. These foes like to stab at you with their swords, doing quite a bit of damage. It is best to hit them with a ranged attack before they can get in close to jab you with their swords! Once you take him down, the gate falls and you can continue along the path to find some Cheese and a few barrels to smash. Follow the road to the left to encounter more Chompies and a Captain K9. The Captain K9's attack does a great deal of damage. Be quick to dodge it! Continue along the path to the left, facing off against Seadog Skippers and Seadog Pirates to reach the next area.

FOUNTAIN SQUARE

Favored Element: Earth

Once you clear out the enemies, head towards the tank. Jump inside and take down the Pirate Frigate. Aim the targeting reticule and fire at the ship until it goes down! Sinking the ship unearths a **Treasure Chest**.

Head down from the fountain and break all the items in the corner to reveal a bounce pad. Use it to reach the raised area you passed before. A **Treasure Chest** and the **Pirate Doo Rag** are here. Once you've collected the loot, head back up and around the path, past the fountain in Fountain Square where Chompies, Seadog Skippers, and Seadog Pirates are waiting for you. Dodge the Skippers' cannonballs while battling the other enemies. Once you've cleared them out, head up the ramp to the left, clearing out the enemies you encounter along the way.

MAYOR'S OFFICE

Favored Element: Earth

There are more Chompies, Captain K9s, and a Life Spell Punk at the top of the ramp. Take out the Spell Punk and the Chompy Pod first. This stems the tide of the Chompies and keeps the Spell Punk from healing your other foes. Once you've cleared the enemies, approach Bandit and get ready for another round of Pirate Cards!

To win the mayor's freedom, you must deal with nine cards in the Cannon Deck. You have one minute to match all the cards. When you match the Blackbeard pair you gain 8 extra seconds! Defeat Bandit to free Mayor LeGrand.

Retrace your steps back down the ramp into Fountain Square, where another pirate duels you in Pirate Cards. Chance's challenge uses the Pirate Curse Deck and has a two minute time limit. This deck contains Two Beard which gives you 10 additional seconds when you match them. The rules are the same with an addition: this time the deck also contains Curse Cards. If you match a pair of Curse Cards, the remaining cards on the table are mixed up! Luckily, you don't need to match them in order to win; match all other pairs and you will win the challenge even

if the Curse Cards remain. Defeat Chance to open up the bridge leading to the next area.

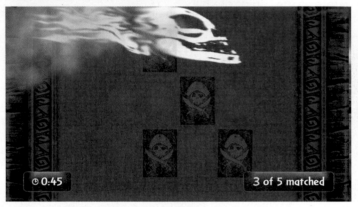

COCONUT ISLANDS

Favored Element: Water

There are two Chompy Pods down the left path. Take them out to stop the Chompies from constantly spawning, and then clear out the Chompies. You must also contend with a few Seadog Skippers and their cannons. Once you have defeated them all, prepare for another Pirate Card challenge.

Woof challenges you to a game of Pirate Cards with his Mermaid Deck. There are 15 cards this time, including Curse Cards! You have 1 minute and 30 seconds to play. In addition to the cards you've seen before, you now have No Beard and Peeky Boo cards to deal with as well. When you match No Beard, you gain 12 additional seconds. Matching Peeky Boo cards gives you an even better bonus—you can briefly see each remaining card.

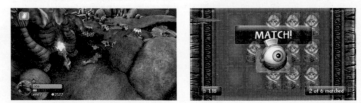

Wild Cards are great for matching with other cards, but they can be dangerous as well. Match a Wild Card with a Curse Card and you may have well matched two Curse Cards! All the cards get shuffled into new positions.

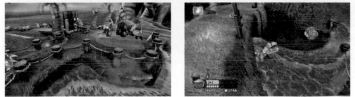

Once you win the game, claim your loot and follow the opened path. Take out the Chompies and the Chompy Pod blocking the path. Continue down to encounter a Captain K9.

Doggerts now challenges you to a game of Pirate Cards with his Lookout Deck. You have 1 minute and 45 seconds to play. This time there are 18 cards and the additional She Beard pair, which gives you an extra 14 seconds when you make a match.

Once you have bested Doggerts, cross the bridge to face two Chompy Pods, Seadog Skippers, and Seadog Pirates. Clear them all out and follow the path until you encounter a Captain K9. Follow the ramp up to reach a Chompy Pod and a Life Spell Punk. Take down the Punk to keep him from healing the Chompy Pod, then take out the Pod.

Switch to a Water Skylander and walk over the water, on the left side of the island. Walk under the small bridge to reach the **Treasure Chest**. Swim back to the foot of the grassy bridge and continue across to reach the next Pirate Card challenge.

Dreadbeard challenges you to a game of Pirate Cards with his Skull Deck. This time you play with 21 Cards and have 2 minutes to play. Defeat Dreadbeard to deal the pirates a substantial blow! Unfortunately, Dreadbeard is a sore loser and he makes off with Jess LeGrand! The pirate hideout is on Plunder Island and the Shipmaster is ready to take you there to teach those pirates a lesson once and for all.

PLUNDER ISLAND

When you arrive at the island you control the ship and must destroy the island's defenses. Move the ship left and right to avoid incoming cannon fire. Their targeting reticule shows up as yellow before they fire and red afterward, so pay attention and quickly move out of danger.

Fire on the pirate fort, and destroy the towers. As you destroy the towers, more cannons come into play for the pirates. As this continues, you must watch for incoming cannon fire as it becomes more difficult to avoid getting hit. Pay close attention, and circle around the island as you fire at the fort. Focus on one tower at a time until you have destroyed all seven towers.

Once the towers fall, you land at the fort. You face Dreadbeard once again at Pirate Cards and the most dangerous deck of all: the Poop Deck!

There are 24 cards in the deck and you have 2 minutes and 5 seconds in which to win. The Sands of Time cards give you an extra 30 seconds when you match them. The Poop Deck also contains a pair of Remove Curse cards which removes the pair of Curse Cards from play. Once you defeat the pirate, you free Jess LeGrand! Return to Cap'n Flynn's Ship knowing you saved the town from the Dreadbeard and his crew.

BURNING QUESTIONS!

Q: How come the pirates here play this card game and not Skystones?

A: Because it's more of a traditional game and these particular pirates fancy themselves as "old-schoolers." They look down on the more modern breed of pirates who play Skystones and buy carnivals and have forgotten the classic ways of pirate life—pillaging, hornswoggling, scallywaggery, and of course, Pirate Cards. I should also point out that while some of these pirates appear to be the same people you meet in Cutthroat Carnival, they are actually not. They just look and sound the same and some have the same name. But that's common in pirate circles, both new and old.

CHAPTER 19
DARKLIGHT CRYPT

STORY GOALS

- ✓ Find the Undead Customer
- ○ Find and Defeat Occulous
- ○ Talk to Gallant

ELEMENTAL GATES

 Fire

DARES	
Time To Beat	12:30
Enemies to Defeat	75

AREAS TO FIND

- ○ Haunted Courtyard
- ○ Forest Walk
- ○ The Dark Labyrinth
- ○ The Parapets
- ○ Haunted Village
- ○ Hedge Maze
- ○ Beyond the Maze
- ○ Hidden Nook

COLLECTIBLES & ENEMIES

Hats		Chef Hat, Pumpkin Hat
Story Scroll		Darklight Crypt
Treasure Chests		4 to collect

 Clipperz

Haunted Knight

 Stump Demon

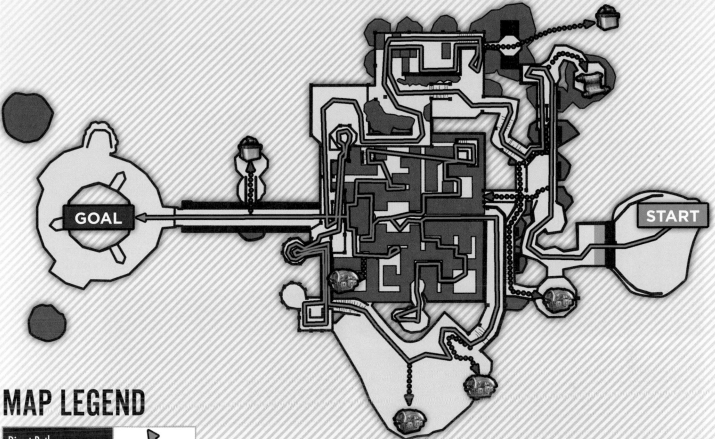

MAP LEGEND

Direct Path	
Optional Path	
Hat Box	
Story Scroll	
Treasure Chest	

HAUNTED COURTYARD

Favored Element: Life

Darklight Crypt is unique in that it's two areas in one! Use the Spectral Shifting Platform to switch between the Real World and the Ghost World. Though the areas are always similar in appearance, there are distinct differences. Certain things and certain enemies appear only in one world or the other. Luckily, you can use this to your advantage. If you don't see a way forward in one world, use the Spectral Shifting Platform to switch to the other. You can also avoid some enemies (or defeat them more easily) by switching worlds.

For example, Haunted Knights are only a threat in the Ghost World. You can smash them in the Real World, gaining some treasure, but no XP. If you want the XP from defeating them, you need to face them in the Ghost World.

Clear out the breakable items around Batterson before stepping onto the Spectral Shifting Platform and entering the Ghost World. Along the path you will have your initial encounter with Clipperz. These small creatures attack you with their sharp claws. Don't let them surround you!

You soon encounter Occulous, a giant eyeball who watches your every move. Follow the path around and drop down to face a Haunted Knight. These walking suits of armor carry a large sword and attempt to pin you to the ground with it. Once you defeat it, push the moveable block up until it forms a bridge.

Use the Spectral Shifter to switch back to the Real World. Head right, watching out for the blocks which move up and down. Follow the path around to the right and down to reach the **Story Scroll: Darklight Crypt**.

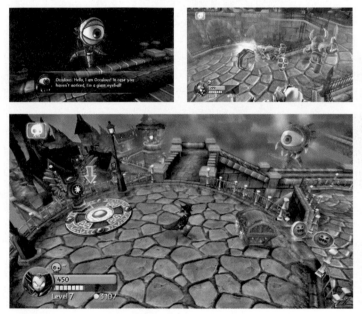

Retrace your steps until you reach the Spectral Shifting Platform. Switch back to the Ghost World, but be ready for a pair of Haunted Knights to attack if you didn't destroy them in the Real World. Climb the nearby stairs and cross the blocks. Pass up the first set of stairs on the right and cross the block you had previously pushed over to reach another Spectral Shifting Platform. Use it to shift back to the Real World to open a **Treasure Chest**.

Shift back to Ghost World and head down the steps to find the Lockmaster Imp. Deal with the Haunted Knight on the way and then engage the Imp to unlock the lock. Inside the lock you see the Imp, as well as his

fiery counterpart. As you turn the lock, don't allow the Imp to touch its fiery counterpart. If this happens, you must start the puzzle from the beginning!

Perfect Lock Puzzle Solution: 8 moves
Left, Left, Left, Right, Right, Left, Left, Right

When the lock opens, be ready to face another Haunted Knight. Follow the path to take on several Clipperz and another Haunted Knight.

FOREST WALK

Favored Element: Fire

Head down the stairs to find another Spectral Shifting Platform. Use it to reach the Real World. Push the nearest block to the edge and then push the other block twice so you can get around it. Walk to the outer edge and push the next block to the left as far as it will go. Push the nearby block up until it can't move anymore and you can access the bounce pad. Use the bounce pad to

reach the top of the blocks. Drop down to grab the loot and climb the stairs. Push the block off, leading down into the Dark Labyrinth.

FIRE ELEMENT GATE:
THE DARK LABYRINTH

Because of the darkness, you aren't able to see anything beyond your immediate vicinity. Follow the path forward until you reach a pressure switch. Immediately after the switch, you encounter Demon Stumps. Head left and down, until you reach a moveable block. Push the block, clearing a way to reach more Chompies and a Chompy Pod.

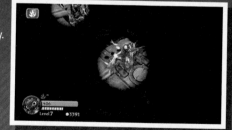

Push the nearby block to complete a bridge to another pressure switch. Retrace your steps and head through the wall near the gated Demon Stumps. Take down the Chompies and Chompy Pods and claim the **Treasure Chest**. Follow the path down until you reach another moveable block. Push it up to create the bridge to another switch. Retrace your steps and head through the wall to the right of the gated Demon Stumps. Be ready for a tough fight as you clear them out of the area. Be on the lookout for their tunneling attack! After you've taken them all out, open the gift box to find the **Chef Hat**! Head all the way back down the hall and use the teleporter to exit the Labyrinth.

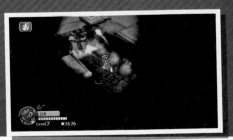

Collect the nearby key and head down the stairs. Push the blocks to close up the bridge and use the bounce pad to walk across it to reach the locked door. Take on the Demon Stumps inside or switch back to the Ghost World to make them inanimate.

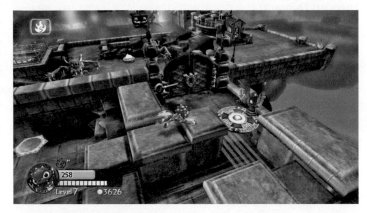

THE PARAPETS

Favored Element: Magic

Enter the door and go up the stairs to the left. Use the bounce pad to reach the coins. Go back down the stairs and head to the right. Avoid the blocks raising and lowering along the path so you don't get crushed.

Face down the Chompy Pods and the Demon Stumps. Take out the Chompy Pods first. The Demon Stumps eat the Chompies it spawns to regain health.

Continue around the house and past another series of moving blocks. When the third block raises up while the second one is down, quickly run through the whole line. Once through, climb the stairs and ride the blocks up to

reach the coins on the chains. After collecting the coins use the Spectral Shifting Platform to switch back to the Ghost World.

Take out the Clipperz and head back across the blocks, which are now resting on the ground. Go through the now open gate and switch back to the Real World. Go through another series of raising and lowering blocks and head down to the Lockmaster Imp. You must be in the Ghost World to activate the lock. Climb the steps and use the cannon to shoot the moving platforms. Switch back to the Ghost World and return to the Lockmaster Imp.

 Perfect Lock Puzzle Solution: 6 moves
Left, Left, Right, Left, Right, Left

HAUNTED VILLAGE

Favored Element: Magic

After you go through the gate you encounter Gallant, one of Batterson's loyal customers. He wants you to help them kick Occulous out of the town for good! In the Real World there are several Demon Stumps wanting a piece of you! After taking care of these foes, there are three doors you can enter: the Coffin House, the Haunted Inn, and the Ghostly Abode.

Here you meet Lugubrious who also wants you to help with Occulous. Take down the Clipperz and collect the loot inside. When you've collected all the loot, exit and head into the Haunted Inn.

Go directly to the second building to find the Inn. Inside the Inn you find several barrels to break, along with some armor. Smash them now to avoid any trouble in Ghost World. Speak with the ghost Nasty and shift to the Ghost World.

If you didn't smash them in the Real World, you have several Haunted Knights to contend with. Take them all down before exiting the Inn.

Exit the Inn and head up, past Gallant, to reach the Lockmaster Imp.

 Perfect Lock Puzzle Solution: 12 moves
Left, Left, Right, Left, Left, Left, Left, Left, Left, Right, Left, Left

For the last two moves to the left, you must rotate the puzzle while the imp is inside the red portal.

Inside the locked area you find a stash of loot!

Head back up the path and past the Inn to reach the Ghostly Abode. There are many Haunted Knights inside. You may want to take advantage of the Real World and smash some of those Knights while they are helpless. If this is the case, head back to the Inn and switch back to the Real World, take care of the Knights, and then switch back to Ghost World. Inside the Ghostly Abode you also find a Lockmaster Imp which can only be accessed in Ghost World.

Perfect Lock Puzzle Solution: 20 moves
Left, Left, Left, Left, Left, Left, Left, Right, Right, Right, Left, Right, Right, Right, Right, Right, Right, Left, Left, Right

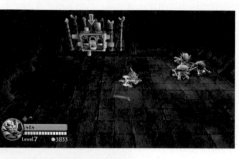

Once you defeat the lock, return to the Inn to switch to the Real World. Head back to the Ghostly Abode and claim your **Treasure Chest**! Exit the Ghostly Abode toward the Hedge Maze.

HEDGE MAZE

Favored Element: Life

Push the blocks out of your way to reach the locked gate. Slide the block to the left to open up a path in the maze. The maze is infested with Chompies and Chompy Pods. Continue up to reach the stone bridge leading to a teleporter, which sends you to the key. Teleport back down once you have it and head back to the locked gate.

On the other side are a Spectral Shifting Platform and a gate with three locks. Shift into the Ghost World and take out the three Haunted Knights standing guard nearby. Don't let the Haunted Knights corner you in the maze. Shifting into the Ghost World opens up a nearby gate. Backtrack a few steps and go to the right. Head through the gate to find another Spectral Shifting platform. If you've had enough of Haunted Knights, shift to the Real World and destroy them in their inanimate form.

When you are finished, switch to the Real World. Follow the path around and take down the Demon Stump. Head up the stairs to reach the teleporter. It takes you to another area of the maze plagued by two more Demon Stumps. Follow the path to grab the key. Push the block forward to reach the door with three locks, use the key, and then collect the one next to the door and use it as well. Head to the left of the door to find a Demon Stump guarding a **Treasure Chest**.

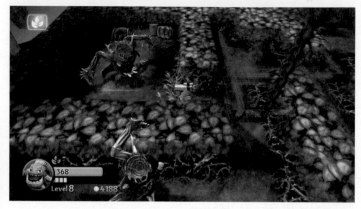

Return to the Spectral Shifting Platform and enter Ghost World. Push the block up and walk around through the now open gate. Shove the block over twice to the hedge wall and push it down into the hole. Retrace your steps and shift back to the Real World and head back across the block you just pushed into the hole. Take down the Demon Stump and collect the third key. Unlock the door and move on to the next area.

BEYOND THE MAZE

Favored Element: Undead

Head down the path until the end. When you reach the second to last set of blocks, you are trapped. When the second set of blocks threatens to trap you, step back one block and wait for the two in front of you to open. Quickly move through, then jump down to face Occulous.

BOSS FIGHT
OCCULOUS

Shift to Ghost World and use the Activator to pull Occulous into the Real World with you. Once you pull Occulous into the Real World, use the cannon to attack him, which is easier said than done. He summons several Demon Stumps to keep you busy. While they are dangerous, don't waste time defeating them as they spawn continually. Avoid their attacks and concentrate on taking down Occulous.

Now that he is vulnerable in the Real World, use the cannons to poke Occulous in his big, old eye! Once you hit him with a cannon, Occulous continually fires his eyebeam until you switch back to Ghost World. Once you have fired a cannon, you cannot shoot another until you have switched back to Ghost World and used the Activator again. Quickly move back to the Shifter to return to Ghost World. Keep on the move and use the bounce pads if you get stuck between Demon Stumps and the eye beam.

After a certain amount of time, Occulous returns to the Ghost World. When this happens, shift into Ghost World and use the Activator again to pull him back into the Real World. Remember to stand behind it to avoid Occulous' gaze. Once Occulous is in the Real World again, use another cannon to shoot him again. Repeat this three times and you defeat the Occulous!

PRO TIP

Keep the Activator between Occulous and you to block his gaze, keeping you safe from his eye beam attack!

After you defeat Occulous, use the bounce pad to head back down the hall which is now open. Take the path to the right to find the Hidden Nook.

HIDDEN NOOK

This very small area is home to some breakable items and a gift box containing the **Pumpkin Hat**! Now that you've collected your hat, return to Occulous' area and speak with Gallant. He transports you back to the Bakery where Batterson is making more pies for the ghosts again.

BURNING QUESTIONS!

Q: Why do the undead like pies so much?

A: Uh, because pies are great. And imagine if you were a ghost or other member of the undead. All you've ever eaten were souls and they apparently taste like a low-grade form of mush. So to go from that to the flavor explosion that are pies? Forget about it! Plus, Batterson's pies are particularly good.

Q: Are Occulous and Eye-Brawl related in any way?

A: I checked and they don't appear to be. Although it's hard to say with Eye-Brawl because he was once two people, the eyeball and the body. And they fought each other for years before finally having the good sense to join forces. When they did, some of their memories got a little mixed up. So it's possible the eye portion of Eye-Brawl is some very distant cousin of Occulous', but it also could just be a coincidence that they are both large, sentient, undead eyeballs. Stranger things have happened, right?

CHAPTER 20

DRAGON'S PEAK

STORY GOALS

- ✓ Find the Dragon's Throne
- ◯ Defeat Vathek's Henchmen

ELEMENTAL GATES

 Air

DARES	
Time To Beat	10:35
Enemies to Defeat	79

AREAS TO FIND

- ◯ Skylands
- ◯ Crystal Falls
- ◯ Obstacle Course
- ◯ The Library
- ◯ Dragon Cliffs
- ◯ Sunburn's Rest
- ◯ Path of Challenges
- ◯ Dragon's Throne

COLLECTIBLES & ENEMIES

Hats	🎁	Winged Hat, Royal Crown
Story Scroll	📜	Dragon's Peak
Treasure Chests	🧰	4 to collect

Chompy

Chompy Pod

Boom Fiend

Arkeyan Hammah

Dragonet

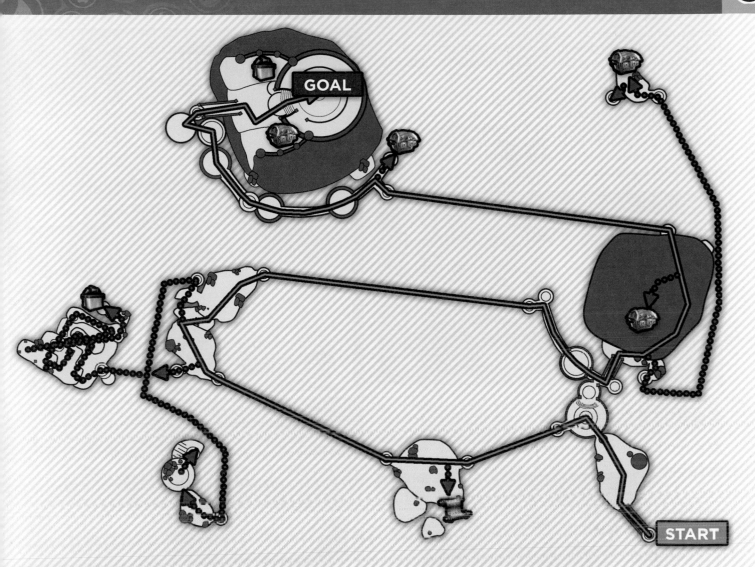

GOAL

START

MAP LEGEND

Direct Path	↖	Story Scroll	🗞	
Optional Path	⬥	Treasure Chest	🧰	
Hat Box	🎁			

SKYLANDS

Flavius gives you a ride to Dragon's Peak. He needs your help to save his ruler, King Ramses, from the curse of his brother Vathek. Head down the stairs toward the Chompy Pods and Chompies. Take on the Chompy Pods to stem the tide of rushing Chompies. There is plenty of stuff to break and a Watermelon if you need to replenish your health.

Use the bounce pad to reach the next platform filled with more Chompies and an Arkeyan Hammah! This enemy tries to smash you with his huge mace. Dodge his swings and hit him while he is recovering from his attack. His weapon is huge and it takes him a second to pick it back up and ready another swing.

Once you have cleared the enemies, awaken Ramses! He asks your help in defeating Vathek. After you have collected any remaining loot, use the Dragon Horn to call Flavius for a ride.

He takes you to the floating island in the distance. On the way, help him steer past obstacles and pick up the Winged Gems. Look out for the Air Mines! If you hit too many obstacles or mines you must restart from the beginning. Use Flavius' fireball to safely detonate the mines before you get close.

CRYSTAL FALLS

Favored Element: Air

Once Flavius drops you off, go down the stairs to face a group of Chompies and a Chompy Pod, along with a couple of Boom Fiends. Boom Fiends run toward you with a lit bomb! Avoid their charge, letting them blow themselves up.

To the left, across the small pond, you find the **Story Scroll: Dragon's Peak**. Collect it to learn more about the history of Ramses' kingdom. On your way to the next Dragon Horn, grab the Cheese if you need to replenish your health. When you are ready, blow the horn to call Flavius for another ride.

As before, you must dodge the floating islands, blow up the Air Mines, and collect the Winged Gems. Flavius soon drops you off on another floating island. To the left there is an Air Element Gate.

Take the teleporter to reach the Obstacle Course. Head to the left and use the bounce pad to reach the raised area. Go right up the ramp, being careful to avoid the spike traps. Drop down and use the bounce pad to reach the raised bridge, then use the bounce pad on the left to reach the platform on the far left with the spike trap. Follow the path and step on the switch to move the block on the right.

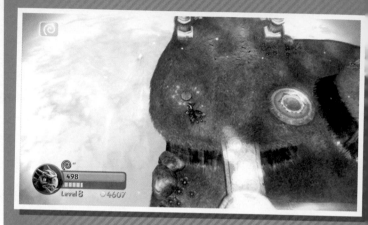

Now use all three bounce pads to your right to reach the bomb. Pick up the bomb and carry it over to the bounce pad and quickly use the other bounce pad to your left, followed by the third one on your left as well. You must be quick to blast down the gate! Watch out for the flame spewing dragons. When the way is clear, grab the key.

Once you have the key, use the bounce pads to make your way back to the right onto the upper bridge. From there continue right, dodging the flame throwing dragons. Before they shoot out a jet of flame, you see fire ignite around their mouths, so you know when to move. Follow the path down and to the right, past the double flame dragons to reach the locked door. Open the gift box inside to collect the **Winged Hat**! Once you collect the hat, head left and drop off the edge to use the teleporter to return to Crystal Falls.

CRYSTAL FALLS

Favored Element: Air

Take down the Boom Fiend and cross the river to encounter the Dragonets. They shoot fireballs, so they can be somewhat troublesome! Make sure you dodge these fiery projectiles! After you've cleared them out, use the bounce pad to reach the area above. Once there, use the bounce pad on your left to reach the next Dragon Horn. Ignore the area to your right for now. You return to it soon. Blow the horn to summon Flavius for another ride. Pick up all the Winged Gems on the way. This time you don't need to worry about any obstacles.

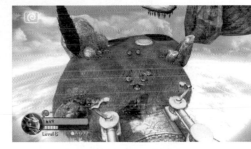

THE LIBRARY

Favored Element: Air

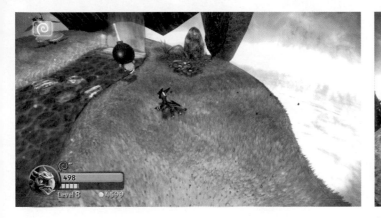

Defeat the Chompies and get ready for a challenge. You must use the bounce pad to hit the rotating bounce pad above you. Time it just right to avoid the spikes and hit the bounce pad. This takes you to another Dragon Horn. Ride with Flavius again to collect a load of Winged Gems. He drops you back at Crystal Falls.

CRYSTAL FALLS

Favored Element: Air

After Flavius drops you off, jump down and use the bounce pad on the right. Take on more Dragonets and an Arkeyan Hammah. Once you've defeated the enemies and collected any loot, use the Dragon Horn to once again call Flavius. Riding on a dragon is riding in style!

Like you did before, avoid obstacles and collect Winged Gems. You don't need to worry about any Air Mines on this flight.

DRAGON CLIFFS

Favored Element: Earth

Make your way carefully through the flaming dragons and down the path. As long as you time your movements carefully you can make it safely through the flames. The path widens into a circle of flaming dragons. Watch the pattern of their firing carefully before moving in. Avoid the flames to reach the breakable items around the circle. Once you've collected your loot, continue down the path and across the short bridge. Here you face a few Chompies. After defeating those toothsome creatures, use the bounce pad and avoid the spikes. Aim right to reach another Dragon Horn. Call Flavius who takes you on another perilous ride.

SUNBURN'S REST

Favored Element: Fire

After you land, deal with the Dragonets. There isn't very much room to dodge their fireballs, so take them down as quickly as you can. Once you've cleared out the enemies, claim the **Treasure Chest**. This opens the gate to the next Dragon Horn. Flavius returns you to Dragon Cliffs.

DRAGON CLIFFS

Favored Element: Earth

This time take the bounce pad to the left, onto the larger island above. Follow the path around to reach another bounce pad. Use it to reach the next **Treasure Chest**. Once you've grabbed the chest, head right to face a couple of Arkeyan Hammahs and a group of Dragonets. After you defeat these enemies, use the Dragon Horn to call Flavius for another ride. Don't forget to dodge obstacles, blow up Air Mines, and grab all the Winged Gems you can!

PATH OF CHALLENGES

Favored Element: Fire

Make your way right, battling the Arkeyan Hammah to reach a **Treasure Chest**. Return to the left, past the entrance and make your way carefully

through the flaming dragons. By now you've got plenty of experience dealing with these. The path opens up into a spinning circular area with flame dragons guarding it. When it spins around to the path, quickly get off the spinning section and once again make your way through flaming dragon statues.

Use the bounce pad to get to the raised area in the middle of the spinning platform. This keeps you safe from the dragon flames while waiting for the bounce pad to get into position. When it comes around underneath the island above, bounce up to face some Dragonets! Cross the bridge to the next spinning platform. As before, use the center and wait until the bounce pad is between the dragon statues. Jump onto it to reach the area above.

Here you find another spinning platform. Stay on the edge and wait for the teleporter to come to you. Quickly use it to reach the Dragon's Throne.

DRAGON'S THRONE

Favored Element: Magic

After listening to Vathek's threats, follow the path and defeat all of the scheming dragon's henchmen! You face Chompy Pods, Chompies, and Arkeyan Hammahs. Once the first group of minions falls to your might, Vathek leaves to prepare more. Use the bounce pad to reach the far right area to reach another **Treasure Chest**.

Head back and use the same bounce pad to reach the spinning bounce pad above. Make sure to time your bounce to avoid the spikes. It bounces you to an identical spinning bounce pad. Aim to the left to reach the small platform containing the **Royal Crown**.

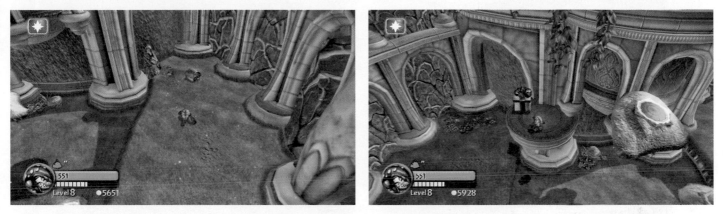

Drop down and use the bounce pads again, this time aiming to the right to reach the top platform. Vathek sends a group of Arkeyan Hammahs, Bomb Fiends, Dragonets, and even Chompies after you. Defeat them to show Vathek that his minions are worthless!

As with most bad guys, his pride is his weakness. Once you defeat his minions, Vathek vacates the throne to face you on the field of battle. Luckily, as soon as he does, Flavius grabs the throne! He takes care of Vathek and makes sure all is right in Dragon's Peak once again.

BURNING QUESTIONS!

Q: So to rule Dragon's Peak, all you have to do is sit on the throne and you're automatically King? That seems, I don't know? Weird?

A: To answer your question, yes, it is weird, and yes, all you have to do is sit on the throne and you automatically become the ruler of Dragon's Peak. But I'm sure you're wondering why it's just that simple and I will tell you. The dragons used to vote for their leaders but their political system became so complex, no one could understand it. Even the act of voting became difficult for most dragons. And those who wanted to rule had to campaign and make speeches and nobody particularly liked it so they finally just said, forget it. Whoever sits on the throne is King. Lucky for them, the first one to do this was Ramses. Not only was he the quickest to sit down but he happened to also be the most qualified to lead.

HEROIC CHALLENGES

Finished the campaign, but still looking for more challenges? Heroic Challenges are the answer! In *Skylanders Giants* there are two types of Heroic Challenges: Skylander Challenges and Purchased Challenges. Each Skylander has their own challenge, but only Series 2 Figures and new characters and the Giants unlock challenges in *Skylanders Giants*. Purchased Challenges are unlocked via Auric's Store.

To play a Heroic Challenge, talk to Cali on Flynn's Ship. Any Skylander that successfully completes a Heroic Challenge earns a permanent benefit to their stats.

Purchasable Challenges

ARACHNID ANTECHAMBER

DESCRIPTION: Defeat eight giant spiders in this dungeon.
BONUS FOR COMPLETION: +4 Speed

FLIP THE SCRIPT

DESCRIPTION: Choose the right path to find the Log of Nort.
BONUS FOR COMPLETION: +4 Speed

CHARM HUNT

DESCRIPTION: Head for the islands and collect 75 charms.
BONUS FOR COMPLETION: +3 Armor

THIS BOMB'S FOR YOU

DESCRIPTION: Fight Trolls to find the 5 singing gems.
BONUS FOR COMPLETION: +5 Critical Hit

CHOMPY CHOMP-DOWN

DESCRIPTION: Head for the mines and take out 100 enemies.
BONUS FOR COMPLETION: +5 Elemental Power

Skylander Challenges

JUMP FOR IT!

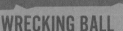

WRECKING BALL

DESCRIPTION: Jump around and collect 90 charms.
BONUS FOR COMPLETION: +4 Speed

THE THREE TELEPORTERS

HEX

DESCRIPTION: Find the correct path to the Golden Spork.
BONUS FOR COMPLETION: +3 Armor

WHERE ART THOU, PAINTINGS?

SPYRO

DESCRIPTION: Destroy the 6 ghostly paintings.
BONUS FOR COMPLETION: +5 Critical Hit

MINING FOR CHARMS

BASH

DESCRIPTION: Find magical ore buried within the rocks.
BONUS FOR COMPLETION: +5 Elemental Power

LAIR OF THE GIANT SPIDERS

PRISM BREAK

DESCRIPTION: Clear this mine of six giant spiders.
BONUS FOR COMPLETION: +5 Critical Hit

DUNGEONESS CREEPS

CHOP CHOP

DESCRIPTION: Search the dungeon for Amber Medallions.
BONUS FOR COMPLETION: +5 Elemental Power

FIGHT, TELEPORT, FIGHT!

LIGHTNING ROD

DESCRIPTION: Fight and teleport your way to the Tribal Mask.
BONUS FOR COMPLETION: +3 Armor

MINING IS THE KEY

IGNITOR

DESCRIPTION: Break rocks to find the keys to find the treasure.
BONUS FOR COMPLETION: +4 Speed

MISSION ACHOMPLISHED

STUMP SMASH

DESCRIPTION: Pick a path and take out the Chompies.
BONUS FOR COMPLETION: +3 Armor

TIME'S A-WASTIN'

SONIC BOOM

DESCRIPTION: Take out enemies for extra time needed to exit.
BONUS FOR COMPLETION: +5 Critical Hit

SAVE THE PURPLE CHOMPIES!

DROBOT

DESCRIPTION: Hit green Chompies, not purple! WARNING: this is tough!
BONUS FOR COMPLETION: +4 Speed

SPAWNER CAVE

TERRAFIN

DESCRIPTION: Take out 100 Chompies by finding the best spawners.
BONUS FOR COMPLETION: +5 Critical Hit

HOBSON'S CHOICE

TRIGGER HAPPY

DESCRIPTION: Fight and teleport your way to find the antique vanity.
BONUS FOR COMPLETION: +5 Critical Hit

ISLE OF THE AUTOMATONS

ERUPTOR

DESCRIPTION: Destroy Automatons and other enemies to score 75 points.
BONUS FOR COMPLETION: +5 Elemental Power

YOU BREAK IT, YOU BUY IT!

DOUBLE TROUBLE

DESCRIPTION: Hit Trolls, not paintings! WARNING: This is tough!
BONUS FOR COMPLETION: +5 Critical Hit

MINEFIELD MISHAP

STEALTH ELF

DESCRIPTION: Make it through the minefield. WARNING: This is tough!
BONUS FOR COMPLETION: +4 Speed

LOBS O' FUN

WHIRLWIND

DESCRIPTION: Earn a tasty treat by taking out Cyclopses.
BONUS FOR COMPLETION: +5 Elemental Power

BOMBS TO THE WALLS

FLAMESLINGER

DESCRIPTION: Use bombs to find 25 magic charms.
BONUS FOR COMPLETION: +5 Elemental Power

JAILBREAK!

GILL GRUNT

DESCRIPTION: Rescue six Mabu from the Cyclops Islands.
BONUS FOR COMPLETION: +3 Armor

ENVIRONMENTALLY UNFRIENDLY

DRILL SERGEANT

DESCRIPTION: Bust 7 of the Troll's pipes.
BONUS FOR COMPLETION: +5 Elemental Power

CHEMICAL CLEANUP

SLAM BAM

DESCRIPTION: Score points by destroying barrels of the right color.
BONUS FOR COMPLETION: +5 Elemental Power

BREAK THE CATS

ZAP

DESCRIPTION: Destroy the cat statues. WARNING: This is tough!
BONUS FOR COMPLETION: +3 Armor

FLAME PIRATES ON ICE

FLASHWING

DESCRIPTION: Defeat the Flamethrower Pirates.
BONUS FOR COMPLETION: +5 Elemental Power

SKYLANDS SALUTE

SPROCKET

DESCRIPTION: Raise all the flags.
BONUS FOR COMPLETION: +3 Armor

S.A.B.R.I.N.A.

TREE REX

DESCRIPTION: Save the Gecko Chorus and their King.
BONUS FOR COMPLETION: +4 Speed

THE SKY IS FALLING

POP FIZZ

DESCRIPTION: Destroy the Troll's large cannon.
BONUS FOR COMPLETION: +5 Critical Hit

NORT'S WINTER CLASSIC

JET-VAC

DESCRIPTION: Make your way around this icy course.
BONUS FOR COMPLETION: +3 Armor

BREAK THE FAKES!

EYE-BRAWL

DESCRIPTION: Put the Trolls out of business by destroying the fakes.
BONUS FOR COMPLETION: +4 Speed

BAKING WITH BATTERSON

SHROOMBOOM

DESCRIPTION: Bring fruit to Batterson for a sweet reward.
BONUS FOR COMPLETION: +3 Armor

SHEPHERD'S PIE

ZOOK

DESCRIPTION: Bring sheep back to their pens.
BONUS FOR COMPLETION: +4 Speed

BLOBBER'S FOLLY

BOUNCER

DESCRIPTION: Help Blobbers escape the dungeon.
BONUS FOR COMPLETION: +5 Elemental Power

WATERMELON'S ELEVEN

HOT HEAD

DESCRIPTION: Dodge bombs to collect 100 watermelons.
BONUS FOR COMPLETION: +5 Elemental Power

DELIVERY DAY

FRIGHT RIDER

DESCRIPTION: Deliver gifts to familiar characters.
BONUS FOR COMPLETION: +4 Speed

A REAL GOAT GETTER

HOT DOG

DESCRIPTION: Go get the Hermit's goats!
BONUS FOR COMPLETION: +3 Armor

GIVE A HOOT

CRUSHER

DESCRIPTION: Return lost owls to their nests.
BONUS FOR COMPLETION: +4 Speed

WOOLY BULLIES

NINJINI

DESCRIPTION: Find the trolls in sheep's clothing.
BONUS FOR COMPLETION: +5 Critical Hit

ZOMBIE DANCE PARTY

CYNDER

DESCRIPTION: Find all the Zombie heads.
BONUS FOR COMPLETION: +5 Critical Hit

THE GREAT PANCAKE SLALOM

CHILL

DESCRIPTION: Race against time through an icy slalom.
BONUS FOR COMPLETION: +4 Speed

SHOOT FIRST, SHOOT LATER

SWARM

DESCRIPTION: Fire cannons at flying barrels.
BONUS FOR COMPLETION: +5 Critical Hit

THE KING'S BREECH

THUMPBACK

DESCRIPTION: Defend King Capybara's castle against an Arkeyan Army!
BONUS FOR COMPLETION: +3 Armor

ACHIEVEMENTS

If you are playing *Skylanders Giants* on Xbox 360 or Playstation 3, you can earn these special achievements in addition to the Accolades the game awards you.

Story Achievements

Earn these Achievements by playing through the game's sixteen Chapters. If you finish the game, they can't be missed.

Rumbletown Ranger	Complete Chapter 3
Skystones Superstar	Complete Chapter 4
Glacier Great	Complete Chapter 5
Vault Victor	Complete Chapter 6
Wilikin Winner	Complete Chapter 7
Security Breacher	Complete Chapter 8
King of the Castle	Complete Chapter 9
Sky Survivor	Complete Chapter 10
Drill-X Defeator	Complete Chapter 11
Molekin Liberator	Complete Chapter 12
Trial Taker	Complete Chapter 13
Copter Captain	Complete Chapter 14
Arkus Adventurer	Complete Chapter 15
Savior of the Skylands!	Complete the Story Mode by recovering the Iron Fist of Arkus and defeating Kaos on any difficulty.

COLLECTIBLES ACHIEVEMENTS

This guide's walkthrough includes the locations of all these collectibles, so earning these Achievements should be no problem!

Soul Surfer	Collect Soul gems for Tree Rex (Chapter 12) and Jet-Vac (Chapter 14).
Seeker Adept	Collect 10 Legendary Ship Parts.
Hint Scholar	Collect 10 Story Scrolls.
Fashionista	Collect 10 Hats.

COMPLETIONIST ACHIEVEMENTS

Nightmare Avenger	Complete the Story Mode on Nightmare difficulty. (Nightmare difficulty unlocks after you beat the game on any difficulty)
Completionist	Earn 3 Stars on any Adventure Level.
To the Max	Level up any Skylander to level 15.
Upgrade Uniter	Purchase all upgrades for any one Skylander.
Spend That Loot!	Amass 65,000 Treasure with any one Skylander

CHAPTER SPECIFIC ACHIEVEMENTS

These achievements are all earned by completing a special goal on one of the game's 16 Chapters.

Elemental Enthusiast	Chapter 1 — Open all the Elemental areas.
Chain Champ	Chapter 2 — Complete the Chain Pull Feat of Strength.
Log Lifter	Chapter 3 — Complete the Log Lift Feat of Strength.
Skystone Sampler	Chapter 4 — Collect all of the Skystones.
Snowman Slammer	Chapter 5 — Destroy 7 snowmen.
Autogyro Pyrotechnician	Chapter 6 — Destroy all the Arkeyan Autogyros.
Talker in a Strange Land	Chapter 7 — Talk to all of the Wilikins.
Cannon Confounder	Chapter 8 — Complete the level without getting directly hit by a cannon.
Kaos Buster	Chapter 9 — Destroy 10 Kaos bust statues.
Mine Menace	Chapter 10 — Shoot down 10 mines.
Pipe Peptard	Chapter 11 — Damage Drill-X by throwing a pipe at him.
Hut Wrecker	Chapter 12 — Destroy 3 enemy huts with boulders Giants can lift.
Column Crusher	Chapter 13 — Destroy all the columns in the second trial.
Pedal of the Medal	Chapter 14 — Collect all 16 speed boosts in "The Long Hall." section.
Freebot Isn't Free	Chapter 15 — Defeat Freebot in a game of Skystones.
Keepin' Cool	Chapter 16 — Complete the chapter without taking damage from fire traps.

MISCELLANEOUS

Skystones Strategist	Capture 2 stones with 1 single stone.
Clean Jersey	Don't take any damage from Kaos' rockets during the mini-game on the Dread-Yacht. (This achievement refers to the mini-game on the Gun Deck of Flynn's ship. After Chapter 7, you gain access to the Gun Deck and you can play one of three random games, including Sheep, Bombs, and Barrels. You must complete the Bombs sequence without getting hit.)
1 and 0	Complete your first Arena Challenge.
Great Gladiator	Complete all 21 Arena Challenges.
Elemental Explorer	Unlock your first Elemental Area.
A New Hero	Complete 1 Heroic Challenge.

SKYLANDERS UNIVERSE

80 page handbook!

SKYLANDERS UNIVERSE
BOOK OF ELEMENTS
MAGIC & TECH

Puzzles, stickers, and games!

SKYLANDERS UNIVERSE
BATTLE FOR SKYLANDS

160 page illustrated novel!

SKYLANDERS UNIVERSE
THE MACHINE OF DOOM

Includes FREE poster!

SKYLANDERS SPYRO'S ADVENTURE
Master Eon's
OFFICIAL GUIDE
Bonus giant poster!

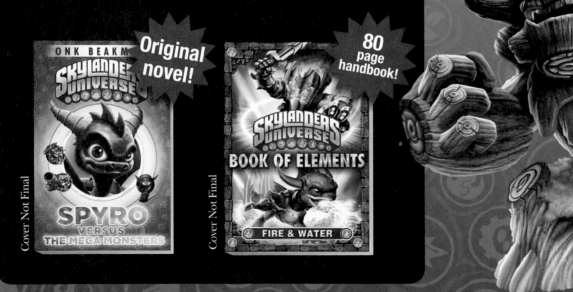

Original novel!

ONK BEAKM
SKYLANDERS UNIVERSE
SPYRO
VERSUS
THE MEGA MONSTERS

Cover Not Final

80 page handbook!

SKYLANDERS UNIVERSE
BOOK OF ELEMENTS
FIRE & WATER

Cover Not Final

$9.99

SKYLANDERS GIANTS

OFFICIAL STRATEGY GUIDE

DIGITAL EDITION AVAILABLE!

After being banished to Earth, Kaos continues to be a nuisance to the Skylanders. Master Eon calls upon all Portal Masters to keep the Skylands safe and this time you have help from all-new Skylanders, including Giants! Plus, there's this handy strategy guide full of tips and hints to ensure the safety of Skylands!

THE DIGITAL EDITION CONTAINS ALL THE CONTENT FROM THE PRINTED GUIDE INCLUDING:

- Meet the Newest Skylanders

- Master Every Level

- Learn everything about the Giants, the Lightcores and the Series 2 Skylanders. Plus, complete coverage of their "Wow Pow" power upgrades!

- Bestiary

- Get the lowdown on all of Kaos's minions.

- Learn what it takes to get 3 stars on every level. Detailed maps reveal all side areas that contain Soul Gems and Legendary Treasures.

- Skystones Strategy, Heroic Challenges, Quests & more.

DIGITAL EDITION AVAILABLE IN THE iBOOKSTORE OR ANDROID MARKET

ACTIVISION.

SKYLANDERS GIANTS

OFFICIAL STRATEGY GUIDE

Written by Thom Denick

DK/BradyGames, a division of Penguin Group (USA) Inc.
800 East 96th Street, 3rd Floor
Indianapolis, IN 46240

ISBN 13 EAN: 978-0-7440-1409-9

Printing Code: The rightmost double-digit number is the year of the book's printing; the rightmost single-digit number is the number of the book's printing. For example, 12-1 shows that the first printing of the book occurred in 2012.

15 14 13 12   4 3 2 1

Printed in the USA.

BRADYGAMES STAFF

PUBLISHER
Mike Degler

EDITOR-IN-CHIEF
H. Leigh Davis

LICENSING MANAGER
Christian Sumner

MARKETING MANAGER
Katie Hemlock

DIGITAL PUBLISHING MANAGER
Tim Cox

OPERATIONS MANAGER
Stacey Beheler

CREDITS

SENIOR DEVELOPMENT EDITOR
Ken Schmidt

MANUSCRIPT EDITOR
Matt Buchanan

SENIOR BOOK DESIGNERS
Carol Stamile
Keith Lowe

PRODUCTION DESIGNER
Areva

ACTIVISION CREDITS

Mireille Gagnon
Daniel Gagnon
Thomas Béland
Christian Morin
Alex "Commander Cool" Ness
Peter "The Kav" Kavic
Chris "The Hippie" Bruno
Ryan Steiner
Shinichiro Ohyama
I-Wei Huang
Vince Castillo
Jennifer Avina
Sasan Helmi
Alexandre Gingras
Elías Jiménez
Vickie Farmer